THE MANAGEMENT
OF GLOBAL DISORDER

READINGS FOR LEADERS

Harlan Cleveland
General Editor

Volume II

THE MANAGEMENT OF GLOBAL DISORDER

Prospects for Creative Problem Solving

Edited, with an introduction, by
Lincoln P. Bloomfield

 UNIVERSITY PRESS OF AMERICA

 EDUCATION FOR REFLECTIVE LEADERSHIP
HUBERT H. HUMPHREY INSTITUTE OF PUBLIC AFFAIRS
UNIVERSITY OF MINNESOTA

Copyright © 1987 by

The Hubert H. Humphrey Institute of Public Affairs
University of Minnesota

University Press of America,® Inc.

4720 Boston Way
Lanham, MD 20706

Co-published by arrangement with The Hubert H. Humphrey Institute
of Public Affairs

Library of Congress Cataloging-in-Publication Data

The Management of global disorder.

(Readings for leaders ; v. 2)
Bibliography: p.
Includes index.
1. International organization.   2. International
relations.   3. United Nations.   I. Bloomfield,
Lincoln Palmer, 1920-   . II. Series.
JX1954.M3427   1987   341.2   87-22997
ISBN 0-8191-6517-4 (alk. paper)
ISBN 0-8191-6518-2 (pbk. : alk. paper)

TABLE OF CONTENTS

Contents

Contents

FOREWORD
Readings for Leaders

This book, *The Management of Global Disorder,* and the series of READING FOR LEADERS of which it is designed to be a part, grows out of an experiment in midcareer education started at the University of Minnesota's Hubert H. Humphrey Institute of Public Affairs.

The experiment started in 1981, and we called it Education for Reflective Leadership. It was designed for, and soon attracted in almost embarrassing numbers, men and women in the part of their lives when they are graduating from specialist excellence to the generalist role in society. They come from government, business, labor, the professions, and nonprofit enterprise—not only Americans but budding leaders from three dozen countries on five continents.

For use during the first academic year in a seminar on Leadership in Public Policy, we assembled readings from many sources (classical literature, scholarly works, thoughtful journalism, and the writings and sayings of reflective practitioners of public affairs, from the insights of the ancient Chinese and Greeks down to the instant history, and histrionics, of recent office-holders).

As we did so, we found that most of the useful insights about the nature of the leadership function were not to be found in academic journals (there exists, in fact, no journal explicitly addressed to generalist leaders) but in the writings of unusually thoughtful people who had been there—whether as leaders themselves or as close observers of the practice of leadership.

Some were statesmen—that is, politicians graduated to responsibility—who, as an exception to the breed, were good at committing to paper what they tried to do, how they did it,

and why they thought it worthwhile to try. The available
insights span the centuries, from Moses and King David and
Julius Caesar down to James Madison, Mahatma Gandhi,
Woodrow Wilson, Winston Churchill and Mao Tse-tung—to
speak only of the dead in order to avoid arguments with the
living.

Some of them were not, in their time, considered "leaders," being more what we would now call "consultants"—such
as Niccolo Machiavelli in fifteenth-century Florence or Liu
Shao, who hired out as a management professional to
princes, to help run their principalities, in the Middle Kingdom
of China during the 3rd century A.D., and wrote The Study of
Human Abilities, the oldest known manual on what we would
now call "human resources management."

Down through the ages the public philosophers, often
people with no yen for public office themselves, have been
leaders too, leaders in thought followed by thousands of
governors and by millions of the governed. K'ung Fu-tsu
(Confucius) was such a one, an anxious but disappointed local
office-seeker who became instead a world-class teachers'
teacher. The thinking of two scholars, Huig de Groot (Grotius)
and Karl von Clausewitz, provides the backdrop to most
modern thinking about war and peace. In our time, John
Gardner and Peter Drucker are examples of two writers who
have provided the basis for an updated philosophy of leadership and the management of complexity.

In reviewing the rich heritage of writings that touch on
leadership, and using them in "education for reflective leadership," we thought it might be useful to build a systematic shelf
of durable readings especially relevant for reflective practitioners—members of the growing "get-it-all-together profes-
sion" who could benefit from prior insights that might help
illuminate the chances leaders are there to take, in whatever
domain they take them.

The premise of READINGS FOR LEADERS is not that
leadership can be taught but that it can be learned. The
largest part of that learning is bound to be "on the hoof," in
the practice of leadership in one's own life and work. But it
helps to take thought; to know what others in analogous
circumstances have faced, and what they did that succeeded

or failed; to learn how to analyze the constraints and loop-holes in the environment for action; to be able to guess where inherited "policy" comes from; to think hard about the future impacts of present actions; and to know by study as well as instinct that everything really is related to everything else. Leaders will do better, it seems, if they reflect on their environment, their purposes and themselves.

A recurring theme in these Readings is that uncertainty is for leaders, somewhere near the center of things. The complexity of relevant factors in any matter touching the public interest, the inherent unknowability of future social and even physical environments, make uncertainty the biggest factor in planning, in decision-making, even in evaluating the effects of actions after the fact.

A program of education for leadership therefore cannot be focussed mainly on how-to-do-it skills, nor can it offer what-to-do prescriptions. Rather, it has to concentrate on helping each leader get used to the assessment of uncertainty, clarify his/her ethical values, and develop for his/her own personal use a comprehensive worldview appropriate for an ambiguous future. More even than practiced skills, leadership is thought-through attitudes, educated instincts.

In the arts and crafts of creating problems that can be solved there has always, as Aaron Wildavsky says, been tension between resources and objectives, between dogma and skepticism, between intellectual reasoning and social interaction. But just now, in the 1980s, the inherent uncertainties of public policy are compounded and our inherited methods for reconciling those contradictions are rusting away.

The reason seems especially to lie in the corrosion of two traditional distinctions that have served us well in the development of modern industrial civilization but are now increasingly indistinct in the world outside our minds. The boundary line between "private" and "public" has been blurred by both private users of public services and public users of private services. And the line between "domestic" and "international" policies and actions is being erased by an interdependence which has become technologically imperative, culturally compelling, economically embarrassing and politically inescapable.

New "facts"—technologies, migrations, cartels, stagflation, terrorism—keep forcing leaders (in both "private" and "public" sectors) to broaden the categories in which "policy" is formulated and leadership exercised. In economic policy, Keynesian demand management and monetarist doctrines have both fallen short of explaining, much less controlling, global epidemics of inflation combined with global unemployment. The world's many experiments in governance (among the republican democracies, the American experiment has so far been the hardiest) still fall far short of "liberty and justice for all."

In the United States, New Deal philosophy and practice, by which the Federal government served as the drivewheel of social justice, needs reappraisal now that we the people seem to want less government even as we insist on more governance. In the great urban regions where three quarters of Americans live, defining "the city" as a single municipality is clearly too small a view. At the same time, the 20th century assumptions that growing complexity requires more centralized systems is in serious question well before the century ends.

In international relations, the invention of a new dimension of violence, incinerating millions of people in a few minutes, may have placed a ceiling on the scale of warfare, for the first time in world history. The rivalry between two governments either of which, if provoked to irrational behavior, could destroy much of the civilized world, hangs as a threatening cloud over world affairs. Yet the collision of economic growth with drives for fairer distribution of its benefits, and with resistance from cultural and religious institutions, creates a worldwide turbulence that cannot be seen clearly, if at all, through the prism of U.S.-Soviet relations.

Education for leadership must therefore be an inquiry into the deeper forces at work, an attempt by leaders themselves to define the broader integrative concepts that can help them connect their small parts of a large complexity with the whole—and thus learn to identify "success" not only with individual or sectoral accomplishments but with general outcomes.

PREFACE

Lincoln P. Bloomfield, the editor of this volume on THE MAN-AGEMENT OF GLOBAL DISORDER, is both scholar and practitioner of international politics, an expert in so many realms that he is among the few people who genuinely deserve to be called foreign policy generalists.

After a wartime stint as a naval officer, he served the State Department as a United Nations expert for more than a decade (1946–57), during the Truman and Eisenhower Administrations. At that time the United Nations was just getting started, and there were not many Americans, experts or amateurs, who thoroughly understood its origins, its purposes and its processes. In those days (it's a little hard to realize now) the U.N. was a major instrument of U.S. foreign policy—and of the foreign policies of half a hundred other founding signatories of the Charter.

Almost a generation later, he returned to another fulltime assignment, this time serving in the Jimmy Carter White House as the person responsible for "global issues" in the National Security Council.

During the first of these tours of public service, Lincoln Bloomfield completed his doctorate in political science, winning Harvard's Chase Prize with the first of his eight books on foreign policy, conflict management and international institutions. In 1957 he joined what was then the nation's most innovative Center for International Studies, at the Massachusetts Institute of Technology; in 1963 he became a lifetime Professor of Political Science at M.I.T.

Somehow the tag "political scientist," which thousands of us wear, doesn't fully connote the wise, imaginative and good-humored contribution which Lincoln Bloomfield has made—teaching a generation of students destined for leadership, writing a series of seminal books, monographs, articles and op-ed pieces, advising governments and lecturing in 36 countries.

His creative scholarship has included pioneering work in adapting "war game" theory and practice to the political relations among nations. He has conducted "conflict-avoidance games" for the U.S. State Department, the Pentagon, the United Nations, and even for the Kremlin. (It is in the interest of the West as well as the East that Soviet leaders, too, understand how governments and peoples might react to Soviet moves on the complex chessboard of inter-state politics.)

Professor Bloomfield's interest has been repeatedly drawn to the idea that government and international agencies should develop the capacity to anticipate potential crises, figure out what to do ahead of time instead of too late, and (as he put it in a recent writing) "enrich the official memory by enabling comparisons and contrasts to be quickly drawn" with comparable prior events. That interest led to the invention of CASCON (Computer-Aided System for Information on Local Conflicts). The computerized CASCON data base contains 520 variables for 67 past conflicts, designed "to link social science techniques to the real-world needs and styles of officials who cope with actual conflicts." He also created the scenario for an award-winning cable television special dramatizing the problem of nuclear war avoidance.

An unusual blend of academic scholarship, hands-on experience, teaching skill and practical common sense thus made Lincoln Bloomfield a "natural" to edit this volume on the management of global disorder. The editor introduces the readings with an original critique of the global nonsystem that is sometimes miscalled "world order."

We are not aware of any comparable anthology of accessible readings, designed for both practicing leaders and students of leadership, on the limitations and potentials of international cooperation.

The range of readings, skillfully shortened to keep the whole within reasonable bounds, is very wide. Yet the editor—in the way he has organized the readings and in his running commentary on them—has imposed on them a paradoxical unity. It is the product of the paradoxes inherent in the subject—the need to manage amid disorder, to organize amid diversity, to govern a pluralistic world, to make a durable and comprehensive peace out of transitory and separable pieces, to reconcile sovereignty with interdependence, to develop by inter-nation negotiation the basis for a global commons, to reflect in action the twin truth that all men are brothers and all brothers are different.

"To make the world safe for diversity"—that was President John F. Kennedy's one-phrase aspiration for American foreign policy. Neither the United States nor any other nation is yet acting out this precept. But it's still a trail for leaders to seek and pursue. These Readings are designed as blazes along that trail.

Two other books are currently being published by the University Press of America in the READINGS FOR LEADERS series.

One is POLITICAL LEADERSHIP IN MILITARY DEFENSE, edited by John P. Craven, the ocean engineer and lawyer who served as Chief Scientist of the Polaris project, the submarine strategic missile system that is still, in its later adaptations, the least vulnerable part of U.S. strategic deterrence. Dr. Craven has also been Dean of Marine Programs and is director of the international Law of the Sea Institute.

The other is LAW, JUSTICE AND THE COMMON GOOD, edited by Sidney Hyman, author of *The American President* and numerous works of biography, history and political analysis, currently a professor at the University of Illinois at Chicago. Professor Hyman also joined his erudition to my practice-oriented mind in editorial collaboration on the whole READINGS FOR LEADERS series.

The launching of the whole project, and the editing and publishing of these three volumes, was made possible by a grant from the EXXON Foundation.

Harlan Cleveland

Dean
Hubert H. Humphrey Institute of Public Affairs
University of Minnesota
301 19th Avenue S.
Minneapolis, MN 55455
September 1986

FRONTISPIECE

AT THE RATE OF PROGRESS since 1800, every American who lived into the year 2000 would know how to control unlimited power. He would think in complexities unimaginable to an earlier mind. He would deal with problems altogether beyond the range of earlier society. To him the nineteenth century would stand on the same plane with the fourth—equally childlike—and he would only wonder how both of them, knowing so little, and so weak in force, should have done so much.

The Education of Henry Adams
Henry Adams

In studying the growths of civilizations we found that they could be analysed into successions of performances of the drama of challenge-and-response and that the reason why one performance followed another was because each of the responses was not only successful in answering the particular challenge by which it had been evoked but was also instrumental in provoking a fresh challenge, which arose each time out of the new situation that the successful response had brought about.

A Study of History
Arnold Toynbee

Article 1

The Purposes of the United Nations are:
1. To maintain international peace and security, and to that end: to take effective collective measures for the prevention and removal of threats to the peace, and for the suppression of acts of aggression or other breaches of the peace, and to bring about by peaceful means, and in conformity with the principles of justice and international law, adjustment or settlement of inter-

national disputes or situations which might lead to a breach of the peace;

2. To develop friendly relations among nations based on respect for the principle of equal rights and self-determination of peoples, and to take other appropriate measures to strengthen universal peace;

3. To achieve international co-operation in solving international problems of an economic, social, cultural, or humanitarian character, and in promoting and encouraging respect for human rights and for fundamental freedoms for all without distinction as to race, sex, language, or religion; and

4. To be a centre for harmonizing the actions of nations in the attainment of these common ends.

United Nations Charter

THE MANAGEMENT OF GLOBAL DISORDER: An Essay

Lincoln P. Bloomfield

INTRODUCTION

THE ENGLISH ANTHROPOLOGIST GEOFFREY GORER, once characterized the difference between British and American approaches to institutions as follows. The British treat an institution the way they treat a tree: plant it, water it, feed it, prune it, let it grow, and hope it will survive into permanence. The Americans treat an institution the way they treat a machine: assemble the pieces, turn the machine on, and if it doesn't run take it apart and try putting it back together differently. At the Massachusetts Institute of Technology, if something goes wrong in the physical plant one merely picks up a phone and dials "FIXIT," and someone comes armed with tools to do just that. This seems an appropriate metaphor for the American "engineering" approach to world problems.

This distinctively American quality has a special meaning when it comes to something called "management." "Management" connotes structures, rules, personnel, budgets—in short, institutional machinery. It is no accident that much of the so-called "world order" machinery of international organizations, created in the mid-twentieth century to deal with greater-than-national or "transboundary" problems, has been of American inspiration and design. Indeed, the very idea of collective "problem-solving" for identifiable global headaches betrays another distinctively American approach

1

to the kinds of difficulties other cultures frequently ascribe to the tragedy of history, to which they must adapt. The institution-building approach, combined with the liberal internationalist ideal of "world order," together reflect the optimism that has been unique to the American culture.

In this spirit, American diplomatic energy was a central element of the post World War II surge of creativity that created today's system of institutions aimed at keeping the peace and fostering human welfare around the globe. That extraordinary five year period from 1944 to 1949 stood in sharp contrast to the earlier 150-year old US view of the outside world's problems as evils to be shunned, not "solved." The postwar arrangements reflected the best available "state-of-the-art" thinking of the times about both collective security and economic and social progress.

In the forty-odd years that have passed, much has changed. But it also needs saying that some things—human nature, for one, attachment to state sovereignty, for another— did *not* undergo the transformations some idealistic reformers confidently anticipated. In the late 1980's the combination of new challenges and old weaknesses has created a widespread sense of system failure. With this disillusionment the earlier optimism seems to have drained out of the "world-order builders." The temptation is great for Americans (and Europeans, Japanese et al.) to turn inward again, and try to go it alone. That trend, if not reversed, can have dangerous consequences not only for international cooperation in general, but for the all-important strategic stability between the nuclear superpowers on which world peace ultimately depends.

It is clearly time to reexamine both the premises and conclusions of a half century ago about multilateral cooperation. Two principles should govern such a reexamination. First, it is evident that simply prescribing "more of the same" is not an adequate prescription for dealing with global-level problems. But second, the objective circumstances of the late 20th century rule out as irrational another binge of isolationism or extreme nationalism. In an age of what I would call "Nationalism Without Autonomy," a new mix is needed which tempers the old optimistic idealism with a constructive realism. For

Americans, this calls for modulating the national passion for comprehensive machinery with a pragmatism that accepts fragmentary "pieces of peace," without either cynicism or abandonment of broader goals. The test of any particular approach is not whether it conforms to our preconceived notions, but rather the extent to which it advances the larger goals of international security, justice, and peace.

DEFINING THE PROBLEM

A constructive pragmatism starts by asking what transboundary tasks need to be accomplished that states cannot successfully manage by themselves.

The transboundary "management" task that dwarfs all others is to avoid a thermonuclear war between the United States and the Soviet Union. Surely the primordial charge for responsible statecraft is to ensure the survival of civilized life. An all-out nuclear war, even if it did not terminate all species except the cockroach, would produce a chain of unimaginable catastrophes ranging from mass annihilation to the "nuclear winter" forecast by scientists. The evidence suggests that nuclear war would most likely come, not from a cold-blooded decision, but from an escalating crisis situation in which either the US or the USSR dares not wait out the crisis for fear it will be struck and unable to retaliate.

So far each has had sufficient invulnerable weapons to ensure its ability to retaliate regardless of the attack. This, for better or worse, means deterrence of nuclear assault. But both sides are busily developing new weapons systems which might for the first time make them fear to ride out a grave crisis. *The possibility of such "crisis-instability" is the single most dangerous threat to world peace.* Regardless of all other issues, the top priority for managing peace must go to avoiding at all costs destabilizing "use it or lose it" weapons systems, and the second priority to finding far better ways to prevent, limit, and terminate armed conflicts between states. Both tasks require cooperative action at bilateral and multilateral levels.

But however overriding the war-prevention imperative, most people are directly affected, not by the theoretical possibility of a thermonuclear exchange, but by such immediate concerns as the prices of goods they need for a decent (or even minimal) existence; the value of their money; the availability of resources from the earth and sea to build their industries, power their activities, and feed their families; and the healthfulness of the air they breathe and the water they drink.

Time was when national governments had at least the theoretical ability to provide these things to their citizens. Next to the transformation in strategic weaponry, the second greatest historic change is the steady erosion in the capacity of governments, even the most powerful, to ensure *by their own actions* the health of the national economy or physical environment, whether in terms of goods in the shop, oil in the furnaces, jobs in the factory, food on the table, savings accounts that keep their value, or lakes and forests that remain viable.

The label "Interdependence" was in vogue in the 1970's as shorthand for this second revolution. That the word has now become a platitude simply confirms the commonplace fact of worldwide *mutual dependence,* and defines the second great international "management" task: to work toward a more stable, prosperous and humane economic and social life in both the developed and developing countries, while preserving for future generations the patrimony of nature now in process of being perilously degraded.

Consciousness-raising about "global issues" involving the welfare—economic, social, or personal—of individuals and groups has caused some to define "security" as embracing the entire human condition. Liberals are correct to criticize the chronic underplaying by national security managers of the socioeconomic-cultural-religious roots of conflict. But while understandable, this has the perverse effect of obscuring the military security problem that remains crucial in an age of unremitting conflict. The security threats of aggressive behavior or governmental terrorism—including cynical outside attempts to exploit popular discontent—can be ignored only at our peril. On the global scale, no less than region by region, "binocular" policy lenses that illuminate both the causes and consequences of conflict are necessary if we are to make sense of the larger problem of international peace and security.

MANAGING THE PROBLEM OF SECURITY

Half a century ago British Foreign Secretary Sir Edward Gray, looking back on the carnage of World War I, said of that war's causes: "Armaments were intended to produce a sense of security in each nation . . . What they really did was to produce fear in everybody. Fear causes suspicion and hatred."(*Twenty-Five Years, 1892–1916,* II., 53) Experts still argue as to whether or not arms races must end in warfare, as well as whether the strategic armaments buildups by the two nuclear giants constitutes a "race." It is true that each side is, to a degree, driven by internal bureaucratic and institutional pressures, and by the inexorable momentum of technology itself. Whether technically a race or not, most would agree with former Secretary of Defense Robert McNamara that a "mad momentum" in the overall action-reaction process has led us to astronomical levels of deliverable nuclear warheads. Henry A. Kissinger has succinctly characterized the risks in a situation where:

> The superpowers often behave like two heavily armed blind men feeling their way around a room, each believing himself in mortal peril from the other, whom he assumes to have perfect vision.

Nuclear Arms Control

Serious efforts were made in the 1960's and 1970's to bring the strategic arms competition under negotiated control. The first landmark agreement was the Limited Test Ban Treaty of 1963 barring nuclear weapons testing in outer space, under water, and in the earth's atmosphere then being dangerously contaminated by radioactive fallout. (France and China continued their testing programs, but in time subsided in the face of international pressures.) Other modest but valuable agreements limited the places where nuclear arms would be placed or tested, starting with the 1959 Antarctica Treaty, and including the 1967 Outer Space Treaty, the 1968 Nuclear Nonproliferation Treaty—NPT—the 1977 Biological Weapons Convention, the 1975 Seabed Treaty, and the 1974 and 1976 agreements to limit underground testing to 150 kilotons TNT equivalent, and control peaceful nuclear explosions.

The first agreement actually to abort a contemplated weapons system was the SALT I Treaty of 1972 limiting anti-ballistic missile systems to two (ultimately one) weapons site for each side, and placing restrictions on development of subsystems recognizably leading to a ballistic missile defense. At the time of writing, that agreement is in process of being subverted by both sides—the Soviets in deploying dual-purpose radars, and both pressing against the limits in their R&D, notably the U.S. under President Reagan's so-called "Star Wars" program. Neither the Carter nor Reagan administrations could bring themselves to complete the Comprehensive Test Ban (CTB) treaty ending underground testing, which would inhibit the development of ever-newer nuclear weaponry. The Soviets concentrated on destabilizing, heavy MIRV'd missiles, prompting a U.S. retreat from the SALT II agreement of 1979. In 1986 both moved closer to renewed efforts to curb offensive missiles.

Other countries are obviously deeply concerned, but a series of UN Special General Assembly Sessions on Disarmament, and indeed three decades of pressure from the great majority of non-nuclear weapons countries, had little or no effect on the plans, programs, and weapons deployments of the Big Two. But the role of the UN has not been entirely inconsequential in the arms control field, in two ways. First, a succession of UN committees on disarmament meeting in Geneva has kept alive important agenda items such as a ban on chemical weapons, to which the powers subsequently have turned. Secondly, the General Assembly, despite its deservedly negative reputation on some counts, has played a significant role in both initially calling for and later "certifying," so to speak, major treaty efforts such as Outer Space and NPT. No other global body exists which can "legitimize" multilateral treaties and other agreements, a function whose value to the international system should not be underrated.

Having said that, the reality is that management (some

would say mismanagement) of the strategic arms competition is entirely in the hands of leaders of two governments whose mutual "suspicion and hatred," in Sir Edward Gray's words, is manifest. Realistically, this means that mankind's hedges against the possibility of massive destruction, at least so far, lie entirely in the rationality, common sense and psychic balance of leaders in Washington and Moscow.

It is important not to minimize the fact that even under conditions of extreme provocation, something has so far inhibited the temptation to use nuclear weapons. The common humanity of individuals in office is the chief defense against annihilation, in the spirit of Bismarck's saying that "a statesman is a politician who thinks of his grandchildren." But perhaps more to the point is the absence of any plausible calculation of political, territorial, economic gain that even begins to justify the prospect of mutual suicide. Every superpower leader since the early 1950s has sooner or later asserted publicly that the use of nuclear weapons is irrational. Statements by Soviet leaders from Stalin to Gorbachev are on the record that a general nuclear war in unwinnable. American presidents from Truman to Reagan have sooner or later taken a public stand in the spirit of John F. Kennedy when he said:

> Hostility today is a fact, but it is not the ruling law. The supreme reality is our indivisibility . . . and our common vulnerability on this planet. (To Irish Parliament, June 28, 1963)

That World War III has not taken place in a half century of ideological struggle unmatched since the religious wars of the 16th century persuades some of the durability of the present system of mutual deterrence (or, put more starkly, mutual terror). The trouble is that no one can know how durable such a system may be. C. P. Snow gave scientific prophesy a bad name when in 1960 he assigned an "absolute certainty" to the probability of a nuclear detonation in anger "within ten years." But a generalized pessimism pervades much of the world as to the capacity of fallible humans in two capital cities indefinitely to manage successfully the fate of the planet. The issue is acutely sharpened by development of new destabilizing systems such as MIRVed ICBMs and space weapons, either of which could undermine the "crisis-stability" that has somehow gotten the world through four decades of tension.

Are there no other alternatives? The U.S. Conference of Catholic Bishops in a magisterial statement in 1983 came close to denouncing deterrence as an inherently immoral policy, given the appalling costs should its mechanism ever fail. But the baffling dilemma remains of how to march back down the nuclear ladder without risking in the process the very tragedy we must avoid. Short of universal brain surgery, as Thomas Schelling once put it, the technical knowledge will remain at hand. What can take the place of mutual deterrence in a conflict-ridden world with an ineradicable memory of how to make nuclear bombs?

The Escape into World Government

Faced with this unprecedented turn in the human condition, some concluded early in the atomic age that nothing but a total revolution in the *political* world would suffice. The spokesman for this view was the great mathematician Albert Einstein. In 1946 he wrote in the *New York Times* that "... The unleashed power of the atom has changed everything except our ways of thinking." (May 25, 1946). The next year he stated that "War will be prevented only when military power in the hands of individual nations is abolished and is replaced by the military monopoly of a supranational organization." In other words, world government.

The following year, the United Nations overwhelmingly endorsed a United States proposal for a giant step along such lines. The so-called Baruch Plan provided for turning over to an international authority the World War II nuclear facilities still exclusively in American hands. Unprecedentedly, the enterprise was to be administered *without a great power veto*. The Soviet Union, by flatly refusing such an offer while moving to develop its own bomb, denied the world its chance to abort the nuclear competition.

Even with the disheartening failure of the UN Atomic Energy Plan, substantial numbers of people were for a time attracted to the vision of world government in the spirit of

Socrates when (according to Epictetus) he counseled: "Never, when asked one's country, to answer 'I am an Athenian or a Corinthian,' but 'I am a citizen of the world'." Some plans were utopian, postulating a world without states and thus presumably free of war. Most discussion focused on more limited proposals such as the Clark-Sohn Plan, which prescribed centralized powers sufficient to manage and enforce a process of disarmament, but with "home rule" for all other functions. (Two hundred years earlier the philosopher Immanuel Kant, in the influential tract *Eternal Peace*, had similarly de-escalated his vision: "Unless all is to be lost, the positive idea of a *world republic* must be replaced by the negative substitute of a *union* of nations which maintains itself, prevents war, and steadily expands." (p. 445))

The mainstream Western internationalist outlook of the early postwar years also challenged the idea of unfettered national behavior, holding, with British Prime Minister Harold Wilson in the mid-1960's, that "a surrender of sovereignty is a mark of an advancing civilization." A decade later a prominent American liberal wrote that:

> Against a background of burgeoning global problems, increasing demands for multilateral action, and actual transnational relationships which increasingly bypass governments, the last true believers in the declining nation-state would, of course, be those holding highest office under it. (Thomas L. Hughes, "Foreign Policy: Men or Measures?", *Atlantic*, Oct. 1974, p.?).

But for at least the current period in political history, a state-centered system continues to prove itself stronger than the so-far abstract threat of cataclysmic warfare which stimulates in turn the idealistic impulse to world "unity." The reasons are three.

First, the proposal by both East and West for "general and complete" disarmament, the logical corollary of which was some form of world government, came and went in the early 1960's as an even semi-serious policy program, and neither West nor East has returned to them. Second, political theory teaches that even limited community institutions involving law and order require first of all a community, meaning a fundamental consensus on some essential human and political values beyond the elemental fear of annihilation. The profound divergence between Western, Eastern and, increasingly, "Southern" concepts of the relation of individual to group have at least so far made such a consensus less rather than more likely.

Soviet suspicions of the non-communist world, and Third World resentment of dependency on the West both seem to carry with them strong assertions of national sovereignty. The national state, elevated in 19th century European thought to a species of deity, became in the 20th century the Holy Grail for the non-European world. And while the national state is correctly indicted as history's prime instrument for organized warfare, it has also supplied the world—including both communist and newly-independent states—a comparatively efficient form of social and industrial organization, substitutes for which have never seemed quite plausible.

Third (and most unsettling to idealists) is the possibility that a supranational authority might generate less, not more, peace than a cooperative effort among states. The ambiguous record of human nature suggests that those in charge of a world order might not be much more enlightened or tolerant or selfless than national leaders. An entirely legitimate fear is that an "international civil war" might well be more destructive than a local conflict that can be isolated. As Ralf Dahrendorf put it, "The power to destroy the earth does not imply the power to run the earth." (*Foreign Affairs*, Oct. 1977).

One should also be warned off at the global level by Hannah Arendt's definition of totalitarianism as "the elimination of all subgroups between the individual and the state." Of course, as the late strategist Herman Kahn once observed, a frightening nuclear crisis, (and certainly a nuclear "Day After") could drastically alter such conclusions. Barring that, we are realistically left with the ambiguity and frustration of voluntary cooperation even in the face of daunting problems states demonstrably cannot resolve alone.

The Concept of Collective Security

The 20th century introduced a rather more limited concept—*universal collective security*—under which all states assumed the obligation to join forces, as a kind of volunteer world police force, to enforce the law against armed aggression. Under the League of Nations and subsequently the United Nations, member states were pledged to assure the "political independence and territorial integrity" of all member states. But under the League Covenant a unanimous vote was required, which of course meant that no action could be taken. Mussolini's invasion of Ethiopia in 1935, Hitler's incremental territorial grabs, and Japan's attacks on China, all might have been successfully deterred by a unified response on the part of a coalition of determined states under a multilateral banner of collective security. That lesson drove much of the wartime planning for postwar machinery. Having presided over the failure of this concept during the slide towards war in the 1930's, the victorious World War II coalition was determined to make collective security a reality.

Chapter VII of the United Nations Charter envisaged countering military aggression with the collective military strength of the victorious powers—the US, USSR and UK, plus France and China—under the flag of the United Nations. But, of course, the situation had changed and, as so often happens, political solutions turn out to be appropriate for solving the problems of the past, and not necessarily those just emerging. The post World War II crises between East and West, far from mobilizing the great powers within the UN Security Council in a coalition for collective security, in fact accurately reflected the enormous schism *between* those great powers. As with disarmament or world government, universal collective security also required a foundation of consensus about at least some basic political values. A "security community" could not exist, other than on paper, if its principal members were in profound disagreement about the nature of the political and economic system to be defended (or defended against).

A coalition of un-likeminded states worked reasonably well during World War II when all were under assault by a common military enemy. But in the postwar world there has so far been insufficient agreement on either basic diagnosis or policy prescription. In the decades since 1945 the fear of nuclear war has steadily increased. But so far that fear has not by itself come close to creating a genuine political community that can support an effective *universal* collective security mechanism. Instead, coalitions of like-minded states have formed non-universal alliances like NATO and the Warsaw Pact, and the world remains in this sense fragmented.

But there is a reassuring irony in the situation. Given the revolutionary change in military power and the realignment of the states in contending coalitions, we should probably be grateful that the hundred or so "small wars" that have taken place since 1945 did *not* face an effective security system under which everyone automatically became involved. In the nuclear age the consequences of dragging in the nuclear powers could be catastrophic. Given what we now know, world peace is more likely to be preserved if the system works to *isolate* and *insulate* conflicts, rather than have them fought by everyone including nuclear weapons powers.

Other Security Issues

Nuclear arms are not the only form of weaponry, nor the only candidates for arms control. *Conventional* armaments are flowing to Third World countries at an increasing rate, and developing countries (LDCs) are themselves becoming significant arms suppliers. Efforts to stem the cost and volume of this flow have been unsuccessful, for several reasons. One reason is because LDCs see no reason why they should not also arm, as a sovereign right. Another reason is because some of them in fact legitimately require arms for defense against predatory neighbors. A third reason is the substantial economic return for the arms suppliers.

Conventional arms control efforts have so far been unsuccessful, perhaps because they are taken by the majority of recipient countries as another form of paternalism by the erstwhile colonial powers, and also because the great powers themselves show no signs of swearing off their own apparently insatiable need for armaments. One potentially useful proposal for multilateral action calls for establishment of a UN "Register" of international arms transactions, at least publicizing what is going on (including growing arms expenditures by countries that simply cannot afford it). But this idea, halfheartedly proposed by some Western powers, has been wholeheartedly opposed by recipient states and so far has gotten nowhere.

Another category of security is the potential spread of nuclear weapons capability to more and more countries. Fortunately, earlier predictions were too pessimistic and only India has added itself to the original list of countries that have exploded a nuclear device—as it happens, the Five Permanent Members of the UN Security Council. Almost 120 countries have signed the 1968 Nuclear Non-Proliferation Treaty (NPT). The UN International Atomic Energy Agency (IAEA) inspects civil nuclear reactors in the non-weapons countries. But several of the most likely proliferators, such as Israel, South Africa and Pakistan, remain outside the treaty, and additional countries are technically capable of making a bomb. There are strong arguments for strengthening the inspection capabilities of the IAEA to make unnecessary any repeats of do-it-yourself antiproliferation actions like the Israeli bombing of a nearly-completed Iraqi nuclear reactor. Equally strong arguments exist for the superpowers to take the kind of serious nuclear arms control measures they promised as their side of the bargain with non-nuclear countries who signed the NPT.

Finally terrorism, particularly "official terrorism" sponsored clandestinely (or even openly) by governments, is on the increase. Major international efforts are taking shape for curbing this scourge starting with the measures against aircraft hijacking initiated by the UN Secretary General and General Assembly in the early 1970's.

Conflict Management

Most conflicts between states (or within the boundaries of states) do not represent clearcut cases of organized warfare in which an identifiable aggressor must be opposed and an identifiable victim aided. Even when they do, the conditions which make universal collective security impossible today also rule out a "law enforcement" approach to the small wars in our world. In this political environment the best way to tackle so-called "local conflicts" is not through any collective military response (which is in any event unavailable) but rather through a neutral third party which can get between the warring parties and, if not actually resolve their dispute, at least cool it down and prevent it from spreading.

What follows makes a distinction between "dispute," meaning quarrel about something of value whether boundaries, resources, political rule, or ideological orientation; "conflict," meaning a dispute that has turned potentially violent; and "hostilities," meaning fighting between organized military units. (These definitions come from the dynamic model developed by Amelia C. Leiss and myself, see *Controlling Small Wars* (NY, Knopf, 1969)).

The small wars and war-generating conflicts that have populated the postwar landscape were until recently very much the concern of the UN system. Except for the invasion of South Korea by Communist North Korea in June 1950, (when in the absence of the USSR a makeshift form of collective security was launched by the Security Council), the provisions of the Charter calling for armed forces to be placed at the disposal of the Security Council have remained a dead letter. In an age of independence movements and "wars of national liberation," one person's aggression or terrorism is another's crusade for freedom. With the great powers invariably taking sides with their small power friends, agreement has usually been impossible on identifying any aggressor in the innumerable small wars that take place. (A UN Committee became deadlocked some time ago in its quest for even an agreed *definition* of aggression).

The international "management" task of local conflict control must deal, not with a revolution as in the nuclear area, but with a melancholy case of "plus ça change, plus c'est la même chose"—the more things change, the more they stay the same. There has been no diminution in the rate at which warfare occurs between and within states in the second half of the 20th century, and little reason to expect much change when the calendar reads "2001." New local conflicts (as they are called by people who are happily distant from them), break out on an average of one and a half times a year.

These are the wars that *do* take place—the conflicts which *do* kill real people.

The other great task involved in managing global conflicts is to develop far more effective ways of preventing, avoiding, limiting, and terminating local conflicts. In this realm of "disorder management" the machinery of international organizations such as the UN, the OAS, and the OAU *have* in fact achieved occasional successes in tranquilizing conflicts. Unlike universal collective security which suffers from a deep conceptual weakness, there exists no *inherent* reason why the processes of conciliation, mediation, and good offices cannot and should not be routinely turned to in helping states to back away from worsening conflict situations and toward some kind of mutual settlement.

The drafters of the UN Charter build into Chapter VI on the Peaceful Settlement of Disputes an obligation to permit discussion of any complaint, and forbade a veto by a party to a dispute. But the Security Council under this heading can only recommend terms of settlement, and we should be clear that such processes are *voluntary* rather than *compulsory*, reflecting the modest nature of the UN system and the limited writ of contemporary international law as well. There exists no central authority to which all states *must* submit their differences, or to which states need even belong (Switzerland still is not a member of the UN). The predominant system of judicial "self-help" means that each state is the judge of whether it even submits to third party consideration a dispute to which it is a party, and whether or not it accepts the majority's recommendations.

Just to list current conflicts and disputes at the time of writing is to illustrate the sad estate to which existing multilateral agencies of peaceful settlement have fallen: outright warfare in Iran-Iraq, Central America, Lebanon, Chad, and Afghanistan, and occasionally violent disputes in the Arab-Israeli area, Korea, South and Southeast Asia, Cambodia, and Cyprus. In recent years Argentina, Iran, Iraq, Israel, the Soviet Union, and the United States have simply ignored calls by the UN Security Council to cease and desist from attacking, invading, annexing, occupying, or whatever. Scores of lesser disputes fester and poison the international climate, in the absence of any established habit of "community" action to deal with them effectively, this despite the ready availability of machinery for international mediation and conciliation, and indeed despite crystal-clear treaty provisions.

The UN Security Council has fallen into disrepute not without reason, given its failure to notice some wars at all, plus its habitual condemnation of Israel on any Middle Eastern questions regardless of merits. But it is also nothing short of scandalous that so few disputes are submitted to the UN Security Council by the great powers with the serious purpose of seeking a fair negotiated settlement—and of fostering the habit of peaceful settlement of disputes. This has been true of France in Algeria, the Soviet Union in Afghanistan, Britain in the Falklands, the US in Indochina and Nicaragua, and China in Vietnam. Perhaps if the larger powers themselves were not so disdainful of the machinery except when it serves their propaganda interests, others would become more serious about it.

Beyond such purely voluntary procedures lie more formal processes, whose record is even less encouraging. The UN system includes a world court—the International Court of Justice—whose judges, garbed in solemn black robes, sit in the Court's impressive chambers in the Hague. But sad to relate, few international disputes of any significance are brought to the ICJ. The reason is not that the Court, despite differences among the 15 judicial backgrounds on the bench, is incapable of analyzing and deciding fairly on the merits of a case, or of giving important and influential Advisory Opinions (as it did on the status of South-West Africa, or Namibia). The reason is rather that almost all disputes today are considered political even if they have major legal questions attached to them.

Indeed, states seem to be moving away from any commitment to even a rudimentary rule of law in the world. The United States has been the voice of global legality, president after president urging on others the rule of law in the world. But the US refusal to acknowledge the Court's 1985 judgment in favor of Nicaragua surely represents a low point, putting the US in the same category as communist Albania which similarly rejected the Court's jurisdiction over, as it happens, a similiar charge of hostile mine-laying. The Ayatollah's Iran similarly scorned the Court when the US sought to bring it to book over the hostage seizure.

More modest, but perhaps of even greater potential value in creating a more orderly and just international system, is the practice of international arbitration. Here two or more parties to a dispute agree to submit their argument to a third party, agreeing in advance to accept the latter's findings as binding, whoever wins or loses. The habit of binding arbitration, which took care of literally hundreds of interstate quarrels in the 1920's, has also declined concomitantly with the decline in international comity and civility. Israel and Egypt agreed to binding arbitration over Taba in 1986. A promising revival of binding arbitration was built into the draft Law of the Sea Treaty largely on US initiative. But it was weakened when the Reagan administration rejected the treaty draft because of its inclusion of a system of international controls over deep seabed mining of hard minerals (also an earlier US initiative).

All of the above is by no means to blame the United States for the present dismal situation, although Washington's recent failure of moral leadership in the general area of international order has further debilitated the prospects for a tolerable global system. Certainly both the communist bloc and many of the new Third World nations explicitly reject the very notion of impartial justice in a framework they identify with the Western tradition they reject in part or in whole.

Multilateral Peacekeeping

One element in the conflict control picture has shown more promise than much else: UN peacekeeping.

In 1956 Britain, France and Israel struck at Egypt in a punitive (and fruitless) attempt to undo President Nasser's nationalization of the Suez Canal and put an end to his cross-border pinprick assults on Israeli territory. President Eisenhower and Soviet leaders found themselves in agreement that this was indeed an unacceptable use of force to redress a political-legal wrong. But the US rejected Soviet Premier Khrushchev's somewhat cynical offer to join forces to crush the three malefactors who incidentally were US allies. Instead, in an extraordinary example of diplomatic improvisation under extreme crisis conditions (Soviet tanks were simultaneously squashing Hungary's bid for freedom), a new quasimilitary device called "UN peacekeeping" was devised by UN Secretary General Dag Hammarskjöld, Canadian Foreign Minister Lester Pearson, the US UN delegation, and others.

Peacekeeping was a halfway house between collective security and dispute settlement (some christened it "Article 6½" of the Charter). UNEF-I and its successors consisted of lightly-armed units of approximately battalion size contributed, not by the great powers but by neutral or otherwise inoffensive small and medium-sized member countries. Their task was not to fight off an aggressor but to interpose themselves between two sides *which had already agreed in principle to stop fighting* (an important point, since such forces are not usable in a combat situation. UN peacekeeping has been effective in helping to end at least three Middle East wars, in Cyprus, and in the former Belgian Congo (now Zaire) when it collapsed in anarchy in the early 1960's.

The drawback of interposing peacekeeping forces between two parties in an extended truce is that it tends to freeze a status quo which probably needs to be changed at least somewhat if the *causes* of war are to be dealt with. But there was for a time in the 1960's and 1970's widespread agreement that by contrast with unchecked national wars (such as Vietnam and Iran vs. Iraq) or situations of unremitting internal chaos and bloodshed (as in Ulster or Lebanon), the benefits of peacekeeping far outweighed its costs whether in financial, political or human terms. A few modest regional multilateral peacekeeping operations were also launched under the auspices of the OAS, the OAU and the Arab League.

Unfortunately, scars were left by Soviet (and, earlier, French) refusal to pay their share of the costs of some peacekeeping operations. Peacekeeping also was buffeted by savage ideological attacks on the UN in the Congo

operation (ONUC) by both Soviets and Western conserva-
tives. The concept suffered with the Turkish invasion of Cyprus
in 1974 despite the presence of a hitherto effective UN force,
and also as a result of the relatively high casualties of the UN
operation in southern Lebanon (UNIFIL) in the late 1970's and
early 1980's at the hands of various destroyers of the peace.
The US and others began to devise non-UN "multinational
forces," one of which succeeded in assisting Egyptian withdrawal from the Sinai in 1978-80, but the other of which was
part of the humiliatingly unsuccessful US intervention in the
Beirut meatgrinder in 1982-84.

The steady decline of multilateral peacekeeping in the
1970's and 1980's as a lively option in the minds of crisis
managers was a costly byproduct of the more general erosion of confidence in the UN as a political institution and the
revival of great power nationalism and unilateralism. Major
efforts of diplomacy and above all of will would be required
to reverse the trend and give multilateral security machinery
another historic chance.

MANAGING THE PROBLEMS OF MUTUAL DEPENDENCE

The idea of international "management" in economic, social
and technological realms is essentially a post-World War II
invention. To the founders of the UN system, the lessons of the
Great Depression added up to the need for far more cooperation in non-military sectors if sources of international tension
such as new tariff wars were to be avoided. Much economic
cooperation has in fact taken place. But one of the most
controversial aspects of contemporary international relations
concerns the wisdom of multilateral agreements that might
interfere with private enterprise and the workings of the
market, and proposals to "tax" the rich countries to benefit the
poor ones. This controversy has slowed the pace of cooperative problem-tackling, while obscuring from view various benefits the US (and everyone else) derives from "functional"
multilateral management where that is appropriate to the
problem.

Most such activities in the economic, social and technological realms fall under the heading of joint or collective *monitoring*, meaning fact-finding, data-collecting, reporting and standard-setting. But the controversy in the early 1980's over international arrangements for seabed mining of hard minerals under the UN Law of the Sea Treaty vividly illustrated the lack of consensus regarding multilateral *regulatory* activity. Some monitoring, and virtually all regulatory acitvities, invariably generate arguments between Third World supporters of multilateral controls, who tend to wield little influence except in concert, and conservative leaders of industralized Western nations who condemn what they interpret as socialism writ large. Such arguments reflect profound differences over the nature of governance, specifically the proper role of state machinery in the economy and with regard to the social order. For perspective, it is helpful to look briefly at some history and political philosophy.

For many centuries the functions of government, even when bloodily contested, were commonly defined. Ever since the demise of the medieval concept of divine right of kings, civil government, whether democratic or tyrannical, has been accepted as existing to render essential common services to the citizenry. Since the appearance of states in their modern form, in the mid-17th century, the list of things central governments exist to do for their citizens has been well understood. The primordial function has always been the physical protection of the citizenry and its property—in the words of the Preamble to the United States Constitution, to "provide for the common defense."

The next category of function of central government was, again quoting from the Preamble, to "promote the general Welfare." Originally this meant fostering commerce and conducting diplomacy (that order reflects the priority found in George Washington's Farewell Address). To do its job, government had to raise taxes—and armies. Soon, governments also took on the protection of domestic industrial and agricultural production from foreign competition. With growing complexity, Western governments by World War I had begun to regulate the size, profits, and working conditions of major domestic enterprises.

More recently, the unprecedented rush of knowledge

and technology stemming from scientific discovery and engineering applications has added yet another dimension to the agenda of governance in technically advanced countries. The newly expanded domestic agenda embraces a range of new problems ranging from uncontrollable inflation to environmental pollution and resource scarcity. Two astounding achievements, one in science and the other in public health, have generated the most daunting consequences for humankind, either for good or for intolerable ill. One set of problems came via physics from the release of nuclear energy. The other set of problems came via medicine from the release of human fertility.

The 1917 Russian Revolution brought special redefinition to traditional concepts of governance. Under "state socialism" the state rather than the individual citizen owned productive property, whether land, factory, or shop. Many governments today, without necessarily owning the means of production à la Marx, nevertheless practice some form of central control over aspects of industrial and agricultural life which in the West represented the most valued and productive private sectors. And almost every country, regardless of ideology, has experienced an accretion of governmental responsibility for the "basic human needs" of the population, ensuring some form of access to food, lodging, health services and education. Both socialist and capitalist societies (and their many mutant combinations) now routinely operate social security programs ranging from child support payments to old age pensions. From this practice has grown the general concept of "entitlements," which implies governmental support to individuals *as a matter of legal right* rather than as charity or transient political whim.

The domestic growth of such "entitlements" has created within some societies a new category of *human rights*. In addition to (and, in non-democratic countries, instead of) the traditional Western catalogue of political and civil rights, an official *obligation* is said to exist to ensure adequate food, shelter, employment, freedom from discrimination, and a variety of other "entitlements."

At the domestic level this has introduced a basic conflict between two philosophies, a conflict subsequently played out on the international stage as well. Countries in the Western tradition believe in *limited* governmental functions and a relatively free marketplace, on the premise that these twin concepts provide the best guarantors of both individual freedom and economic prosperity. The socialist bloc and many poor countries give paramountcy to *state-directed* economic and social welfare above the political rights and individual "freedom from violation of the person" so highly valued in the West. Their contention is that the rights on which Western political society rests are a luxury unaffordable by others until "basic human needs" are met. Needless to say, some in the West believe in the idea of entitlements, while some in the East and South highly value political liberty and personal freedom from governmental abuse. But no one seems to have suggested a truly satisfactory way to combine economic equity with economic growth *and* personal freedoms.

Whether the issue is economic entitlements or social rights, a major quarrel is inevitable between states whose public philosophy rests on such vastly different ideological foundations. The *international* debates today faithfully mirror those differences concerning the expansion of the "welfare" function, above all the extent to which regulation, not to mention redistribution of wealth and production, represent legitimate qualities of either domestic governance or global "management." The so-called "New International Economic Order" (NIEO), advanced programmatically by a coalition within the UN of developing countries known as the "Group of 77" (now numbering around 120), implies an equalization of wealth between rich and poor as a matter of obligation. The demands for equity and redistribution embodied in the NIEO drive much of the North-South debate, and still provide the idiom in which much UN rhetoric is couched.

Non-controversial "Trans-Boundary" Cooperation

The subjects for international "management" of global economic, social and technological disorders can be divided into several levels. The level usually called "functional" is the least infected by rhetoric about "monopoly capital" and "international socialism." Here are found programs for dealing with "common goods" types of functions which individual states are manifestly unable to manage by themselves, and which on any calculus of costs and benefits argue for cooperating to serve one's own best interests.

The list of what might be termed "non-optional cross-boundary functions" include some thoroughly familiar tasks: the international delivery of mail and of telecommunications, the allocation of shared space on the electromagnetic spectrum, the control of epidemic diseases that know no political frontiers, the protection of travellers along international sea and air routes, and the dissemination of information regarding weather and crops. The recognizably commonplace nature of these "neighborhood" chores has made it natural to assign to multilateral agencies missions familiar to one's own local community.

Reaching back into the 19th century, the Universal Postal Union, headquartered in Bern, Switzerland sets international postal standards and provides technical assistance to developing countries. For Americans, it represents the assurance that a letter mailed with a US stamp will be delivered anywhere in the world. It is difficult to imagine a less controversial function, and much the same can be said of the International Telecommunications Union, successor to another 19th century agency. Located in Geneva, it sets and regulates assignment of frequencies for all international radio, telephone, TV and satellite communications, acts as an international information and training center, and is currently instituting a worldwide dialing system.

But a word of caution: as the electromagnetic spectrum recently appeared to be running short of new frequencies for the exponentially increasing links among people and among countries, cooperation gave way for a while to accusations and threats. In addition, with the growing capacity for direct downlink broadcasting via satellites into peoples' homes, governments bent on controlling their own citizens' access to information felt threatened. The spectrum proved flexible, thanks to sideband and other technologies plus computerization of frequency allocation, and the pressure eased. But we have not heard the end of arguments for government control over all received communications, and, if the drive for a New International *Information* Order persists, over journalistic reporting as well.

It has been said with some justice that all contributions to all UN agencies could be justified by the World Health Organization's dazzling success in eradicating the scourge of smallpox from the face of the earth. The WHO, based in Geneva, conducts immunization campaigns, sets international health regulations, runs an epidemic warning system, helps improve health education and public health facilities; and fosters medical research. This all sounds non-controversial, and it is. Even during the decades-long US-led boycott of the Peoples Republic of China from UN membership, the WHO's epidemic control programs inevitably had to include the country containing a quarter of the human race.

But even technical agencies have not entirely escaped recent moves by militant Third World leaders to politicize their proceedings with contentious debates regarding Palestinian rights and Apartheid. Such posturing succeeded in poisoning two UN specialized agencies—the International Labor Organization and UNESCO—to the point where the US at least temporarily withdrew from both. The good news is that other Third World governments have joined Western member states in helping to protect technical programs from destructive tampering. It also helps that technical agencies such as the WHO are staffed and their meetings attended by the global medical and public health fraternity, and by scientists whose professional instinct is to keep political quarrels at arms length. In this sense some intergovernmental organizations, particularly where scientists and technicians have access to information on a global basis, can take shelter from the storms that sweep over political agencies such as the General Assembly and Security Council.

Other relatively non-controversial UN specialized agencies reflect the pragmatic need to get together to take care of common tasks no one can handle alone. The International Civil Aviation Organization—ICAO—in Montreal promotes safe and efficient civilian air travel by setting standards for aircraft operation safety and navigation equipment, pilot training, the use of a common language (English) and noise levels over land areas. It also provides rescue and communications facilities and technical assistance to LDCs. The obvious interest in a jet-propelled world in avoiding political controversy in the air was strained—as were great power relations—by the Soviet Union's destruction of an off-course Korean civil airliner full of passengers in September, 1983. ICAO investigated the incident, criticized the brutal Soviet act, and worked to avert such disasters in the future. The Inter-Governmental Maritime Consultative Organization in London serves a comparable purpose. IMCO also sponsors treaties to curb ocean pollution through dumping, and to establish liability for damage caused by oil spills. And the highly successful World Weather Watch was in fact initiated in the UN General Assembly.

The UN Food and Agriculture Organization in Rome— FAO—has worked chiefly in the developing regions, helping to improve agricultural and fishing techniques. The FAO like other specialized agencies seems to do best in the fields of research and technical assistance to developing countries. But, despite varying degrees of success, the problem of supplying adequate food for growing populations increasingly exceeds the capabilities of individual countries acting alone. Land, favorable climate, investment capital, foreign currency reserves, and human skills are unequally distributed among countries. A handful of food exporters generates vast agricultural surpluses, while the per capita food supply for many countries, notably in subSaharan Africa, continues to decline.

In a major international commitment to help improve food security for all, the 1974 Rome World Food Conference started new programs and created new institutions including the World Food Council and World Food Program to address such problems as emergency shortages, unpredictable price fluctuations, and the need to improve the capabilities of developing countries to feed themselves. The short-term results of these efforts have been discouraging. Negotiations for an international grain reserve petered out and the minimum target for international food aid has never been reached except in emergencies such as the 1985 African famine.

Many people recognize the need for more rational and humane international arrangements for distributing food to those who need it, while helping agricultural producers avoid costly supply and demand cycles. To act on these insights requires a recognition on the part of the chief grain producers, above all the US, that they too stand to gain from cooperative arrangements. It *also* requires a better showing by advocates of international management that the costs of tampering with the market need not outweigh the benefits.

MANAGING THE ECONOMIC AND SOCIAL AGENDA—PLUSES AND MINUSES

During the postwar period two agencies acquired reputations among both Western bankers and LDC recipients as indispensable actors on the global developmental scenes. The World Bank and the International Monetary Fund (IMF) were for some years independent of the UN system. Recently affiliated with the UN, both still represent the premier international agencies in their fields. But controversy concerning their adequacy mounts on two scores. The World Bank has a so-called "soft-window" affiliate, the International Development Association, which makes long-term, low-interest loans to governments and private enterprises in LDCs. The US contribution against which others are pegged recently failed to keep up with needs, particularly in a period of US deemphasis of international aid, and indeed of cooperative multilateral programs in general.

Even while becoming a prime force in reform efforts by nations facing financial insolvency, the IMF was increasingly criticized for threatening political stability in poor debtor countries by imposing onerous domestic restrictions. Its currency stabilization efforts seem less and less sufficient to the kind of episodic turmoil in international capital markets which can undermine national budgets overnight. Here too, with the US dollar reemergent as king of world currencies, the chances for improved monetary stability and predictability depend largely on American willingness to engage in serious negotiations aimed at restructuring the global monetary system.

Some of the same points can be made with respect to another major sector of world economic life which stands in serious need of fresh cooperative approaches. International trade is regulated primarily, if imperfectly, by the market, as it should be. The ancient market-undermining cycle of escalating competitive tariff barriers, leading to shared domestic misery, was substantially broken by the liberalization trend started by President Franklin Roosevelt in the 1930's. Despite strains, the US remains committed to freer trade, thanks to its growing dependency on export sales. A certain amount of inter-nation cooperation to avoid mutual economic suicide takes place bilaterally, notably among the US, Japan, and the European Community, as well as through special multilateral arrangements such as the Lomé Convention tying the Community with several score LDCs in preferential ways. Globally, a modest framework of cooperation is fostered by agreed trade arrangements under the Generalized Agreement on Tariffs and Trade—GATT.

But a host of new difficulties has arisen with which the current system cannot cope. The advanced nations of the industrial North are defensively inflicting economic damage on one another as their machinery wears out and their aging smokestack industries become non-competitive. Diplomatic bandaids keep trade warfare from breaking out. But the present "non-system" may prove simply unable to handle strains growing out of the transition of industrial societies to high technology, information and service sectors. Nor are current inter-state agreements on trade adequate to incorporate the spectacular transformation of some hitherto underdeveloped LDC's into major producers and exporters of manufacturers and consumer goods, plus high technology. Protectionism comes in new "non-tariff" forms related to subsidies plus pollution and safety standards. It threatens not only the newly-industrialized countries, but others who still rely on agricultural trade to finance their development and pay their debts.

THE BOUNDARIES OF ACTION

This overview of the management of global disorder highlights the central paradox in world affairs today. President Dwight Eisenhower once said that "the people want peace so badly governments better get out of their way and let them have it." But human nature comes with two faces, only one of which is pacific and constructive. The philosopher William James wrote pessimistically that "our ancestors have bred pugnacity into our bone and marrow, and thousands of years of peace won't breed it out of us." Perhaps this is what Immanuel Kant meant in his 18th century essay "Eternal Peace" when he argued that "The state of peace must be founded; for the mere omission of the threat of war is no security of peace. . . ."

As we have seen, security has many meanings, and towering over them all is the question of how best to avoid nuclear war. For the present, there appears to be no substitute for direct dealings between the two nuclear superpowers. The sooner both make the fundamental decision to get along on a live and let live basis, the sooner they will take the prudent risks essential to any serious reduction of nuclear weaponry. Each giant lacks trust in the other. But trust is relative. As the old Arab proverb has it, when the Prophet was asked by someone if he should let his camel loose in the desert and trust in Allah, he replied "first tie up your camel, and then trust in Allah."

UN Secretary General Dag Hammarskjöld once defined the overriding problem of our time as the "relations of man to man, of man to his environment, and of groups to groups." Tensions between East and West are so fraught with peril that they constantly claim the top of the agenda. Relations between the industrialized partners of the West are increasingly troubled, and may not always conform to the rule that when Moscow growls, the West draws together regardless of differences. As we have seen, the North-South relationship generates tension across the whole international security and welfare agenda.

The post World War II organizational arrangements—the UN system of agencies plus regional and functional bodies—

together form an unprecedented nexus of actual and potential cooperation. International organizations have brought great benefits to their members, along with major headaches. The result of three decades of decolonization has been the creation of almost a hunded new states which form a numerical majority in the UN General Assembly and the assemblies of the specialized agencies. Using the parliamentary devices learned from the West, this majority seeks through unity to convert individual weaknesses into economic strength through a form of political judo.

Indeed, as two scholars have written:

> Over their longer history, the greatest potential for change from international organizations may lie in the opportunity they give the less powerful to influence the climate of opinion and the accepted values according to which action is determined . . . they may become a means of giving the less powerful majority of countries a greater collective voice in the management of world affairs . . . (Robert W. Cox and Harold K. Jacobson, *The Anatomy of Influence*, p. 428)

But this potential empowerment of the powerless is one reason the great powers spurn UN opportunities and disdain UN exhortations and injunctions. The US no less than the Soviet Union, China no less than France and Britain, reject the idea that a numerical majority has the right to force action. Communist countries successfully align their votes with the majority almost regardless of the issue, but fundamentally distrust the processes of an institution whose control is shared with capitalist states. For their part, the major Western states chafe under the drumbeat of militant criticism, and increasingly conclude that Adlai Stevenson's hopes for a "Parliament of Man" were misplaced on the grounds that "a Parliament of Man composed largely of men who do not believe in Parliaments may not be a promising institution." (Naomi Bliven in the *New Yorker,* Apr. 28, 1980).

The sad estate to which international organization has fallen was reflected in Secretary General Perez de Cuellar's first annual report in which he spoke of "the crisis in the multilateral approach in international affairs and the concomitant erosion of the authority and status of world and regional intergovernmental institution." "We are," he concluded, "perilously near to a new international anarchy." Editor Lewis Lapham recently wrote in the same vein that "In an age of anxiety, the forces bearing forward into the unknown future sponsor countervailing forces beating backward into the familiar past. The more complex and civilized the advance, the more simple-minded and barbarous the retreat." (Harper's, March 1984, p. 11).

In rethinking our predicament, several principles are worth keeping in mind. Organizational solutions may not always be the correct pathway to genuine problem-solving. Theologian Reinhold Niebuhr deplored the "increasing tendency among modern men to imgine themselves ethical because they have delegated their vices to larger and larger groups." (Atlantic Monthly, 1927, p. 639). More practically, Harlan Cleveland counseled that "a multipolar world of independent nations—a world of protected variety—would constitute the safest environment . . . we want to be sure that no nation or group of nations ever gains the exclusive right even to define world order, let alone to manage it." (The Obligations of Power, p. 6). In short, safety and freedom lie in diversity, rather than in the global unity idealists once sought.

In this world, which like it or not is the one we have to work with, the American proclivity for pragmatic "problem-solving" looks more promising than the other American proclivity for institutional machinery operating under precise written rules. The method used successfully by the fathers of contemporary Europe such as Jean Monnet and Walter Hallstein was to ensure that "the parties all range themselves on one side of the table to confront the problems on the other side." (Robert R. Bowie in Shaping the Future, NY: Columbia U. Press, 1964, p. 15). No problems better lend themselves to this treatment than the control of nuclear weapons both superpowers build while decrying them, or the instabilities no one really benefits from in international trade, finance, food and energy supply or, for that matter, terrorism.

In this sense logic still points to the need for cooperative strategies even in an era when unilateralism and closed alliance relations are dominant over the multilateral variety. Attempts to build watertight compartments of unfettered state sovereignty confront porous national borders through which

leak in quickening pace such boundary-disregarding commodities as technology, information, finance capital, illegal
aliens and pollution. These objective trends make nonsense of
a strategy of "go-it-alone," however much the right to act
unilaterally is celebrated by leaders in Moscow and Washington, Tripoli and Jerusalem, Pretoria and Havana.

The 18th century philosopher Kant completed the passage quoted earlier about the need to "found" a state of
peace by concluding that "a neighbor may treat his neighbor
as an enemy unless he has guaranteed security to him, which
can only happen within a state of law." ("*Eternal Peace*," p.
436). Realistically, law follows rather than precedes the existence of a community which shares values extending beyond
the abstract fear of annihilation or anarchy. But "law in
pieces," like peace in pieces, is eminently practical, and found
everywhere about us.

Given even a minimal expansion of its presently constricted vision, the United States government would lose no
time in mobilizing a new coalition of moderate states of all
regions and persuasions to resume progress, however modest, in constructing pieces of a more workable and durable
international order. The pragmatic prescription calls for concentrating on building essential "fragments of community"
rather than designing new master blueprints. The vital first step
would be to reinstate a serious belief in the efficacy of
equitable and verifiable negotiated arms reductions, without
making that commitment dependent on achieving strategic
"superiority," or on transforming the Soviet system into something more acceptable to us, and vice versa. Another important US step in the direction of encouraging constructive
international behavior would be to rejoin the human race, as
it were, by offering to renegotiate the virtually completed Law
of the Sea treaty developed under three American administrations, but discarded on ideological grounds by a fourth.

Will a change in the American approach produce the
improvements in the international climate so ardently desired
by the people of whom General Eisenhower spoke? Not
necessarily. But we have control only over our own attitudes
and actions and, more to the point, we are still the richest and
most powerful nation in the world. "Progress," a writer recently argued, "does not march broadly and uniformly, like a

Roman legion but, rather, sends out scouts, in ones and twos, darting ahead of the main body" (Anthony Bailey in *The New Yorker*). It is time once again for the United States of America, even as it keeps its powder dry, to give a fresh boost to the intensified international cooperation on which our interests and security realistically depend.

READINGS ON THE MANAGEMENT OF GLOBAL DISORDER

I

LOOKING AHEAD

I. LOOKING AHEAD

THE GREAT PRIORITY TASKS IN THE MANAGEMENT OF PEACE ARE TWO, one negative, one positive. The first charge on leadership is to avoid a thermonuclear war in which all humankind would suffer intolerably. The second charge is to devise far better ways to foster international cooperation in dealing effectively with the international challenges that confront all humankind.

These great tasks require clear thinking on the part of both leaders and informed citizens. But the primary obstacle is the lack of consensus on the nature of the challenge, the kind and amount of international "order" that is necessary or desirable, and the need for adaptation to an unprecedented rate of change. To act effectively also requires knowledge of the essential facts and issues, against the backdrop of three crucial background elements.

The first such issue has to do with how to define the problem. In section IA (whose all-inclusive title for our dilemma—the "Problematique"—I have borrowed from the Club of Rome) three keen observers describe the consequences of global change that insistently call for better ways of coping. The late Charles W. Yost, one of America's most experienced diplomats, lists five critical factors that, in combination, bring all peoples under unprecedented siege. Second, veteran economist Miriam Camps focuses on the contradictions inherent in the concept of a global community. Third, Zbigniew Brzezinski, innovative scholar and National Security Adviser to President Carter, identifies two schools of thought that share some basic premises about global interdependence, but diverge sharply between mindsets that he labels "power realism" and "planetary humanism." Many of the writers in the sections that follow fall into one or the other of these broad categories.

The second background element is the balance of limits

and possibilities in the human condition. Political scientist Cyril F. Black starts the discussion in section IB with the thesis that much of the violence characteristic of the modern era has come from the effort to integrate people possessing contrasting value systems and political institutions; he concludes that genuine security will require some transfer of loyalties from national to international and transnational institutions. It is interesting to compare the view, articulated three centuries earlier, of the Reverend Thomas Hobbes, writing in violent seventeenth-century England. Hobbes set the tone for a depressing view of human nature that without adequate social and political controls adds up to a war of all against all. The late American anthropologist Clyde Kluckhohn suggests that social science can shed light on the baffling dilemma of how people can get along together peacefully despite their differences. Finally, the late historian Hans J. Morgenthau is the *locus classicus* for the concept of power as the fuel for all sociopolitical engines.

The third essential background component is a set of mind-stretching—and sobering—glimpses into the future that reflective leaders must help shape. Writer Francis A. Beer supplies an analytic framework for a future that assumes nations will develop in ways consistent with past experiences. He holds that if peaceful periods are longer, international polarization will nevertheless increase. In 1980 the U.S. Department of State and the Council on Environmental Quality startled Presidents and citizens alike with their so-called "Global 2000" report. Among the conclusions: the rich-poor gap will increase, there will be fewer resources to go around, the environment will lose important life-supporting capacities, prices will rise, vulnerability to natural disaster and human disruptions will increase, and the population explosion may overshoot the earth's carrying capacity. Former World Bank President Robert S. McNamara sketches the dire consequences of that unchecked population growth.

Management professor Peter F. Drucker argues that on the economic front the world has *already* changed in three crucial ways: primary products are uncoupled from manufacturing, production no longer determined employment, and capital, not trade, drives the global economy.

Others are optimistic if—and it is a crucial if—people will take on more individual responsibility. Harlan Cleveland, Dean of the Hubert Humphrey Institute of Public Affairs of the University of Minnesota (and general editor of this series) pictures the world in which nobody is in charge, and which seems to many of its less affluent inhabitants to be essentially leaderless, dangerous, uneconomic, unjust and even ungovernable. He considers it imperative for citizens and, more important still, candidates for high office, to wrap their minds around these complexities, and develop their own "strategic global agenda."

A.

PROBLEMATIQUE

HISTORY & MEMORY

Charles W. Yost

THERE ARE NOW PRESENT IN OUR GLOBAL SOCIETY five factors, all direct or indirect consequences of the scientific revolution, which no previous human society, no earlier century, has ever had to confront. These five factors, taken together, represent a qualitative change in 'our condition and our predicament.

The first is the presence and proliferation of nuclear weapons, which, if used on a wide scale, could profoundly cripple or wholly destroy our civilization.

The second factor is the population explosion which, unless comprehensively curbed before the end of the century, could place such intolerable burdens on the environment and on the structures of society that both might break down.

The third factor, arising partly from the second and partly from the extravagances of modern industrialism, is that certain raw materials on which modern societies depend both for sustainment and for political stability may be dangerously diminished before either substitutes are devised or greater austerity becomes politically tolerable.

The fourth factor is that a global juxtaposition of peoples, an uncomfortable interdependence of disparate and sometimes hostile societies, has been created by the revolution in communications brought about during the past half-century by the airplane, radio, television, satellites, computers, and the new habits and appetites these have generated.

The fifth factor is the drastic compression in time of the social strains and transformations that flow from the coincidence of the several revolutions of modern times.

If these five novel factors, profoundly disquieting as they are, are nevertheless confronted soberly and resolutely by all of us individually and collectively, there is no essential reason why all of them should not be successfully dealt with and overcome. Nuclear weapons, despite our addiction to them, certainly need not be used. Population growth can be slowed and stabilized, late but not too late. Critical raw materials can be conserved, recycled, even forgone if necessary, until substitutes are found or life-styles adjusted to their absence. International interdependence, exasperating as it may often be, can be accommodated to and effectively managed to the mutual advantage of most if not all peoples. Social transformations, disruptive and violent as they will often be in our times, can nevertheless be contained and eventually digested. There is nothing intrinsically insoluble about any of these problems.

The question is whether human societies as currently organized, nationally and internationally, as psychologically conditioned by their past and present social environment, *will* deal with these problems rationally and decisively, *will* make the necessary psychological, political, and structural adaptations in time.

[*History and Memory,* 1980, pp. 281–82]

COLLECTIVE MANAGEMENT

Miriam Camps

IMPLICIT IN THE CONCEPT of global or world community
there are the ideas not only that the world's welfare is to be
optimized, (rather than that of a particular state or group of
states), but also that it is the individual rather than the nation
whose interests are of primary concern. Again, this is not a
concept that commands general support today: it is openly
attacked in some societies and honored more by words than by
deeds in most societies. Almost everywhere, the nation-state is
still the political and social structure that commands the most
loyalty and disposes of the most power. Nevertheless, although
the claim of the individual rather than the state to be the
essential component of the world system will not become widely
accepted in the years ahead, there is a detectable shift in the way
individual claims are regarded today as compared to the
situation even a relatively few years ago. This has become
conspicuous recently in the new attention given to human rights
and in the emphasis put on reshaping assistance to the
developing countries to ensure that the basic needs of the
poorest people within those countries are met.[12]

We live in a time of many contradictions, most of which
show every sign of continuing throughout the eighties. On the
one hand, we have new demands placed on governments. On
the other, we have a pervasive distrust of governments—a
dualism characterizing the international as well as the national
sphere. At the international level, the problems of governance
become compounded by the further contradiction that despite
the emphasis on the new need for collective management there
is little willingness to delegate any power to international or
supranational agencies. Some of the more ambitious attempts to

do so, such as the European Community, are in conspicuous difficulty. The new emphasis on the need to give reality to the concept of the world as a community by accepting an obligation to organize international relationships to meet the basic human needs of all people coexists with insistent demands for recognition of the sanctity of unfettered national action. Diversity, resurgent nationalism, and the proliferation of entities called states but sharing few common characteristics create a sense of a more fragmented world. Yet the evidences of the global cobweb of interconnectedness in which we are all caught up are everywhere about us.

[*Collective Management: The Reform of Global Organization*, 1981, pp. 25–26]

[12]The following quotation from a speech by Secretary of State Vance to the OECD ministerial meeting, June 24, 1977, is also indicative of the shift: "We are in transit to a new era of cooperation and common action. In practical terms our journey will involve going beyond new directions for industrial democracies, new discourse with state-trading nations, and new relationships with developing countries. It will take us to a firmer focus on people. It is the individual and collective hopes of people, their rights and their needs that deserve the fullest measure of our dedication." Official text issued by U.S. Information Service, June 24, 1977.

US FOREIGN POLICY

Zbigniew Brzezinski

A BROAD AND UNDEFINED NOTION of global interdependence seems to represent the general principle which most Americans share.

This underlying consensus, however, is vague. It lacks a sharp focus defining, as was the case in the past, the character and thrust of America's relationship to the world. Moreover, the shared notion of global interdependence is given philosophical and political substance in significantly divergent ways by two contending schools of thought which today represent the principal lines of division among the concerned and articulate public. The outlook of these two contending schools—each of which initially starts with the same basic premise of global interdependence—may be best capsulated by the terms "power realism" and "planetary humanism."

The power realists, generally more conservative in their values, tend to be preoccupied with the more traditional concerns of international affairs, particularly with such issues as strategy, the relationship of forces, the balance of power, diplomacy and monetary policy; they attach a very high value to stability, both as a concept and as a norm. They may often disagree on prescriptions and priorities, but they do hold a basic view in common in that they see the world as still dominated by *international* politics.

In contrast, the planetary humanists tend to think of the globe more as *a unit* beset by certain common problems. When attempting to translate into policy their basic predispositions, they tend to concentrate on such matters as ecology, nutrition, development, social justice and equality, or limits to growth.

There are thus overtones in the above division of the older debate in America between "realists" and "idealists," but the differences are important: the new power realists accept more

45

and more the notion of political interdependence, and their concern with stability preempts to some extent the idealists' earlier preoccupation with peace. Planetary humanists, unlike their predecessors the idealists, are much more concerned with social change—rather than peace—in a world which they see as beset by dynamically mounting socio-economic crises, and their remedies focus on socio-political reforms. Many of them decry stability and accept the desirability in some cases even of violent change.

The former tend to be older, and hence an element of generational conflict is doubtless involved here (providing a parallel to Klingberg's cycles). This generational variance in perspectives is in large measure a consequence of the historical discontinuity experienced lately by American society. The thrust of any society into a new age for which established generalizations are lacking creates a situation of uncertainty and division ably expressed by novelist Hermann Hesse, whose writings have been sensitive to historical change:

> Human life is reduced to real suffering, to hell, only when two ages, two cultures and religions overlap. . . . There are times when a whole generation is caught in this way between two ages, two modes of life, with the consequence that it loses all power to understand itself and has no standard, no security, no simple acquiescence.

Much of what has happened in America during the last decade and a half fits that evocative statement. It is no exaggeration to state that America has lately experienced—probably more so than any other contemporary society—a true cultural revolution. In the short time span of slightly more than a decade the United States has undergone a significant change in its social values, racial relations, sexual mores, esthetic and artistic standards; all of that is bound to produce especially sharp generational gaps, including disagreements about America's role in the world.

["U.S. Foreign Policy: The Search for Focus",
1973, pp. 712–13]

B.

THE NATURE OF HUMAN SOCIETY

WORLD ORDERS: OLD AND NEW

Cyril F. Black

II. *The Process of Global Transformation*

The Scientific and Technological Revolution.

Underlying both the unprecedented opportunities and the potential catastrophes characteristic of the modern era is the scientific and technological revolution that has already transformed some societies and seems likely in the long run to transform the way of life of all human beings if they survive long enough. The essence of this revolution is an increase in per capita productivity in most spheres of human activity that has almost completely changed the way of life of peoples affected by it—not always for the better. This is not the place to describe this process of change except to say that it has involved increasing specialization, and hence interdependence, starting with the family and extending out in all directions until some aspects of human activity are now globally interdependent. It will be a great many decades before this process works itself out fully, but several of its characteristics are worth noting as they affect the world order in the immediate future.

(1) The growing necessity for interdependence, radiating out from the family to ever larger structures of organization, has ineluctably involved the destruction of institutions developed during the premodern level of science and technology. The agony of violence that this transformation has engendered reflects the profound difficulties involved in adapting institutions inherited from an earlier time to the levels of achievement made possible by the scientific and technological revolution. The application of this new knowledge to human affairs holds out the possibility that for the first time in history all human beings can be adequately fed, housed, and cared for. At the same time, progress toward the achievement of this level of human welfare has been accompanied by unprecedented changes in the way

beliefs have had to give way to modern values. Institutions based essentially on local communities have gradually lost their influence, as human activity has come to be organized in ever larger frameworks until even the largest states must now cooperate closely to meet all of their needs. Much of the violence characteristic of the modern era has come from the effort to integrate peoples with contradictory value systems and political institutions. The competition for resources to meet the needs of rapidly growing economies, and the massive movements of peoples from the countryside to cities, from agriculture to industry, and from ignorance to education, have also led to much conflict.

(2) The effectiveness of institutions depends on the loyalty accorded to them by individuals. An important aspect of the global prospect of transformation is the change in values that enables individuals to transfer their loyalties from old to new institutions.

Action is motivated by values—by a choice of goals that is based on an understanding of what the world is like and on faith in principles by which it should be ordered. Values must change with the advancement of knowledge resulting from experience and study, but since they are firmly rooted in the past they change only with great difficulty. In an era in which societies are being rapidly transformed, established values frequently become an obstacle to the adaptation of traditional ways called for by new knowledge. People are cautious about transferring their loyalties from established ways to those that have not been fully tried.

For most people the highest values are the maintenance and advancement of their personal welfare and that of their immediate families. For this value they have been willing to sacrifice the lives of those dear to them in the civil struggles accompanying the creation and modernization of national states, and in the international wars in which the integrity of these states has been perceived to be at stake. Loyalty to the national state has been the most intense and persistent form of identity reflecting the search for personal welfare in the modern era. One of the most challenging problems in the near future will be to achieve a significant transfer in loyalties from national to international and transnational institutions so that the latter can gain acceptance as a necessary means to achieving personal security and other common objectives.

A broadening focus of individual loyalties reflects and is accompanied by the growing relevance of the world order to individual welfare. The value once placed on the large family as a source of mutual security is giving way to an acceptance of family planning as a means of assuring that populations will not outstrip the food available to support them. The majority of the people of the world who live in poor countries now expect to achieve within one lifetime the level available to the few in rich countries. The political, economic, and social rights of individuals that were once handled by local custom have now become matters of international concern. In these and other respects, as a result of increasing specialization and the ever-expanding exchange of goods and services, values relating to elemental human needs that were once a matter of local concern have been placed on the world agenda.

["World Orders, Old and New", 1977, pp. 4–6]

LEVIATHAN

Thomas Hobbes

WHATSOEVER THEREFORE IS CONSEQUENT to a time of Warre, where every man is Enemy to every man; the same is consequent to the time, wherein men live without other security, than what their own strength, and their own invention shall furnish them withall. In such condition, there is no place for Industry; because the fruit thereof is uncertain: and consequently no Culture of the Earth, no Navigation, nor use of the commodities that may be imported by Sea; no commodious Building; no Instruments of moving, and removing such things as require much force; no Knowledge of the face of the Earth; no account of Time; no Arts; no Letters; no Society; and which is worst of all, continuall feare, and danger of violent death; And the life of man, solitary, poore, nasty, brutish, and short. . . .

To this warre of every man against every man, this also is consequent; that nothing can be Unjust. The notions of Right and Wrong, Justice and Injustice have there no place. Where there is no common Power, there is no Law: where no Law, no Injustice. Force, and Fraud, are in warre, the two Cardinall vertues. Justice, and Injustice are none of the Faculties neither of the Body, nor Mind. If they were, they might be in a man that were alone in the world, as well as his Senses, and Passions. They are Qualities, that relate to men in Society, not in Solitude. It is consequent also to the same condition, that there be no Propriety, no Dominion, no *Mine* and *Thine* distinct; but onely that to be every mans, that he can get; and for so long, as he can keep it. And thus much for the ill condition, which man by meer Nature is actually placed in; though with a possibility to come out of it, consisting partly in the Passions, partly to his Reason.

The Passions that encline men to Peace, are Feare of Death; Desire of such things as are necessary to commodious living; and a Hope by their Industry to obtain them. And Reason suggesteth convenient Articles of Peace, upon which men may be drawn to agreement. These Articles, are they, which otherwise are called the Lawes of Nature.

[*Leviathan,* pp. 103–106]

MIRROR FOR MAN

Clyde Kluckhohn

ANTHROPOLOGY PROVIDES A SCIENTIFIC basis for dealing with the crucial dilemma of the world today: how can peoples of different appearance, mutually unintelligible languages, and dissimilar ways of life get along peaceably together? . . .

What common ground is there between human beings of all tribes and nations? What differences exist? what is their source? how deep-going are they? . . .

The new stage of development of the social sciences, still largely unrealized by the general public, may prove to have consequences as revolutionary as those of atomic energy. However, it would be fantastic to anticipate any immediate molding of world civilization to human desires and needs. Cultures and beliefs, attitudes, and feelings of men change slowly even in the accelerated modern tempo . . .

Human life should remain as a home of many rooms. But the world with all its variousness can still be one in its allegiance to the elementary common purposes shared by all peoples. Those boundaries that block mutual understanding will be worn dim by much international traffic in ideas, in exchange of goods and services. Within each society the use of scientific methods in the study of human relations can adjust our culture patterns to the changes brought about by technology and world-wide economic interdependence. This can happen. It probably will happen. But when?

[*Mirror for Man*, 1957, pp. 9, 220]

POLITICS AMONG NATIONS

Hans J. Morgenthau

INTERNATIONAL POLITICS, like all politics, is a struggle for power. Whatever the ultimate aims of international politics, power is always the immediate aim. Statesmen and peoples may ultimately seek freedom, security, prosperity, or power itself. They may define their goals in terms of a religious, philosophic, economic, or social ideal. They may hope that this ideal will materialize through its own inner force, through divine intervention, or through the natural development of human affairs. They may also try to further its realization through nonpolitical means, such as technical co-operation with other nations or international organizations. But whenever they strive to realize their goal by means of international politics, they do so by striving for power. The Crusaders wanted to free the holy places from domination by the Infidels; Woodrow Wilson wanted to make the world safe for democracy; the Nazis wanted to open Eastern Europe to German colonization, to dominate Europe, and to conquer the world. Since they all chose power to achieve these ends, they were actors on the scene of international politics . . .

Political power is a psychological relation between those who exercise it and those over whom it is exercised. It gives the former control over certain actions of the latter through the influence which the former exert over the latter's minds. That influence derives from three sources: the expectation of benefits, the fear of disadvantages, the respect or love for men or institutions. It may be exerted through orders, threats, persuasion, the authority or charisma of a man or of an office, or a combination of any of these. . . .

The political objective of military preparations of any kind is to deter other nations from using military force by making it too risky for them to do so. The political aim of military preparations is, in other words, to make the actual application of military force unnecessary by inducing the prospective enemy to desist from the use of military force. The political objective of war itself is not per se the conquest of territory and the annihilation of enemy armies, but a change in the mind of the enemy which will make him yield to the will of the victor. . . .

The aspiration for power being the distinguishing element of international politics, as of all politics, international politics is of necessity power politics. While this fact is generally recognized in the practice of international affairs, it is frequently denied in the pronouncements of scholars, publicists, and even statesmen. . . .

In recent times, the conviction that the struggle for power can be eliminated from the international scene has been connected with the great attempts at organizing the world, such as the League of Nations and the United Nations.

[*Politics Among Nations,* 1967, pp. 25–30]

C.

SKETCHES OF THE FUTURE

PEACE AGAINST WAR

Francis A. Beer

OUR DESCRIPTION AND EXPLANATION of the dynamics of peace and war provide a basis for predicting the future and a strategy that might control it.

PROJECTIONS

Projections of the future are always risky. If we attempt to draw lessons from history, we may assume that the future will be like the past. Such extrapolations are useful only if there are no major surprises. If we suspend our doubts about continuity in history and allow ourselves to assume that the future will develop in a way consistent with our historical experience, the major factors of violence and technology—aggregation, polarization, and militarization—should tend to develop along a particular natural course.

Violence

There may be a long-run trend toward peace diffision and concentration and aggravation. Peaceful periods may be longer today while wars may have become less frequent and shorter. War casualties may have increased both in absolute terms and relative to population. The actual existence of such a trend is open to question. If it does exist, however, the map of future international relations will show longer, lower valleys of peace together with sharper, higher peaks of violence.

Peaceful life will become more and more the norm. Wars will become less frequent and, when they do occur, they will be shorter than in the past.

59

Declining general incidence of war or the termination of any particular military conflict is obviously welcome. Yet neither one necessarily implies the elimination or even reduction of the human or material costs of war. War will not go away. International violence will continue to be a problem of much more than historical interest.

Longer interwar periods will be way-stations for subsequent wars that may inflict even greater casualties than the ones that preceded them. There will be more war-related deaths both absolutely and relative to population because of the higher destruction wrought by wars when they do occur, and the chances for the average citizen to complete his or her life in peace will be reduced.

If the pattern of domestic violence follows international violence, there will be fewer civil wars. Yet again, when domestic violence does occur, it will tend to be more massive and pervasive than in the past, and it will kill and wound larger numbers of individuals and higher percentages of domestic populations.

Much international violence will occur in the gray zone between peace and war. Governments will continue to intervene clandestinely in the affairs of others. Secret services and mercenaries will try to intimidate or eliminate opponents, using violence in counterinsurgency operations. Assassination and torture will be important weapons (cf. Little, 1975; Klare, 1972).

Guerrillas and terrorists will threaten organizations of all kinds—governments, cities, corporations, schools. Nuclear capabilities in the hands of terrorists will pose grave problems for highly concentrated urban or nuclear stockpile areas (cf. Beres, 1979; Norton and Greenberg, 1979; Blair and Brewer, 1977; Krieger, 1975).

Wars may be most common in the Third World, where the logic of modern technology is weaker. International violence should be relatively frequent in Southeast Asia, Africa, and Latin America. Such wars will imply relatively low casualties because they will usually center around conventional or limited nuclear capabilities.

Wars at North-South seams will be rarer but more serious. One possible area of friction is the Middle East, located at the juncture of Europe, Asia, and Africa, the center of religious conflict and energy resources. One can imagine a scenario, the early stages of which include Arab leaders raising the price of oil to new heights and using the revenues to accelerate modernization. Simultaneously, they undertake increasingly militant actions against Israel and the Western powers. These nations pay the price for oil and military defense in declining production, rising inflation, and unemployment. At some point the Palestinians, the Arab states, and their Northeastern allies attempt a final military solution to the Israeli problem. Alternatively, Israel and the Northwestern allies use military force to seize critical oil fields. Violence expands in terms of both weapons and geography. Each side undertakes nuclear strikes against the other. Fighting spreads north through Turkey and west across the Mediterranean to southern Europe and North Africa.

Unlike energy reserves, food is a problem that is geographically diffuse. If mass starvation reaches major proportions, and if the global South continues to develop military capabilities, Third World governments may threaten, provoke, or undertake nuclear war to obtain nourishment for their populations.

Wars in the Northern hemisphere should occur least often, but will carry the most dangerous implications. Possible wars in Northeast Asia include violence between the Soviet Union, China, and possibly Japan. In Northern Europe, the status of Berlin might again threaten to bring the Soviet Union and the Eastern European states to blows with the North Atlantic powers (cf. Hackett et al., 1979; Salisbury, 1970).

A portion of future organized warfare will be fought with the most advanced means of mass destruction—if only because they exist. Such wars will produce massive direct casualties as whole cities are destroyed. They will generate even larger indirect, long-term damage. The use of nuclear weapons will permanently raise global radioactivity. Nuclear effects will show up over the long term in statistics for various diseases, including genetic defects in the newborn (cf. Lewis, 1979).

If atomic, biological, and chemical warfare expands to its natural boundaries, it may cover all areas of the globe and involve the use of all weapons in national stockpiles. It may destroy large portions of existing human civilization and cause serious disabilities to that portion which remains.

Such war will be more terrible than any that humankind has ever experienced. Yet it will probably not permanently destroy global humanity. At the present time this seems technically impossible.

Aggregation

Aggravated international violence, together with the exhaustion of natural resources, might destroy modern technology. Humanity might not follow the dinosaurs into extinction, but it could be thrown backward to an early industrial or preindustrial period. The world of modern global technology may end as a lost civilization like the Garden of Eden, Atlantis, or Mayan society (cf. Stavrianos, 1976; Meadows et al., 1974; Vacca, 1974).

The logic of our argument suggests, however, that aggregation will continue to grow in the future as it has in the past. International law and organization will gradually become more supranational. International legal theory and practice will include new sectors: space, the oceans, and resources are issue areas where legal growth is likely to occur. Additional international actors—supranational organizations, nation-states, various kinds of transnational groups, and individuals—will be recognized and will make use of the expanding international legal framework.

The number of international courts will grow, and with them, personnel and resources available to the international legal sector. This expanded network of international courts will help settle an increasing number of disputes within the law of peace. International court decisions will be increasingly accepted as having the authoritative force of law. International actors will find the stakes in many cases less important than the value of ongoing institutions for resolving disputes.

International courts will also act more authoritatively on the law of war. War victims in the future may seek legal redress for alleged violations of *jus ad bellum* or *jus in bello*. International criminal courts may further develop the principles of tribunals like the one convened at Nuremberg after World War II and use them more actively to punish individuals for international crimes (cf. Ferencz, 1979; Johnston, 1974; Falk, 1971b).

Other forms of international organization will continue to grow in a similar way. There may be short-run drops in support for particular institutions. Over the long run, however, existing international organizations at all levels will add to their staffs and their treasuries. New functional and regional organizations, multinational corporations and conglomerates will appear.

International organizations will contribute more extensively to dispute settlement and conflict management. They will provide more assistance to direct negotiations as well as such services as good offices, inquiry, mediation, concilation, and arbitration. They will also supply expanded peacekeeping forces and war relief.

As international bureaucratic activities expand, they will help national governments. Many people believe that there already is too much domestic government. The future promises more rather than less.

Exchange will also continue to grow. The future will see the gradual emergence of a New International Economic Order (cf. Cline, 1979a, 1979b; Cox, 1979; Bergsten, 1975). The NIEO will include higher levels of international trade, investment, assistance, and migration. There will be an overall rise in material welfare. Global, regional, and national trade and development programs and planning will all contribute to a general increase in the standard of living. The U.N. Specialized Agencies and Regional Economic Commissions as well as various regional economic communities will continue to work to this end.

Scientific discoveries and inventions will benefit us materially. And we will increasingly find ways to deal with the critical problems of energy, pollution, food, and overpopulation. The fact that we are much more aware of these problems is itself a strong force for their amelioration and resolution (cf. Leontieff et al., 1977; Kahn et al., 1976).

The exhaustion of fossil fuels poses a short-term threat to man's energy reservoir. In the long run diverse methods will generate new energy. Among the most promising is the development of much more efficient techniques for using solar energy. Massive solar collection stations may be built in the world's great deserts or on ocean or space platforms. A breakthrough in photovoltaic technique would allow each building and vehicle itself to generate much of the energy it requires to operate (cf. Stobaugh and Yergin, 1979; Lovins, 1977; Willrich, 1975).

Advances on these and other fronts should dissipate or transform many of the present problems of pollution. The replacement of fossil fuels must inevitably reduce the automobile exhaust fumes clouding major cities. Advanced emission control and industrial filtration systems will further protect air, earth, and water. The pollution problems of nuclear energy sources will be hard to solve. As yet, they have not been dealt with in a way that can inspire great confidence. The current state of the nuclear energy industry implies radioactive contamination and thermal pollution, and the possible impairment of life in the oceans. One hopes, however, that over time the efficiency of nuclear plants will gradually increase and their harmful emissions will substantially decline.

Agriculture will expand and diversify. New food sources will be cultivated and processed. New techniques of weather modification and water dynamics will increase agricultural yeilds. Desalination and the development of salt-water technology will allow people to use water resources previously inhospitable to human agriculture.

The problem of overpopulation will adapt to the solutions of technology as well. The global death rate will continue to decline—at least during peacetime, but eventually the global birth rate may level off or decline as well. The development and distribution of new and more efficient birth control devices will make family planning much easier. Child-rearing may become increasingly expensive—as a result of both market forces and government policies, including taxation—and this will also help bring overpopulation under control. State-supervised reproduction and child-rearing may even take much family planning and decisionmaking out of individual hands.

Language will continue to expand. International communications will increase. The growth of international bureaucracy and exchange implies a corresponding increase in international communications at all levels. Devices like space satellites and sensors will provide increasingly complete and sophisticated coverage of the earth's surface, allowing close monitoring of, and informed rapid intervention in, all dimensions of collective life.

Multilateral diplomacy will cover new arenas of international activity. International media, business, educational, and leisure communications will grow. Scientists and artists will improve international information transmission at all levels, from presidents and prime ministers to ordinary citizens. These international developments will feed back into domestic communities, producing some homogenization of culture as well as increasing the promulgation of the values of cooperation and peace at all levels of society.

Polarization

The direct effects of further aggregation should help to limit war and militarization. At the same time, however, continued aggregation will also work to increase polarization. Differentiation, inequality, and instability will all become more pronounced.

Major groups will become more distinct. Their boundaries will be firmer. Their connections with external groups will be weaker, their internal relations denser. The global Northwest, Northeast, and South will further develop their own separate international legal blocs, organizational coalitions, transaction networks, and ideologies. These will both bind them closer together and separate them further from each other.

Nation-states will become increasingly centralized. Central national governments will dominate regional, provincial, and local political communities. National markets will become further concentrated. Populations will be more densely packed. National myths will be more pervasive as modern education and communications assimilate different ethnic and religious groups into a homogenized culture. Dissident belief systems will become rare and unpopular.

As the logic of mass politics, economics, and culture works itself out, national communities will grow at the expense of the autonomy of groups and individuals. Centralized national political systems may involve more popular participation in collective decisions and expanded formal political rights for minority groups and individuals. Advanced technology will also allow increased popular participation in decisionmaking; and such participation will increase over time—including more and more people and increasing numbers and kinds of issues—political and military as well as social, economic, and cultural. Two-way interactive television hooked into central computer facilities will allow face-to-face discussion and rapid voting (cf. Campbell, 1974).

Paradoxically, however, the application of computerized communications technology to politics may increase individual feelings of powerlessness and isolation. Many votes on many issues provide individuals with only a small portion of control. Though individuals may be increasingly included in decision-making about collective matters, they will also be increasingly excluded from decisionmaking about private matters. In spite of increased opportunities for participation in collective decisions, individuals may feel that their own lives are increasingly beyond their own control and subject to the arbitrary dictates of the external society. The individual will have a shrinking sector of his or her own life under his or her autonomous, private, and sole command. People will remain more and more at a physical distance, with less and less reason to leave their isolated spaces and mingle constructively with others.

Inequality will become more obvious. The powerful and rich will move further away from the weak and poor. Those who hold political power at different levels will be increasingly distant from those who do not. The rich will grow richer, and the poor will grow richer—but the rich will grow richer at a faster rate, and the poor will feel poorer.

Some presently poor states with scarce resources like oil may improve their positions through hard bargaining. Most of the world's poor, however, will travel in accommodations that are more and more distant from first class (cf. Hardin, 1977a, 1977b; Nagel, 1970).

Class inequality will advance within domestic societies as well. Bureau-technocrats will use their control of collective property to consolidate and advance their own interest (cf. Kahn et al., 1977).

Instability will become more pronounced. If growth continues, change will become more rapid as new discoveries and inventions build on each other. If growth slows, different groups will win or lose substantial amounts of cherished values (cf. Deutsch, 1975).

Militarization

The polarization of the system will be related to its further militarization. More differentiated international legal blocs and international organization coalitions will contribute to more legal justification of war and military alliances. Stronger international transaction networks will channel military transfers between nations, either through overt military trade and aid or more indirect means, including related knowledge and equipment for supposedly nonmilitary purposes.

Expanded exchange supergroups and common markets will use the boycott, embargo, and blockade in more subtle forms to exert pressure on opponents. Different sides will attempt to apply the resources they control for bargaining purposes—food, ocean and space resources, weather modification, directed pollution, energy, or perhaps the forcible exportation of surplus population (cf. Abrahamsson and Steckler, 1973; Redick, 1974). Global ideologies may expound values and plans for peace, but they will also convey hostility toward those in other camps (cf. Hsin, 1972).

National differentiation will go together with national militarization. Governmental centralization, market concentration, and mythology will keep company with more military regimes, military complexes, militant attitudes and beliefs.

As national communities become harder and more tightly bound, military regimes will become more common. Large segments of the globe will be under direct or indirect military rule.

Political communities will become more coercive, moving in the direction of garrison states. The velvet language of democracy or socialism will hide a good deal of intimidation. Repressive political regimes will rely less on prison, torture, and killing than they do today. More indirect and sophisticated methods will use the advanced technology of information gathering and presuasion to reach the end of political control more efficiently.

National military complexes will expand. The military will increasingly diversify, associating itself with widely desired social goals, including material welfare. National resources will be cultivated with an eye to their direct military application. Military managers will develop even more sophisticated political and administrative skills to generate and supervise massive budgets and personnel. Nongovernmental organizations, including business corporations, will increasingly serve military ends and use military methods.

National mythology will be increasingly militant. Individuals will be expected to identify more exclusively and completely with their nation-states than they now do. Military values, images, and attitudes will also be much more important.

Greater international and national inequality also imply the greater necessity of military capabilities. Military might will help maintain and increase such inequality. Nations with large military establishments will use them to coerce others to provide what they want. Within nation-states, the military and its allies will increasingly dominate other components of society.

Instability will continue to interact with militarization. International alliance races will continue.

The growth of international aggregation implies progress in arms control. The future will see the expansion of a network of arms control treaties bringing new international actors and new areas of the arms race into the growing network of international law. Existing international organizations will expand their jurisdiction in the area of arms control. New specialized international agencies for arms control at global, regional, and bilateral levels will appear and take hold an monitoring and attempting to enforce the provisions of these agreements. Alleged violations will gradually, be brought before legal tribunals.

Arms control efforts may hinder arms races, but the competitive development of weaponry will continue. The diffusion in ownership and use of atomic, biological, and chemical weapons will go forward. Third and Fourth World leaders of the future will come to possess at least the weapons of the present. If nuclear power plants are used extensively to meet future energy needs, their byproducts will accelerate the diffusion of nuclear weapons. Figure 6-1 projects that 40 countries will have nuclear capabilities by 1985 (see Gompert et al., 1977).[1]

Weapons will gradually expand into space beyond the earth's atmosphere (cf. Salkeld, 1970). On the earth itself, there will be air, land, and sea surveillance systems with tracking ranges of thousands of miles and automatic alarms. Advanced location systems will enable decisionmakers to pinpoint geographical placement of units and individual soldiers. Spaceborne television cameras will allow zoom closeups, bringing political leaders and military staffs right down on the action (Dickson, 1976).

Automated battlefield command and control systems with computer controlled tactics will be operational. Future military arsenals will rely heavily on remote control, miniaturized electronics, and bionics. They will include remotely piloted vehicles, "smart" bombs, and self-planting land and ocean mines. There will be advanced laser designator systems for homing devices and fire control; new generations of antimissile, antiradar missiles; disintegrator lasers and follow-on "death ray" technology; as well as advanced techniques for the military modification of climate, weather, pollution, water, food, and energy supplies (cf. Barnaby, 1976; Weiss, 1975).

Civil defense may lead to the construction of vast underground living complexes. If nuclear war occurs on a substantial scale, those most susceptible to radioactively generated disease will die off in large numbers. Others with higher natural resistance may be relatively immune to high levels of radioactivity and will survive and prosper.

The rapidity and pervasiveness of communications will contribute to the maintenance of international image races and will concentrate and accentuate image crises. The simultaneity of future communications will mean that events that earlier would have taken months, weeks, or days, and whose evaluation would have been limited to a relatively small number of decisionmakers, will now take hours or minutes and involve whole populations. Escalation will occur much more rapidly.

National military regimes will turn over relatively quickly; military complexes will contribute to high rates of inflation and sudden shifts in national employment and national mood. Active policies of disdevelopment may serve as powerful political tools to defuse potential disorder. Governments may use planned recession as a political weapon against dissident segments of the population. National militance may become more volatile as advanced media help shift popular moods between hostility and friendliness.

[*Peace Against War*, 1981, pp. 302-11]

[1]*Note:* Figure 6-1 is not included in this volume.

ENTERING THE TWENTY-FIRST CENTURY: THE GLOBAL 2000 REPORT

Council on Environmental Quality and
U.S. Department of State

THE WORLD IN 2000 WILL BE DIFFERENT from the world today in important ways. There will be more people. For every two persons on the earth in 1975 there will be three in 2000. The number of poor will have increased. Four-fifths of the world's population will live in less developed countries. Furthermore, in terms of persons per year added to the world, population growth will be 40 percent *higher* in 2000 than in 1975.

The gap between the richest and the poorest will have increased. By every measure of material welfare the study provides—per capita GNP and consumption of food, energy, and minerals—the gap will widen. For example, the gap between the GNP per capita in the LDCs and the industrialized countries is projected to grow from about $4,000 in 1975 to about $7,900 in 2000. Great disparities within countries are also expected to continue.

There will be fewer resources to go around. While on a worldwide average there was about four-tenths of a hectare of arable land per person in 1975, there will be only about one-quarter hectare per person in 2000 (see Figure 11 below). By 2000 nearly 1,000 billion barrels of the world's total original petroleum resource of approximately 2,000 billion barrels will have been consumed. Over just the 1975–2000 period, the world's remaining petroleum resources per capita can be expected to decline by at least 50 percent. Over the same period world per capita water supplies will decline by 35 percent because of greater population alone; increasing competing demands will put further pressure on available water supplies. The world's per capita growing stock of wood is projected to be 47 percent lower in 2000 than in 1978.

The environment will have lost important life-supporting capabilities. By 2000, 40 percent of the forests still remaining in the LDCs in 1978 will have been razed. The atmospheric concentration of carbon dioxide will be nearly one-third higher than preindustrial levels. Soil erosion will have removed, on the average, several inches of soil from croplands all over the world. Desertification (including salinization) may have claimed a significant fraction of the world's rangeland and cropland. Over little more than two decades, 15–20 percent of the earth's total species of plants and animals will have become extinct—a loss of at least 500,000 species.

Prices will be higher. The price of many of the most vital resources is projected to rise in real terms—that is, over and above inflation. In order to meet projected demand, a 100 percent increase in the real price of food will be required. To keep energy demand in line with anticipated supplies, the real price of energy is assumed to rise more than 150 percent over the 1975–2000 period. Supplies of water, agricultural land, forest products, and many traditional marine fish species are projected to decline relative to growing demand at current prices, which suggests that real price rises will occur in these sectors too. Collectively, the projections suggest that resource-based inflationary pressures will continue and intensify, especially in nations that are poor in resources or are rapidly depleting their resources.

The world will be more vulnerable both to natural disaster and to disruptions from human causes. Most nations are likely to be still more dependent on foreign sources of energy in 2000 than they are today. Food production will be more vulnerable to disruptions of fossil fuel energy supplies and to weather fluctuations as cultivation expands to more marginal areas. The loss of diverse germ plasm in local strains and wild progenitors of food crops, together with the increase of monoculture, could lead to greater risks of massive crop failures. Larger numbers of people will be vulnerable to higher food prices or even famine when adverse weather occurs. The world will be more vulnerable to the disruptive effects of war. The tensions that could lead to war will have multiplied. The potential for conflict over fresh water alone is underscored by the fact that out of 200 of the world's major river basins, 148 are shared by two countries and 52 are shared by three to ten countries. Long standing conflicts over shared rivers such as the Plata (Brazil, Argentina), Euphrates (Syria, Iraq), or Ganges (Bangladesh, India) could easily intensify.

Finally, it must be emphasized that if public policy continues generally unchanged the world will be different as a result of lost opportunities. The adverse effects of many of the trends discussed in this Study will not be fully evident until 2000 or later; yet the actions that are necessary to change the trends cannot be postponed without foreclosing important options. The opportunity to stabilize the world's population below 10 billion, for example, is slipping away; Robert McNamara, President of the World Bank, has noted that for every decade of delay in reaching replacement fertility, the world's ultimately stabilized population will be about 11 percent greater. Similar losses of opportunity accompany delayed perceptions or action in other areas. If energy policies and decisions are based on yesterday's (or even today's) oil prices, the opportunity to wisely invest scarce capital resources will be lost as a consequence of undervaluing conservation and efficiency. If agricultural research continues to focus on increasing yields through practices that are highly energy-intensive, both energy resources and the time needed to develop alternative practices will be lost.

The full effects of rising concentrations of carbon dioxide, depletion of stratospheric ozone, deterioration of soils, increasing introduction of complex persistent toxic chemicals into the environment, and massive extinction of species may not occur until well after 2000. Yet once such global environmental problems are in motion they are very difficult to reverse. In fact, few if any of the problems addressed in the Global 2000 Study are amenable to quick technological or policy fixes; rather, they are inextricably mixed with the world's most perplexing social and economic problems.

Perhaps the most troubling problems are those in which population growth and poverty lead to serious long-term declines in the productivity of renewable natural resource systems. In some areas the capacity of renewable resource systems to support human populations is already being seriously damaged by efforts of present populations to meet desperate immediate needs, and the damage threatens to become worse.

Examples of serious deterioration of the earth's most basic resources can already be found today in scattered places in all nations, including the industrialized countries and the better-endowed LDCs. For instance, erosion of agricultural soil and salinization of highly productive irrigated farmland is increasingly evident in the United States, and extensive deforestation, with more or less permanent soil degradation, has occurred in Brazil, Venezuela, and Colombia. But problems related to the decline of the earth's carrying capacity are most immediate, severe, and tragic in those regions of the earth containing the poorest LDCs.

Sub-Saharan Africa faces the problem of exhaustion of its resource base in an acute form. Many causes and effects have come together there to produce excessive demands on the environment, leading to expansion of the desert. Overgrazing, fuelwood gathering, and destructive cropping practices are the principal immediate causes of a series of transitions from open woodland, to scrub, to fragile semiarid range, to worthless weeds and bare earth. Matters are made worse when people are forced by scarcity of fuelwood to burn animal dung and crop wastes. The soil, deprived of organic matter, loses fertility and the ability to hold water—and the desert expands. In Bangladesh, Pakistan, and large parts of India, efforts by growing numbers of people to meet their basic needs are damaging the very cropland, pasture, forests, and water supplies on which they must depend for a livelihood. To restore the lands and soils would require decades—if not centuries—*after* the existing pressures on the land have diminished. But the pressures are growing, not diminishing.

There are no quick or easy solutions, particularly in those regions where population pressure is already leading to a reduction of the carrying capacity of the land. In such regions a complex of social and economic factors (including very low incomes, inequitable land tenure, limited or no educational opportunities, a lack of nonagricultural jobs, and economic pressures toward higher fertility) underlies the decline in the land's carrying capacity. Furthermore, it is generally believed that social and economic conditions must improve before fertility levels will decline to replacement levels. Thus a vicious circle of causality may be at work. Environmental deterioration caused by large populations creates living conditions that make reductions in fertility difficult to achieve; all the while, continuing population growth increases further the pressures on the environment and land.

The declines in carrying capacity already being observed in scattered areas around the world point to a phenomenon that could easily be much more widespread by 2000. In fact, the best evidence now available—even allowing for the many beneficial effects of technological developments and adoptions—suggests that by 2000 the world's human population may be within only a few generations of reaching the entire planet's carrying capacity.

The Global 2000 Study does not estimate the earth's carrying capacity, but it does provide a basis for evaluating an earlier estimate published in the U.S. National Academy of Sciences' report, *Resources and Man*. In this 1969 report, the Academy concluded that a world population of 10 billion "is close to (if not above) the maximum that an *intensively managed* world might hope to support with some degree of comfort and individual choice." The Academy also concluded that even with the sacrifice of individual freedom and choice, and even with chronic near starvation for the great majority, the human population of the world is unlikely to ever exceed 30 billion.

Nothing in the Global 2000 Study counters the Academy's conclusions. If anything, data gathered over the past decade suggest the Academy may have underestimated the extent of some problems, especially deforestation and the loss of deterioration of soils.

At present and projected growth rates, the world's population would rapidly approach the Academy's figures. If the fertility and mortality rates projected for 2000 were to continue unchanged into the twenty-first century, the world's population would reach 10 billion by 2030. Thus anyone with a present life expectancy of an additional 50 years could expect to see the world population reach 10 billion. This same rate of growth would produce a population of nearly 30 billion before the end of the twenty-first century.

Here it must be emphasized that, unlike most of the Global 2000 Study projections, the population projections assume extensive policy changes and developments to reduce fertility rates. Without the assumed policy changes, the projected rate of population growth would be still more rapid.

Unfortunately population growth may be slowed for reasons other than declining birth rates. As the world's populations exceed and reduce the land's carrying capacity in widening areas, the trends of the last century or two toward improved health and longer life may come to a halt. Hunger and disease may claim more lives—especially lives of babies and young children. More of those surviving infancy may be mentally and physically handicapped by childhood malnutrition.

The time for action to prevent this outcome is running out. Unless nations collectively and individually take bold and imaginative steps toward improved social and economic conditions, reduced fertility, better management of resources, and protection of the environment, the world must expect a troubled entry into the twenty-first century.

[*Entering the Twenty-First Century: The Global 2000 Report to the President*, 1980, pp. 39–42]

THE POPULATION PROBLEM

Robert S. McNamara

POPULATION GROWTH RATES IN MOST DEVELOPING COUNTRIES fell significantly in the 1970s. This has led many to believe that the world in general, and most countries in particular, no longer face serious population problems and that efforts to deal with such problems can therefore be relaxed.

Such a view is totally in error. Unless action is taken to accelerate the reductions in the rates of growth, the population of the world (now 4.7 billion) will not stabilize below 11 billion, and certain regions and countries will grow far beyond the limits consistent with political stability and acceptable social and economic conditions. Africa, for example, now with less than a half billion people, will expand sixfold to almost three billion; India will have a larger population than China; and El Salvador will grow from five million to 15 million.

Rates of population growth of this magnitude are so far out of balance with rates of social and economic advance that they will impose heavy penalties on both individual nations and individual families. Nations facing political instability of the kind already experienced in Kenya, Nigeria and El Salvador—instability in part a result of high population growth rates—will more and more be tempted to impose coercive measures of fertility regulation. Individual families will move to higher levels of abortion, particularly of female fetuses, and higher rates of female infanticide.

Developed and developing countries have a common interest in avoiding the consequences of current population trends. . . . Governments bear a heavy responsibility, and rightly so, in fashioning any effective and humane solution to the world's population problem.

There is also, of course, an important role for the international community. The most important help that community can give is to increase its support for high rates of economic and social advance throughout the developing world and, in particular, in the low-income countries.

This will require far stronger resistance to the increasing pressure for protectionist barriers to the exports of the developing countries, a longer-term approach to the debt crisis and to the future financial requirements of the middle-income countries, and a much greater recognition of the need of the low-income countries for larger flows of concessional aid.

["Time Bomb or Myth: The Population Problem," 1984, pp. 1107–1129]

THE CHANGED WORLD ECONOMY

Peter F. Drucker

THE TALK TODAY IS OF THE "changing world economy." I wish to argue that the world economy is not "changing"; it has *already changed*—in its foundations and in its structure—and in all probability the change is irreversible.

Within the last decade or so, three fundamental changes have occurred in the very fabric of the world economy:

—The primary-products economy has come "uncoupled" from the industrial economy.

—In the industrial economy itself, production has come "uncoupled" from employment.

—Capital movements rather than trade (in both goods and services) have become the driving force of the world economy. The two have not quite come uncoupled, but the link has become loose, and worse, unpredictable.

These changes are permanent rather than cyclical. We may never understand what caused them—the causes of economic change are rarely simple. It may be a long time before economic theorists accept that there have been fundamental changes, and longer still before they adapt their theories to account for them. Above all, they will surely be most reluctant to accept that it is the world economy in control, rather than the macroeconomics of the nation-state on which most economic theory still exclusively focuses. Yet this is the clear lesson of the success stories of the last 20 years—of Japan and South Korea; of West Germany (actually a more impressive though far less flamboyant example than Japan); and of the one great success within the United States, the turnaround and rapid rise of an industrial New

England, which only 20 years ago was widely considered moribund.

Practitioners, whether in government or in business, cannot wait until there is a new theory. They have to act. And their actions will be more likely to succeed the more they are based on the new realities of a changed world economy. . . .

It is much too early to guess what the world economy of tomorrow will look like. Will major countries, for instance, succumb to traditional fears and retreat into protectionism? Or will they see a changed world economy as an opportunity?

Some parts of the main agenda, however, are fairly clear by now. Rapidly industrializing countries like Mexico or Brazil will need to formulate new development concepts and policies. They can no longer hope to finance their development by raw material exports, e.g., Mexican oil. It is also becoming unrealistic for them to believe that their low labor costs will enable them to export large quantities of finished goods to developed countries—something the Brazilians, for instance, still expect. They would do much better to go into "production sharing," that is, to use their labor advantage to become subcontractors to developed-country manufacturers for highly labor-intensive work that cannot be automated—some assembly operations, for instance, or parts and compoments needed only in relatively small quantities. Developed countries no longer have the labor to do such work, which even with the most thorough automation will still account for 15 to 20 percent of manufacturing work.

Such production sharing is, of course, how Singapore, Hong Kong and Taiwan bootstrapped their development. Yet in Latin America production sharing is still politically unacceptable and, indeed, anathema. Mexico, for instance, has been deeply committed since its beginnings as a modern nation in the early years of this century to making its economy less dependent on, and less integrated with, that of its big neighbor to the north. That this policy has been a total failure for 80 years has only strengthened its emotional and political appeal.

Even if production sharing is implemented to the fullest, it would not by itself provide enough income to fuel development, especially of countries so much larger than the Chinese "city-states." We thus need a new model and new policies.

Can we learn something from India? Everyone knows of

India's problems—and they are legion. Few people seem to realize, however, that since independence India has done a better development job than almost any other Third World country: it has enjoyed the fastest increase in farm production and farm yields; a growth rate in manufacturing production equal to that of Brazil, and perhaps even of South Korea (India now has a bigger industrial economy than any but a handful of developed countries); the emergence of a large and highly entrepreneurial middle class; and, arguably, the greatest achievement in providing schooling and health care in the villages. Yet the Indians followed none of the established models. They did not, like Stalin, Mao and so many leaders of newly independent African nations, despoil the peasants to produce capital for industrial development. They did not export raw materials. And they did not export the products of cheap labor. Instead, since Nehru's death in 1964, India has followed a policy of strengthening agriculture and encouraging consumer goods production. India and its achievement are bound to get far more attention in the future.

The developed countries, too, need to think through their policies in respect to the Third World—and especially in respect to the "stars" of the Third World, the rapidly industrializing countries. There are some beginnings: the debt proposals recently put forward by Treasury Secretary James A. Baker, or the new lending criteria recently announced by the World Bank for loans to Third World countries, which will be made conditional on a country's overall development policies rather than on the soundness of individual projects. But these proposals are aimed more at correcting past mistakes than at developing new policies.

The other major agenda item is—inevitably—the international monetary system. Since the Bretton Woods Conference in 1944, the world monetary system has been based on the U.S. dollar as the reserve currency. This clearly does not work any more. The reserve-currency country must be willing to subordinate its domestic policies to the needs of the international economy, e.g., risk domestic unemployment to keep currency rates stable. And when it came to the crunch, the United States refused to do so—as Keynes, by the way, predicted 40 years ago.

The stability supposedly supplied by the reserve currency

could be established today only if the major trading countries—
at a minimum the United States, West Germany and Japan—
agreed to coordinate their economic, fiscal and monetary policies, if not to subordinate them to joint (and this would mean
supranational) decision-making. Is such a development even
conceivable, except perhaps in the event of worldwide financial
collapse? The European experience with the far more modest
European Currency Unit is not encouraging; so far, no European government has been willing to yield an inch for the sake
of the ECU. But what else can be done? Have we come to the
end of the 300-year-old attempt to regulate and stabilize money
on which, after all, both the modern nation-state and the international system was largely based?

We are left with one conclusion: economic dynamics have
decisively shifted from the national economy to the world economy.

Prevailing economic theory—whether Keynesian, monetarist or supply-side—considers the national economy, especially
that of the large developed countries, to be autonomous and the
unit of both economic analysis and economic policy. The international economy may be a restraint and a limitation, but it is not
central, let alone determining. This "macroeconomic axiom" of
the modern economist has become increasingly shaky. The two
major subscribers to this axiom, Britain and the United States,
have done least well economically in the last 30 years, and have
also had the most economic instability.

West Germany and Japan never accepted the "macroeconomic axiom." Their universities teach it, of course, but their
policymakers, both in government and in business, reject it.
Instead, both countries all along have based their economic
policies on the world economy, have systematically tried to
anticipate its trends and exploit its changes as opportunities.
Above all, both make the country's competitive position in the
world economy the first priority in their policies—economic,
fiscal, monetary, even social—to which domestic considerations
are not normally subordinated. And these two countries have
done far better—economically and socially—than Britain and
the United States these last 30 years. In fact, their focus on the
world economy and the priority they give it may be the real
"secret" of their success.

Similarly the "secret" of successful businesses in the developed world—the Japanese, the German carmakers like Mercedes and BMW, Asea and Erickson in Sweden, IBM and Citibank in the United States, but equally of a host of medium-sized specialists in manufacturing and in all kinds of services—has been that they base their plans and their policies on exploiting the world economy's changes as opportunities.

From now on any country—but also any business, especially a large one—that wants to prosper will have to accept that it is the world economy that leads and that domestic economic policies will succeed only if they strengthen, or at least do not impair, the country's international competitive position. This may be the most important—it surely is the most striking—feature of the changed world economy.

["The Changed World Economy", pp. 768, 788–791—]

FOREIGN POLICY AND PRESIDENTIAL SELECTION

Harlan Cleveland

THE WORLD OF THE 1980s, and probably beyond, seems leaderless, dangerous, uneconomic, unjust and ungovernable. The problem for the "executive committee," and especially for its sometime chairman, is to exercise leadership in moderating its dangers, enhancing its efficencies, rectifying its injustices, and arranging the governance of its necessarily international functions.

—It is a world with nobody in general charge. That is, of course, the way we Americans wanted it. We didn't want the Kaiser or Adolph Hitler or Josef Stalin to be *über alles*—but we also didn't want to be global policemen or overseers ourselves. Through alliances and aid programs, we have done what no leading power in history has done—shared our power with others, tried to build up other nations (including recent ex-enemies) and international agencies. Let's not be carried away with our own generosity, because it was really enlightened selfishness: we didn't want all those foreigners on our back. We wanted our brothers to keep themselves.

We succeeded—too well, some would say. The world is not managed from Washington or anywhere else. Its governance is an exercise in the management of pluralism. It is an American-style outcome: it's what James Madison was trying to describe in Federalist No. 10, and it's what we have been trying to make work in the United States for 200 years past.

"A civilization," Raymond Aron wrote, "is usually composed of combative states or of a universal empire." But what we have achieved is much more complicated: ". . . quarreling states, more

subjected to asymmetric interdependence than they would like,
. . . too different to agree, too interconnected to separate."

—It is a world full of frustrated leaders, their frustration
the psychic fallout of the transition we are in, a transition
compounded of changing values, changing technologies
(especially information technologies), changing attitudes toward
growth, work, sex and leisure, the horizontalization of process
and the globalization of problems, producing a widespread
sense of incapacity to cope. Denis Brogan, the British scholar of
American politics, once wrote of "the illusion of omnipotence."
A fairer description of the U.S. popular mood in the 1970s and
early 1980s might be an illusion of impotence.

Evidence of the macrotransition is to be found in every
domain and dimension. We seem to be moving from
bureaucratic pyramids to horizontal systems of "consensus,"
"collective leadership," and committee work; from Keynesian
economic management to doctrines not yet invented; from a
man's world to equality of the sexes; from more centralization to
more devolution and separatism; from colonial struggles to
struggles to make independence work; from local technologies
to global technologies; from an ethic of quantitative growth to
qualitative growth; from preoccupation with physical "growth
limits" to a new thinking about information as an expandable
resource; from military strategies for the use of nuclear
weapons to strategies that assume nuclear weapons are militarily
unusable; from notions like the "inner logic" of technological
change and the "invisible hand" of market choice to social
direction-setting for new technologies and political bargaining
as the dominant force in the marketplace; from a useful
distinction between "domestic" and "international" to the
internationalization of domestic affairs and vice versa; from the
idea of national security as military defense to a concept of
world security comprising oil embargoes, wheat deals,
environmental risks, international crime, nuclear proliferation,
population movements, religious and cultural identity, a
world-wide "fairness revolution," and periodic global epidemics
of inflation and unemployment.

—It is a world full of dangerous weapons. Nearly two-thirds
of a trillion dollars of annual defense spending worldwide. Five

nuclear weapons states, two more presumed to have nuclear
weapons, two dozen more with a "nuclear mobilization capacity"
if they wish. One nation per year gone nuclear for energy
production, producing as a by-product the starting kit for
several thousand Hiroshimas a year—if they wish. A massive
trade in conventional arms, amounting to more than $13 billion
per year in 1982—with American ingenuity and marketing skills
accounting for 37.7 percent of that worldwide. The prospect of
terrorists brandishing much bigger bangs than any terrorist has
yet found it useful to set off. An eerily stable strategic stalemate,
rooted in the uncertainty of response combined with the certainty of devastation if a response is provoked. And an escalating
capacity by smaller nations—or guerilla groups, criminal con-
spiracies or individual desperadoes—to make a less-than-global
mess of the complexity we call civilization.

—It is a world full of wars. In 1980-82, six new wars started
and only two were turned off. In 1983 there were 40 major and
minor conflicts in the world, involving 45 of the world's 164
nations—ten conflicts in the Middle East and the Persian Gulf,
ten in Asia, ten in Africa, seven in Latin America and three in
Europe. As many as four and a half million soldiers (of the 25
million in standing armies worldwide) are engaged in combat.
The total casualties in these wars are uncounted, but estimates of
deaths run from more than one million up to five million. The
number of wounded could be three times the number of dead.
The financial cost of these wars runs into many hundreds of
billions of dollars. (The 45 nations involved in the 40 wars spend
more than $500 billion a year on their armed forces).

—The industrial democracies face a chronic crisis of governance—their leaders baffled by the dirt, danger and disaffec-
tion that urban systems seem to generate, their young people
educated for nonexistent jobs, their middle classes periodically
squeezed by inflation, disemployed by recession and harassed by
bureaucracy, their industries and farms hosting an enormous
migratory proletariat, their governments revolving in endless
and ineffective coalitions. The leading "centrally-planned economy" is, by contrast, so stable as to be static—its leaders unable to
generate the morale or productivity to compete in the trading
world, incapable 65 years after the Bolshevik Revolution of

feeding their own people, incompetent to enforce their system dependably on their key neighbors, let alone create a durable market for it around the world.

—The rich nations—and the rich people in the poor nations—face a global fairness revolution, multiplying the demands on a world economic system that knows how to include only a minority of humankind in its benefits. We are witness in consequence to a shredding of international law by those who think markets are unjustly rigged to favor the already favored, and a growing resentment of a money system that helps the rich get richer by making more and more unrepayable loans to the poor. Both among and within the nation-states of the twentieth century, the old French warning retains its relevance: *Entre le fort et le faible, c'est la liberté qui opprime et la loi qui affranchit.* In relations between the strong and the weak, it's freedom that oppresses and law that liberates.

The arguments (and terrorism, and wars) are about what kind of law liberates. The kind we have had, the law that was written by the big brothers in the brotherhood of man—sanctity of contract, property rights, nondiscriminatory trade, freedom to use and exploit the international commons—is being shredded by nonobservance. Reiteration of the principles is about as operational as the mandatory health warnings on cigarette advertising seems to be. What is happening is an ironic extension of another legal doctrine—*rebus sic stantibus,* the notion that a change of conditions justifies a fresh shuffle and a new deal. The prime threats to world security, inside nations and among nations, arise when newcomers to the political bargaining table reach for the cards before the earlier arrivals are ready to make room for more chairs.

—A world population of 4,677 million is already programmed to double in four decades. The world food situation—not yet organized enough to call it a "system"—is too dependent on the North American granary, where public policy is still afflicted with a hundred-year bias in favor of scarcity. The world energy economy still discourages plentiful solar sources, draws down too fast on the complex petroleum molecules that are really too valuable and versatile to be burned, and might have to settle in desperation for coal (which risks overheating the earth through the "greenhouse effect" of spewing carbon dioxide into the global atmosphere) or nuclear power (which facilitates the proliferation of nuclear weapons and produces radioactive wastes for which no garbage dump has yet been found).

—It is a world in which a growing number of functions that simply have to be performed cannot be contained in national decision systems at all—the management of transborder data flows, the allocation of radio frequencies, the regulation of satellite communications, global pollution, ocean fishing and mining, weather forecasting and modification, the nuclear fuel cycle, the potentials of earth-sensing space vehicles, and a complexity of transnational corporations which provide much of the enterprise in world trade and investment yet remain the most popular villains in world politics.

—It is, in sum, a world whose international institutions and practices are not yet able to cope with the international functions modern science and technology have made possible, or resolve the conflicts generated by the modernization process itself.

In a polity where ultimately the people make the policy, even individual citizens have to try to get their minds around the whole of this complexity. *A fortiori*, a President or a candidate for the presidency has to wrap his/her mind around the world, develop for his/her own personal use a strategic global agenda— which can serve both to help educate the American constituency and to guide the day-to-day tactical actions and reactions that constitute "American foreign policy."

["Foreign Policy and Presidential Selection", 1980, pp. 4-10]

II

ORGANIZING AMID DIVERSITY

II. ORGANIZING AMID DIVERSITY

ORGANIZING HAS TO MEAN SOMETHING MORE TANGI-
BLE THAN A SPIRIT OF COOPERATION, INDISPENSIBLE as
that is if people around the world are to cope with their
common problems. The United Nations system (meaning the
Security Council, General Assembly, Economic and Social
Council, Trusteeship Council, Secretariat, and World Court,
plus the approximately fifteen specialized agencies dealt with
under Part IV in discussing "functionalism"), is the contemporary global expression, however imperfect, of the historic
movement to organize the nations for collective security and
the common welfare.

To set the stage, Harvard scholars Robert Keohane and
Joseph Nye, in one of the longer excerpts in this volume,
provide a pragmatic overview of the contemporary role and
value of international organizations. In doing so they draw
heavily on their earlier work in identifying so-called "regimes"
that give some structure to disorderly functions affecting the
life of nations.

Rival visions of the world are sharply illuminated by the
contending positions taken toward the United Nations in Part
IIA. There are doubtless other views, but major differences
about the correct road toward common goals are obvious in
these selections. The center of the road preferred by Westerners is reflected in a section I have labelled the "democratic
internationalist" position. Former cabinet official Elliot L. Richardson quotes a statement in support of the UN by six
former Secretaries of State, seven former US Permanent
Representatives to the UN, and four former National Security
Advisers. Richardson (who is Chairman of the UN Association
of the USA) thinks anti-UN sentiment in the US indicates a self-
crippling vision in a situation in which scarcely any important

American interest is within our power to manage alone or with just a few friendly allies. The President of the same UNA-USA, Edward C. Luck, sets forth the centrist argument in favor of United Nations activities that he argues serve the narrower as well as the larger U.S. national interest.

The doctrinal Soviet view stands in sharp contrast. Perhaps the existence of nuclear weapons explains the not insignificant difference between the famous apocalyptic assertion by Lenin in 1919, and the contemporary expression of the Soviet doctrine of "peaceful coexistence" by Soviet premier Nikita S. Khrushchev, as well as the at least rhetorical support for the UN by one of his successors, Premier Konstantin Chernenko.

In contrast to both is a Third World view in the form of the statement delivered to the opening session of the 1984 U.N. General Assembly by its newly-elected president, Paul J.F. Lusaka, Permanent Representative of Zambia to the UN. Lusaka reflects the increasingly balanced view of the UN, and indeed of the West generally, that characterizes moderate voices from the developing countries.

The Western radical left, represented here by Richard S. Falk and Samuel S. Kim, believes that nuclear and ecological anxieties, plus ethical considerations, make states obsolete in favor of a communitarian global order—an obviously premature conclusion. What might be called the American nationalist right airs two major grievances. The first, Richard Grenier, sees in the UN hypocritical support of leftist radical movements but silence regarding Communist tyranny. Former US Ambassador to the UN Jeane J. Kirkpatrick typifies the right's allergy to what some among them indict as "international socialism." She notes a recent explosion of UN regulatory activity, some in response to legitimate needs but much entailing ideological distortion.

Finally, veteran UN Secretariat official Brian Urquhart echoes the late Dag Hammerskjöld's view that the smaller, relatively powerless countries find political strength and essential technical assistance in the UN system. He authoritatively surveys the Security Council's potential.

A special strain in Western thinking that for a time attracted support but has substantially receded, is the utopian dream of world government. Five writers examine the logic of world government in relation to plans for disarmament, and discuss the glaring obstacles. New Yorker writer Jonathan Schell defines the nuclear Hobson's Choice as a matter of either living with nuclear terror or unrealistically seeking to institute a true global state. In their classic proposal for UN Charter revision, reformer Grenville Clark and law professor Louis B. Sohn blueprint a system of enforceable world law resting on general and complete disarmament.

In an exposition of the arguments about world organization, Prof. Cecil V. Crabb Jr., criticizes the tendency to let the desire for supranational communities become proof of their existence, while the late British journalist Leonard Beaton advances the thesis that governments can move toward a working international system through common organization of military forces.

TWO CHEERS FOR MULTILATERISM

Robert O. Keohane and Joseph S. Nye Jr.

UNREALISTIC VISIONS

SEVEN MAXIMS MAY HELP THE UNITED STATES develop an effective strategic approach to international regimes.

Do not try to recapture the past

Nostalgia for a simpler, more neatly arranged world leads Americans periodically to propose "grand designs" to solve foreign-policy problems. But postwar visions are now unrealistic. The U.N. General Assembly, with its one state, one vote rule, is not sufficiently amenable to American influence to be a reliable instrument of foreign policy. And policymakers' recent dreams of a "new Bretton Woods" meeting or of a large conference to rewrite and strengthen the NPT might make matters worse. Even during the period of American dominance, universalistic approaches were often unsuccessful: Myths to the contrary, numerous doctoral dissertations have established that the United States did not have an "automatic majority" in the General Assembly, even during the period before the entry of so many Third World states. The diffusion of power that has taken place in recent years makes large-conference diplomacy even more unwieldy than before and therefore more likely to disappoint. The number of contradictory demands often destroys all possibility of a satisfactory resolution, as the troubled outcome of the Law of the Sea Conference, after more than a decade of effort, demonstrates.

In today's world, universal international organizations are more valuable as sounding boards than as decision-making bodies. If the United States listens carefully, but not naively, these organizations may tell it something about the intensity of, and shifts in, others' views. These forums do influence the agenda of world politics. They may legitimate important decisions reached elsewhere (an example would be some of the arms control treaties negotiated by the United States and the Soviet Union and subsequently blessed by a General Assembly vote). But only rarely are universal international organizations likely to provide the world with instruments for collective action.

Ask whether the world really needs it

Regimes are needed only when uncoordinated behavior by governments has much worse results than coordinated action. Issues lacking serious conflicts of interest may need very little institutional structure. Some international problems are more like the question of whether to drive on the left or the right side of the road than like the issue of which car goes first at an intersection. Once a society has decided on which side cars will drive, practice becomes largely self-enforcing. No one but a suicidal maniac has an interest in deviating from the agreement. Many international regimes are similarly self-enforcing—for example, arrangements for delivery of letters, the location of shipping lanes, or specification of which languages will be used in international air traffic control. No one, after all, has an interest in sending mail to the wrong place, inviting collisions by using the wrong shipping lanes, or suddenly switching to French while landing in Chicago.

The more significant regimes, however, concern subject areas where each government would prefer that everyone cooperate except itself. For instance, when a country default seems likely, the common interest calls for a collective effort to save the system. Nevertheless, it is in the interest of each bank to cease lending or even to close out its loans to questionable borrowers. If each bank acts in this way, default is inevitable and the system will surely collapse. A cooperative regime governing bank lending is therefore desirable to the banks themselves. Likewise, international arrangements for the security of energy consumers may . . . reduce incentives for countries to bid against one another for oil during a shortage. Regimes for debt and oil resemble the stoplights needed at busy intersections: Without rules, pursuit of self-interest by each leads to disaster for all.

To incorporate explicit provisions for monitoring and enforcing rules, regimes that are not self-enforcing usually require international organizations. Such organizations, however, do not have the capability themselves to enforce rules—this must be done by governments—but rather only to exercise surveillance to identify deviations from previous agreements and to engage in planning so that governments will be better prepared to cope with future emergencies. Often the most effective international organizations are surprisingly small. In 1980 the IMF had a staff of only 1,530 persons and GATT employed only 255 individuals. Yet the IMF and GATT arguably accomplish more than certain other international organizations with more than twice the number of personnel, such as the International Labor Organization, the FAO, and UNESCO. And they compare favorably with a number of national bureaucracies as well.

The key question is how well an international organization and the regime of which it is a part structure incentives for governments. A sophisticated strategic approach to international regimes does not assume that international bureaucracies must be large or directive. On the contrary, sometimes an international organization can be most effective by seeking to provide incentives for governments to rely more on markets than on national bureaucratic management. The GATT trade regime, for example, expands the scope of market forces by restricting unilateral protectionism by governments. The IMF stresses the role of market discipline in countries that borrow heavily from it; in the 1970s it shifted from trying to help manage fixed exchange rates to a loosely defined role in a market-oriented system of flexible rates. International organizations are worthwhile only if they can facilitate bargaining among member states that leads to mutually beneficial cooperation. They are not desirable for their own sake.

Build on shared interests

To flourish, regimes must enhance the goals of governments. On many issues, governments may regard their interest as so divergent that no worldwide agreement can possibly be reached.

Under these conditions, efforts to negotiate regimes are likely to lead eventually to painful choices between poor agreements and negotiation failure. Deliberations on a new international economic order foundered on the heterogeneity of interests in the world—not only between rich countries and poor countries, but within each of those groupings.

The collapse of various global negotiations, however, does not mean that the era of new regimes has closed. During the last decade a number of new institutions and sets of rules affecting relations among the advanced industrialized countries have emerged. Examples include agreements on export credits negotiated during the late 1970s, various codes agreed upon during the Tokyo Round of trade negotiations, and adaptations in the nuclear proliferation regime in the mid-1970s to establish supplier guidelines for safer nuclear commerce.

These regimes and others, such as the IEA, have two key features. All these regimes were designed to resolve common problems in which the uncontrolled pursuit of individual self-interest by some governments could adversely affect the national interest of all the rest. All these regimes were formed not on a universal basis, but selectively. The export-credit and nuclear-suppliers "clubs," for example, include only countries that are major suppliers of credit or nuclear material; the IEA deliberately excluded nonmembers of the Organization for Economic Cooperation and Development.

When establishing smaller clubs, those participating must consider their effect on the larger regime. Nuclear suppliers, for example, were concerned that formation of their group would exacerbate resentment among other adherents to the nonproliferation regime. Yet sensitivity to issues of exclusion can help resolve these problems. Once they had agreed on export guidelines in 1978, members of the nuclear suppliers group emphasized quiet, bilateral diplomacy in order to maintain broad commitment to the nonproliferation regime.

If a relatively small number of governments have shared interests in a given issue greater than their differences, it can make sense to limit membership, or at least decision-making power, to those countries. Sometimes, meaningful agreements can be reached only by excluding naysayers. Every effort should be made, however, as in the GATT code, to allow for the eventual universalization of the regimes. Further, particular attention should be paid to the long-term interests of developing countries, so that a legitimate desire to make progress on specific issues does not turn into a general pattern of discriminating against the weak.

A crazy quilt of international regimes is likely to arise, each with somewhat different membership. Better some roughness around the edges of international regimes, however, than a vacuum at the center. Poorly coordinated coalitions, working effectively on various issues, are in general preferable to universalistic negotiations permanently deadlocked by a diverse membership.

Use regimes to insure against catastrophe

Insurance regimes are less satisfactory than effective regimes that control events and thereby eliminate adversity rather than simply share its burdens. It is better, other things being equal, to prevent floods by building dams than merely to insure against them. Likewise, IEA members would prefer to prevent oil embargoes than merely to share diminished supplies in response to them. Yet in some situations, having adequate insurance may deter hostile action by reducing the potential gains from "divide and conquer" strategies. And in any event, regimes that are able to control events often cannot be constructed. When this is the case, insurance strategies may be better than relying on unilateral action or merely hoping for the best. In thinking about international cooperation, governments are often well advised to "elevate them sights a little lower," accomplishing what they can rather than bemoaning their inability to do more.

The best enforcement is self-enforcement

Centralized enforcement of rules in international regimes through hierarchical arrangements is normally out of the question: There is no police force and only a tiny international bureaucracy. If states are to comply with regime rules, they must do so on the basis of long-term self-interest.

Arranging enforcement is not so difficult as it may seem.

The major advanced industrialized countries deal with each other on a large number of issues over an indefinite period of time. Each government could "get away with" a particular violation. But viable regimes rely, in one form or another, on the principle of long-term reciprocity. No one trusts habitual cheaters. Over time, governments develop reputations for compliance, not just to the letter of the law but to the spirit as well. These reputations constitute one of their most important assets. As the economist Charles Kindleberger once remarked, "In economics bygones are bygones, but in politics they are working capital."

Reciprocity is harder to institutionalize in multilateral settings than in bilateral settings. It often is difficult to agree on "equivalent" contributions. When arguing with its NATO allies about burden sharing, for instance, the United States concentrates on financial efforts, while European states stress contributions in kind through expropriated land or national service. Moreover, a tradeoff provided in one contest may lead to demands for compensation from other countries or on other issues. Nevertheless, the practice of reciprocity does provide incentives for compliance, and in a well-functioning regime, standards exist to govern reciprocity. The subsidies code devised during the Tokyo Round, for example, not only specifies conditions under which countervailing duties can be applied in response to subsidies, but also sets limits on the severity of such duties.

In the design of institutions, enforcement should rest on provisions for information sharing and reciprocity rather than on nominal powers of coercion through centralized enforcement. Despite extensive voting rules, the IEA has never taken a formal vote, but its members share information about oil-company and government behavior. The IAEA has helped deter misuse of nuclear fuels by threat of discovery through its inspection system rather than by assured sanctions in the event of violation. Other contemporary regimes—whether for surveillance of exchange rates by the Group of Five, for maintaining bank lending to debtor countries, or for export credits—also depend on self-enforcement through the generation and dispersal of information, rather than on the wielding of supranational powers.

Failure to notice this point can lead governments to downgrade what international regimes can do—provide a framework for decentralized enforcement of rules. If countries focus instead on the fact that regimes cannot enforce rules through supranational machinery, the international community may miss opportunities to develop new institutions that, by generating information about reputations, may allow practices of greater reciprocity to evolve in world politics.

Look for the right moment

In the life cycles of international regimes, erosion takes place gradually, as governments and transnational actors find loopholes in the rules. Defenders of regimes spend their time putting their fingers in the dike.

Occasionally, crises threaten to burst the dike and destroy the established order. The inadequacy of existing regimes becomes evident; old conceptions of reality are shattered and entrenched interests and coalitions shaken or torn apart. The prospect of a world financial crisis can concentrate a banker's mind.

In periods of crisis, opportunities for the construction of international regimes characteristically arise. "Creative destruction," in the economist Joseph Schumpeter's phrase, can result from the collapse of the presuppositions underlying old regimes or from a shattered complacency about the absence of regimes. Thus the first serious discussions of international monetary coordination, which led eventually to Bretton Woods, took place in the ominous depression years before World War II. Economic crises in the 1970s and 1980s saw not only the collapse or erosion of old regimes, but also the founding of the IEA in 1974, after the oil crisis, and the strengthening of the IMF after 1982, in the wake of threats of default by Third World countries.

The period from 1929 to 1933, however, demonstrates that creative responses to crises are not automatic. During crises, policymakers may not look for innovative solutions but may try to muddle through from week to week. Caught unprepared, they may have no time to draw up well-conceived plans for institutional change. Yet if policymakers have thought through the fundamental issues in advance, they may be able to use the opportunities created by crises to devise immediate solutions that support long-term strategy.

In other words, if American foreign policy is to take advantage of crises rather than merely react to them, there is need to think about the desirable evolution of institutions before lightning strikes. No grand design for a broad array of new rules and institutions is necessary. Grand designs stir up objections from many interests, domestic as well as international. Nevertheless, thinking ahead can be used to turn particular crises, even those limited to particular problems, into openings for constructive change. It may not be possible to create comprehensive regimes with an enormous impact, but partial regimes may emerge with constructive effect in particular areas.

For at least the last 25 years the U.S. government has not been known for effective long-range planning. American policymakers can do better than they have at this task. But much thinking about future regimes will be done outside government; at the same time, the effectiveness of the outsiders' work will depend on the receptivity of insiders. Likewise, executive-branch planning must involve key congressional figures. Such links not only help secure legislative support for foreign-policy initiatives, but also help bring new ideas into the policymaking process.

Use regimes to focus U.S. attention on the future

In the eyes of its critics, American foreign policy is notoriously unreliable. Does it make sense to talk about strategies for international regimes when America cannot seem to avoid confusing and confounding its allies by engaging in erratic, often ideological behavior?

But these shortcomings in American foreign policy reinforce the need to use crises in a sophisticated way to carry out constructive change. During these crises the president's leeway for getting decisive measures through Congress becomes wider, often dramatically so. The United States has always had difficulty keeping sight of its own long-term interests. The division between executive and legislature and the splits within branches of government make it particularly hard for the United States to pursue far-sighted self-interest. Attempting to lay out the principles of international regimes can clarify the country's long-term, internationalist interests. Like the Constitution, international regimes can remind the country of its fundamental purposes, for they can legitimate a broad conception of the national interest that takes into account others' values and policies.

This effort at long-range planning also helps the United States retain its alliance leadership. Constraints imposed by constructive international regimes make America a more reliable partner internationally than if it followed unilateralist policies. Credible promises can be made and extracted by partners with solid reputations. In addition, regimes often provide leaders of allied countries with opportunities to influence the domestic debates of alliance states by holding each to the regime's standards. This strengthens alliances by giving participating governments the opportunity to exercise "voice," in the economist Albert Hirschman's phrase, rather than simply to "exit." Since America's allies have some influence over its policies, they are more willing to commit themselves to alignments with the United States. The impressive strength and durability of America's alliances can be attributed in part to its commitment to the constructive constraints of international regimes.

Regime Maintenance

In world politics today actors are many, and a bewildering array of issues overlap. Diffusion of power has reduced America's ability to establish international regimes as it pleases. No matter now high the defense budget, the United States cannot recapture the preponderant position it held in the 1950s. Further, maintaining military strength is only part of a viable foreign policy. As the pre-eminent political and commercial power, America also has a strong national interest in building and maintaining international regimes. Yet recent foreign-policy debates have given little attention to this dimension of national interest.

Major international regimes continue to reflect U.S. interests, by and large because of U.S. influence in establishing and perpetuating them. But unless the United States takes the lead in maintaining them, it is unlikely that other countries will have the interest or ability to do their share. As Great Britain found in the 1930s, when the leading trading country closes its market, the protectionist scramble is on. When Washington extended U.S. jurisdiction over new areas of the seas, as it did in 1945, it should have expected others to go it one better—as several coastal states in Latin America did. If the United States relaxes its standards for nucler exports, other suppliers will relax theirs, probably even more. American restraint is no longer sufficient to build or maintain rules, but it almost certainly remains necessary.

This U.S. interest in regime maintenance does not mean the United States need remain passive as others in pursuit of narrow national interests chip away at existing rules and arrangements. Indeed, there is much to be said for reciprocity as an effective way to maintain cooperation in world politics. And sometimes reciprocity will entail retaliation, as it does increasingly in international trade. But the ultimate objective of retaliation should be to reinforce compliance by others with general rules, rather than to seek exemptions for oneself—exemptions that will be only temporary and that will contribute to the decline of international order, which all should be striving to avoid. Thus the United States should design its strategies to provide realistic incentives to others, behaving in their self-interests, to support international regimes that the United States finds valuable. . . .

Dreams of a slow, even unsteady march toward the world order envisaged by the founders of the U.N. are obsolete. But the United States cannot simply exchange these dreams for the alluring promise of a world without the frustrations of multilateral cooperation. Economic and security interdependence is a reality that cannot be wished away. The United States is not strong enough to be able safely to assume that other countries will acquiesce in its unilateral attempts to reshape the world. Global unilateralism in the 1980s could therefore be as expensive an illusion as isolationism was half a century ago.

What global unilateralism misses is the continuing American interest in international regimes. In addition to worrying about military power and Soviet intentions, the United States needs to be concerned about other dimensions of power and relations with the whole international system. To deal effectively with issues involving international regimes—such as how to deal with UNESCO, what to do about nuclear proliferation, and whether to rescue or abandon the nondiscriminatory provisions of GATT—the United States needs a coherent strategy based on a realistic understanding of the conditions for effective multilateral cooperation. Such a strategy should emphasize reciprocity—which means being tough on rude violators as well as being willing to cooperate with those who wish to cooperate. The United States must support international institutions that facilitate decentralized enforcement of rules, without naively believing that enforcement will be automatic or easy. The United States should reflect, in advance of crises, on how international institutions can help achieve cooperation, and it must be ready, in crises, to put forward proposals that have been devised in quieter times.

Such a combination of institutional strategy and tactical flexibility could be simultaneously visionary and realistic. It would be opportunistic in the best sense: ready to seize opportunities provided by crises to make regimes more consistent with America's interest and values. It is a viable alternative to recurring fantasies of global unilateralism.

["Two Cheers for Multilaterism" (pp. 154-169)]

A.

THE UN AND THE PROBLEM OF WORLD LAW AND ORDER: CONTENDING POSITIONS

DEMOCRATIC
INTERNATIONALIST

STATEMENT BEFORE HOUSE COMMITTEE

Elliot L. Richardson

MANY PEOPLE CONTINUE TO QUESTION the usefulness of the world organization, and the Senate recently voted to make debilitating cuts in US support for the UN. In recent days there has been a series of intemperate remarks about the UN, going so far as to question whether it should remain in the United States. These comments have been unfortunate, it seems to me, in all respects but one, namely that they do provide an opportunity for reflection on the underlying causes of the problem and the true attitudes of the American people.

I should like at this time to read to the subcommittee a brief statement on these issues by six former Secretaries of State, seven former United States Permanent Representatives to the UN, and four former National Security Advisers:

> "The United Nations is an important instrumentality in the conduct of American foreign policy. Our experience, both in our public and private roles, has brought this home to us. The United Nations provides this country with a forum for protecting and promoting our own interests as well as for seeking solutions to problems we share with other countries. It is appropriate as well that this country should be the site of the United Nations, given the vision that has guided us as a nation and given the role we play, on all levels, in the world today. We all recognize the shortcomings of the United Nations, but we live in a very imperfect and increasingly dangerous world and we must make the best use possible of whatever means we have for managing the problems that beset us."

It is generally accepted that President Roosevelt pressed to have the headquarters of the UN in this country because he wanted to do all that he could to thwart efforts by American isolationists—of whom there seems always to be a vocal if not large contingent—to keep the US from joining the organization. But that is history. What is more important is that there are good reasons today for keeping the UN headquarters here. Some of them are practical—the UN contributes about $700 million to the New York area economy alone, nearly as much as the US portion of the UN budget. In addition, UN development programs spend substantial sums for US goods and services.

Secondly, it is useful to the US to have delegates from virtually every country in the world experience American society at firsthand. Those of us who have genuine confidence in the strength and attractiveness of our system can only welcome this unique opportunity to impress the rest of the world.

What I believe to be the most important considerations, however, are less tangible. This country is the proper site for the preeminent world organization because of the role America plays in the world. The United States is not just the leader of a coalition, nor just a leader of a certain group of countries that share our values and political system, it is *the* leading country in the entire world community. It is regarded as such by all, though the fact may not always be admitted or rejoiced in. As such it is our proper function and our responsibility to be the home of the United Nations.

We should all recognize, however, that the argument is not really about the site of the UN. It is about the organization itself, and our relationship to it, and in turn it is about how we see ourselves in relation to the rest of the world and how we believe the problems we face should be dealt with.

To some extent, of course, the thought that the UN might take itself elsewhere reflects exasperation at criticism by others, and it evaporates with the first sober thought about what the UN means for us. As such, it is inconsequential. At another level, however, it reflects the persistent presence in this country of a narrow nationalism that once was called isolationism. Although it has long been a feature of the American political scene, it is not a characteristically American viewpoint. It is a form of ideology, and we are a people who have generally shunned ideology, and who developed pragmatism to a fine art. It emphasizes fear and suspicion of the outside world, and we are a people who have thrived on confidence and an openness to the rest of the world. It is at heart a rejection of cooperative ways of dealing with problems, while no people in the world has prided itself more, or with more reason, for knowing how to make things work by cooperative effort.

The rallying point for this narrow viewpoint is hostility to the United Nations, though it is not the UN itself that is fundamentally at issue. Like other attempts to adjust to the realities of global interdependence, the UN is the target of a sense of frustration and resentment. These feelings spring from a number of simplistic assumptions, all of them wrong:

—that the US is still consistently able, as we like to think it once was, to protect and promote its own interests solely by its own efforts;

—that organized, multilateral means of solving or dealing with problems are not only in the main unnecessary, but are to be distrusted; and

—that unilateralism is forced on us by an essentially hostile world.

This is a crippling vision of the world for a superpower with global responsibilities. Whether we like it or not, our fate is indissolubly bound up with the actions of countries with different economic, political and social systems, as well as with other developed Western countries. In today's world, scarcely an important American interest, and no serious threat to our well-being, is within our power to manage or control by ourselves or with a few friends. Native American pragmatism, faced with that reality, would see only one sensible course—to employ every available means, including the use of multilateral organizations, to bring to bear on these concerns the joint efforts of the countries necessary to their successful management.

What the public seems to be saying in its pragmatic way is that there are critical problems the US cannot deal with alone, that the UN can help with them, and that we should not get too upset about the rhetoric. On the other hand, the public also seems to be saying that the UN is not dealing adequately with these problems. The poll results speak of increasing the UN's powers. This translates, in part, into an increased commitment by the member governments to use the UN for solving problems. It also means finding ways to make the organizations that make up the UN system work better, as well as devising new means to address new or changing problems.

The focus of debate in this country about the UN should be on these practical issues. It too seldom is. We are diverted from serious purposes by such irrelevancies as petulant comments about the UN's presence in this country. Not nearly enough creativity and energy is being expended on generating policies that will shape the institutional means to meet future crisis.

[Statement before House Subcommittee on Human Rights and International Organizations, Sept. 27, 1983, pp. 1-4]

THE U.N. AT 40: A SUPPORTER'S LAMENT

Edward C. Luck

ALTHOUGH THE UNITED NATIONS IS DEDICATED to resolving problems that have escaped solution through other means, its performance has inevitably fallen short of its founding vision. It is an arena in which a majority composed of the less powerful try through persuasion and rhetoric to convince a determined minority of the more powerful to do things they have long refused to do. Buffeted by competing visions of its role in the world, as well as by competing claims on its services, the United Nations has become an organization in search of an identity. Trying to be all things to all people, the United Nations has ended up disappointing most and disaffecting some, most importantly the United States.

Yet the United States is itself a country in search of a strategy. Having long ceased to exploit multilateral options or to build international institutions, American policymakers now complain of the ineffectiveness and political orientation of these bodies. U.S. officials know what they do not like about the United Nations—that is easy—but they appear much less certain about what they want it to accomplish. In stressing vote counts, budget limits, and ideological debates, American officials have lost sight of what the United Nations should be and how the United States could improve it. It is neither fair nor productive to complain about the impotence of the United Nations and then to act to undermine its capabilities.

The United Nations, after all, will never be more than what its members allow it to be. The United States and other key member states must decide what kind of a United Nations they want and are willing to pay for, financially and politically. Do they really want a strong United Nations and, if so, to do what?

COMPETING VISIONS

After almost four decades, it is time to articulate a new vision of the missions and capabilities of the United Nations. Three such basic visions already exist today regarding the organization's purpose, beyond its important role as a universal political forum. These visions are not incompatible, but different blocs assign them different priorities, preventing the emergence of any consensus.

Performing Functional Activities

The Reagan administration recognizes, and even stresses, that U.N. agencies perform a variety of useful functions in facilitating the international flow of communications, technology, and humanitarian and development assistance. Agencies such as the International Atomic Energy Agency (IAEA), the International Civil Aviation Organization, the International Labor Organization (ILO), the International Telecommunications Union, the U.N. Development Program, the U.N. High Commissioner on Refugees, UNICEF (U.N. Children's Fund), the World Health Organization, and many others carry out day-to-day functions that are essential to the smooth working of the international system or that serve basic human needs. The International Monetary Fund and the World Bank, more loosely affiliated with the United Nations, play absolutely critical roles in the world economy.

Promoting Systemic Change

From the outset, the United Nations, with American support, served as a major catalyst for decolonization. Having succeeded in this effort, the organization has been transformed by the influx of former colonies that now seek to use the United Nations as a vehicle for reordering international economic, social, and political relationships.

Implementing Collective Security

The U.N. charter stresses collective security, as practiced by the victorious Allies during World War II, as the organization's fundamental purpose. Human rights and economic and social goals are also recognized in the charter, but implicitly are assigned a lesser priority.

Under the Reagan administration the United States has applauded the United Nations as a functional organization but has bitterly opposed efforts by the majority of members to promote systemic change. In theory, the United States would also prefer a strong U.N. role in peace and security, but, like other members, its enthusiasm has been selective. Washington has discouraged U.N. involvement in regions where its own strategic objectives might be brought into question, such as the Middle East, Central America, and, in earlier years, Indochina. Of course, the United States has advocated a higher U.N. profile on issues embarrassing to the Soviet Union, such as Afghanistan, yellow rain, and the September 1983 downing of an unarmed South Korean airliner by Soviet fighters.

Conversely, Moscow has welcomed nonaligned efforts to promote systemic change since the debate costs the Soviet nothing and fans anti-Western sentiment in the Third World. The Soviets, however, put relatively modest resources into U.N. functional activities and development programs. They advocate a strict interpretation of the charter, stressing the veto in the Security Council and the priority of peace and security issues. Thus the Soviets vigorously champion disarmament resolutions but rarely support a more active role for the secretary general and refuse to pay for many peace keeping operations in the field.

For the less-developed and nonaligned countries, international institutions are very important as avenues for economic assistance, as forums in which they can express their viewpoints alongside the major powers, and as potential buffers for enhancing their security from external threats. Relatively few conflicts among nonaligned countries themselves, however, have been brought to the attention of the Security Council. It was Argentina, not the United Kingdom, that balked at the secretary general's plan to avert more bloodshed in the crisis over the Falkland Islands (Islas Malvinas). At the same time, the more militant nonaligned states have managed to put issues of systemic change at the top of the nonaligned agenda, calling for steps that many Westerners consider unrealistic and even radical.

For the United Nations as an institution, the first vision offers the least risk but chances political irrelevance; the second, high risk, polarization, and little chance of achievement; and the third, high risk but much potential gain. If current trends continue, U.N. agencies will continue to perform useful functions, but even these agencies will gradually lose political support if the organization fails to address constructively the broader, more difficult issues in the political realm. The United Nations will remain an uneasy amalgam of a debating society and a collection of functional entities. To become a stronger organization, the United Nations will have to make a difference to the central issues of peace and security facing humankind as well as maintain its useful functional activities. Achieving this goal will entail creating a new vision that leaves sweeping efforts at systemic change for future agendas and more propitious climates, while encouraging the more incremental and conciliatory approaches to North-South political disputes. If a vision based on consensus and compromise does not emerge, the United Nations will have less and less to celebrate on future birthdays. . . .

U.S. STRATEGY

Before it can develop a coherent strategy toward the U.N. system, the United States will have to address three fundamental questions on which it has wavered over the years. First, does it have a long-term commitment to strengthening the U.N. system from within or will it withdraw step by step and seek alternative means of coping with multilateral issues? Second, what really counts at the United Nations in terms of American interests and what should the United States expect from the system? Third, how should the United States go about getting what it wants out of the United Nations?

American officials have been ambivalent toward the United Nations since its early days, rarely turning to multilateral diplomacy until all else failed. The threat or act of withdrawal has become an accepted American tactic in agencies such as the IAEA, the ILO, the U.N. Educational, Scientific, and Cultural Organization (UNESCO), and even the United Nations itself. When the Senate votes overwhelmingly to slash U.S.-assessed contributions unilaterally—which would be tantamount to withdrawal—when an American representative speaks of bidding the United Nations a "fond farewell" and the president applauds his statement, when the U.S. permanent representative terms the United Nations "a dangerous place," and when the United States turns its back on the World Court and on the Law of the Sea Treaty, it is clear why even American allies wonder whether the United States will support multilateral institutions and approaches when the going gets tough. They ask whether American criticism of the United Nations is meant to strengthen the institution or to provide a rationale for eventual withdrawal. Given the extent of problems in the U.N. system, its best friends should be vocal critics, but with the clear intent to build, not undermine, the institution. This theme has been reflected in several recent public opinion polls, which show a growth in public frustration about the inability of the United Nations to fulfill their high expectations along with a very high and steady level of support for remaining in the organization and for seeking to strengthen it. Most Americans neither love the United Nations nor want to leave it.

Sometimes it seems as if the U.S. government does not really want what it needs out of the United Nations and does not need what it wants. In the long term, the United States needs stronger multilateral institutions to buttress the stability and predictability of international relations in an essentially turbulent era. Too often, however, the United States and other countries have stressed using multilateral forums to persuade other countries to endorse their foreign-policy actions and to condemn those of their adversaries. Votes in the General Assembly tend to be interpreted by American officials in an ethnocentric manner, as if they were referendums on the conduct of U.S. foreign policy and votes for or against the United States, though often they reflect routine internal U.N. bargaining or expressions of national views and interests that have little to do with the United States. These defensive attitudes have contributed to the weakening of the institution and to American isolation within it.

Moreover, the United States appears to be particularly inept at multilateral diplomacy, as U.S. Permanent Representative Jeane Kirkpatrick herself has stated on occasion. In part, this reflects America's status as the world's greatest power and the largest target in forums composed largely of small countries. But the problem also stems from the frequent turnover in U.S. representation at the United Nations—12 permanent represent-atives in the last five administrations—and in the relative inexpe-rience of many Americans serving at the U.S. mission. America's difficulties are also rooted in an innate American reluctance to engage in the kind of subtle give-and-take style of diplomacy that characterizes one-nation, one-vote forums.

The decline in Washington's ability to get its way has been most striking in the General Assembly, where the percentage of votes in which the United States sided with the majority—excluding consensus votes and abstentions—has declined from more than 40 percent in 1977 and 1978 to barely more than 15 percent in 1982 and 1983. The style and the priorities of U.S. representatives, the conservative shift in U.S. policies, and in-creasing polarization on issues relating to the Middle East and southern Africa are all responsible. Delegates from many coun-tries contend that U.S. representatives should listen more, talk less, and refrain from lecturing other states about their values and interests. They complain repeatedly that Kirkpatrick spends too little time in New York and that she and her staff have made insufficient effort to keep contact with their counterparts, espe-cially those from the Third World.

American laws linking foreign assistance levels to the recipi-ent's General Assembly voting pattern may be psychologically gratifying, but they have not been able to win votes or to make friends. In a March 13, 1984, press conference, Kirkpatrick claimed that America's get-tough tactics were working and that the portion of General Assembly votes in which the majority sided with the United States rose from 1977-1978 to 1983. The actual voting records, however, show just the opposite trend, and the U.S. mission issued a little-noticed correction the next day. Yet this press release did little to dispel the widespread misimpression that Washington's coercive policies have succeeded. Similar Soviet tactics, such as efforts to reverse the General Assembly's votes on Afghanistan, have also backfired. One reason for the American failures is that carrot-and-stick tactics do not work unless both carrots and sticks are offered.

The United States will remain in a minority position in most General Assembly votes on the Middle East, southern Africa, and North-South economic issues until diplomacy begins to resolve the underlying issues. Although the rhetoric of more radical states is often offensive and should be rebutted strongly, American criticisms should be aimed at those states and not at the forum itself. The latter is tantamount to killing the messenger for delivering bad news. The United States still has great influence in the Secretariat, the Security Council, and most specialized agencies.

UNESCO has been an exception, although not an unredeemable one. It is widely acknowledged in the U.N. system—and confirmed in a recent study by the U.S. General Accounting Office—that UNESCO is one of the weakest specialized agencies in terms of management practices, personnel morale, budget restraint, and politicization. It has done much good work but is badly in need of reform. Yet instead of staying and fighting for needed changes, the United States has announced its intention to withdraw at the end of 1984, citing its inability to induce sufficient reform from within. More puzzling, the U.S. decision followed UNESCO's 22nd General Conference session that blunted attacks on Israel and press freedom, suggesting that U.S. pressure was already having a positive effect. Moreover, the United States only at the last minute specified a long list of sweeping changes UNESCO would have to make this year to prevent an American walkout. UNESCO has made some effort to respond to the U.S. criticisms of its day-to-day operations, including beginning an administrative review, establishing advisory groups, and hiring a Washington public relations firm to enhance its image in the United States. Still, unless there is a significant breakthrough, the United States will walk away from the agency having failed, not succeeded, in making its point stick. [It walked. ed.]

FILLING THE LEADERSHIP VOID

While U.S. leadership is essential to strengthening international institutions, other states have contributed to the decline of the United Nations and bear important responsibilities for turning the situation around. The Soviets, after almost two decades of painful isolation, today enjoy a comfortable position in the world body. While Moscow has suffered numerous defeats on political issues, such as Afghanistan, Kampuchea, and the downing of the South Korean airliner, it has managed to deflect most nonaligned criticism and direct it toward the United States and its allies. While initiating relatively few programs or resolutions—and paying for even fewer—the Soviets have managed to identify themselves as champions of nonaligned proposals. Seeing little risk in endorsing economic, political, and disarmament resolutions that will never be implemented, Moscow has steered a hypocritical but highly effective path through U.N. debates. But the Soviets' refusal to provide financial support for most peace keeping operations may soon put them far enough in arrears to bring into question their General Assembly voting privileges and quite possibly trigger a major constitutional crisis.

The individually weak nonaligned countries recognize that unity is their key to political leverage in multilateral bodies. But in order to maintain consensus they too often have allowed their more radical colleagues to shape the agenda and set the tone for their participation in the U.N. system. The nonaligned countries have put forward relatively few constructive proposals, particularly concerning peace and security. General Assembly resolutions on the Middle East have become so slanted as to make that body irrelevant to peace efforts in that region. This trend has begun to undermine the credibility of the Security Council and the Secretariat in dealing with the Middle East, though the Israelis have recently revived proposals for strengthening U.N. peace keeping troops in Lebanon.

Recognizing the futility of confrontational approaches to North-South issues, moderate nonaligned countries have recently begun to reassert themselves. But the nonaligned as a whole need to recognize that their actions in the United Nations have consequences for relations with the United States and for multilateralism. The alienation of Western public opinion and the polarization of U.N. political discussions will only further undermine the very institutions on which their prosperity and security depend in the long run.

Who will begin to fill the leadership void at the United Nations? Until the United States begins to reassert itself, clearly the other industrialized free-market countries, with their stated desire to bolster international norms and institutions, will have to fill the bill. To a certain extent, this has already happened in many of the functional agencies and on financial and management question. Yet Japan and most West European countries are still reluctant to take a high profile on the war-and-peace issues on which the future of international organization hinges.

All countries have a stake in making the system work and each needs to contribute to turning the system around. No country, the United States included, can remake international bodies in its own image. None should expect multilateral institutions to serve their unilateral interests consistently. But they should recognize that the United Nations is an instrument, not an ideal, that must be used and cared for through good times and bad if it is to work well when needed most.

"The U.N. at 40: A Supporter's Lament" (pp. 144-148, 154-159)

SOVIET

REPORT OF CENTRAL COMMITTEE

V.I. Lenin

WE ARE LIVING NOT MERELY IN A STATE, but in a system of states, and the existence of the Soviet Republic side by side with imperialist states for a long time is unthinkable. One or the other must triumph in the end. And before that end supervenes, a series of frightful collisions between the Soviet Republic and the bourgeois states will be inevitable. That means that if the ruling class, the proletariat, wants to hold sway, it must prove its capacity to do so by military organization also.

[Report of the Central Committee at the Eighth Party Congress, p. 33]

ON PEACEFUL COEXISTENCE

Nikita S. Khrushchev

WE ALL OF US WELL KNOW THAT TREMENDOUS CHANGES have taken place in the world. Gone, indeed, are the days when it took weeks to cross the ocean from one continent to the other or when a trip from Europe to America, or from Asia to Africa, seemed a very complicated undertaking. The progress of modern technology has reduced our planet to a rather small place; it has even become, in this sense, quite congested. And if in our daily life it is a matter of considerable importance to establish normal relations with our neighbors in a densely inhabited settlement, this is so much the more necessary in the relations between states, in particular states belonging to different social systems.

You may like your neighbor or dislike him. You are not obliged to be friends with him or visit him. But you live side by side, and what can you do if neither you nor he has any desire to quit the old home and move to another town? All the more so in relations between states. It would be unreasonable to assume that you can make it so hot for your undesirable neighbor that he will decide to move to Mars or Venus. And vice versa, of course.

What, then, remains to be done? There may be two ways out: either war—and war in the rocket and H-bomb age is fraught with the most dire consequences for all nations—or peaceful coexistence. Whether you like your neighbor or not, nothing can be done about it, you have to find some way of getting on with him, for you both live on one and the same planet . . .

What, then, is the policy of peaceful coexistence?

In its simplest expression it signifies the repudiation of war as a means of solving controversial issues. However, this does not cover the entire concept of peaceful coexistence. Apart from the commitment to non-aggression, it also presupposes an obligation on the part of all states to desist from violating each other's territorial integrity and sovereignty in any form and under any pretext whatsoever. The principle of peaceful coexistence signifies a renunciation of interference in the internal affairs of other countries with the object of altering their system of government or mode of life or for any other motives. The doctrine of peaceful coexistence also presupposes that political and economic relations between countries are to be based upon complete equality of the parties concerned, and on mutual benefit.

It is often said in the West that peaceful coexistence is nothing else than a tactical method of the socialist states. There is not a grain of truth in such allegations. Our desire for peace and peaceful coexistence is not conditioned by any time-serving or tactical considerations. It springs from the very nature of socialist society in which there are no classes or social groups interested in profiting by war or seizing and enslaving other people's territories. The Soviet Union and the other socialist countries, thanks to their socialist system, have an unlimited home market and for this reason they have no need to pursue an expansionist policy of conquest and an effort to subordinate other countries to their influence . . .

Contrary to what certain propagandists hostile to us say, the coexistence of states with different social systems does not mean that they will only fence themselves off from one another by a high wall and undertake the mutual obligation not to throw stones over the wall or pour dirt upon each other. No! Peaceful coexistence does not mean merely living side by side in the absence of war but with the constantly remaining threat of its breaking out in the future. *Peaceful coexistence can and should develop into peaceful competition for the purpose of satisfying man's needs in the best possible way.*

We say to the leaders of the capitalist states: Let us try out in practice whose system is better, let us compete without war. This is much better than competing in who will produce more arms and who will smash whom. We stand and always will stand for such competition as will help to raise the well-being of the people to a higher level.

The principle of peaceful competition does not at all demand that one or another state abandon the system and ideology adopted by it. It goes without saying that the acceptance of this principle cannot lead to the immediate end of disputes and contradictions which are inevitable between countries adhering to different social systems. But the main thing is ensured: the states which decided to adopt the path of peaceful coexistence repudiate the use of force in any form and agree on a peaceful settlement of possible disputes and conflicts, bearing in mind the mutual interests of the parties concerned. In our age of the H-bomb and atomic techniques this is the main thing of interest to every man.

["On Peaceful Coexistence", 1959, pp. 1-4]

SPEECH TO CENTRAL COMMITTEE

Konstantin U. Chernenko

THE SOVIET UNION AS A GREAT SOCIALIST POWER fully realizes its responsibility to the peoples for preserving and strengthening peace. We are open for peaceful, mutually beneficial cooperation with the states in all continents. We are for a peaceful settlement of all disputable international problems through serious, equal and constructive talks. The U.S.S.R. will cooperate in full measure with all states which are prepared to assist through practical deeds to lessening international tensions and creating an atmosphere of trust in the world; in other words, with those who will really lead things, not to preparation for war, but to a strengthening of fundamentals of peace. We believe that with these aims, full use shall be made of all the existing levers, including, certainly, such as the United Nations, which has been created precisely for preserving and strengthening peace.

[Speech to Central Committee, Feb. 13, 1984]

THIRD WORLD

ADDRESS TO THE U.N. GENERAL ASSEMBLY

Paul J. F. Lusaka

CONVENTIONAL WISDOM SUGGESTS that the greatest of Powers do not need the United Nations to survive. Indeed, some even assert that international security since the founding of the Organization has been guaranteed by the nuclear "balance of terror" and that the existence of this Organization, has had nothing to do with it. While it can be argued that this balance of terror has played a role in preventing total war, it has contributed very little to the creation of real peace. In contrast, the United Nations has made substantial contributions. Certainly, a strong case can be made to show that a world without the United Nations would be a much more dangerous place in which to live. Even the balance of terror itself operates within a context of diplomacy and international exchange; and to this extent, at least, all States depend upon this context within which the United Nations is a major element.

However, whether one or another State could possibly survive without the United Nations is not the central or crucial issue. The small and medium-sized States need the United Nations. This is not because they are confident that the United Nations can assure their security and independence or indeed their very survival. On the contrary, the cumbersome methods of the Security Council and its increasing difficulties in taking timely and effective decisions, offer no firm hope in that direction. Rather, and I hope that this is true also for the Great Powers, they need the United Nations because it still represents mankind's most imaginative structure for using cooperative methods to tackle man's ancient enemies: war, disease, poverty and the denial of basic human rights and freedom.

Under favourable circumstances, the United Nations creates the setting within which States can use their common wisdom to enunciate the norms which, when observed, provide for the maintenance of international peace and security.

It is tempting for Member States, perhaps relying too much on their own military, industrial, economic and moral authority, to believe that they can, not only ensure their own security, but that they can also impose their own particular concepts of peace and security on the world community. History, in its long display of the rise and fall of great empires, teaches us a different lesson. No state, however awesome its military power, or however great its industrial and economic strength, can have a unique grasp on common sense, nor can it unilaterally command the strength of purpose and the tenacity of commitment required to safeguard the peace and security of the world community. Of course, I am aware that a single state might be well placed to obstruct international efforts to strengthen the global machinery for peace and security. But we should never forget, that obstruction is no substitute for leadership.

The approach of the fortieth anniversary of our Organization affords us an uncommon opportunity to rededicate ourselves to the important truth that the world needs the United Nations. The conceptual framework which gave birth to the Organization is still as vital and essential as when it was formulated in the critical period of the struggle against Nazism and Fascism. Nonetheless, it is incumbent upon all of us to candidly recognize that all is not well in our Organization under present circumstances.

Earlier on I alluded to the crises we are now experiencing. It is true, of course, that since its inception, the Organization has been buffeted to and fro, and has gone through many trying periods. We have experienced various crises of confidence and disenchantment.

We have been able to come through these crises.

However, what we are faced with today is more serious: some Member States are questioning the very legitimacy of our Organization. Some assert that the United Nations' deliberative organs have ceased to honour the principle of objectivity, sobriety and fairness. It is even being suggested that these organs have served as instruments for the exacerbation of conflicts rather than for promoting understanding and reconciliation among States. Others bemoan the prevalence of double standards and absence of consistency in decisions. The imposition of collective sanctions is judged to be totally effective in certain situations but is assessed as impractical and counter-productive in others. Surely, such perceptions, even though they may not be totally accurate, do not enhance the credibility of our Organization.

But the time is long past for name-calling, for blaming one another, or for pointing accusing fingers in efforts to dissect the ills of our Organization. What is required at this critical juncture is a time to pause, to reflect deeply and to re-evaluate the direction in which we must move if our Organization is to regain its credibility and full acceptance. This is not the time for fractious rhetoric. Nor is it the time for facile or evasive answers or indeed ostrich-like behaviour. We should be united in our conviction that the United Nations remains an essential human instrument in the conduct of international relations. And within the context of this conviction, we should examine our actions and systems in order to bring about whatever reforms are necessary, to implement the objectives for which the Charter was designed.

[Address to U.N. Assembly September 18, 1984 (pp. 4-8)]

RADICAL LEFT

WORLD ORDER STUDIES—NEW DIRECTIONS

Richard A. Falk and Samuel S. Kim

THE WORLD ORDER STUDIES APPROACH: POINTS OF DEPARTURE

THE ESSENTIAL FEATURES OF THE WORLD ORDER approach can be indicated by briefly setting forth its main assumptions.

(1) *Contest of Emergency/Obscenity:* The world order approach arises in a context of grave social concern for the state of the world today. This concern emphasizes the inadequacy of the traditional focus of inquiry and policy into international issues. As such, the world order approach reflects anxieties about nuclear war and ecological hazards, as well as about the scandal of avoidable mass misery. It seeks deliberately to put these issues at the center of its intellectual efforts, conceiving education as social mobilization, as well as abstract learning.

(2) *Normativity.* Closely associated with (1) is the central idea that the global situation is being seriously deteriorated by *avoidable evils.* The world order approach establishes its identity by postulating values: peace, social and economic justice, human rights, ecological balance, humane governance. Politics as a value-realizing process provides a new type of coherence. Policy in a global setting is evaluated by reference to the human interests at stake rather than associated only with national interests. Normativity implies, also a critical stance toward knowledge (for what valued end?) rather than one based on detachment and the accumulation of skills (the sharpening of tools). The role

of knowledge is to transform the context of emergency/obscenity in specified ways.

(3) *System Discontinuities.* Traditional approaches to international political life emphasize the continuities and essential resilience of the state system. In contrast, the world order approach stresses positive and negative discontinuities, that is, the linked opportunities for drastic global reform and the dangers of statist collapse. This approach is concerned with alternatives to the pattern of war and repression that currently dominate international life. It seeks images and designs of what else might be coming into being in international political life that could appreciably realize world order values. As such, it assesses trends and cumulative effects arising out of existing dynamics, as well as the description and explanation of persistent patterns of statist behavior.

Normative futurism based on the altered frameworks of comprehensive value-realization can be contrasted with technocratic futurism that finds "fixes" (e.g. space colonies, nuclear fusion energy) to solve the problems of human society within existing economic, cultural, political, and ecological frameworks. In somewhat oversimplified form, normative futurism tends toward progressive politics, emphasizing popular movements for social change, whereas technocratic futurism seeks to persuade existing elites to invest capital creatively at the technological frontier. The world order approach is wary of, although not unalterably opposed to, technocratic futurism.

(4) *Globalist Perspective.* The world order approach presupposes that the world can be conceived of as a whole and that the human species shares bonds and is, in fact, bonded by a shared legacy and destiny. As such, the statist structure of the world is treated as transient and conditional, a fragmentation of a potential global social reality. This fragmentation arose at a given time in human history and is in the process of being superceded. Such globalism does not dismiss the role of the state in preserving autonomy and diversity in the world as now constituted, achieving national cohesion (internally) and safeguarding independence (against external actors).

For most peoples, the most notable feature of recent world history has been the struggle to become a viable state. The anticolonial movement involved the preliminary quest for formal independence, including the right to one's own flag and to participate in international arenas. More recently the struggle has involved efforts to achieve economic, cultural, and political viability in the face of internal dissension and transnational penetration of various sorts. Too little statism (e.g. Lebanon, post-Shah Iran), as well as too much (e.g. the Soviet Union, Argentina) pose serious value problems in the world today. Notions of self-reliance, collective self-reliance, and non-alignment represent efforts to secure the virtues of statism in the present world order system.

A globalist perspective also gives due accord to non-state actors, including those associated with intergovernmental arrangements (e.g. the United Nations, international financial institutions), transnational activities (e.g. multinational corporations, banks), and nongovernmental operations (e.g. Red Cross, Amnesty International). The world is seen as becoming more complicated and confusing, the various trends and activities being evaluated by reference to their effect on the values at stake and by their relationship to desired networks and regimes.

Globalist thinking associated with the world order approach tries to avoid "globaloney," that is, preaching pieties or touting pipedreams. It does not want to discredit holistic orientations in the annals of serious reflective or activist thought by appearing irrelevant to the practical concerns of men and women worried by the context of danger and hardship. Concrete preoccupations can benefit, however, from utopian explorations. We may need to develop alternative visions of the future to facilitate transformation. In this regard, imaginative writers and artists, such as Ursula LeGuin and Doris Lessing, have more to offer world order studies than the more constrained speculations of social scientists.

(5) *Praxis.* The entire shape of the world order enterprise is premised on active social engagement. It is not a matter of learning for learning's sake, of fulfilling careerist objectives, or helping out the global managers and grand strategists. A strength of Marxism is that it moves from critique to practice with a theory that will explain how to realize proximate goals. World order studies has a comparable ambition, although it presently lacks a comprehensive view of praxis. It rejects romantic politics that sets forth a wish list for the future. World order

politics emphasizes the credibility of its transition imagery by which the present might become the preferred future. In this regard, knowledge is purposive, possibly partisan, to be mobilized for "the oppressed," against "the oppressor" on behalf of "human interests" and "world order values." This partisanship, deeply challenging to mainstream academic conventions about the "neutrality" of inquiry, is directly linked to the belief that current global problems confront us with an emergency situation. The relevance of knowledge to action may not be nearly so evident in other historical contests.

(6) *Structuralist Orientation.* The nature of the challenge posed by the array of "avoidable evils" (hunger, war, repression, environmental decay) is such that the structure of international political life is drawn into question. In relation to war and mass poverty, for instance, the state system, with its hierarchically arranged territorial units, cannot be expected to fashion arrangements based on non-violence and resource-sharing. World order value-realization presupposes system-change, that is, frameworks of institutions, procedures, and rules that give due weight to the globalist orientation, although not necessarily to centralization. As well, a weakening of materialist incentives and a strengthening of cooperative behavior and moral incentives seems essential for a world political system that solves concrete problems in a manner responsive to criteria of the human interest. These developments should be understood as adjustments to the pressures of context rather than as ethical imperatives.

(7) *Transition and Transformation prospects.* The world order approach has not been consistent about its conception of positive global reform. Much of the earlier depictions of a better world political system were apolitical in the sense of having no idea about how to achieve transition and an eventual global transformation. Subsequently, the implicit approach was an appeal or rational argument designed to persuade influential people. This top-down view of global reform has been recently supplanted by a more bottom-up view based on the global potential of ongoing movements for social change and liberation. Hence, "the oppressed," to the extent mobilized for global reform, become "the proletariat," the social force promoting a progressive realization of values, including whatever structural adjustments are

needed. Given dangers of nuclear war and ecological decay and the refusals of existing leaders to take appropriate "precautions," the category of oppression becomes universal, that is to say, species-wide. Such an actuality seems genuinely unprecedented, and could, in time, eventuate in a new politics congruent with the aspirations of world order values.

There is no claim being made that mobilized movements among the oppressed are consistently or self-consciously dedicated to world order values. Their horizons are generally narrower, characteristically focused on radical revisionings of the domestic political structure. The world order approach contends, however, that these movements can have wider implications which are now just beginning to be understood. Indeed, it is becoming clearer that movements of national revolution are being thwarted after they "succeed," partly because of the hostile character of the existing international political system. Other movements, such as the growing West European movement against nuclear weapons and militarism, can only be successful by spreading everywhere and by adopting wider projects of transformation. Given increasingly linked global realities, partly as a consequence of technological capacity and scale, progressive changes at the national level are very vulnerable to disruptive reactions. The struggle against oppression in all its forms seems increasingly likely to merge with the quest for a new world order.

(8) *The Drift of History.* Increasingly, the world order approach does not itself claim to be an independent force. Rather, to the extent it offers hope for transcending the structures of oppression, this hope arises from an interpretation of the drift of history. Of course, "drift" is a subjective category. Furthermore, the historical process does not pull all in one direction. Yet, the world order approach contends that systemic discontinuities of a specific sort are taking place in international life that make its description of "reality" more satisfactory than those of the Machiavellians or Marxists. Oddly enough, then, given the WOMP stress on normativity, it is a mode of descriptive analysis, giving an interpretation to the cumulative weight of emergent anti-statist trends, that deserves special emphasis: World order studies as counter-cultural journalism.

More concretely, the drift of history is interpreted as favoring the continuing dynamics, however troubled, of self-determination and national revolution. More broadly, this drift seems likely to unleash a widening movement against oppression that is transnationally guided, given the agenda set by the menace of nuclear war and by environmental contamination of various kinds. It is unlikely that the 1980s will end without a major transnational ecological/nuclear disaster of some kind. If so, then the latent popular energies of those who feel victimized could easily become an explosive force in the 1990s. The first stirrings of such a prospect are evident in Western Europe and Japan, and are beginning to surface in established institutions of moral concern, especially in religious organizations. As one small illustration, the Catholic Archbishop of Seattle, Raymond Hunthausen, recently urged citizens to refuse to pay 50 percent of their Federal income tax as a protest against nuclear arms which he described as "demonic weapons which threaten all life on earth"; in a letter Lutheran, United Methodist, United Presbyterian, and United Church of God leaders endorsed this proposal.

The world order approach does not predict a positive outcome, but it does anticipate pervasive turmoil of a sort that will alter decisively the political frameworks for problem-solving in the decades ahead, quite possibly in a regressive manner. The polemical point is that the modes of inquiry that presuppose the persisting solidity of these frameworks will not help us understand what is really happening in the world.

["World Order Studies: New Directions and Orientations",
1981, pp. 8-10]

RADICAL RIGHT

YANQUI, SI! UN, NO!

Richard Grenier

THE UNITED NATIONS IS AN ORGANIZATION that actively supports the violent overthrow of sovereign states by revolutionary movements. But not all states and not all movements. It is highly selective. To qualify, a movement must be radical and Marxist, and, of course, terrorists are welcome. In 1970 the U.N. General Assembly approved a resolution encouraging "colonial peoples" and national liberation movements to use "all necessary means at their disposal" to overthrow sovereign governments. In 1974 Yasir Arafat of the PLO, pistol on his hip, received a standing ovation when he addressed the General Assembly. The PLO and SWAPO (the Marxist-terrorist "South West Africa People's Organization") are now not only official "permanent observers" at the United Nations, they are partly funded by it. Since 1977 SWAPO has been granted an estimated $40 million of U.N. money, and a pro-PLO "Division for Palestinian Rights" has spent more than $6 million. The PLO—get this—took part in a U.N. conference on civil aviation and airplane hijacking. The ANC and PAC, communist-dominated guerrilla and terrorist groups operating across the South African border, receive a biannual U.N. subsidy of at least $9 million. The major nonviolent black opposition to the South African government, however, is the Inkatha, led by the head of the Zulu Nation. It receives no U.N. support.

Notice the odd concentration of U.N. activity around the organization's two pariah states, South Africa and Israel, as if they were the only trouble spots on the globe. In the *Through the Looking Glass* world of the U.N., words mean only what the U.N. says they mean. I have no idea why the Afghans struggling desperately to free their country from Soviet occupation do not qualify as a national liberation movement, but I have never heard them mentioned once in the corridors of the U.N., except by the United States. Nor have I ever heard talk of the Kurds, who have been fighting everyone around them for generations. And again, except from the U.S., I have never heard a whisper about such obvious non-nations as Poland, Czechoslovakia, Hungary, Estonia, Latvia, Lithuania, Moldavia, Uzbekistan, Kirghīzīa.

["Yanqui, Si! U.N., No !", 1984, pp. 28-29]

GLOBAL PATERNALISM

Jeane J. Kirkpatrick

THERE HAS BEEN, IN RECENT YEARS, A VERITABLE EXPLOSION of UN regulatory activity. It has occurred for a number of reasons, some very good and obvious ones. Important among these is the emergence of a number of new areas of activity that seem to many to require some sort of multinational agreement. The driving forces have included technological advance and, of course, growing interdependence in the world economy. These are very real forces and require a response . . .

Within the UN context, even when genuine problems are being addressed, there are invariably some powerful factors and motives at work pushing UN regulatory initiatives in some very unfortunate directions. The process of regulation in the United Nations is distorted at several levels—at the ideological level, the political level, the technical level and, finally, at the level of implementation.

IDEOLOGICAL DISTORTION

The first distortion occurs, I think, at the ideological level. How an issue is defined has obvious consequences for how it is going to be dealt with. And in the UN context the definition of the issue gets shaped, naturally, by the dominant ideology. Unfortunately for Americans—and for anyone interested in economic growth and development—the dominant ideology in the United Nations concerning economic regulation is a version of class war that has been developed by a kind of gross adaptation of Marxist categories to relations among nations. According to this version of class war, the many poor nations are locked in a bitter and ongoing struggle with the few rich nations, very much as the working class or proletariat is, according to Marxist ideology,

149

locked in an ongoing struggle with the few capitalists inside nations.

According to this theory, if property isn't theft, it is something very much like it. And because poverty, in this view, is caused by exploitation, the very fact of underdevelopment is seen as proof that a nation has been exploited. Wealth, on the other hand, is seen as won by exploiting others. The very fact of affluence proves that a nation has been guilty of exploitation. Disparities of wealth, in this view, are seen as intrinsically unjust. Justice, therefore, requires redistributing wealth from the rich nations to the poor nations. That is another way of saying that the political culture that prevails in the UN system on economic matters has two distinctive characteristics: It asserts the need for a more equal distribution of the world's wealth and it provides a moral justification for that redistribution. It is hostile or at best indifferent to the production of wealth in general and to those corporations in particular which operate across national boundaries (transnationals) or whose ownership is multinational.

Political distortion

These ideological factors inevitably come into play as regulatory negotiations are undertaken and carried out under UN auspices. To this ideological context is added the political structure of the United Nations, a very important and very little understood factor. The United Nations is not simply a body in which representatives of 157 sovereign nations meet. It is a body in which groups interact very much as individuals form parties in legislatures.

Nations in the United Nations are organized into a series of overlapping groups, or blocs, and the business of the United Nations takes place through the interaction of these groups. There is, for example, the Soviet bloc, there is the European Community bloc, there is the Nonaligned bloc, there is the Group of 77. (The G-77 is the third world organized for economic purposes; the Nonaligned is the third world organized for political purposes.) Each of these blocs has its own particular dynamic. Each of them has a problem, too—which is to maintain its own internal unity and cohesion. The blocs are formed as small nations try to develop greater strength by joining together, and they get that strength only at the price of maintaining their own internal unity.

But each of the blocs is filled with internal contradictions because of their members' conflicting interests and very different perspectives. They maintain unity chiefly by aggregating concern for all the specific interests of all the specific members. At last count, the G-77 had 126 members, and it is not much of an exaggeration to say that the G-77's bargaining positions very frequently turn out to be the sum total of all those members' demands. That adds up to a lot of demands. This method of establishing a negotiating position by accumulation, so to speak, naturally results in some very unrealistic demands. It also gives the most extreme positions of the most extreme members of the group a decisive effect on the negotiating position of the total group. A bloc's unity—particularly the unity of a big bloc, and to a certain extent of a smaller bloc, too—is bought, in many cases, at the price of the group's acquiescence in the most extreme demands of its most extreme members.

TECHNICAL DISTORTION

And that is not all. There is also distortion at the technical level where, it is important to note, the people who shape the negotiations and the debates concerning regulation almost invariably utterly lack technical expertise about the matters to be negotiated, to be regulated. Therefore, political concerns dominate. The process of goal-setting and problem-defining is governed not by consideration of what is technically necessary, desirable, or feasible, but quite simply by the politics of the blocs, in the political culture of international class struggle.

Politics at the UN takes a rather pure form, worthy of our state legislatures at the turn of the century. There is a good deal of vote trading, arm-twisting, demagoguery, playing to the galleries, a certain amount of buying and selling, logrolling, and pork-barreling. All those highly developed political skills are very much in fashion at the UN. There is widespread cynicism and tacit understanding that a good many of the declarations of intentions that are made there will never be implemented.

The result of all this is that the problems that are going to be addressed by the regulatory mechanisms are often defined ideologically, unrealistically, and in a manner that is technically inappropriate. In most legislatures, such political dynamics exist of course, but their distorting impact is moderated once the technical experts take over and try to translate into technically meaningful terms the broad commands of general policy. Unfortunately, that does not necessarily happen in the UN context. There, the technical level, too, is not only bureaucratic and suffers from all the problems endemic to bureaucracies, but there is another problem: inside the United Nations, technicians are drawn from 157 countries. Not all technical bodies have technicians from all 157 countries, but there are always a good many nations represented and all the major blocs are represented. To the usual array of bureaucratic problems, such as red tape and duplication are added the conflicting codes of international civil service behavior. Whether you think you ought to represent your technical expertise or your nation is an open question. Whether the conflicting national codes of bureaucratic and technical behavior can be made harmonious is also an open question and frequently, unfortunately, it is a question that cannot be answered in the affirmative.

IMPLEMENTATIONAL DISTORTION

Finally, even at the level of implementation, we find another distorting factor. Many of the regulations enacted by the United Nations have consequences for the member states. And since the people who are implementing these regulations are representatives of member states, some of which think it is the job of all their citizens to work all the time for their own state, there is a level of nationalist distortion that takes place at the implementation level and affects everything that goes on. The consequence is a hodge-podge of ideological, political, bureaucratic, and national practices—and theories—that frequently distorts the regulatory process in the UN context beyond anything dreamed of in the national regulatory context . . .

Transnational corporations, as they are usually called in the UN, are regularly tried and found guilty of the most extraordinary range of crimes. Naturally, therefore, punitive regulation of transnational corporations becomes a kind of a good in itself. The rhetoric used gives the game away—rhetoric like "killing babies for profit" and that sort of thing. Some people apparently think that that rhetoric has greater resonance in the West than do the standard third world appeals about redistributing wealth, which may be one of the reasons it is emphasized.

An interesting role is played in this regulatory process by nongovernmental organizations—which, loosely defined, include numerous public interest groups from both ends of the political spectrum. Apparently, some of the nongovernmental organizations that do not achieve much success in this country, or in other Western countries, have focused very heavily on the United Nations as the point at which to try to secure adoption of the regulatory and punitive policies they cannot get adopted in their own political systems. It has been observed, at the UN, that there is emerging a kind of recognizable "iron triangle" uniting nongovernmental organizations, third world representatives (particularly of the radical third world countries), and ideologically sympathetic international bureaucrats in quest of restrictive international health and safety regulations. Interestingly, this new international paternalism almost invariably advocates adoption in the UN of restrictions on activities which could just as easily, in principle, be adopted within the specific countries of the member nations, if those countries chose to do so. If, for example, the countries of Africa did not desire the marketing and advertising of infant formula, there is no reason in the world that their governments could not so decide, and adopt such policies at the national level.

The fact that this regulatory thrust is focused at the level of the international bureaucracy is, I think, a suggestive clue about the strategy for establishing this new global socialism, this new paternalism, in which an international bureaucracy believes it knows what is better for everyone—better for us, better for the third world, better for everyone. In the UN system, the view is widespread that the institutions of the United Nations itself are the arena in which the "new international economic order" can be achieved. They are, after all, the institutions in which a majority exists that can be counted on—on the basis of one country, one vote—to favor projects that are highly discriminatory from the point of view of the most powerful nations in the world, including our own. The powerful nations are outnumbered in the UN; we constitute a reliable minority. There has been a lot of talk about the automatic majority in the UN. But for every automatic majority there is an automatic minority, and that's us.

UN agencies, then, are the scene of a struggle that we seem doomed to lose. Regulation is the instrument for the redistribution of what is called the world's wealth. The international bureaucracy functions as the "new class" to which power is to be transferred. Global socialism is the expected and, from the point of view of many, the desired result.

The problem with this is, of course, that it is bad theory. it is bad theory in the technical sense that its major terms do not accurately describe the world with which they deal. Wealth is not created by theft or transfer from less developed countries to more developed countries. It is created, as Adam Smith well understood, by innovation, investment, entrepreneurship. Wealth is created by growth. Computers, automobiles, aviation, looms, locomotives, the steam engine itself were not stolen from the third world. They were invented in the first world. Neither was the poverty of the least developed countries caused by the ravages of multinationals, or even by colonialism—for which, by the way, we Americans had no responsibility. The theory of international class war is equally misleading with regard to development. Poverty cannot be ended by redistribution. It can only be ended by economic development which, as we all know, is a creative process in which all sectors of a society become involved.

Finally, at the core of this theory of international class struggle lies another very curious notion: the idea that there is such a thing as the world's property—sea, space, whatever—and that the United Nations has a right to it. On exactly this theory rests the claim, the United Nations' claim, of sovereignty over oceans and space. The argument is that whatever belongs to no one belongs to the United Nations. It is a strange doctrine of property, a mistaken theory of development, and a destructive doctrine of regulation. Doubtless, international regulation is needed in a good many domains. Doubtless, consumers in remote places need protection against unscrupulous multinationals. (They need protection in ways that do not inhibit economic development and growth, I may say, as well.) And doubtless, too, all of us need protection against the arrogance of the new international "new class."

["Global Paternalism: The UN and the New International Regulatory Order", 1983, pp. 17-22]

FROM THE INSIDE

INTERNATIONAL PEACE AND SECURITY

Brian Urquhart

"THE POLICY LINE AS I SEE IT," Hammarskjöld wrote in 1959, "is that the U.N. simply must respond to those demands which may be put to it. . . . The United Nations should respond and have confidence in its strength." An important part of this approach was his feeling that the smaller powers had a particular stake in the Organization. Thus he wrote in 1960:

> The UN has increasingly become the main platform—and the main protector of the interests—of those many nations who feel themselves strong as members of the international family but who are weak in isolation. . . . They look to the Organization as a spokesman and as an agent for principles which give them strength in an international concert in which other voices can mobilize all the weight of armed force, wealth, an historical role and that influence which is the other side of a special responsibility for peace and security.

And again, three months before his death:

> I would rather say that I see the future of this Organization very much as one of an organ which primarily serves the interests of smaller countries which otherwise would not have a platform in world affairs—these smaller countries, however, within the Organization intimately cooperating with the big powers.

This part of his vision of the United Nations, as the platform for the majority of smaller powers, has certainly been amply fulfilled in the intervening years. And the cooperation within the Organization between them and the big powers, if not as yet exactly intimate, is certainly increasing on a wide range of essential subjects.

But the second part of his vision—which is the subject of

159

this article—has been a different story. Hammarskjöld's basic view of international peace and security was that a reliable and just world order could only be built pragmatically by making precedents and by case law. By this process he hoped that the United Nations would be gradually transformed from an insitutional mechanism into a constitutional instrument recognized and respected by all nations.

He considered that the Secretary-General had a special role to play in that transformation. While this role might be applicable to any form of international conflict, it had special relevance as regards the great powers and the cold war. As he said in 1959:

> I consider it a very natural function for the Secretary-General to keep problems as much as possible outside the cold war orbit and on the other hand, of course, to lift problems out of the cold war orbit to all the extent he can. That is for many reasons. One of them is that it is one way in which we can get over the difficulties created for the UN and UN operations by the cold war. It is one way, so to say, if not to thaw the cold war, at least to limit its impact on international life.

In his second term, Hammarskjöld began to speak of the emergence of an "independent position" for the Organization rooted in the existence at the United Nations of "an opinion independent of partisan interests and dominated by the objectives indicated in the UN Charter." He believed that some kind of international order and international conscience were taking shape at the United Nations for which he, as Secretary-General, was best placed to be the spokesman and even the executive—because, by the nature of his office and his election as Secretary-General, he was lifted above the conflicts that divided the Organization. He spoke of "imaginative and constructive constitutional innovations" to encompass this new nature of the United Nations. Sovereign governments were on the whole not enchanted by such heady notions.

Hammarskjöld lost no opportunity to put before the member governments the choice of alternatives for the future of the United Nations. On the one hand, it could be simply "a vast conference machinery . . . a framework for public multilateral negotiations . . . robbed of its possibilities of action in the preservation of peace"—a reversion to the pattern of the League of Nations—or, on the other, the active peace organization that had slowly been emerging during the previous five years. . . .

IV

Twenty years later, it is clear that we are still far from achieving even the first stage of Hammarskjöld's vision of the United Nations as a more active and comprehensive peace organization. Governments, where their own interests are involved, tend to go their own way, getting as much as they can, acting, if necessary, with little respect for the U.N. Charter and sometimes becoming involved in costly and futile conflicts. Expediency tends to be the order of the day—expediency born of fear or opportunism and of conflicting economic, political and military interests and the increasing economic interdependence of countries and continents. Armaments and the arms race continue to spiral out of all control. The rule of law is still a dream on the international stage. The United Nations, often ignored in normal times as the central instrument of an agreed world order, is relegated, in the political sphere at least, to the position of last resort—last resort for the great powers when nuclear confrontation looms, last resort for the weak and the threatened, and the upholder, all too often impotent, of the rights of the dispossessed and of the victims of conflict.

This is not a negligible function, and it is one which deserves far more recognition and respect than it gets, but it is hardly the role that the chastened victors of World War II had in mind for the future world Organization. The sequence of events leading to the foundation of the United Nations is all too well known—the steady erosion, after a promising start, of the League of Nations and in its place a growing and deadly cynicism about international organization and the capacity of nations to do something sensible together; the collapse of dreams of disarmament; the disastrous failure of collective will in facing the aggressions—Japanese, Italian and German—of the 1930s, and the descent into world war; and finally the rise, like a phoenix from the ashes, of the old discredited idea of a world organization for the maintenance of international peace and security. Are we doomed, with our newfound capacity for nearly total destruction, to repeat this disastrous cycle one final time?

The Charter was written with the disasters of previous years in mind. Not surprisingly, it did not foresee accurately the shape and balance of the postwar world. The apotheosis of the major victors of the war (China, France, the United Kingdom, the United States, and the U.S.S.R.) as permanent members of the Security Council with the power of veto, in itself put a limitation on the powers of the new world Organization for political action and even for political development. On the other hand, without such preferential status it is unlikely that the world's two most powerful states would have joined the Organization. It can also be argued that this recognition of the realities of power serves to balance the other extreme of international democracy, the one country-one vote system in the General Assembly.

Did Roosevelt, Stalin, Churchill and, later on, de Gaulle, really believe that they were founding an Organization which would "save succeeding generations from the scourge of war"? And, if so, knowing all too well the nature of sovereign states, how did they think it could work in practice?

The primary theme of the Charter is the peaceful settlement of international disputes and the mobilization of the international community to deal with threats to the peace and acts of aggression. In the postwar situation, clear acts of aggression were hard to identify and even harder to agree on. In fact, the main current of threats to peace flowing from the East-West competition for power and influence ran through the very heart of the Security Council which was supposed to deal with threats to peace.

The Charter describes a system for maintaining international peace and security which assumes that all governments will play the roles assigned to them. Those involved in disputes will avail themselves of the means available in the Charter to settle those disputes peacefully. If they fail to do this the membership of the United Nations, under the guidance of the Security Council, will take a series of steps designed to persuade them to do so. The governments concerned will heed and obey the injunctions of the Council. And if in the end the threat to peace persists, the Council, led by its permanent members, will apply enforcement measures, ranging from economic sanctions to military action, to restore peace and security.

This, in simple terms, was the plan the founders put their signatures to. Admittedly the veto power meant that the council would be unable to mount an enforcement operation against one of its own permanent members—a precaution which is as much in the interests of the smaller powers as of the large ones, because it eliminates the possibility of their being required by the Security Council to take part in a war against a great power. But aside from that, the founders do not seem to have wished to consider how far the Security Council could in reality be expected to act as a body united by a higher responsibility for world peace and security, and how far its performance would inevitably be limited and its unity denied by the conflicting national interests of its members. Thus, from the outset the various conflicts between the interests of its members, and especially those arising from the cold war, have often made it difficult, if not impossible, for the Council to fulfill its true role. In times of crisis, the separate lines of individual national interest have tended therefore to come together, if at all, only in cautiously worded and sometimes ambiguous resolutions of the Council or in a more or less vague delegation of responsibility to the Secretary-General . . .

VI

Is it realistic to suppose that the Security Council will be able, in the foreseeable future, radically to improve the quality of its guardianship of international peace and security? It is customary to answer this question by suggesting that the peace-keeping and mediating capacity of the United Nations be increased and rendered more effective, or that in some unexplained way the Secretary-General should act more decisively. Such suggestions avoid the basic issue, which is one of govenmental intention and will.

It is understandable enough that governments who have an adventure in mind and believe they are strong enough to carry it through do not come first to the Security Council. It is also often difficult for governments who suspect they may be threatened to come to the Council in time, for this may trigger off the very threat they are trying to avoid. The permanent members of the Council, however, with their special position and responsibilities, might be expected to be looking for means to overcome these problems in the interests of preserving the wider peace.

Current experience seems to show the opposite tendency. Indeed, there appears to be an increasing reluctance to mobilize the Council in situations where there is a clear danger of conflict or even when fighting has actually broken out. Recently it took several initiatives by the Secretary-General in the form of letters to the Security Council President to bring the Council even to consult upon the Iran-Iraq war, on which the Council finally supported the Secretary-General's initiative to send to the area a Special Representative, Olof Palme of Sweden, to pursue a peaceful settlement. There was a somewhat similar reluctance over the violent situation in Lebanon in the mid-1970s, which the Secretary-General also brought to the Council's attention. Lebanon came formally onto the Council's agenda only after the Israeli military intervention in south Lebanon in 1978. It was also the Secretary-General, in the absence of an initiative by any of the members, who brought the Cyprus situation to the Council during the disasters of 1974 on the island—a situation incidentally with which the United Nations was intimately concerned because of the presence of a U.N. peace-keeping force there.

What are the springs of this reluctance, especially among the permanent members of the Council, which so often debilitates the capacity of the Security Council to carry out its primary function, the maintenance of international peace and security? The natural human tendency not to get involved in trouble in the hope that it will somehow go away certainly affects many governments, but this is surely not the real problem. The ramifications of the international relationships of most major powers nowadays are so complex as to make them often reluctant in many situations to take a firm stand on one side or the other, or on a matter of principle. "What will it do to our relations with 'X'?" is at the root of much of the expediency which gnaws at the basic principles of the Charter. Domestic politics also play a primary role in involvement or noninvolvement in most international questions.

The permanent members of the Security Council are certainly also inhibited by their relationship with each other. On a wide variety of international conflicts or potential conflicts, it is axiomatic that the East will be on one side and the West on the other. If a forthright resolution is before the Council on such matters, it is therefore likely to be vetoed by one side or the other. Permanent members are naturally cautious about precipitating such a situation, which publicly displays the built-in limitations of the Council. Nor are they eager to find themselves outvoted by a majority opposed to their policies, forcing them to use the veto in a politically damaging manner. On the other hand, the Council is capable on occasion of responding unanimously to a serious situation, as for example over the American hostages in Iran or in the recent call for a cease-fire in Lebanon.

Other groups of members also have problems about resorting to the Security Council. There is a natural desire that regional problems should be handled, if at all possible, by regional organizations. Indeed, the Charter provides for this. This sometimes means that a regional organization holds on to a problem too long before admitting that it may require treatment in the wider context of the United Nations. There seems no good reason why the action of regional organizations should not, when necessary, be reinforced by partnership with the Security Council. The relationship should be a mutually supportive one.

Moreover, governments as a rule prefer to solve their problems by the most direct possible method and if possible without the publicity, not to mention the political involvement, that is inevitable in a recourse to the Security Council. This is a perennial reason why serious problems tend to be brought before the Security Council only at a late stage when they are correspondingly more difficult to deal with.

All this being said, the question inevitably arises whether governments really believe in the machinery they set up after the last world war or indeed in collective action for the maintenance of peace through the United Nations, except when things have come to such a pass that there is no other resort or alternative. It is well to recall that a basic lack of confidence in collective action, more than anything else, effectively killed the League of Nations and led to World War II. Will history repeat itself? This question is important unless one assumes that the United Nations—or any other fledgling system of world order for that matter—is a quixotic and fundamentally superfluous activity to which lip service must be paid while the real business of international relations goes on elsewhere. We have surely had enough lessons in this century alone to show that this is an extremely short-sighted and dangerous belief.

The Security Council has certainly developed and changed since the public confrontations, dramas and walkouts of its earlier days. It is a more cautious, less dramatic body than it was, and it is worth considering the advantages and disadvantages of this tendency in terms of its future development. A large proportion of the Council's working time is now spent in informal consultations in a room recently built for this purpose—and in waiting for those consultations to start. In fact, the Council now almost never holds a public meeting without consulting informally in advance, collectively and in smaller groups, on the scenario and the decisions to be taken. Sometimes the consultations maximize the Council's reluctance to meet to the point where it decides not to meet publicly at all. On such occasions it is in effect reduced to mumbling behind closed doors on issues affecting international peace and security—which does little to increase its prestige or the public respect in which it should be held. Although this trend tends to increase the role of the Secretary-General in international crises—and Secretary-General Waldheim has made persistent efforts to provide leadership and initiative in successive crises—it does not provide him with the strong and consistent backing necessary for his effectiveness in difficult situations.

If the consultation process, in which the Council members discuss matters very frankly and informally, in the end has the effect of consolidating the will of the Council and turning it into the united peace-maintaining body it was originally set up to be, it will prove to have been an important stage in the Council's development. If on the other hand the consultation process is principally a means of escaping public disagreement and adopting an increasingly expedient and evasive approach to world problems, it may in the end reduce the Council to a level of impotence and disrespect from which it will not be able to recover in time the influence necessary to play a decisive role in a desperate crisis.

["International Peace and Security", 1981, pp. 2-15]

B

WORLD GOVERNMENT VS. PLURALISM

THE ABOLITION: A DELIBERATE POLICY

Jonathan Schell

THE CONSENSUS, AMONG SO MANY of those who have thought deeply about the nuclear predicament, that nuclear weapons cannot be abolished unless world government is established seems to find support in traditional political theory: in the distinction between the so-called state of nature, in which men live in anarchy and resolve their disputes among themselves, with war serving as the final arbiter, and the so-called civil state, in which men live under a government and submit their disputes to its final arbitration. In reflecting on the formation of states out of warring tribes or principalities, political thinkers have often observed that the transition from the state of nature to the civil state is usually radical and abrupt, frequently involving some act of conquest or other form of violence, and admits of no partial or halfway solutions, in which, say, a central authority is given the legislative power to "decide" the outcome of disputes but not the executive power to enforce its decisions. We seem to be faced with the same radical, either-or choice in the world as a whole, in which nations, although each constitutes a civil state within its own borders, have, according to the traditional view, always lived in an anarchic state of nature in their relations with each other.

Nations do not dare to give up war and disarm until world government, or some equivalent, is in place because if they did they would be left without any final arbiter for settling disputes. This situation would be inherently unstable, because as soon as a serious dispute arose—concerning, for example, who was to control a certain piece of territory—nations would reach for the instruments of war, and the impotent, halfway civil measures would be ignored or swept aside (as happened, for example, to

171

the League of Nations in the nineteen-thirties). That is why the political thinkers of our time have, with rare unanimity, declared that either total disarmament or full nuclear disarmament is impossible without the simultaneous establishment of world government—and we are left with the unfortunate choice between living with a full balance of nuclear terror, which we would like to get away from, and instituting a full global state, which we would like to avoid. If a lawless government were to assume control of the world and such slaughter were to be carried out in the global darkness of the oppression of all mankind the horror of the situation would be beyond all imagining.

Nevertheless, most people are agreed that the immediate poltical choice before us is between an anarchic state of nature, in which nations possess nuclear weapons, and the civil state, or world government, in which they would not.

[*New Yorker,* January 9, 1984, pp. 43-44]

WORLD PEACE
THROUGH WORLD
LAW

Grenville Clark and Louis B. Sohn

THIS BOOK COMPRISES A SET OF DEFINITE AND IN-
TERRELATED PROPOSALS to carry out complete and universal disarmament and to strengthen the United Nations through
the establishment of such legislative, executive and judicial institutions as are necessary to maintain world order.

Underlying Principles

First: It is futile to expect genuine peace until there is put into
effect an effective system of *enforceable* world law in the limited
field of war prevention. This implies: (a) the complete disarmament, under effective controls, of each and every nation, and (b)
the simultaneous adoption on a world-wide basis of the
measures and institutions which the experience of centuries has
shown to be essential for the maintenance of law and order,
namely, clearly stated law against violence, courts to interpret
and apply that law and police to enforce it. All else, we conceive,
depends upon the acceptance of this approach.

Second: The world law against international violence must
be explicitly stated in constitutional and statutory form. It must,
under appropriate penalties, forbid the use of force by any
nation against any other for any cause whatever, save only in
self-defense; and must be applicable to all individuals as well as
to all nations.

Third: World judicial tribunals to interpret and apply the
world law against international violence must be established and

173

maintained, and also organs of mediation and conciliation,—so as to substitute peaceful means of adjudication and adjustment in place of violence, or the threat of it, as the means for dealing with all international disputes.

Fourth: A permanent world police force must be created and maintained which, while safeguarded with utmost care against misuse, would be fully adequate to forestall or suppress any violation of the world law against international violence.

Fifth: The complete disarmament of all the nations (rather than the mere "reduction" or "limitation" of armaments) is essential for any solid and lasting peace, this disarmament to be accomplished in a simultaneous and proportionate manner by carefully verified stages and subject to a well-organized system of inspection. It is now generally accepted that disarmament must be universal and enforceable. That it must also be complete is no less necessary, since: (a) in the nuclear age no mere reduction in the new means of mass destruction could be effective to remove fear and tension; and (b) if any substantial national armaments were to remain, even if only ten per cent of the armaments of 1960, it would be impracticable to maintain a sufficiently strong world police force to deal with any possible aggression or revolt against the authority of the world organization. We should face the fact that until there is *complete* disarmament of every nation without exception there can be no assurance of genuine peace.

Sixth: Effective world machinery must be created to mitigate the vast disparities in the economic condition of various regions of the world, the continuance of which tends to instability and conflict.

The following supplementary principles have also guided us:

Active participation in the world peace authority must be universal, or virtually so; and although a few nations may be permitted to decline active membership, any such nonmember nations must be equally bound by the obligation to abolish their armed forces and to abide by all the laws and regulations of the world organization with relation to the prevention of war. It follows that ratification of the constitutional document creating the world peace organization (whether in the form of a revised

United Nations Charter or otherwise) must be by a preponderant majority of all the nations and people of the world.

The world law, in the limited field of war prevention to which it would be restricted, should apply to all individual persons in the world as well as to all the nations,—to the end that in case of violations by individuals without the support of their governments, the world law could be invoked directly against them without the necessity of indicting a whole nation or group of nations.

The basic rights and duties of all nations in respect of the maintenance of peace should be clearly defined not in laws enacted by a world legislature but in the constitutional document itself. That document should also carefully set forth not only the structure but also the most important powers of the various world institutions established or authorized by it; and the constitutional document should also define the limits of those powers and provide specific safeguards to guarantee the observance of those limits and the protection of individual rights against abuse of power. By this method of "constitutional legislation" the nations and peoples would know in advance within close limits what obligations they would assume by acceptance of the new world system, and only a restricted field of discretion would be left to the legislative branch of the world authority.

The powers of the world organization should be restricted to matters directly related to the maintenance of peace. All other powers should be reserved to the nations and their peoples. This definition and reservation of powers is advisable not only to avoid opposition based upon fear of possible interference in the domestic affairs of the nations, but also because it is wise for this generation to limit itself to the single task of preventing international violence or the threat of it. If we can accomplish that, we should feel satisfied and could well leave to later generations any enlargement of the powers of the world organization that they might find desirable.

While any plan to prevent war through total disarmament and the substitution of world law for international violence must be fully adequate to the end in view, it must also be *acceptable* to this generation. To propose a plan lacking in the basic essentials for the prevention of war would be futile. On the other hand, a plan which, however ideal in conception, is so far ahead of the times as to raise insuperable opposition would be equally futile. Therefore, we have tried hard to strike a sound balance by setting forth a plan which, while really adequate to prevent war, would, at the same time, be so carefully safeguarded that it *ought* to be acceptable to all nations.

It is not out of the question to carry out universal and complete disarmament and to establish the necessary new world institutions through an entirely new world authority, but it seems more normal and sensible to make the necessary revisions of the present United Nations Charter.

[*World Peace Through World Law,* 1960, p. 2]

POLICY-MAKERS AND CRITICS

Cecil V. Crabb, Jr.

AMONG PROPONENTS OF MACROPOLITICS, for example, there is often a tendency to let an obvious *desire* for new political communities beyond the nation-state level to be offered as proof that such communities actually exist or are emerging. The benefits supposedly accruing from higher forms of political community are sometimes cited as evidence not only that new forms of political community are in fact evolving but that—since the "future of civilization" is held to depend upon their emergence—the impulse toward macropolitics is powerful and "inevitable." Much "integration theory," Patrick Morgan has observed, posits the idea that progress toward the creation of supranational forms of political community is "an inevitable or logical 'next step' in hunman-community development." In evaluating the evidence on the subject, devotees of this theory are continually in danger of falling victim "to their wishes." Integration theory thus comes perilously close at times to being a modern species of social Darwinism: Its basic premise is that, in response to the needs of an increasingly complex environment, human society is evolving novel forms of political community above the nation-state level to meet its needs. Considerable evidence that this is *not* occurring tends to be either disregarded or explained away.

Another vulnerable aspect of integration theory is a recurrent tendency to equate the growing and easily demonstrated *interdependence* of societies and peoples throughout the world with the emergence of a global sense of "shared values" and consensus, the hallmarks of community. Here, a tendency often exists to confuse a *characteristic* of a community relationship with its basic *cause*. Within advanced societies, for example, the relationship between labor and management normally is a highly interdependent one. The failure of a major business corporation, for example, would adversely affect the interests of both, although perhaps in different ways. Yet the fact of such interdependence does not necessarily prove the existence of an emerging sense of "shared values" between labor and management, creating ever tighter bonds of community between them. As conditions in the Republic of South Africa, where a high degree of economic interdependence exists between whites and Bantus (blacks), illustrate, interdependency *per se* does not automatically produce a sense of political community. Many advocates of integration theory tend to be indifferent to the *kind*, or what might be called the *quality*, of the interrelationship existing among peoples. An essentially *unequal* one—a condition in which one group feels discriminated against, or exploited by, another—may as easily generate alienation, suspicion, and conflict as it engenders a feeling of "shared values."

Another tacit premise underlying much integration theory is the assumption that the ideal of higher forms of community *is a universally shared value throughout human society*. Some cultures and religious groups throughout the world, however, do not accept Aristotle's idea that humans achieve their highest potentialities by functioning as members of a community. Hinduism, for example, exalts an individual's "withdrawal" from the world in order for the believer to achieve "identity with Brahman." Similarly, in only an ultimate and very long-range sense can it be said the [sic] Marxism extols the idea of community. According to its ideological tenets, after a "classless society" has been created, a true community will come into existence. Until then, however, and for an indefinite period in the future, Marxism anticipates that class conflict will be ubiquitous in human relationships, both within non-Marxist societies and between Marxist and non-Marxist states. In modern history, movements like fascism and Nazism have exalted war and other forms of violence and have been predicated on the theory that a "superior race" is destined to dominate the world. It would of course be comforting to believe (as the Victorians tended to think about the possibility of global war) that mankind has discarded, outgrown, or otherwise abandoned such ideas. Yet no evidence exists that this is the case. In the more recent period, disciples of

Gaullism in France, and throughout Europe generally, tended to venerate the nation-state and to call for a "Union of Fatherlands" (*Europe des patries*), with France of course playing the leading role. At the other extreme, in many societies outside the West (the Indian subcontinent and a number of Black African states provide conspicuous examples), ethnic, tribal, linguistic, and religious minorities not only show little discernible interest in supranational forms of political integration; frequently, they evince little loyalty even to the *national* political community, whose bonds remain tenuous and fragile. As much as any other challenge inherent in the idea of "nation-building," political leaders in such countries are hard pressed to win the support of these "subnational actors" for the concept of national political integration.

Still another questionable assumption underlying many theories of political integration is the idea that war, violence, and political instability have their origins mainly in conditions of economic scarcity and deprivation among the world's peoples. On that premise, it follows that the elimination of global poverty should appreciably reduce the risk of violence throughout the international system. It will be recalled that Secretary of Defense Robert S. McNamara correlated the incidence of sub-nuclear violence throughout the world with the zone of global poverty. To his mind, the existence of global poverty was perhaps the leading cause of violence throughout the world.

Now, this is the kind of statistical correlation that may mean something—or nothing at all. As a logical proposition, it is conceivable that both global poverty and global violence have their origins in independent (and thus far, unidentified) causations. Even if a correlation of this kind is statistically valid, it provides us with no convincing evidence concerning the *origins* of violent patterns of human behavior. We know from innumerable anthropological and psychological studies, for example, that the human propensity for violence most probably has multiple and complex origins. Americans have become acutely aware in recent years that, as their standard of living has risen, so has the index of various kinds of crime, with some of the most rapid increases occurring among middle- and upper-income groups! On the international level, again it was the wealthiest nation in history, the United States, that participated massively in the two most prolonged and destructive conflicts witnessed since World War II, the Korean War and the Vietnam War. (Significantly, in the latter if not in the former, critics of America's role often asserted that it was precisely *because* the United States was wealthy, and believed that its economically dominant position in Asia was threatened, that it engaged in this protracted military encounter. Or, as a variant interpretation, it was sometimes charged that America sought to *expand* its economic position in Asia, perhaps by gaining access to the newly discovered oil reserves in Southeast Asia.) As a more general phenomenon, one authority argues that in modern history regional and global peace have been threatened more frequently (and certainly more ominously) by the "developed" than by the less advanced societies. World War I and World War II erupted mainly in Europe, with another advanced state, Japan, playing a key role in triggering the latter. Nazi Germany, in some ways the most advanced society on the European Continent, deliberately embarked upon the path of military aggrandizement, aimed at annexing and subordinating other societies.

McNamara's reasoning tends to obscure a pivotal fact about the relationship of poverty to political behavior. In many respects (if admittedly not in all), *poverty is a relative condition.* Poverty may be variously defined, but it is a term often applied to those groups at the bottom of the income scale vis-à-vis other groups. Thus, the term poverty may be applicable to the inhabitants of America's ghettos, as well as to the Untouchables of India, although the standard of living of the former is substantially higher than that of the latter. But this fact does *not* necessarily make poverty-striken groups in America more "content with their lot" than Indian villagers. As Richard Rosecrance observes, human motivations and political expectations normally "relate to *relative* status and economic welfare rather than absolute status and welfare." It is quite possible, and the experience of a number of countries in recent years makes it seem probable, that jealousies, alienation, tensions, and conflicts among groups—the antithesis of political community—will *increase* as a given society makes economic progress.

At any rate, experience has demonstrated rather convincingly that national development is not the "key to peace" which McNamara's statistical correlation would suggest. The available evidence offers little credence to the simplistic formula: global security = global development. Indeed, as some commentators have suggested, if global or regional *peace* is deemed the paramount goal of human society, a strong case could be made for the contention that the quest for global development ought to be abandoned! Poverty-striken groups, Rosecrance notes, "are not in a position to wage large-scale war against their neighbors." Conversely, the process of national development *per se* is apt to prove destabilizing and to furnish a new impetus toward political upheaval and violence.

Globally, income differentials between the wealthier and poorer societies are already wide, and *these disparities are likely to become even more pronounced in the future.* Bruce Russett has predicted that many parts of Asia and Africa are rapidly becoming a "huge slum." Relative to the gains anticipated for societies in advanced countries, the position of millions of people in most Third World nations is declining. A generation from now, the citizen of America or Western European nation will be relatively better off than a resident of Asia or Black Africa. Meanwhile, with the rapid extension of global communications facilities, such income disparities are becoming widely publicized. To the extent that the idea of community presupposes a rough egalitarianism or "sharing of benefits" among its members, the tendency in the international environment is clearly in the contrary direction. The same tendency is evident *within* several regions. The oil-rich states of the Middle East, for example, are accumulating wealth at a pace that other countries in the area cannot match. Within a decade or so, Iran expects to have achieved a standard of living equal to Western Europe's. In Latin America, an economically dynamic Brazil forges rapidly ahead; to the minds of other Latin Americans, Brazil threatens to become a "South American Colossus." In Black Africa, Nigeria possesses a potential for development that few of its neighbors can rival. As time passes, the disparities existing among the states within the major regions may exceed those separating the advanced from the less developed nations as a whole.

Serious questions can also be raised about another aspect of integration theory: the extent to which the level or volume of "transactions"—the exchange of information, the volume of mail, trade and commerce, tourism, and the like—between or among nations serves as an accurate indicator of supranational community bonds. Even Karl Deutsch, the principal exponent of this idea, in time became pessimistic about its value as a reliable gauge of community sentiment. He conceded, for example, that such transactions *within* states were often increasing more rapidly than those between states. But even if this were not so, the relationship between international transactions and the impulse to political integration seems at best tenuous.

The supposition that a rising level of "transactions" among peoples indicates the presence of, or strengthens, community bonds between them is a variant of a very old idea in the American ethos. During World War I President Wilson repeatedly distinguished between the attitudes of the German *people* and their supposedly misguided and aggressive *leaders*. After World War II, many Americans made the same distinction about the Soviet regime: Presumably, the Russian people's aspirations and intentions were the same as those of the American people; the cold war ensued because of the totalitarian and expansive impulses of Russia's Communist hierarchy. Conversely, the Kremlin reasoned in a basically similar fashion about the United States: The American "proletariat" longed for peace and coexistence, whereas the "warmongers" fomented tensions and conflicts with the Communist world. Accordingly, the United States, the Soviet Union, Communist China, and many smaller nations have sponsored various kinds of educational, cultural, and scientific exchange programs, people-to-people movements, and the like on the premise that, as people "get to know each other better," the prospects for global peace and security are enhanced. The key fact often overlooked about such programs, however, is that *governments are motivated to engage in them primarily to enhance the achievement of their own foreign policy goals.* Such cultural diplomacy is an instrument of *national* policy, designed to strengthen national institutions and sovereignty.

Another aspect of integration theory that requires critical examination is the concept of the "spillover effect." As we have already explained, this idea holds that, as nations learn to collaborate successfully in limited spheres (like trade, economic policy, and the production of selected commodities), such cooperation will in time be extended to ever widening areas, leading eventually to the creation of new forms of political community.

"Neofunctionalists" believe that the spillover effect generates irresistible momentum toward political integration. The history of the most successful form of regionalism witnessed in the postwar period, the European Economic Community, is most frequently cited to illustrate the point. Beginning with modest European collaboration on tariff and trade issues in the early postwar period, EEC has evolved into a numerically large and complex organization promoting economic, financial, and other forms of cooperation among its members. With Great Britain's entry into EEC (accompanied by the disappearance of the rival European Free Trade Area, or EFTA), the organization's membership grew from six to ten members, making EEC in some respects the most influential trading nexus in the world. EEC's ultimate goal is *political union* among its members. Neofunctionalists are convinced that even now, as a result of decision-making on important economic questions, there exists a considerable degree of *de facto* political collaboration among the EEC partners. According to neofunctionalist theory, as time passes the tendency toward more explicit and elaborate forms of political integration will become irreversible.

Yet advocates of the spillover concept overlook or disregard considerable contrary evidence. From the inception, certain members of EEC have looked upon the organization as an instrument mainly for achieving important national goals. One major motive for establishing EEC and other forms of supranational cooperations in postwar Europe, for example, was to preserve the security and sovereignty of France and smaller states, which were apprehensive about the implications of West Germany's phenomenal economic revival. Under de Gaulle particularly, France looked upon European integration as a device for *limiting* Germany's sovereignty and regional political influence, while enhancing its own. Besides, France regarded EEC as a counterweight to American influence on the Continent; insofar as Paris supported the goal of European integration at all, it sought to maximize French, and more broadly European, influence in dealing with the United States. By contrast, even after it joined EEC, Britain was conscious of, and dependent upon, its "special ties" with the United States, which, in a period of declining British power, were still viewed as vital.

Impassioned rhetoric favoring European political integration aside, studies of public opinion within the EEC area have revealed no significant popular sentiment in favor of European political union or support for the belief that supranational economic cooperation must be followed by political integration. One of the earliest advocates of the idea of European political community, David Mitrany, came to the conclusion that the numerous and complex mechanisms of financial, economic, and other forms of supranational collaboration existing on the Continent after World War II made the European environment extremely fragmented, posing a serious obstacle to the region's ultimate *political* unification. The success of the European Economic Community to date may merely prove the validity of what has been called the "law of inverse salience." As J. S. Nye defines it, "the less important the task politically . . . the greater the prospects for the growth of the organization's authority vis-à-vis the member states." In the same vein, Stanley Hoffmann distinguishes between "high" (or very important) and "low" (or relatively minor and technical) political decisions. EEC has exhibited a high degree of consensus among its members with respect to the latter, but not with respect to the former.

Many of the observations we have made about the experience of the European Economic Community apply with even greater cogency to other regional organizations and to the concept of regionalism generally. Sometimes viewed (largely on the basis of EEC's accomplishments) as the most "promising" form of supranational political cooperation among states, regionalism encounters a number of existing and future obstacles. Not the least of these is a problem to which we have already alluded: The necessity in a true community for relations among its members to be governed by the principle of approximate egalitarianism. The history of the Organization of American States has demonstrated that whatever consensus unites its members is most apt to be directed against the disproportionate influence of the strongest member, the United States. Insofar as the OAS is designed to provide its members with security, the smaller states seek protection mainly from the "North American Colossus"; conversely, the United States is primarily interested in enhancing Western hemispheric security against the Soviet Union, Red China, or perhaps Castro's Cuba. Experience with regional cooperation in Central and West Africa indicates that supranational economic cooperation *per se* will not solve most of the area's pressing economic problems; for a long time to come, Africa is likely to remain economically dependent upon the advanced nations (particularly Western Europe); and there is little evidence to date of any significant degree of political collaboration among members of African regional organizations. Similarly, thus far experience in Asia (while impressive in terms of the number of regional institutions and mechanisms established) affords little evidence indicating the emergence of a common regional "identity" among the diverse peoples of the area. One commentator remarks that in the Asian environment a stronger sense of "national identification" will have to precede effective regional cooperation. After detailed study, Nye's overall verdict on regionalism is that it is *not* likely to provide a "master key to a peaceful world order." Rosecrance concurs in this general conclusion, holding that regionalism "appears to be the *least* likely area of future cooperation" among nation-states. Another study has found that, despite the movement toward regional integration since World War II, "nationalist fervor is at an all-time peak in certain parts of the world."

As for the United Nations, which by the 1970s was experiencing several different "crises of confidence" in terms of the attitudes of the members toward it, in Richard W. Sterling's words the organization "faithfully reflects the fragmented structure of the international political system." From the beginning, the U.N.'s effectiveness has depended upon the concurrence of the "parochial sovereignties" comprising it. As a former American U.N. official has conceded, the U.N. is "a reflection of a turbulent and divided world, an arena for the interplay of *national power,* a limited instrument for the *voluntary association of nations* in areas where the interests uniting them are stronger than the interest dividing them."

A number of commentators are, like Inis Claude, extremely dubious about the U.N.'s ability to evolve into the "potential master-controller of the international system—a superstate, a government over governments" in the future. In Claude's view, such multilateral political institutions work "no moral alchemy"; no evidence exists that their decisions "will be suffused with wisdom and decency" or that they will lead "to justice and order." The U.N. was created to be, and it remains, an organization representing "a collection of states, a creature of states, an instrument of states, and a property of states"; in relations with its members, the U.N.'s role "is that of servant, not that of master." The point is often overlooked by advocates of macropolitics that many U.N.-sponsored programs are designed *to strengthen the nation-states* belonging to the organization; to the extent that they succeed, such programs quite possibly enhance *national* capabilities and loyalties. Given the U.N.'s inherent limitations and the political realities affecting its role, in the view of several commentators, the superpowers may actually *strengthen* the organization when they appear to by-pass it by engaging in *dètente* or other forms of peaceful negotiations in which the U.N. plays little part. At any rate, for an indefinite period in the future, the stability of the international system is likely to be affected decisively by decisions made and enforced by the superpowers.

What are the prospects that the highest form of political integration—world government—will promote international peace and contribute to the Good Life for the members of human society? The question really poses two others. Initially, what are the chances that a global political authority is emerging and will be established in the foreseeable future? The probability of even that seems absolutely *nil*. The trends in international politics today, Rosecrance has said, "are as much centrifugal as centripetal"; nationalism remains a potent rival to supranationalism; throughout the world, ethnic minorities, tribal units, and dissident groups still actively challenge the authority of *national* political institutions. After a generation's experience the history of the United Nations offers little evidence that it is evolving into, or will soon be superseded by, a truly sovereign global authority. To the contrary, as the "crisis of confidence" in American attitudes toward the U.N. illustrates, the challenge perhaps is to make that body's limited authority effective!

Yet even if it were probable or feasible, it seems unlikely that a global political authority would necessarily inaugurate a Golden Age of peace and stability for human society. World government would evoke strong opposition from two extremist groups in the contemporary world. On the political left wing, many groups are suspicious of *all* authority and political "establishments" generally. At the other pole, right-wing forces remain

devoted to principles like individual rights and "limited" government; they advocate "law and order" as a corrective for many of
society's current ills; and they are congenitally opposed to governmental programs designed to benefit poorer segments of the
population—the stratum that would of course constitute the
majority in any system of world government. Moreover, experience to date with certain United Nations activities affords little
ground for hope that evils like "bureaucratic imperialism" would
be lacking in a system of world government. As one study of
U.N. health programs has concluded: "It would be a mistake to
assume that national and international administrators concerned with world health do not exhibit the same aggressiveness
and vested interest that bureaucrats in other fields exhibit."
Indeed, there would be logical grounds for supposing that a
global bureaucracy might be less attuned to the needs of ordinary people and more interested in its own self-serving objectives than a national bureaucracy.

     As a number of critics of world government and other
forms of macropolitics have pointed out, the premise upon
which most such schemes rest is that supranational forms of
political community will resemble the American, or possibly a
European parliamentary, political system. The emerging macropolitical system, it is assumed, will operate as American or
European national systems ideally *ought to function.* Tacitly, the
idea is almost always present that macropolitical systems will be
democratic, stable, and "responsive" to the wishes and needs of
the world's people. It is further assumed that these new systems
will be "constitutional" regimes, as Americans have commonly
understood that concept: The powers of the government will be
limited, and safeguards will protect individual rights against
arbitrary governmental power. This conception ignores the fact
that the concept of limited government enjoys little support
outside the West. As Lincoln Bloomfield has observed: "It is . . .
by no means clear that world-government enthusiasts have
sufficiently examined the implications of tyranny on a global
scale."

     Still another claimed advantage of world government—its
ability to control war and violence throughout the international
system—also seems largely illusory. As Philip Jessup has observed: "Civil War, revolution, [and] mob violence are more

frequent manifestations of man's unruly and still savage nature than are wars between states." A global political authority might well have a *higher* susceptibility to civil upheavals, insurrections, and other forms of strife—the ultimate causes of which might be more difficult for a global than a national political authority to remove—than does the existing nation-state system.

[*Policy-Makers and Critics*, 1976, pp. 149-159]

THE REFORM OF POWER

Leonard Beaton

AN INTERNATIONAL SECURITY STRUCTURE which claims to be the agent and trustee of world security as a whole cannot for long confine itself to the essentially political, scientific and industrial problems of nuclear power or of chemical and biological weapons. There remain the immense security problems created by the world's armed forces and the great armouries of weapons. However unsatisfactory the official plans for the reform of power may be, they bring all armed forces within their scope. A world security structure such as is contemplated here must move step by step, allowing its authority to grow as it gains the confidence of an effective consensus of states; but a new approach to these problems cannot be seriously considered if it does not show how it would handle the traditional problems of military power if a consensus emerged.

Two main issues arise. The first is to find a long-term solution to the organization of nuclear weapons which can preserve the security they are thought to provide. The second is to construct a system of international security which can be extended widely. Obviously, the achievement of either objective will be the work of decades and the fruit of immense political skill and effort. Earlier chapters have also subjected it to certain limits: it cannot and will not come from the establishment of some central monopoly of power; it will always be subject to the ability of the greatest powers (at least) to take their own security back into their own hands; and it must be developed on the basis of the present system of security. On these assumptions, how can governments anxious to develop a working international system move forward?

The answer is to find technical and military arrangements

in which states can subject part or all of their military forces to common organization while retaining ultimate ownership and control of these forces in their own hands. This would require the invention and refinement of a political and military device by which forces could have a dual character: national recruitment, pay and purposes combined with international planning and organization. The technique proposed here is that, where possible, armed forces should be committed or assigned to the international security structures. To the extent that national governments could see that their security objectives were being achieved by the collective body, they would commit their forces to it; to the extent that they felt they must use their forces for purposes inconsistent with the international arrangements, they would maintain them under purely national control. Although this suggestion may sound theoretical and unrealistic, the technique has been developed and refined in the orthodox military atmosphere of the North Atlantic Treaty Organization and has been practiced there for nearly 20 years.

An international security order can only be the sum of a great number of individual security situations. It may be that at times the states of the world, weary with detailed negotiation, will see some virtue in a general reduction of armed forces or in careful elimination of certain classses of weapons. But in general it is likely that a conscious international order will advance by detailed efforts to meet the anxieties of governments about security. The commitment of the sources of others' insecurity could give men devoted to this task a chance to show that a conscious world order is possible and can make the general desire for security into an enduring system.

In this way, world security could grow a new skin, and over the years the old one might die. As with any political artifice, success would depend on the skill and understanding of those who developed and worked it. There can be few clear outlines or anything like a blueprint. But there are basic requirements, most of which can be filled without asking governments to scrap their forces and weapons. A method of growth from the present must be found.

[*The Reform of Power,* 1972, pp. 201-06]

III

MANAGING
SECURITY

III. MANAGING SECURITY

IN RECENT YEARS THE NOTION OF SECURITY has been substantially redefined by those who focus on economic and social problems, failure to manage which certainly affects the security of people and states everywhere. Nevertheless, for clarity we need to identify and understand security in its primary meaning—the use or threat of force by states or groups against other states or groups.

Perhaps because it is so self-evident, I have not included a selection spelling out the obvious need for defense against armed aggression, direct or indirect. Rather, the emphasis is on original thinking that illuminates the *meanings* of security.

In section IIIA the problem is first discussed in philosophical terms by Leonard Beaton, who believes true security cannot come from alliances but only through disarmament and an improved international regime. Of quite a different order is Astronomer Carl Sagan's widely-reported argument that climatic catastrophe and cascading biological devastation could result from nuclear war above a certain level of weaponry.

Political scientist Richard Ned Lebow draws on historic cases of "the paranoia of the powerful" to underscore each superpower's excessive concern for its credibility and exaggeration of the malevolent capabilities of the adversary. Another increasingly familiar dimension of contemporary violence is international terrorism, which author James B. Motley foresees continuing, and against which he skteches several possible responsive strategies. One-time government official Thomas Wilson appeals for a holistic perspective on security, and World Policy Institute president Robert Johansen ends the section with an idealistic vision which, though clearly unrealistic by today's standards, he thinks would become possible given a war-free security system.

Arms control is dealt with in depth in the companion volume to this one edited by John Craven. For our purposes here only the larger issues are sketched in IIIB. Physicist Freeman Dyson wants the diplomat's skill at finding a workable compromise between international order and balance of power to be applied to dilemmas of nuclear policy. Veteran American diplomat and historian George F. Kennan questions whether nuclear weapons are weapons at all in the traditional sense.

The American debate was sharpened when the Catholic Bishops of America, in a widely-discussed pastoral letter updating the church's 16th century definitions of just and unjust wars, reluctantly accepted the concept of deterrence, but agonized over its reliance on threatening the innocent. They also urged agreements to halt testing, production and deployment of nuclear weapons and called for deep cuts in nuclear inventories. In an acerbic response, strategist Albert Wohlstetter fails to see how one can be committed never to use nuclear weapons and yet have them deter, particularly when not all superpower differences are negotiable.

Section IIIC touches on five crucial "pieces of peace" relevant to international security. World War III could start from a local conflict spinning out of control, with the two superpowers on opposing sides, so conflict prevention is more important than ever, but progress has recently been running in reverse gear. UN Secretary General Javier Perez de Cuellar sees the UN's primary responsibility to act as an effective and impartial instrument of conflict control—obviously an imperfectly realized hope.

The armed but non-fighting peacekeeping technique invented by the UN in 1956 to deal with the Suez war is one of the few success stories of our times. British scholar Alan James critically reviews the growing tendency to reinvent peacekeeping outside of the UN system (for example the Lebanese fiasco of 1982-83), and suggests a reasonable balance between inside-outside and military–civilian.

Regional organizations have not done much better than the UN as peacemakers, but make considerable political sense and may represent the future. The regionalist approach appealed to Westerners when after World War II it became clear that the UN could not handle superpower conflicts. Prof. Seyom Brown of Brandeis University summarizes the concepts involved, and Mahnaz Z. Ispahani discusses the new phenomenon of "micro-regional" groups now acquiring flexibility thanks to the larger stalemate.

Local conflicts could escalate catastrophically unless nuclear proliferation continues to be prevented. The record is not bad, but there are signs of possible breakouts in the near future. An influential report by the United Nations Association of the USA warns against complacency and urges strengthening of the UN specialized agency that monitors peaceful uses of nuclear materials, the International Atomic Energy Agency.

A.

THE SECURITY PROBLEM

THE REFORM OF POWER

Leonard Beaton

ALL GOVERNMENTS SEEK SECURITY for their country
and people. Keeping out the invader and maintaining the civil
peace are the first duties of those who hold political power. If
challenged, most peoples are prepared to sacrifice much of their
wealth and many lives to protect their security as they understand it. Armed forces are permanently maintained in case some
external or internal menace may develop and sustain broader
arrangements which are thought to keep the country safe.
Security was the original business of monarchs and rulers and it
remains fundamental to modern governments.

For states, as for individuals, security can seldom be an
absolute condition. Most people who live in orderly societies
would consider that they had reasonable personal safety; yet
they are subject to the perils of personal accident, earthquakes
or drunken drivers. All that they can ask of their society, and all
that they generally expect, is a reasonable prospect of survival
and a high probability of living the sort of life they choose. The
same can be said of states. They do not seek some absolute level
of security through the arrangements they normally make—
armaments, military forces in being, alliances, international
institutions. They seek what they calculate will be a reasonable
likelihood that they can design and operate their own institutions in their own territory. Governments generally want to
preserve their monopoly or near-monopoly of force over a
defined area against any long-term or short-term threats from
inside or outside. They may become convinced of the importance of certain friendly governments to their security or the
need to prevent others from acquiring weapons or raising forces
to a level they find threatening. Strong powers also tend to

construct security policies on wider assumptions: that, for example, strategic areas should be kept friendly. They may also react to a change in the military posture or sympathies of a rival or neighbour. It can be argued that Germany went to war in 1914 because her strategic theory compelled her to do so in the face of Russian mobilization. More recently, a President of the United States could state* that "nuclear weapons are so destructive, and ballistic missiles are so swift, that any substantially increased possibility of their use or any sudden change in their deployment may well be regarded as a definite threat to the peace".

The anxiety to achieve a safer system of power in the world—an effective international order—has been prominent for many years and particularly since the full horror of nuclear arms was demonstrated beyond doubt. The emergence of weapons of such destructive power has convinced many people that a security system built on sovereign governments is too prone to break down to be sustained for long. Others console themselves with the hope that the use of nuclear and thermonuclear weapons is and will be so intolerable that it becomes all but impossible: and this, they feel, will also rule out any action which might lead by sure steps to the employment of these weapons. In all the significant powers, these essentially radical and conservative schools of opinion have had a long debate about the best system of security. Most governments make a place for both in their policy: they build their security on national or alliance foundations; and they proclaim that this is temporary and inadequate and that the security of the future must be based on disarmament and a new international order.

These two positions are usually seen as opposites and those favouring one commonly mistrust the other—the hard line and the soft line, the tough nationalists and the complaisant internationalists, the pessimists and the optimists. But it can be argued that they are opposed in their means and not their ends. For the end of each is security. The central objection of the internationalists to the world system as it is now operating is that it cannot provide security. Though it is less often stated in so many words, this is also the main objection of the nationalists to disarmament plans. Each side has its case. Those who look to world institutions to operate a system of international security seldom speculate on the security problems this would create if it was achieved; and those who put their faith in the present order tend to ignore the problems which technology, political change, nuclear proliferation and miscalculation are increasingly loading on to it.

NOTES

*This statement was made by President Kennedy in October, 1962, in explanation of his decision to impose a quarantine on the movement of Soviet ships to Cuba.

[*The Reform of Power,* 1972, pp. 9-11]

NUCLEAR WAR AND CLIMATIC CATASTROPHE

Carl Sagan

THESE FINDINGS WERE PRESENTED IN DETAIL AT A SPECIAL CONFERENCE in Cambridge, Mass., involving almost 100 scientists on April 22-26, 1983, and were publicly announced at a conference in Washington, D.C., on October 31 and November 1, 1983 . . .

They point to one apparently inescapable conclusion: the necessity of moving as rapidly as possible to reduce the global nuclear arsenals below levels that could conceivably cause the kind of climatic catastrophe and cascading biological devastation predicted by the new studies. Such a reduction would have to be to a small percentage of the present global strategic arsenals . . .

There is a real danger of the extinction of humanity. A threshold exists at which the climatic catastrophe could be triggered, very roughly around 500-2,000 strategic warheads. A major first strike may be an act of national suicide, even if no retaliation occurs. Given the magnitude of the potential loss, no policy declarations and no mechanical safeguards can adequately guarantee the safety of the human species. No national rivalry or ideological confrontation justifies putting the species at risk. Accordingly, there is a critical need for safe and verifiable reductions of the world strategic inventories to below threshold. At such levels, still adequate for deterrence, at least the worst could not happen should a nuclear war break out.

National security policies that seem prudent or even successful during a term of office or a tour of duty may work to endanger national—and global—security over longer periods of time. In many respects it is just such short-term thinking that is responsible for the present world crisis. The looming prospect of the climatic catastrophe makes short-term thinking even more dangerous. The past has been the enemy of the present, and the present the enemy of the future.

The problem cries out for an ecumenical perspective that rises above cant, doctrine and mutual recrimination, however apparently justified, and that at least partly transcends parochial fealties in time and space. What is urgently required is a coherent, mutually agreed upon, long-term policy for dramatic reductions in nuclear armaments, and a deep commitment, embracing decades, to carry it out.

["Nuclear War and Climatic Catastrophe", 1983-84, pp. 259, 292]

THE PARANOIA OF
THE POWERFUL

Richard Ned Lebow

BY THE LATE 1980s the world may witness the bizarre and frightening phenomenon of two awesomely powerful but painfully vulnerable superpowers, each acutely sensitive about its own sources of weakness and deeply fearful of the other's efforts to exploit them. If this portrayal of the superpowers seems farfetched, the reader is reminded of the historical precedent of Wilhelminian Germany, awesomely powerful for its day but so insecure in its power that it acted in ways that made it the principal menace to the peace of Europe.

The paranoia of the powerful can and has constituted a profound source of international instability. As Thucydides demonstrated, policymakers in such circumstances tend to exhibit an exaggerated concern for their credibility, convinced that any sign of weakness will only encourage further challenge from their adversaries. In the case of Germany, this concern found expression in a series of aggressive foreign policy ventures that brought about the very situation of encirclement German leaders feared and ultimately led to war.

If anything is more disturbing than a great power acting in this manner, it is the prospect of *two* superpower adversaries doing so. Both already display tendencies in this direction. The United States has a remarkable, some call it pathological, concern for its credibility. Democratic and Republican policymakers alike also exaggerate the extent to which Soviet or Soviet-Cuban machinations lie behind every threatening Third World upheaval. The Shaba invasion, Nicaragua and, most recently, El Salvador, are all cases in point. A series of foreign policy setbacks, among them Indochina, Angola and Iran, have promted American leaders to cast about for cheap and dramatic ways of displaying resolve. They have succumbed to what could be called "the Mayaguez mentality," named after the first effort to do this in the immediate aftermath of the collapse of American influence in Indochina. The most recent example of this phenomenon was the invasion of Grenada which came hard on the heels of the disaster in Lebanon.

Soviet policymakers also appear to exaggerate the malevolent influence their adversary is capable of exercising. Soviet spokesmen have repeatedly charged the United States with responsibility for the turmoil it confronts in both Afghanistan and Poland. Some of these charges are propaganda, but there is no reason to doubt that to some extent it actually reflects the real views of Soviet officials, as sincerely held if equally farfetched as some of the anti-Soviet charges made by their American counterparts. This may be particularly pronounced with respect to the Polish situation which must pose a serious cognitive dilemma for Soviet leaders. To recognize it for what it was, a workers' revolution against a bureaucratic dictatorship imposed and maintained by Moscow, would entail calling into question the most fundamental myths of Soviet-style Marxism. The men of the Kremlin have, therefore, every psychological and political incentive to explain away Polish developments by any means they can. The long arm of American imperialism can play a useful role in this regard just as the Soviet-Communist conspiracy was invoked by Americans a generation earlier to explain their "loss" of China. Unfortuantely, such illusions, while comforting, also tend to have damaging long-term foreign policy consequences.

["The Paranoia of the Powerful", 1983, pp. 14-15]

INTERNATIONAL TERRORISM

James B. Motley

TERRORISM IS AN EXTREMELY COMPLICATED PHE-
NOMENON and has appeared in many guises. Terrorism is
now a "politically loaded term," i.e., one nation's terrorism is
another nation's national liberation movement. In recent years,
terrorism has undergone major reorganization and redefinition
and emerged as a sophisticated strategy for use as a political
weapon. Throughout the years, there have been successes, as
well as failures, for terrorist actions. However, political changes
which have had "lasting effect" have been made only in rare
circumstances when political mass movements used terrorist
tactics in the framework of a wider strategy. Terrorists see
themselves as legitimate actors; thus, from their perspective,
they are entitled to use diplomacy or force. The fundamental
difference between the terrorist and the criminal rests with their
respective objectives. The terrorists' ultimate justification is the
furtherance of political cause; the criminals' motivation is selfish
material gain. Finally, contemporary terrorists are a different
breed from their historical 19th century predecessors. The
former are young, well-educated, middle class, and belong to a
highly structured organization. However, as with their forerun-
ners, modern-day terrorists are motivated by some political
philosophy and devoted to a particular cause.

Contemporary terrorism embraces a wide variety of political phenomena. It involves a group of individuals who are
products of affluent industrialized society. They seek to destroy
that society in the name of some revolutionary concept. Examples of such groups would include the Italian Red Brigade,
German Baader-Meinhof gang, Japanese Red Army, and the
U.S. Weather Underground. A second group of terrorists would

be those espousing more traditional political causes—unification of Ireland, a homeland for the Palestinians, majority rule for Rhodesia, and independence for Puerto Rico. Acts of "international terrorism" are committed to terrorize nations and governments into compliance or complacency.

International terrorism is distinguished by three characteristics. First, it embodies a criminal act. International terrorism may take the form of an assortment of acts which are generaly regarded by nations as criminal, e.g., assassination, bombing, kidnapping, hijacking. Second, international terrorism is politically motivated. An extremist political group, convinced of the rightness of its "cause," resorts to violent means to advance that cause. Normally, this violence is directed against innocent persons who have no personal connections with the grievance motivating the terrorist act. Finally, international terrorism transcends national boundaries through: (a) the choice of a foreign victim or target, (b) the commission of the terrorist act in a foreign country, or (c) an effort to influence the policies of a foreign government. . . .

International terrorism, one may posit, may well be the kind of low-level conflict confronting the United States in the years ahead. "A diffusion of power is taking place in the world today. Ethnicity vies with nationality as a basis for legitimate political authority." If the trend of United Nations membership continues to grow at the current rate of three new nations a year, by 1990 the inhabited portion of the planet will be subdivided into more than 200 independent political communities; 300 by the year 2000. The majority of these will be "ministates"— economically dependent and vulnerable to external pressures— but capable of using force against other nations. Such states, unable or unwilling to mount challenges on the battlefield, may adopt the tactics of the terrorist—or form alliances within such terrorist groups—as a mode of surrogate warfare against their opponents.

Surrogate warfare is a weapon that would favor the non-democratic powers, and if skillfully used could give them a marked advantage. Totalitarian societies, China and the Soviet Union, are much less vulnerable to disruption by terrorists than are democratic societies. These societies are much more capable of coercing and controlling their populations.

Terrorism has entered the mainstream of world politics and as such the fact that it could become a new form of warfare must be accepted. With the availability of relatively small and inexpensive means of destruction, a handful of men could have an enormous impact upon states and societies worldwide. It is not unrealistic to envision some countries preferring to arm and use terrorists to pursue their foreign policy objectives, rather than accept the stigma of direct and visible involvement in a conflict with another state. As one author has stated, such countries "might view terrorist activities as a continuation of warfare by other and more effective means, in which the constraints applying to conventional warfare under accepted standards of international behavior and law could be conveniently disregarded." Terrorism is a relatively inexpensive and efficient way of doing a great deal of harm, and doing it without the political embarrassment that can be attached to many overt state actions. Specifically, terrorism could be intentionally used to: (a) instigate an international incident, (b) provoke an enemy, (c) carry out acts of sabotage, or (d) incite a repressvie reaction against a specific group in a country. In many ways, terrorism could become an alternative to conventional wars—not necessarily an undesirable step. In the past, the "mercenary soldier" has appeared wherever there were battles to be fought and armies willing to hire him. Tomorrow, the "terrorist-on-contract" may be a very likely possibility which will confront governments. Contract terrorism is not an attractive concept but when compared with the havoc of full-scale warfare, it may well be the lesser of two evils.

Efforts by the United States to enlist the aid of the United Nations to combat international terrorism has not made any serious headway. "To a large majority of states in the United Nations, terrorism is perceived as a political rather than a humanitarian issue." This is a very critical distinction, i.e., the disagreements that arise are over basic values rather than technical questions. In other words, inasmuch as terrorism is linked to a myriad of issues—imperialism, racism, and economic exploitation—its political implications are that there is no agreement that the phenomenon in question is a problem. If international terrorism could be viewed as a serious problem—a humanitarian issue—the only disagreements among states would be the technical questions of how to best deal with the problem. However, within the contemporary international system there does not exist—nor is it likely to exist anytime in the near future—a consensus among the community of nations that terrorism is a serious problem requiring effective countermeasures.

There will always be grievances that are used to indict the state or the world system and to justify strategies of terrorism. "Moreover, even if such grievances were soluable in principle, they would certainly not yield to treatment in the short run." There are, however, three strategies that can be followed in the short run to inhibit the use of violence by terrorists. First, states must demonstrate that they will not submit to intimidation. This is easier said than done and would require sacrifices, individual pain, and suffering. Such actions would show terrorists that their inclination to violence is ineffective. Second, steps can be taken to render terrorists more responsive to threats of deterrence. There is, even to the terrorist, a threshold beyond which certain costs become intolerable. Counterterrorist measures can succeed once the threshold of unacceptable damage is understood and the terrorist population has been identified and isolated. Finally, steps can be taken to impede the growing cooperation among terrorist groups. Such steps would include a broad range of options: (a) infiltration of terrorist organization, (b) improved international border checks, (c) use of the media to publicize patterns of terrorist cooperation, and (d) separate negotiations with selected terrorist groups to destroy their bonds and atomize their operations. . . .

There are those who advocate that if acts of international terrorism are "to be faced squarely," such acts must be viewed as international peacekeeping problems—not domestic law enforcement challenges. A well-conceived, highly trained, and versatile "international paramilitary force" must be an on-the-shelf ability. Individual nations should not be expected to bear the miltiary and political burdens of terrorist activities alone.

["International Terrorism: A New Mode of Warfare", 1981, pp. 32-39]

WORLD SECURITY AND THE GLOBAL AGENDA

Thomas W. Wilson Jr.

THE DANGER OF POLITICAL PARALYSIS

THE SECURITY IMPLICATIONS OF STATE-OF-THE-PLANET ISSUES are not difficult to grasp. Already there is a dawning awareness of a security component in man's rising capacity to bring about disasters analogous to major natural calamities—or, for that matter, conventional wars—without resorting to weapons at all. We can begin now to understand that the burning of fossil fuels might trigger a change in the global climate with an impact on the United States comparable to a major military defeat. We can comprehend that man-made damage to the ozone layer could produce long lists of casualties. We can start to glimpse the potential consequences of headlong destruction of tropical forests, or the steady deterioration of environmentally crucial coastal zones. And we can hear rising voices from the scientific community warning of potential threats to human survival implicit in the rapid disappearance of animal species and the accelerating loss of genetic diversity in the world of plants that provide energy for life on Earth. Military defense is clearly not the only security game in town.

Indeed, one is tempted to wonder what national security can possibly mean for inhabitants of a living planet whose basic biological systems—croplands, pastures, forests, fisheries—are deteriorating steadily under man-made pressures. These clear and present dangers to the security of Planet Earth cannot be met by doubling or redoubling the defense budget or by deploying military forces abroad. Manifestly, our notions of "vital national interest" need a drastic overhaul; and, in that process,

210

protection of the Earth's basic systems must become an integral part of a modern concept of security for this and other nations.

But there is another, more subtle and insidious threat to enduring security in the world today—and it rivets the new global agenda directly to the issue of world peace and security. The name of this menace is political paralysis. It is a much more credible threat to the future viability of this world than is instant disaster from either military or nonmilitary sources. And it is largely the product of a failure to manage the range of problems bearing on the human condition that are now part of the global agenda and at the heart of North-South relations.

As things stand now, both sides have painted themselves into corners. The developing countries agree that they want to participate in economic decisions that affect their interests, but they cannot agree on just how the system should be redesigned or just where to take hold of the problem. Their demands, therefore, are cast in general terms in order to maintain the "solidarity" they perceive to be their only source of bargaining strength.

The market-economy industrialized nations complain that the new order demanded by developing countries is a slogan without recognizable substance: and that, whatever it means, economic reform is not an event to be declared by majority resolution but is a process of adaptation to be negotiated on a technical basis over a period of time. In this defensive posture, most of the developed countries have managed to appear as stand-pat defenders of an international economic system that, it is plain to see, no longer works in the interest of either rich or poor. For their own reasons, the socialist bloc nations remain on the side lines.

So, in effect, nothing happens. This is the anatomy of political paralysis. It poisons an international environment already polluted by ancient feuds, strategic conflicts, and recurrent violence. It accelerates the drift into a general crisis in the world's capacity to handle contemporary problems. And it reinforces disintegrative tendencies that undermine world peace. This is the context in which political paralysis can be seen most clearly as a dangerous threat to national security—and every bit as "real" as military hardware in the hands of unfriendly nation-states.

"Security" Is a Widening Concept

No one of sound mind would deny that military capability is an indispensable part of any plausible concept of national security in a disorderly world that is armed to the teeth. Nor does anyone argue that security rests exclusively upon military force.

But the ascendancy of a new political agenda of global problems poses what looks at first glance to be a paradoxical imperative: the need to reexamine concepts of national security in the light of transnational problems. So far, this has been resisted effectively in a near-obsession with the strictly military aspects of the security problem. Governments appear virtually oblivious to the security implications of a failure to cope with the new global agenda. "Defense" issues are still kept in one compartment of policy analysis and though—along with "strategy" and "vital interests"—while "development," "topsoil," and "hunger" remain in their segregated realms of perception, expertise, and action. This, after all, is how we have been taught to organize and to think about our affairs.

Now this way of thinking has itself become a threat to security. For an extended failure to take positive action on global problems can only contribute to a breakdown of that minimal state of order essential to the peaceful conduct of human affairs—and, hence, to the security of nations and peoples. Indeed, an obsession with the military dimension imperils security on three counts: First, it is limited to perceptions, policies, and modes of behavior that have led, during this century, to two world wars, a nuclear balance of terror, the survival of traditional warfare, unheard-of levels of armament, and a conceptual trap from which there seems to be no escape and no outcome save war or the tyranny of massive armament for the indefinite future. Second, it withholds resources—material and human—from urgent tasks in defense of planetary security, without which the very meaning of national security is called into serious question. Third, near-exclusive concern with the military aspect of security contributes to political paralysis and, hence, to a dangerous neglect of those disintegrative forces that pull the world toward the unmarked boundary between a state of peace and a state of war.

CONCLUSIONS

In a nutshell, then:

- The traditional correlation between military strength and national security has been attenuated over recent decades by many factors, including a pervasive diffusion of military capabilities, the heightened vulnerabilities of an increasingly interdependent world, and the emergence of new sources of power and influence in international affairs.
- Demographic, economic, political, and environmental world trends have combined in recent years to create a qualitatively distinct class of unavoidable world-level problems that were virtually unknown to traditional diplomacy; that are beyond the reach of national governments; that cannot be fitted into accepted theories of competitive interstate behavior; that are coming increasingly to dominate world affairs; that cannot be wished away; and that are indifferent to military force.
- The emergence of these issues raises unfamiliar dangers: on the one hand, physical threats to planetary systems that support all life; and, on the other hand, dangers of an irreversible slide into anarchy, tyranny, violence, and even war, through a political paralysis induced largely by preoccupation with traditional military concepts of national security.
- A draft agenda of some of these global problems was identified during the 1970s, but national governments have not yet recognized the far-reaching implications of world-level problems for peace, security, and the conduct of international relations.

In the final decades of the twentieth century, national security is inconceivable without global security which clearly requires an active defense of planetary life support systems, a positive strategy for breaking out of a political paralysis that abandons the field to disintegrative forces in world affairs, a much strengthened capability for managing an ascendant agenda of transnational problems, and the management of sustainable growth worldwide.

["World Security and the Global Agenda", 1981, pp. 303-306]

TOWARD A
DEPENDABLE PEACE

Robert C. Johansen

IF WIDESPREAD EDUCATION AND ATTITUDINAL CHANGE are stimulated by a global social movement, the limits of the possible could widen sufficiently to achieve a new system with the following characteristics:

1. All nations are protected against the threat or use of violence by any other nation.
2. Such protection can be guaranteed in part because the production and the possession of all military weapons are prohibited. (Law-enforcement equipment necessary for the maintenance of domestic tranquility is, of course, not prohibited.) Extremely hazardous non-weapons materials, such as fissionable substances, are also strictly regulated according to universally applied rules.
3. A world security organization functions with the power to enforce the rules against the possession of weapons or the misuse of fissionable materials. It presides over enforcement activities of a transnational police force and administers the arms-reducing process in its final stages. Officials acting on its behalf have the authority to prevent weapons violations anywhere in the world. The organization, operating within a system of checks and balances to insure accountability, is responsible to a global assembly.
4. A global monitoring agency inspects for violations of weapons prohibitions. Information regarding possible violations can be given directly to the agency by any citizen of any country.
5. Countries are required to settle disputes through non-violent political, social, or judicial processes.

6. A standing, individually recruited transnational police or peace force enforces the globally established rules for war prevention.

7. The diversion of resources from the manufacture of military equipment into the production of food and the abolition of poverty enables most families on earth to have adequate nourishment and shelter.

—People could feel less alienated from other nationalities. There would be no need to be ready and willing to destroy generic brothers and sisters in Moscow on fifteen minutes notice. Nor could people need to fear that their wheat or computer components sold abroad will help some "foreigners" gain a military advantage over them. Travel could be less encumbered by political and military chauvinism.

—There would be pervasive internal consequences for some militarized societies. Military dictators and racist regimes would be deprived of one of their major rationales—security needs—as well as of the military hardware they have used to help maintain their power. Starting the process to abolish the warfare system would give new life to the movement for achieving human rights around the world.

—Because military dominance in world affairs could not continue without large national arsenals, forms of non-military influence would take on new importance. Although the industrial giants would continue to possess great power, the presently weak states would no longer suffer the disadvantage of being military inferior.

—The advance of human rights and global self-determination would be aided by the demise of covert political interventions by groups like the CIA and KGB. Such activities could no longer be justifies on national security grounds, nor would overseas collaborators be so readily found in a climate where military regimes would no longer prosper.

—A decline in the role of military power would also contribute to economic justice. To be sure, the economically powerful societies would not be much more eager to share wealth equitably, but with military power and covert intervention diminished, the rich would be less able to force their will on the poor. Rich elites could no longer rationalize opposition to social reformers on grounds that the latter were a threat to national security. The success of a new ideology in any country could not become a military threat to its neighbors.

Favorable though most of these prospects sound, such a world would be no utopia. There doubtless would be controversies over establishing trade and immigration policies, transferring technology, pricing food and energy resources, and disposing of hazardous wastes. There would be fears that one society might develop powerful non-military means for exerting dominance over other groups. Some disputes will arise that are presently unforeseen. *Yet, all of these conflicts will exist even if we continue the arms buildup.* Resolving them will be far easier if nations are securely unarmed than if they are armed. The proposed system will establish a better climate for cooperation and make available more resources than a global system heavily burdened by armaments.

A global peace system clearly seems desirable. What strategy could make it possible?

[*Toward A Dependable Peace,* 1978, pp. 25-28]

B.

ARMS CONTROL

WEAPONS AND HOPE

Freeman Dyson

THE DIPLOMATIC HISTORY of the last two centuries has been a story with two alternating themes—international order and balance of power. The purpose of international order is to keep the world peaceful; the purpose of the balance of power is to keep it stable. The dilemma of the diplomats arose because a peaceful world is usually not stable and a stable world is usually not peaceful. When diplomats created institutions of international order and neglected the balance of power, international order became impotent and there was no stability. When they pursued the balance of power and neglected international order, national power became irresponsible and there was no peace. And the world blundered repeatedly through the same tragic cycle—from a failed international order to the emergence of a new balance of power, from the balance of power to competitive alliances and war, from the disasters of war to a new attempt at international order.

Nuclear weapons have arrested the cycle. This is the great blessing that nuclear weapons have brought the world. Because there are nuclear weapons, the cycle is stuck. There is a balance of power with competitive alliances but no world war. Instead of war, there is the threat of nuclear annihilation. The threat of annihilation keeps the cycle from turning. But the old dilemma of the diplomats persists. Mankind recognizes that it cannot live forever under the threat of nuclear annihilation. If it is to survive, the threat must be removed sooner or later. "Ban the bomb" says that mankind must establish an international order to remove the threat before the threat destroys mankind. "Don't rock the boat" says that mankind just preserve the threat in order to maintain the balance of power that keeps the world stable. It is the same choice the diplomats always faced—either an unstable international order or a stable balance based upon

219

the threat of violence. Only the magnitude of the violence has changed.

The great diplomats, from Metternich to Harriman and Kennan, have known that wisdom lies in compromise—that the pursuit of international order without power is futile, and that the pursuit of power without international order is barbarous. To find the workable compromise between international order and balance of power is the diplomat's high art. And the same art is needed to find the middle way through the dilemmas of nuclear policy. There is no safe path. But the path of compromise is likely to be safer than either the naive recklessness of "Ban the bomb" or the blind conservatism of "Don't rock the boat."

["Weapons and Hope", 1984, p. 99]

A PROPOSAL FOR INTERNATIONAL DISARMAMENT

George F. Kennan

ADEQUATE WORDS ARE LACKING to express the full seriousness of our present situation. It is not just that we are for the moment on a collision course politically with the Soviet Union and that the process of rational communication between the two governments seems to have broken down completely; it is also—and even more importantly—the fact that the ultimate sanction behind the conflicting policies of these two governments is a type and volume of weaponry which could not possibly be used without utter disaster for us all.

For over 30 years wise and far-seeing people have been warning us about the futility of any war fought with nuclear weapons and about the dangers involved in their cultivation. Some of the first of these voices to be raised were those of great scientists, including outstandingly that of Albert Einstein himself. But there has been no lack of others. Every president of this country, from Dwight Eisenhower to Jimmy Carter, has tried to remind us that there could be no such thing as victory in a war fought with such weapons. So have a great many other eminent persons.

When one looks back today over the history of these warnings, one has the impression that something has now been lost of the sense of urgency, the hopes, and the excitement that initially inspired them, so many years ago. One senses, even on the part of those who today most acutely perceive the problem and are inwardly most exercised about it, a certain discouragement, resignation, perhaps even despair, when it comes to the question of raising the subject again. The danger is so obvious. So much has already been said. What is to be gained by reiteration? What good would it now do?

Look at the record. Over all these years the competition in the development of nuclear weaponry has proceeded steadily, relentlessly, without the faintest regard for all these warning voices. We have gone on piling weapon upon weapon, missile upon missile, new levels of destructiveness upon old ones. We have done this helplessly, almost involuntarily: like the victims of some sort of hypnotism, like men in a dream, like lemmings heading for the sea, like the children of Hamlin marching blindly along behind their Pied Piper. And the result is that today we have achieved, we and the Russians together, in the creation of these devices and their means of delivery, levels of redundancy of such grotesque dimensions as to defy rational understanding.

I say redundancy. I know of no better way to describe it. But actually, the word is too mild. It implies that there could be levels of these weapons that would not be redundant. Personally, I doubt that there could. I question whether these devices are really weapons at all. A true weapon is at best something with which you endeavor to affect the behavior of another society by influencing the minds, the calculations, the intentions, of the men that control it: it is not something with which you destroy indiscriminately the lives, the substance, the hopes, the culture, the civilization, of another people.

What a confession of intellectual poverty it would be—what a bankruptcy of intelligent statesmanship—if we had to admit that such blind, senseless acts of destruction were the best use we could make of what we have come to view as the leading elements of our military strength!

To my mind, the nuclear bomb is the most useless weapon ever invented. It can be employed to no rational purpose. It is not even an effective defense against itself. It is only something with which, in a moment of petulance or panic, you commit such fearful acts of destruction as no sane person would ever wish to have upon his conscience.

There are those who will agree, with a sigh, to much of what I have just said, but will point to the need for something called deterrence. This is, of course, a concept which attributes to others—to others who, like ourselves, were born of women, walk on two legs, and love their children, to human beings, in short— the most fiendish and inhuman of tendencies.

But all right: accepting for the sake of argument the profound iniquity of these adversaries, no one could deny, I think, that the present Soviet and American arsenals, presenting over a million times the destructive power of the Hiroshima bomb, are simply fantastically redundant to the purpose in question. If the same relative proportions were to be preserved, something well less than 20 per cent of those stocks would surely suffice for the most sanguine concepts of deterrence, whether as between the two nuclear super-powers or with relation to any of those other governments that have been so ill-advised as to enter upon the nuclear path. Whatever their suspicions of each other, there can be no excuse on the part of these two governments for holding, poised against each other and poised in a sense against the whole northern hemisphere, quantities of these weapons so vastly in excess of any rational and demonstrable requirements.

How have we got ourselves into this dangerous mess?

Let us not confuse the question by blaming it on our Soviet adversaries. They have, of course, their share of the blame, and not least in their cavalier dismissal of the Baruch Plan so many years ago. They too have made their mistakes; and I should be the last to deny it.

But we must remember that it has been we Americans who, at almost every step of the road, have taken the lead in the development of this sort of weaponry. It was we who first produced and tested such a device: we who were the first to raise its destructiveness to a new level with the hydrogen bomb: we who introduced the multiple warhead; we who have declined every proposal for the renunciation of the principle of "first use"; and we alone, so help us God, who have used the weapon in anger against others, and against tens of thousands of helpless non-combatants at that.

I know that reasons were offered for some of these things. I know that others might have taken this sort of a lead, had we not done so. But let us not, in the face of this record, so lose ourselves in self-righteousness and hypocrisy as to forget our own measure of complicity in creating the situation we face today.

What is it then, if not our own will, and if not the supposed wickedness of our opponents, that has brought us to this pass?

The answer, I think, is clear. It is primarily the inner momentum, the independent momentum, of the weapons race itself—the compulsions that arise and take charge of great powers when they enter upon a competition with each other in the building up of major armaments of any sort.

This is nothing new. I am a diplomatic historian. I see this same phenomenon playing its fateful part in the relations among the great European powers as much as a century ago. I see this competitive buildup of armaments conceived initially as a means to an end but soon becoming the end itself. I see it taking possession of men's imagination and behavior, becoming a force in its own right detaching itself from the political differences that initially inspired it, and then leading both parties, invariably and inexorably, to the war they no longer know how to avoid.

This is a species of fixation, brewed out of many components. There are fears, resentments, national pride, personal pride. There are misreadings of the adversary's intentions—sometimes even the refusal to consider them at all. There is the tendency of national communities to idealize themselves and to dehumanize the opponent. There is the blinkered, narrow vision of the professional military planner, and his tendency to make war inevitable by assuming its inevitability.

Tossed together, these components form a powerful brew. They guide the fears and the ambitions of men. They seize the policies of governments and whip them around like trees before the tempest.

Is it possible to break out of this charmed and vicious circle? It is sobering to recognize that no one, at least to my knowledge, has yet done so. But no one, for that matter, has ever been faced with such great catastrophe, such inalterable catastrophe, at the end of the line. Others in earlier decades, could befuddle themselves with dreams of something called "victory." We, perhaps fortunately, are denied this seductive prospect. We have to break out of the circle. We have no other choice.

How are we to do it?

I must confess that I see no possibility of doing this by means of discussions along the lines of the negotiations that have been in progress, off and on, over this past decade, under the acronym of SALT. I regret, to be sure, that the most recent SALT agreement has not been ratified. I regret it, because if the benefits to be expected from that agreement were slight, its disadvantages were even slighter, and it had a symbolic value which should not have been so lightly sacrificed.

But I have, I repeat, no illusion that negotiations on the SALT pattern—negotiations, that is, in which each side is obsessed with the chimera of relative advantage and strives only to retain a maximum of the weaponry for itself while putting its opponent to the maximum disadvantage—I have no illusion that such negotiations could ever be adequate to get us out of this hole. They are not a way of escape from the weapons race: they are an integral part of it.

Whoever does not understand that when it comes to nuclear weapons the whole concept of relative advantage is illusory—whoever does not understand that when you are talking about absurd and preposterous quantities of overkill the relative sizes of arsenals have no serious meaning—whoever does not understand that the danger lies not in the possibility that someone else might have more missiles and warheads that we do but in the very existence of these unconscionable quantities of highly poisonous explosives, and their existence, above all, in hands as weak and shaky and undependable as those of ourselves or our adversaries or any other mere human beings: whoever does not understand these things is never going to guide us out of this increasingly dark and menacing forest of bewilderments into which we have all wandered.

I can see no way out of this dilemma other than by a bold and sweeping departure—a departure that would cut surgically through the exaggerated anxieties, the self-engendered nightmares, and the sophisticated mathematics of destruction, in which we have all been entangled over these recent years, and would permit us to move, with courage and decision, to the heart of the problem.

President Reagan recently said, and I think very wisely, that he would "negotiate as long as necessary to reduce the numbers of nuclear weapons to a point where neither side threatens the survival of the other.". . .

Now I have, of course, no idea of the scientific aspects of

such an operation, but I can imagine that serious problems might be presented by the task of removing, and disposing safely of, the radioactive contents of the many thousands of warheads that would have to be dismantled. Should this be the case, I would like to see the President couple his appeal for a 50 per cent reduction with the proposal that there be established a joint Soviet-American scientific committee, under the chairmanship of a distinguished neutral figure, to study jointly and in all humility the problem not only of the safe disposal of these wastes but also the question of how they could be utilized in such a way as to make a positive contribution to human life, either in the two countries themselves or—perhaps preferably—elsewhere. In such a joint scientific venture we might both atone for some of our past follies and lay the foundation for a more constructive relationship.

It will be said: this proposal, whatever its merits, deals with only a part of the problem. This is perfectly true. Behind it there would still lurk the serious political differences that now divide us from the Soviet government. Behind it would still lie the problems recently treated, and still to be treated, in the SALT forum. Behind it would still lie the great question of the acceptability of war itself, any war, even a conventional one, as a means of solving problems among great industrial powers in this age of high technology.

What has been suggested here would not prejudice the continued treatment of these questions just as they might be treated today, in whatever forums and under whatever safeguards the two powers find necessary. The conflicts and arguments over these questions could all still proceed to the heart's content of all those who view them with such passionate commitment. The stakes would simply be smaller: and that would be a great relief to all of us.

What I have suggested is, of course, only a beginning. But a beginning has to be made somewhere: and if it has to be made, is it not best that it should be made where the dangers are the greatest, and their necessity the least? If a step of this nature could be successfully taken, people might find the heart to tackle with greater confidence and determination the many problems that would still remain.

It will also be argued that there would be risks involved.

Possibly so. I do not see them. I do not deny the possibility. But if there are, so what? Is it possible to conceive of any dangers greater than those that lie at the end of the collision course on which we are now embarked? And if not, why choose the greater—why choose, in fact, the greatest—of all risks, in the hopes of avoiding the lesser ones?

We are confronted here, my friends, with two courses. At the end of the one lies hope—faint hope, if you will—uncertain hope, hope surrounded with dangers, if you insist. At the end of the other lies, so far as I am able to see, no hope at all. . . .

In the final week of his life, Albert Einstein signed the last of the collective appeals against the development of nuclear weapons that he was ever to sign. He was dead before it appeared. It was an appeal drafted, I gather, by Bertrand Russell. I had my differences with Russell at the time as I do now in retrospect; but I would like to quote one sentence from the final paragraph of that statement, not only because it was the last one Einstein ever signed, but because it sums up, I think, all that I have to say on the subject. It reads as follows:

> We appeal, as human beings to human beings: Remember your humanity, and forget the rest.

["A Proposal for International Disarmament", 1981]

THE CHALLENGE OF PEACE

Catholic Bishops of the U.S.

MORAL PRINCIPLES AND POLICY CHOICES

178. Targeting doctrine raises significant moral questions because it is a significant determinant of what would occur if nuclear weapons were ever to be used. Although we acknowledge the need for deterrent, not all forms of deterrence are morally acceptable. There are moral limits to deterrence policy as well as to policy regarding use. Specifically, it is not morally acceptable to intend to kill the innocent as part of a strategy of deterring nuclear war. The question of whether U.S. policy involves an intention to strike civilian centers (directly targeting civilian populations) has been one of our factual concerns.

179. This complex question has always produced a variety of responses, official and unofficial in character. The NCCB Committee has received a series of statements of clarification of policy from U.S. government officials. Essentially these statements declare that it is not U.S. strategic policy to target the Soviet civilian population as such or to use nuclear weapons deliberately for the purpose of destroying population centers. These statements respond, in principle at least, to one moral criterion for assessing deterrence policy: the immunity of noncombatants from direct attack either by conventional or nuclear weapons.

180. These statements do not address or resolve another very troublesome moral problem, namely, that an attack on military targets or militarily significant industrial targets could involve "indirect" (i.e., unintended) but massive civilian casualties. We are advised, for example, that the United States strategic nuclear targeting plan (SIOP—Single Integrated Operational Plan) has identified 60 "military" targets within the city of Moscow alone, and that 40,000 "military" targets for nuclear weapons have been identified in the whole of the Soviet Union. It is important to recognize that Soviet policy is subject to the same moral judgment; attacks on several "industrial targets" or politically significant targets in the United States could produce massive civilian casualties. The number of civilians who would necessarily be killed by such strikes is horrendous. This problem is unavoidable because of the way modern military facilities and production centers are so thoroughly interspersed with civilian living and working areas. It is aggravated if one side deliberately positions military targets in the midst of a civilian population. In our consultations, administration officials readily admitted that, while they hoped any nuclear exchange could be kept limited, they were prepared to retaliate in a massive way if necessary. They also agreed that once any substantial numbers of weapons were used, the civilian casualty levels would quickly become truly catastrophic, and that even with attacks limited to "military" targets, the number of deaths in a substantial exchange would be almost indistinguishable from what might occur if civilian centers had been deliberately and directly struck. These possibilities pose a different moral question and are to be judged by a different moral criterion: the principle of proportionality.

181. While any judgement of proportionality is always open to differing evaluations, there are actions which can be decisively judged to be disproportionate. A narrow adherence exclusively to the principle of noncombatant immunity as a criterion for policy is an inadequate moral posture for it ignores some evil and unacceptable consequences. Hence, we cannot be satisfied that the assertion of an intention not to strike civilians directly, or even the most honest effort to implement that intention, by itself constitutes a "moral policy" for the use of nuclear weapons.

182. The location of industrial or militarily significant economic targets within heavily populated areas or in those areas affected by radioactive fallout could well involve such massive civilian casualties that, in our judgement, such a strike would be deemed morally disproportionate, even though not intentionally indiscriminate.

183. The problem is not simply one of producing highly accurate weapons that might minimize civilian casualties in any single explosion, but one of increasing the likelihood of escalation at a level where many, even "discriminating," weapons would cumulatively kill very large numbers of civilians. Those civilian deaths would occur both immediately and from the long-term effects of social and economic devastation.

184.   A second issue of concern to us is the relationship of deterrence doctrine to war-fighting strategies. We are aware of the argument that war-fighting capabilities enhance the credibility of the deterrent, particularly the strategy of extended deterrence. But the development of such capabilities raises other strategic and moral questions. The relationship of war-fighting capabilities and targeting doctrine exemplifies the difficult choices in this area of policy. Targeting civilian populations would violate the principle of discrimination—one of the central moral principles of a Christian ethic of war. But "counterforce targeting," while preferable from the perspective of protecting civilians, is often joined with a declaratory policy which conveys the notion that nuclear war is subject to precise rational and moral limits. We have already expressed our severe doubts about such a concept. Furthermore, a purely counterforce strategy may seem to threaten the viability of other nations' retaliatory forces, making deterrence unstable in a crisis and war more likely.

185.   While we welcome any effort to protect civilian populations, we do not want to legitimize or encourage moves which extend deterrence beyond the specific objective of preventing the use of nuclear weapons or other actions which could lead directly to a nuclear exchange.

186.   These considerations of concrete elements of nuclear deterence policy, made in light of John Paul II's evaluation, but applying it through our own prudential judgements, leads us to a strictly conditioned moral acceptance of nuclear deterrence. We cannot consider it adequate as a long-term basis for peace.

187.   This strictly conditioned judgment yields *criteria* for morally assessing the elements of deterrence strategy. Clearly, these criteria demonstrate that we cannot approve of every weapons system, strategic doctrine, or policy initiative advanced in the name of strengthening deterrence. On the contrary, these criteria require continual public scrutiny of what our government proposes to do with the deterrent.

188.   On the basis of these criteria we wish now to make some specific evaluations:

1) If nuclear deterrence exists only to prevent the *use* of nuclear weapons by others, then proposals to go beyond this to planning for prolonged periods of repeated nuclear strikes and counterstrikes, or "prevailing" in nuclear war, are not acceptable. They encourage notions that nuclear war can be engaged in with tolerable human and morel consequences. Rather, we must continually say "no" to the idea of nuclear war.

2) If nuclear deterrence is our goal, "sufficiency" to deter is an adequate strategy; the quest for nuclear superiority must be rejected.

3) Nuclear deterrence should be used as a step on the way toward progressive disarmament. Each proposed addition to our strategic system or change in strategic doctrine must be assessed precisely in light of whether it will render steps toward "progressive disarmament" more or less likely.

189.   Moreover, these criteria provide us with the means to make some judgments and recommendations about the present direction of U.S. strategic policy. Progress toward a world freed of dependence on nuclear deterrence must be carefully carried out. But it must not be delayed. There is an urgent moral and political responsibility to use the "peace of a sort" we have as a framework to move toward authentic peace through nuclear arms control, reductions, and disarmament. Of primary importance in this process is the need to prevent the development and deployment of destabilizing weapons systems on either side; a second requirement is to insure that the more sophisticated command and control systems do not become mere hair triggers for automatic launch on warning; a third is the need to prevent the proliferation of nuclear weapons in the international system.

190.   In light of these general judgments we *oppose* some specific proposals in respect to our present deterrence posture:

1) The addition of weapons which are likely to be vulnerable to attack, yet also possess a "prompt hard-target kill" capability that threatens to make the other side's retaliatory forces vulnerable. Such weapons may seem to be

useful primarily in a first strike; we resist such weapons for this reason and we oppose Soviet deployment of such weapons which generate fear of a first strike against U.S. forces.

2) The willingness to foster strategic planning which seeks a nuclear war-fighting capability that goes beyond the limited function of deterrence outlined in this letter.

3) Proposals which have the effect of lowering the nuclear threshold and blurring the difference between nuclear and conventional weapons.

191. In support of the concept of "sufficiency" as an adequate deterrent, and in light of the present size and composition of both the U.S. and Soviet strategic arsenals, *we recommend:*

1) Support for immediate, bilateral, verifiable agreements to halt the testing, production, and deployment of new nuclear weapons systems.

2) Support for negotiated bilateral deep cuts in the arsenals of both superpowers, particularly those weapons systems which have destabilizing characteristics; U.S. proposals like those for START (Strategic Arms Reduction Talks) and INF (Intermediate-range Nuclear Forces) negotiations in Geneva are said to be designed to achieve deep cuts; our hope is that they will be pursued in a manner which will realize these goals.

3) Support for early and successful conclusion of negotiations of a comprehensive test ban treaty.

4) Removal by all parties of short-range nuclear weapons which multiply dangers disproportionate to their deterrent value.

5) Removal by all parties of nuclear weapons from areas where they are likely to be overrun in the early stages of war, thus forcing rapid and uncontrollable decisions on their use.

6) Strengthening of command and control over nuclear weapons to prevent inadvertent and unauthorized use.

192. These judgments are meant to exemplify how a lack of unequivocal condemnation of deterrence is meant only to be an attempt to acknowledge the role attributed to deterrence, but not to support its extension beyond the limited purpose discussed above. Some have urged us to condemn all aspects of nuclear deterrence. This urging has been based on a variety of reasons, but has emphasized particularly the high and terrible risks that either deliberate use or accidental detonation of nuclear weapons could quickly escalate to something utterly disproportionate to any acceptable moral puspose. That determination requires highly technical judgments about hypothetical events. Although reasons exist which move some to condemn reliance on nuclear weapons for deterrence, we have not reached this conclusion for the reasons outlined in this letter.

193.   Nevertheless, there must be no misunderstanding of our profound skepticism about the moral acceptability of any use of nuclear weapons. It is obvious that the use of any weapons which violate the principle of discrimination merits unequivocal condemnation. We are told that some weapons are designed for purely "counterforce" use against military forces and targets. The moral issue, however, is not resolved by the design of weapons or the planned intention for use; there are also consequences which must be assessed. It would be a perverted political policy or moral casuistry which tried to justify using a weapon which "indirectly" or "unintentionally" killed a million innocent people because they happened to live near a "militarily significant target."

194.   Even the "indirect effects" of initiating nuclear war are sufficient to make it an unjustifiable moral risk in any form. It is not sufficient, for example, to contend that "our" side has plans for "limited" or "discriminate" use. Modern warfare is not readily contained by good intentions or technological designs. The psychological climate of the world is such that mention of the term "nuclear" generates uneasiness. Many contend that the use of one tactical nuclear weapon could produce panic, with completely unpredictable consequences. It is precisely this mix of political, psychological, and technological uncertainty which has moved us in this letter to reinforce with moral prohibitions and prescriptions the prevailing political barrier against resort to nuclear weapons. Our support for enhanced command and control facilities, for major reductions in strategic and tactical nuclear forces, and for a "no first use" policy (as set forth in this

letter) is meant to be seen as a complement to our desire to draw a moral line against nuclear war.

195. Any claim by any government that is pursuing a morally acceptable policy of deterrence must be scrutinized with the greatest care. We are prepared and eager to participate in our country in the ongoing public debate on moral grounds.

196. The need to rethink the deterrence policy of our nation, to make the revisions necessary to reduce the possibility of nuclear war, and to move toward a more stable system of national and international security will demand a substantial intellectual, political, and moral effort. It also will require, we believe, the willingness to open ourselves to the providential care, power and word of God, which call us to recognize our common humanity and the bonds of mutual responsibility which exists in the international community in spite of political differences and nuclear arsenals.

[The Challenge of Peace: God's Promise and our Response",
1983, pp. 56-62]

BISHOPS, STATESMEN AND OTHER STRATEGISTS ON THE BOMBING OF INNOCENTS

Albert Wohlstetter

THE BISHOPS PASS LIGHTLY over or further confound many already muddled and controversial questions of fact and policy. In a world where so many intense, deep, and sometimes mutually reinforcing antagonisms divide regional as well as superpowers, are there serious early prospects for negotiating the complete, verifiable, and permanent elimination of nuclear or conventional arms? If antagonists don't agree, should we disarm unilaterally? If we keep nuclear arms, how should we use them to deter their use against us or an ally? Might an adversary in some plausible circumstance make a nuclear attack on an element (perhaps a key non-nuclear element) of our military power or that of an ally to whom we have issued a nuclear guarantee? Might such an enemy nuclear attack (for example, one generated in the course of allied conventional resistance to a conventional invasion of NATO's center or of a critical country on NATO's northern or southern flank) have decisive military effects yet restrict side effects enough to leave us, and possibly our ally, a very large stake in avoiding "mutual mass slaughter"? Could some selective but militarily useful Western response to such a restricted nuclear attack destroy substantially fewer innocent bystanders than a direct attack on population centers? Would any discriminate Western response to a restricted nuclear attack—even one in an isolated area on a flank—inevitably (or more likely than not, or just possibly, or with some intermediate probability) lead to the destruction of humanity, or "something little better"? Or at least to an unprecedented catastrophe? Would it be less or more likely than an attack on population to lead to unrestricted attacks on populations? Can we deter a restricted nuclear attack better by threatening an "unlimited," frankly suicidal, and therefore improbable attack on the aggressor's cities, or by a limited but much more probable response suited to the circumstance?

The bishops' authorities slip by or confuse almost all these questions.

The bishops, their defenders, and the strategists on whom they rely all talk of the uncontrollability of nuclear weapons as a deplorable but unavoidable fact of life. However, they make a virtue of this supposed necessity. John Garvey, columnist for the Catholic *Commonweal*, knows that one may not threaten what one does not intend to do, and grants that "if your enemy knows that you will absolutely refuse to use a weapon, what you have is no longer a weapon and is therefore useless"; but he claims that "it would be naive to think that we are so fully in control of ourselves that in the event of an attack we would not say, 'What the hell,' and hit them with everything we've got." Which apparently would give the threat, however immoral, some use as a deterrent.

However, it would be naive or worse to suppose that we cannot impose controls over both initial and subsequent uses of nuclear weapons. "Permissive action links," which we place on all our weapons overseas and which microchips and other electronic advances are constantly improving, can make it essentially infeasible for military commanders to use nuclear weapons without release by a remote political authority. Moreover, if we really thought political authority were reckless, we could make this release mechanism as elaborate as we liked and even divide the releasing codes so that they would require the agreement of many parties. But the processes of consultation in the Alliance are now complex, and would affect not only the initial, but also subsequent releases. It is most unlikely that we would simply say "Whee!" and let everything go. In Europe the problem is quite the opposite. We should not and do not rely on the threat of losing control to deter either nuclear or conventional attack. But

MAD and the fictions of uncontrollability it has propagated encourage us to rely on the threat of losing control as a substitute for dealing with the dangers of conventional conflicts. In short, they have led us to be less serious about conventional war as well.

The bishops' strategists, who believe that one can deter even if one is plainly committed never to use nuclear weapons, first, second, or ever, would maintain a capability but never use nuclear weapons at all. McNamara, when he changed from the doctrine of his first two years to talk of capabilities for mutual assured destruction, said he would maintain the capability to kill Russian civilians but would actually use nuclear weapons against certain military targets. That's rather different. Nonetheless it was a long step on the way to the present absurdities and evasions of the moral and prudential problems of discouraging a nuclear attack on the U.S. or one of its allies. Or a conventional attack.

The Soviets see the lasting independence of Western democracies side by side with their own system as a permanent danger to its maintenance, not to say its expansion toward an international utopia. Meanwhile, there is little evidence that some plausible arrangement would lead them to surrender so powerful an instrument of coercion or defense. That, after all, was indicated in their rejection of the Baruch-Acheson-Lilienthal plan for international control of atomic energy. Stalin exhibited none of the anguish sincerely felt by Western leaders and none of their momentary hopes for a world authority governing Communists and non-Communist nations side by side. The contrast of his private view with that of Western leadership is illustrated by the accounts of such privileged and reliable witnesses as Milovan Djilas: "He spoke of the A-bomb, 'That is a powerful thing, pow-er-ful!' His expression was full of admiration . . ."

Nor have Soviet leaders since Stalin shown any lesser awareness of the value of nuclear weapons as an implicit or explicit means of intimidation in a hostile world they do not dominate. Their value is only enhanced by the contrasting Western scruples on the same subject. If Western political as well as religious leaders take Western possession of nuclear weapons as justified only if there is progress toward agreement with the Russians to eliminate them altogether, they place in Soviet hands the decision as to whether the West will continue to maintain a nuclear deterrent.

Not all differences are negotiable. Pretending that they are suggests a willingness to disarm unilaterally—either because the Soviets prevent agreement or because they agree only to a disarmament which would be purely nominal for them but real for the West.

We should recognize that utopian hopes for total nuclear disarmament cannot excuse a Western failure to defend its independence soberly without using reckless threats. Unfortunately, our elites now link the phrase "arms control" not only to millennial dreams of early complete nuclear disarmament, but to the strategy of using threats to annihilate cities as a way of deterring attack; and to a perverse myth of the "arms race" that suggests that nuclear war is imminent because our nuclear arms have been spiraling exponentially and will continue to do so unless we limit our objectives to the destruction of a fixed small number of vulnerable population centers. (No one has ever suggested that the only way to avoid an exponential race in conventional arms is to train our fire on villages rather than enemy tanks. But when it comes to nuclear arms our elites will believe almost anything.) That is not the "arms control" Donald Brennan had in mind. "Arms control," as he and the Princeton physicist, Freeman Dyson, have understood it, should aim at the more traditional and more sensible goal of restraining the bombardment of civilians. But the phrase is now loaded with wishful and mistaken prejudices. It suggests that without arms agreements our spending on defense inevitably will rise exponentially and uncontrollably; and that with arms agreements Soviet arms efforts will diminish. Experience for nearly two decades after the Cuban missile crisis illustrates the opposite.

A serious effort to negotiate agreements with the Soviets might enable us to achieve our objectives at lower levels of armaments that might otherwise be possible. (Improved active defenses, as J. Robert Oppenheimer observed, could facilitate such bilateral agreements since they would make us safer from cheating or assaults by third countries. Being serious about arms agreements, however, is not the same as being desperate. Even without agreements the West is quite able to deter war and defend its independence against a formidable and persistently hostile adversary committed, as the Soviet Union has been, to changing the "correlation of forces" in its favor. The contrary view is deeply pessimistic and ultimately irresponsible, leading easily to treaties and "understandings" which only worsen the situation of the West.

For a serious and indeed sincere pursuit of arms negotiation by the West calls for a sober assessment of how any arrangements contemplated in an agreement are likely to affect the West's long-term objectives of security and independence, and its intermediate objective of redressing the balance which worsened during the period of détente. These are not merely technical matters. The actual results of arms negotiations have, in the past, contrasted sharply with our expectations and desires. The negotiations of the last two decades started with Western expectations that the agreements achieved would reduce arms spending on both sides without any change in the balance. We assumed that the Soviets, like ourselves, had, as a principal objective, the desire to reduce the percentage of their resources devoted to arms spending and that they would choose "arms control" rather than arms competition. The record plainly shows that Western assumptions were wishful. The Soviets pursued arms agreements as a method of limiting Western spending—which did decline as a proportion of GNP by nearly half in the period after the missile crisis—while they themselves steadily increased their spending and did succeed in changing the balance. Now the West has the problem of catching up and that is especially hard to negotiate.

Serious negotiations today must recognize the limits to what they can accomplish. We and the Soviets share an interest in avoiding mutual suicide, an interest which each of us will pursue whether or not we reach genuine agreement in various understandings and formal treaties. But the Soviets also have interests in expanding their influence and control and, in the process, destabilizing the West, if necessary by the use of external force rather than simply by manipulating internal dissension. Arms agreements might temper, but are unlikely to eliminate, this reality. In particular, there seems scant basis to hope for major economies in our security effort through negotiated limits or reductions.

Experience suggests that when the Soviets agree to close off one path of effort, they redirect their resources to other projects posing differing but no lesser dangers. On the other hand, many of the ostensible goals of arms agreements are best achieved through measures which we can and should implement on our own. Our current efforts—which a freeze would stop—to design and deploy nuclear weapons which are more accident-proof and more secure against theft or unauthorized use, are a good example. Measures to improve the safety, security, and invulnerability of nuclear weapons can be implemented by both sides individually because they make sense for each side independently of formal treaties or elaborate verification measures. These need not mean a net increase in the numbers or destructiveness of nuclear weapons in our stockpile. . . . If we increase precision further, we can drastically further reduce the number and destructiveness of our nuclear weapons. Increased precision can also improve the effectiveness of conventional weapons so that they may increasingly replace nuclear brute force. And it would improve our ability to avoid the unintended bombing of innocents with nuclear or conventional warheads. It would enlarge rather than foreclose our freedom to choose.

But many strategists in our foreign-policy establishment prefer to foreclose choice. The orthodox view, expressed by editors of our magazines dealing with foreign affairs, liberal Senators, scientists, and many former officials, holds that any use of nuclear weapons by us will almost surely end in a disaster leaving almost everybody dead or worse than dead; yet that we should have no alternative other than to threaten the bombing of cities; and that we should therefore make clear to our adversaries and allies that we will never fight a nuclear war. Anyone who holds that as the true faith will want to believe that he has no other choice. If he cannot say, like Flip Wilson, "The Devil made me do it," he can introduce the *deus ex machina* of technology: Nuclear Technology makes me do it. He is likely to be outraged by any heretic who dares suggest we might have choices.

[Bishops, Statesmen and Other Strategists", 1983, pp. 16-35]

C.

PIECES OF PEACE

CONFLICT
PREVENTION

REPORT OF THE SECRETARY GENERAL 1983

Javier Perez de Cuellar

THE CHARTER OF THE UNITED NATIONS clearly gives priority to dealing with threats to international peace and security and to the commitment of all nations, especially the permanent members of the Security Council, to cooperate within the framework of the United Nations towards this end. It is the weakening of this commitment that has, perhaps more than any other factor, led to the partial paralysis of the United Nations as the guardian of international peace and security.

Furthermore, when East-West tension is superimposed on regional conflicts and serves to exacerbate them, the already destructive nature of such disputes is likely to be aggravated and the danger of widening strife becomes an ominous prospect. On some occasions this process has gone so far that regional conflicts have been perceived as being wars by proxy among more powerful nations. In situations of this kind, the deliberative organs of the United Nations tend to be bypassed or excluded or, worse yet, to be used solely as a forum for political exchanges.

There have been, at any given time in past years, several regional situations with grave potential implications for international peace. At the present time, for example, such situations exist in South-East Asia, Afghanistan, Central America, Namibia and several other parts of Africa including Chad, in the Middle East and Lebanon, Cyprus and in the Iran-Iraq war. . . .

Neither the Security Council nor any other international organ can in all cases hope to resolve in short order acute international conflict situations that may involve serious clashes of interest between the actual parties as well as between the members of the Council. The Security Council under the Charter has, however, the obligation to assist the parties in the search for solutions to international disputes. But above all it is the council's duty to ensure tht this process should remain peaceful, lest it endanger the wider peace. Even though the members of the Council may be profoundly divided about the merits of a given case, it is their duty to find ways and means of keeping the situation under control, without prejudice to the shape of an eventual setttlement. Seen in this perspective, conflict control is a basic element of the primary responsibility of the United Nations for the maintenance of international peace and security.

For their part, States and other parties to international disputes have a primary obligation at all stages to co-operate with the Security Council and the Secretary-General in suitable forms of conflict control. However, the willingness of the parties to co-operate with the United Nations will inevitably be contingent upon the capacity of the Organization to act as an effective and impartial instrument of peace. Only if this essential condition is achieved will Member States come to the realization that in times of trouble they can rely on the United Nations to help to restore or maintain the peaceful conditions in which negotiated solutions of the basic issues can be sought as part of a civilized and rational international order.

Aside from conflict control, the main objective of the Security Council, particularly of its permanent members, should be to develop an effective common approach to potential threats to international peace and security, to assist and, if necessary, to put pressure on the conflicting parties to resolve their differences justly and by peaceful means. Such a concerted approach would dispose of great resources of persuasion and, if necessary, of practical leverage. That, surely, is the approach to important conflict problems which the authors of the Charter had in mind. This approach would go a long way to developing in practice a system for international peace and security designed to supersede arms races, military and other forms of conflict and the inherent risk of ultimate disaster. This is, after all, the basic idea of the Charter.

Unfortunately, we are in danger of becoming accustomed to a very different situation. All too often the members of the

Security Council tend to be so divided on the matter at hand and so apprehensive of each other's reaction to it that agreement on how to proceed remains elusive. When we consider how to improve the performance of the United Nations we must give priority to the cohesion and co-operation of the membership in facing threats to international peace. We should recognize that such threats are of an importance which should override the differences of interest and ideology which separate the membership. The Council must be primarily used for the prevention of armed conflict and the search for solutions. Otherwise it will become peripheral to major issues, and in the end the world could pay, as it has before, a heavy price for not learning the lessons of history.

If this analysis seems Utopian, it is certainly preferable to a course of action which risks, through partisanship, the elevating of a local conflict into a world confrontation. Indeed the habit of adopting a concerted approach to problems of international peace and security might lead to the statesmanlike co-operation which will be essential in bridging the great present divisions of our international society and in turning the tide in crucial matters such as disarmament and arms control. . . .

[Report of the Secretary-General 1983, pp. 4,5]

MULTILATERAL PEACEKEEPING

THE POLITICS OF
PEACEKEEPING

Alan James

PEACE-KEEPING IS A TERM which has come into general use during the past twenty-five years to describe a particular type of activity in the cause of international peace. The activity itself goes back a long way beyond this period, but it is only since the mid-1950s that it has attracted a distinctive verbal characterization. What it encompasses is the non-forceful deployment in tense or potentially difficult situations of inspectors, intermediaries, or interposers. The fact that their method of operation does not rely on the use of force means that their very presence requires the assent of the parties, and this basic fact about such missions also sets the condition for their success: that the parties respect and cooperate with them. In turn this requires that the peace-keepers should act impartially and be seen to be acting impartially.

The main vehicle for peace-keeping activity has been the United Nations, but the world organization has not enjoyed a monopoly. After the 1954 agreements regarding Indo-China, for example, three non-UN Commissions were set up to watch over and assist the return of peace. Again, in 1973, the cease-fire agreement regarding Vietnam was accompanied by the establishment of an International Commission. In 1965 a US-dominated Inter-American Force (quickly re-named the Inter-American Peace Force) was sent to the Dominican Republic, and four years earlier an Arab League force had appeared in Kuwait. But on the whole it has been the UN to which states have turned when they have been in need of peace-keeping services.

In responding, the UN has normally made use of military personnel. When a force of several battalions has been set up, this has been the only practical way to proceed, appropriate member states being looked to for the required contingents. Observer groups, where the constituent component is the individual observer, have also usually been made up of military men, officers of suitable rank being seconded from the armed forces of member states. However, in some cases, for one reason or another, such military observers have sometimes come from civilian life, having served previously in the armed forces. And observer groups of a basically civilian nature have been used by the UN, as in the Balkans in the late 1940s and in Laos in 1959. Furthermore, UN activity in the field of a conciliatory kind has typically involved civilian personnel.

Recent developments, however, have raised a couple of questions—one so far small, the other already rather bigger—about the assumption that in the usual way peace-keeping activity will be conducted by the UN through the medium of military people. The small question concerns the assumption that peace-keeping is generally an activity which is best conducted by those who are currently on active military service.

MILITARY V. CIVILIAN PERSONNEL

There is no necessary reason why the role of a passive observer should be filled by a military person. It may be easier to obtain such a person's services, but if the nature of that which is to be observed is essentially non-military—the movement of people and vehicles, for example—then a civilian might do the job just as well. Moreover, if the observation is heavily dependent on technological devices of a sophisticated sort, civilians who are versed in their use may be more readily available. While, therefore, there were strong political reasons for the despatch of a US civilian mission (of up to two hundred men) to the Sinai in 1975 in connection with the second Egyptian-Israeli disengagement agreement, the particular nature of their task made the use of civilians functionally appropriate.

However, their subsequent use was more surprising. The Egyptian-Israeli Peace Treaty of March 1979 had envisaged the continued use of a UN Peace-Keeping Force and Military Observers in eastern Sinai during the final stage of Israel's occupation and withdrawal. When this scheme collapsed on account of the threat of a Soviet veto in the Security Council, the task of positive observation—inspection and verification—was, by easy agreement between Egypt, Israel and the United States, given to the existing civilian mission. This was a job which on past experience would certainly have gone to military personnel. Admittedly, some of the American civilians involved had had military experience, but even so it was an unusual development. Moreover, it was a success. Of course, the fact that the civilians acquitted themselves well was in no small measure due to the fact that they were working in a very congenial political environment. But it was a possibly significant straw in the wind, and it had a sequel.

The Peace Treaty provided that when Israel finally withdrew from Sinai in April 1982, a narrow band of territory on the Israeli side of the international frontier, in which there were certain limitations on permissible forces, should be watched over by UN observers. The assumption was that Military Observers of the usual type would be used. As, however, the UN was unable to supply the Force which was to operate on the other side of the frontier it was agreed that once again the US should supply civilian observers. Only thirty-five were required. About half were recruited from US agencies dealing with international matters, and the rest are Americans with technical expertise and, often, military experience.

Thus during the rest of the 1980's and beyond there could be an increased use of civilians for peace-keeping activities of an observational kind, especially if more use is made in peace-keeping operations of modern technology. In itself this is unlikely to be of political significance. The nationality of civilian peace-keepers will be no less sensitive an issue than that of military personnel doing the same sort of job. A potential host state might be slightly more willing to accept a civilian than a military observer, on the ground that a civilian might be rather less militarily perceptive. But as against that the potential host would have to weigh the fact that injury or death to a civilian could have slightly greater political repercussions than if the same thing happened to a military man. However, there is unlikely to be much in these calculations. If an observer mission is acceptable in principle it is most unlikely to be less or more so on account of a civilian as against a military composition.

UN v. Non-UN Forces

The larger question which was referred to above concerns the auspices under which peace-keeping takes place, and, more particularly, whether the UN is in danger of being toppled from its position as the usual source of peace-keeping forces. The further question which arises is whether the source of such a force is an issue of any importance. As long as the job is done, does it matter who does it?

This question has come on to the international agenda on account of the relative spate of non-UN peace-keeping forces which have appeared during the last few years. Thus the February 1980 election which prefaced the independence of Zimbabwe was watched over by a non-UN Monitoring Force of about 1500 men. Most of them came from the British Army—1250—but they were supplemented by small detachments from Australia, New Zealand, Kenya, and Fiji. The election was also watched by a civilian Commonwealth Observer Group drawn from 11 countries, observers nominated by 13 states and two international organizations, and a number of independent and non-governmental observers.

A year later the Organization of African Unity (OAU) decided to send an African peace-keeping force to Chad to monitor an earlier agreement that the country should be governed transitionally by a regime of national union. Six states initially offered to contribute forces but in the event only Nigeria (the largest contributor), Zaire, and Senegal provided contingents which made up the 3250 strong force. The US, France, Britain, and Algeria helped with money or supplies, and by the end of 1981 the force was in place. Additionally, Kenya, Zambia, and Guinea-Bissau sent observers on behalf of the OAU. Both force and observers were withdrawn half way through 1982.

By this time another non-UN peace-keeping force had appeared on the scene, the Multinational Force and Observers (MFO). It was deployed in Sinai in March 1982 in preparation for Israel's final withdrawal in the following month, with the task of undertaking the verification and inspection activities which the Egyptian-Israeli Peace Treaty had anticipated would be done by the UN. The Observer element of this entity has already been mentioned. The 2600 strong Force element is made up of light infantry battalions contributed by the United States, Columbia, and FIji, and smaller military units from the US, Australia and New Zealand, France, Italy, the Netherlands, Britain, and Uruguay. Additionally, Norway provides the Force Commander and a few staff officers. The MFO is a separate international organization under the overall control of its Director-General who, with his international staff, is based in Rome. The costs of the MFO (after its first year, for which a different basis was adopted) are divided equally between Egypt, Israel, and the US, and participating states are reimbursed the extra costs which arise from their participation. The Director-General, who has been appointed for a four-year-renewable term, is a retired American foreign service officer.

Later in 1982 two Multinational Forces (which for convenience will be distinguished as MNF I and MNF II) were sent to Beirut in the wake of Israel's invasion of that country. In mid-June the Israeli forces stopped at the outskirts of Beirut and laid siege to the Western part of the city, where about 11,000 Palestinian guerrillas were interspersed with about half a million civilians. After lengthy negotiations amidst a continuing bombardment it was agreed that a three-nation force should supervise the withdrawal of Palestinian forces from the city. The US contributed about 800 military personnel, France the same number, and Italy about 400. The evacuation began on 21 August and was completed within eleven days. The MNF left shortly afterwards.

Then, however, came the massacre of Palestinian civilians in two refugee camps in Beirut and a similarly composed MNF II was soon on its way back to Beirut. It was, however, larger than before, comprising 3400 men divided more or less equally between the three contributor states. Subsequently France increased the size of its contingent to take the Force to about 4000 men, and early in 1983 a small British unit of 80 troops joined MNF II . . . at the time of writing there are two and a half UN peace-keeping forces. The UN Force in Cyprus (UNFICYP) has been in that country for the last twenty years, and since 1974 has watched over the buffer zone between the forces of Cyprus and those of Turkey. It has about 2300 men, with battalions from Austria, Britain, Canada, Denmark, and Sweden, and token units from Finland and Ireland. There are also 34 civilian police from Australia and Sweden.

On the eastern part of the Golan Heights the UN Disengagement Observer Force (UNDOF) is deployed between Syria and Israel in consequence of a 1974 cease-fire and disengagement agreement. It has about 1300 men from four countries: Austria, Canada, Finland, and Poland.

The half-force is in fact twice as big as the other two put together, the UN Interim Force in Lebanon (UNIFIL), which went to southern Lebanon following the Israeli invasion of March 1978, the Israelis withdrawing within the next few months. It has units from Fiji, Finland, France, Ghana, Ireland, Netherlands, Norway, Senegal, and Sweden, and a small Italian helicopter unit. . . .

Additionally, there are two UN Military Observer Groups. the UN Truce Supervision Organization (UNTSO) was set up in 1948 and is still in being as a separate group with a strength of about 300. Operationally, however, it is to all intents and purposes now confined to working with UNDOF and UNIFIL.

The other Observer Group is the UN Military Observer Group in India and Pakistan (UNMOGIP), which has been posted along the cease-fire line in Kashmir since 1949. After the Indo-Pakistan war of 1971, however, India stopped cooperating with the peace-keeping activities of UNMOGIP, and in consequence, while it remains in place, it is unable to make any significant contribution to the maintenance of calm. Presently it comprises about 40 officers.

What, then, are the reasons which account for the UN, in a sense, being bypassed so frequently in recent years in respect of an activity for which it had come to be widely regarded as particularly suitable? Putting it in other words, what, from the point of view of the maintenance of peace, are the advantages of non-UN forces over those set up by the Organization? And what advantages does the UN still retain, vis a vis non-UN sources, so far as the mounting of peace-keeping forces is concerned? The issues may conveniently be considered under four sub headings: factors relating to the establishment, the efficiency (in an organizational sense), the effectiveness (operationally viewed), and the ending of peace-keeping forces. The implicit and sometimes explicit theme of the ensuing discussion will be that non-UN forces have elements of political concentration and exposure which sometimes give them advantages over UN forces and sometimes not. And, turning the coin over, UN forces are marked by elements of political diversification and dilution which can sometimes be a disadvantage when compared to non-UN forces but are on other occasions a strength.

A. Establishment

So far as the establishment of peace-keeping forces is concerned, it may sometimes be easier or more appropriate to operate outside the UN, or even necessary to do so if a force is to be set up. In certain circumstances, for example, a regional or non-regional body may be felt to be the most suitable organizational parent. Some such feeling may have been behind the use of a Commonwealth Force and Observer Group in Rhodesia/ Zimbabwe, in that this kept the matter within the Commonwealth family—although undoubtedly there were other more important factors which pointed in the same direction. Certainly this feeling was present in respect of the OAU's decision to send its own force to Chad: Africa was handling its own problems.

Furthermore, a group of like-minded states (like-minded, that is, on the issue in question) may sometimes find that the way a UN peace-keeping force is difficult or blocked by one or more of the hazards of the UN's procedures. In which case, the setting up of their own force through multilateral negotiations may be the obvious way forward. A veto may be threatened or cast in the Security Council, as happened in respect of the intended extension of the UN Force in Sinai in 1979. The task, in these circumstances, of trying to get a two-thirds majority in the General Assembly may be too disheartening to attempt, and may look assuredly futile. The 1979 situation certainly fell into one or other of these categories.

Even if there is no obstacle within the UN, the Organization may be *persona non grata* to one of the disputants which, as peace-keeping rests on consent and cooperation, means that the UN cannot be used. The British Conservative Government of 1979 would not have looked kindly on the idea of calling in the UN to monitor an election in the territory which had been temporarily restored to its bosom. Indeed, at first Britain seemed to think that some of her policemen would be sufficient for the job. And in Beirut in 1982 Israel refused to have anything to do with the idea of a UN force. In August she even prevented the full execution of a UN Security Council decision to deploy observers in the city. Thus the United States, very reluctantly, and in face of Soviet protests, came around to the idea of organizing a multinational force herself. She was no more enthusiastic about this after the September massacres had brought the issue of Beirut back to her front door, but once again felt obliged to tread the multinational paths, given the continued unavailability of the UN. . . .

In the case of the two MNF's, the formal host state was Lebanon. So dire was her plight that she would have been willing to welcome almost any kind of international force. Other potential hosts, however, may be very wary of the multinational or even the regional idea. States almost always worry about the presence of foreign troops on their soil, and a multinational force, which represents nothing more than its members, could seem a more threatening prospect than one controlled by the UN. The way in which the Syrian-dominated Arab Deterrent Force (which went to Lebanon in 1976) turned against the local Muslims at one early stage will not be an attractive precedent, notwithstanding the fact that the Force may perhaps not fall into the peace-keeping category. There is also the consideration that a regional or continental force may be more easily used than a UN force to pay off old (or newly-discovered) intra-regional or continental scores. President Goukouni of Chad certainly felt betrayed by the OAU, as well he might, given that he was overthrown during the presence of the OAU force—which promptly left once his successor had taken office.

It is also the case that potential contributor states may be more reluctant to join a multinational than a UN force. Participation in a multinational force probably represents a more overtly political act in relation to the dispute, and in the case of smaller participants may suggest too close an identification with the policies of the prime mover(s) behind the multinational idea. Joining a UN force, on the other hand, can be expressed as giving general support to the world Organization and its high ideals. In the case of the MFO, for example, the US required a letter from the President of the Security Council, saying that the UN was unable to establish a force, before she would make a substitute move. And then, once Egyptian and Israeli consent had been secured, enormous difficulty was encountered in lining up other contributors. Only Fiji came forward readily with the offer of a battalion—provided that its members could be provided with certain basic equipment, which the US was only too happy to supply. Columbia also offered a battalion in due course, completing the requirement for ground troops. However, other participants were needed, both for specialist units and political cover, and this is where the real problems set in. It was over this matter that the US Secretary of State was alleged to have accused the British Foreign Secretary (in the US National Security Council) of duplicity. But eventually all was settled— and then it was only the US Congress that had to be strongly prodded to pass the necessary enabling law in time.

In the case of MNF II, the Lebanese Government spoke on a number of occasions towards the end of 1982 about the possible quadrupling of the Force and an expansion of its role. Press reports suggested that about a dozen countries had been approached for troop contributions, and Morocco was reported to have offered 2000—only to be vetoed by Israel. The Dutch Government replied with a firm 'no', saying it preferred UN forces, and was supported by its Parliment. Sweden took the same line. The only thing to emerge from this activity was that Britain, after having initially declined to contribute on the ground that it was already participating in the MFO (with 35 men), and reportedly having received strong military advise to stay out, eventually came up with a reconnaissance unit of 80.

One other, lesser, factor regarding the establishment of peace-keeping forces which may count in favor of the UN is that the body has now had a lot of experience in setting them up. Its expertise will probably be available to others, and the US certainly drew on the peace-keeping section of the UN Secretariat in planning for the MFO. But even so, do-it-yourself is never easy for the novice, even with the fullest instructions. And the experience of the OAU in respect of Chad is a particularly doleful one, where it took almost a year to get the Force in place, and even then it continued to face considerable logistic and financial problems.

B. Efficiency

In theory, it might be expected that a multinational or regional peace-keeping force would be able to organize itself more efficiently than a UN force, on account of the fewer number of states involved and the likelihood of their having a more coherent political purpose. The UN, for example, has sometimes supplied its forces with exceedingly vague, contradictory, or impractical mandates, and this has sometimes led to subsequent trouble on the ground. The Congo Force (1960) was supposed to 'assist' the Congolese Government in the restoration of law and order, while staying out of internal quarrels. UNIFIL (1978) was charged with restoring calm in an area over which it was most unlikely to obtain full control. Not surprisingly, difficulties and recriminations followed in both cases. Moreover, the interpretation of any mandate can give rise to problems where, as is usual, a UN force is made up of contingents supplied by governments of very different political hues. For, although it is frowned upon, contingents naturally keep in close touch with their home governments, and this can lead to different local reactions to similar situations. In southern Lebanon PLO activity was responded to somewhat diversely, and one critical observer has been heard referring to one UN contingent as 'PLObatt'. Obviously, this type of thing obstructs the emergence of a clear and efficient structure of command and control. One might expect that the problem would be less troubling for a multinational force.

A connected point refers to relations with the disputants. The UN has always operated on the principle that it is up to it to determine the composition of its forces, although it has prudently never tried to force a contingent of an unacceptable nationality on a host state. But where one of the disputants is on foreign soil, the UN has not felt iself so constricted. Thus in UNDOF, and also in the UN Force which was in Sinai from 1973 to 1979, contingents were included from states not in diplomatic relations with Israel. But this means that on account of Israel's refusal to cooperate with such contingents, they would only be used on the Syrian and Egyptian sides of the cease-fire lines and disengagement zones. This gave rise to operational difficulties,. In multinational forces, on the other hand, all disputants might be expected to have a bigger say about the composition of the force. Israel's rejection of a Moroccan contingent for MNF II has already been mentioned. In the case of the MFO one of the difficulties was that only countries acceptable to Israel were considered. This gave rise to problems at the time, but has probably increased the operational efficiency of the Force. It might be added that where the disputants' wishes are consulted in this way it is also less likely that they will view any of the contingents with the contempt which Israel has shown for one or two of those in UNIFIL, on account of such matters as hair length and alleged drug taking. The lack of such an attitude should also add something to the efficiency of a non-UN force.

The points made in the previous paragraph do seem to have some force (although they may also have some consequential disadvantages, to be considered below). But those which were raised in the first paragraph of this section do not seem as strong as were theoretically supposed. The mandates of the two MNFs have hardly been crisp—to assist Lebanon to ensure the PLOs safe departure in the first case, and to enable Lebanon to resume full sovereignty over its capital in the second. And MNF II, like its predecessor, has no overall command structure at all. Everything turns on regular liaison meetings in Beirut of the Ambassadors of the contributing countries and the Commanders of the contingents. This seems to have worked reasonably well so far, but it is not hard to envisage developments in which it could fall apart relatively easily. And it is difficult to see how this form of control arrangement could effectively accommodate many more than the present relatively small number of contributing states. The mandate of the OAU's Chad Force also appears to have been noticeably vague. It did have a Commander—a Nigerian—but this does not appear to have greatly reflected or facilitated its cohesion.

The other two non-UN forces of recent years present a different picture, but there is no reason to think that they, rather than the Chad Force and the MNFs, will be typical. In the case of the Commonwealth Monitoring Force, its brief was detailed and clear, and it was directly under the authority of the British Governor, who in turn was a servant of the British Government. The MFO's mandate (originally intended for the UN) was also clearly set out, and its command structure in the field is very similar to that of a UN force. The Commander, however, does not report to a political body via the UN Secretary-General, but simply to the MFOs Director-General in Rome—a US national. So long as the parties cooperate, as they have done so far, this arrangement can work smoothly. But if there was trouble, and US interests were involved, the MFO scheme could attract appreciable controversy.

C. Effectiveness

One obvious possible advantage of non-UN forces, and especially of multinational forces, is that, within the generally accepted principles of international peace-keeping, they might be able to take a more resolute line on the ground. The orders to the individual contingents will come more directly from the home Defense Ministries than in the case of contributors to a UN force; and participation in the multinational enterprise will probably reflect a more immediate national stake in the maintenance of calm in the area in question. The result should be a tougher and a more cohesive force than those which the UN usually fields. It is also the case—looking at much the same point from a different angle—that the disputants may be more reluctant to make trouble for a multinational force in that the several contingents will, to a greater extent than with UN forces, be seen as virtually the direct representatives of their governments. There will, as it were, be no UN dilution. Especially if one or more of the contributors are states which are either significant in themselves or for one or both of the parties, this should give the multinational force a greater deterrent value.

Recent experience, however, has not wholly borne out these prognostications. MNF II has not always been notable for its cohesion. It may not be much more than routine military complaining, but remarks have been heard about the tendency of the French to show off and to regard the enterprise as one of national competition rather than cooperation. On the other hand, the Americans have been charged with pussyfooting and a reluctance to take risks. Certainly there have been some differences in approach on the ground, and the US contingent has not had the air of representing the world's leading power. . . . Possibly all this reflects little more than the unfamiliarity of the

American Army with peace-keeping techniques and problems. For, apart from a handful of officers with UN observer missions, the US has had virtually no experience, either abroad or at home, of the sort of situation with which the UN has been dealing as a matter of routine for many years. . . .

This draws attention to a problem at the very heart of the multinational idea. It may seem an excellent thing from the point of view of the maintenance of peace to have a force in place which is somewhat more awe-inspiring than the usual type of UN force. But as against this, it may well be the case that such a force may not be equally appealing to all the disputants. Or one of them, while satisfied with the idea at the time of its proposal, may apprehend a change of heart on the matter at a later date. This has two consequences. The first is that disputants may not always consent to the proposed establishment of a multinational force, and as peace-keeping depends above all on consent and cooperation this means that even if it was possible to go ahead with the idea it would be most unwise to do so. The second is that if disputants show an imbalance of enthusiasm for a multinational force because of its strength, there is a danger that the force will be seen as partial to the side which favors a strong force. In turn this will reduce both the likelihood of cooperation from the other party and the general credibility of the force as a peace-keeping agency.

Viewed more generally, one can say that from the perspective of peace-keeping a conflict between toughness and impartiality (and there is no necessity for such a conflict, but it could arise) should be decided in favor of impartiality. Peace-keeping can be conducted in different circumstances with varying degrees of resolution, but there is a fundamental distinction between peace-keeping on the one hand and deterrence and enforcement on the other. Peace-keeping depends essentially on the cooperation of all the parties, and that will only be forthcoming if the peace-keeping forces' reputation for impartiality is well established and firmly maintained. The UN has been a large, if unsung, success story in this area, and the requirement for impartiality is no less in respect of peace-keeping forces of a multinational kind. This crucial consideration should not be lost to sight in an enthusiasm for the extra strength which a multinational format might be presumed to bring.

D. Ending

The experience of the withdrawal of the UN Emergency Force in 1967 from the Egyptian-Israeli border at the request of the Egyptian President has had a deep effect on general attitudes to peace-keeping. Accordingly, multinational forces might be seen as advantageous on the ground that they can be got rid of less easily. The protocol establishing the MFO, for example, provides that it can only be removed by the mutual agreement of Egypt and Israel. However, as against this it might be borne in mind that MNF I was restricted to a term of thirty days, and the despatch of MNF II was stated to be 'for a limited period' only— although here the term limited is taking on that special ambience which attaches to words about time and expectations when they appear in a peace-keeping context. Furthermore, there is no reason why safeguards about withdrawal should not be built into UN peace-keeping forces if the parties are agreeable and the Seecurity Council has no objection. Thus the Egyptian-Israeli Peace Treaty provided that the UN Force and Observers which were to be placed in eastern Sinai should only be withdrawn with the consent of both Egypt and Israel or by the Security Council with the affirmative vote of the five permanent members. Thus, each permanent member would have had a veto on the withdrawal of the UN force.

However, too much can be made, and is made, of the whole issue of security against withdrawal. Peace-keeping, it has been emphasized, is not enforcement or deterrence. Accordingly, if a host state or one of the parties wants a peace-keeping force to leave, it is not going to do much good by staying, or trying to stay. Cooperation from at least one side is likely to be lost, and in consequence the force would have lost its peace-keeping raison d'etre. Pointing to the lack of a terminal date in the constitutive document, or to a provision requiring mutual agreement on withdrawal, will not be much help. Of course, such provisions may have much diplomatic and psychological value when a force is set up. And peace-keepers should not take their leave too easily. But too much emphasis on a legal right to stay put, come what may, is unlikely to be productive. Indeed, it may be counter productive, in that potential host states will usually be very suspicious of suggestions that peace-keeping forces should be able to outstay their welcome, which may reduce their willing-ness to invite them in the first place. Especially might this be so if one or two powerful states are closely interested and involved in the establishment of such a force, as is more likely in the case of a multinational than a UN force.

A more immediate and perhaps more serious problem concerning the ending of peace-keeping forces relates to the possibility of their erosion and perhaps collapse through the withdrawal of contingents. It might be thought that multina-tional forces would be relatively immune to this danger, on account of the political interest of the contributing states in the work of such forces. However, an equally plausible argument to the contrary could be advanced. A change in foreign policy or domestic regime could lead to a multinational contingent being withdrawn on the ground that its involvement is no longer in the state's direct interest. Domestic criticism or unease about the state's participation might also find fairly immediate expression. For in neither case would the claim that the state was acting as a good UN member be available. Furthermore, in a multinational force made up of a few contingents, or a few key contingents, the loss of one might be particularly telling as a replacement might be hard to find (see the discussion above regarding the establishment of such forces). This problem of the withdrawal of contingents is one which the UN has met on several occasions, but has always managed to weather. Partly this is because the Organization has a relatively wide range of possible replacement contributors to approach, and such states are not usually op-posed in principle to helping the UN out. And partly it is because a number of states participating in UN forces continue to do so not just out of a general concern for peace and an interest in broadening their armed services' experience, but also out of a feeling of loyalty to the UN.

BALANCE SHEET

The above discussion suggests that sometimes a non-UN peace-keeping force may be more appropriate than a UN one, and that occasionally it may be the only way of dealing with a peace-keeping task. In itself, there is no need to be concerned about this. If a contribution towards the maintenance of peace can best or only be made by a non-UN agency, it is vastly better that it should be made in this way than not at all. Moreover, even if it could be established that a trend has been established whereby the UN's peace-keeping facilities were being bypassed, it would not be self-evident that this is, in the recent description of the UN Secretary-General, a 'dangerous' development. However, there are two reasons for thinking that despite the recent crop of non-UN forces, it is going rather too far to talk in terms of the emergence of a trend away from the UN.

In the first place, all the non-UN forces can be reasonably attributed to special circumstances. The Zimbabwe/Rhodesia Force was established in very much a one-off situation, and the OAU is unlikely to be keen to repeat its chequered peace-keeping experience in Chad. Nor are other regional bodies strong contenders for this kind of exercise. The Organization of American States is always worried about the possibility of US dominance; the Arab League is as divided as ever; and the Association of South-East Asian States is chiefly concerned about a problem to which peace-keeping techniques are not the most relevant. And so far as three multinational forces which have appeared in the Middle East is concerned, it is notable that all involve, on the one hand, Israel's hostility to the UN and, on the other, the acceptability of the US as the major peace-keeper. It is unlikely that there will be many other circumstances in which such a conjunction of events, or something comparable to them, will occur.

However, it *is* the Middle East where the UN has been in the past (and remains) most active in its peace-keeping role. And after a while any special circumstances argument tends to look a bit suspect. But there is a second reason for thinking that a trend away from the UN has not been established. It is that the more general arguments which have been considered in this paper do not suggest that non-UN peace-keeping forces have a marked advantage over those mounted by the world Organization. There are some advantages to be had from the rather more politically concentrated multinational forces, but the political dilution and diversification which the UN offers usually provides a more appropriate way of responding to the task of peace-keeping. It may not be called upon to do so very often, for peace-keeping is very much an ad hoc affair, arising in response to some crises as and when they occur, and suitable crises may not occur with much frequency. But nonetheless they are likely to crop up from time to time, and it would be surprising if the UN was more often than not ignored as a peace-keeping agency.

Moreover, other things being equal, there are certain not-yet-discussed advantages in turning to the UN rather than to an ad hoc group or even to a regional agency. The first is that on account of the UN's institutional continuity a UN peace-keeping force (or observer group) can easily be run down to a minimal level but maintained in being as a basis for possible expansion later if the circumstances require it.

The way in which UNTSO has had a continuous but very varying life in the Middle East for the last thirty-five years is a testimony to this point, as is UNMOGIP in its present rather reduced circumstances in Kashmir. UNIFIL too, although hardly reduced in size, is presently maintained in southern Lebanon rather in the manner in which a resting actor might more or less take up residence outside the doors of a promising agency.

Then, secondly, there is the argument that the world being what it is, it is likely (as suggested in the last paragraph but one) that the UN will continue to be looked to for peace-keeping aid—an organization of last or crisis resort and a dumping ground for difficult problems. Accordingly, it is highly desirable that the UN's procedures in this area should be kept well oiled by occasional use, and that those with experience of these matters should not be dispersed about the UN Secretariat on other tasks. As the Americans found, and continue to find, running a peace-keeping force is not the most straightforward of tasks. At present the UN knows very well how to go about it. This asset should not be squandered, which requires that the UN be employed now and then on the alleviatory techniques of peace-keeping.

Lastly, the UN does stand, among other things, for the value of peace. It is, of course, a highly political organization. But it is also generally seen as having a rather special standing, representing man's aspirations for a less conflict-ridden world. And in the field, as a peace-keeper, it has shown that it is fully capable of acting with the full impartiality of the true international civil servant. Therefore, both for the UN as an organization and for the members' perceptions of it, it is important that the UN be manifestly seen, from time to time, to be making some contribution towards the maintenance of peace. Peacekeeping is the activity of this which has come to be distinctively associated with the UN. Its value in actually keeping the peace should not be overemphasized: it is secondary rather than primary. But it is undoubtedly valuable. There is no need for the UN or anyone else to be snooty if this job is sometimes done outside the world Organization. But there is ground for claiming that where such a role is open to the UN, that is the body which should be the preferred peace-keeping organization.

["The Politics of Peacekeeping in the 1980's", 1983, pp. 27–41]

REGIONAL
APPROACHES

ON THE FRONT BURNER

Seyom Brown

A WORLD OF REGIONS

THE GROWING REALIZATION in the decades following World War II that human society is nowhere near being able to institute the world order designs of either the advocates of a world state or the champions of a substantially strengthened United Nations has been accompanied by the flowering of the idea of regional integration as an alternative to the universal designs. For some, the regionalist alternative is a way station on the road to a universal system of governance. For others it is a sufficient concept of world order, the idea being that wherever there is a voluntary intermeshing of societies across nation-state lines, it is likely that disputes between the involved nations will be inhibited from escalating to war and that when there is a intraregional conflict, the presence of conflict control mechanisms within a region will reduce incentives for superpower intervention and confrontation.

Indeed, the regionalist idea has been the most popular idealistic concept animating the international activists in the United States policy establishment since the late 1940s when it became obvious that the cold war was probably here to stay for the indefinite future. It was not enough to be simply *against* the expansion of communism. Regional institution building thus became the *positive* rationale for some of the major cold war initiatives of the United States—the Marshall Plan, NATO, and various regional associations in Latin America, the Middle East, and Africa.

The high positive value placed on regional political integration was reflected in the strong support of official Washington

271

for the consolidation of the European Economic Community (EEC), even though the regional common market would mean discrimination against imports from the United States as the EEC moved to achieve free trade among its members. . . .

Since the 1960s, however, the regionalist concept has suffered a decline in the United States policy community. Experience with the European Community and with other regional efforts has shown that substantial political unification is a long way off, even for the Europeans, and that negative attitudes toward outsiders often constitutes a large part of the incentive for regional cooperation, and this may work against concrete economic and security interests of the United States.

For Western Europe, the most optimistic forecasts for the remainder of the twentieth century envision a loose confederacy with minimal supranational functions, primarily for coordinating monetary and trade policies. The enlargement of the starting group of seven countries (France, the Federal Republic of Germany, Italy, Belgium, the Netherlands, Luxembourg, and Portugal) to include Britain, Denmark, Ireland, and Greece has diluted the political-cultural homogeneity of the original continental core and encouraged the intensification of crosspressures. There is as much dissonance today in the EEC as there is harmony; and when harmony is attained by EEC members on international issues, it frequently is engendered by disputes with the United States.

Elsewhere the prospects are even less favorable for regional integration because the preconditions of a common political orientation, a generally homogeneous level of economic development, and basic trust between the members of their cooperative intentions are inadequately developed.

The members of the Association of Southeast Asian Nations (ASEAN), for example, have little in common apart from the fact that they all border the strategically important waterways connecting western and southern Asia with the vast open Pacific and that most of their peoples have a racial physiognomy which is basically similar. The differences in national culture are large. Indonesia is primarily Muslim; Thailand is 95 percent Buddhist; and the Philippines are 75 percent Roman Catholic. The only language in which the leaders of the region can communicate with each other is English—but not because of a common colonial experience. Indonesia was part of the Dutch empire; Singapore and Malaysia were mostly under British control; the Philippines were under Spanish and then U.S. rule; and Thailand has been an independent country for two centuries. The former French colonies of Indochina (Vietnam, Laos, and Cambodia) do not belong to ASEAN, and their professedly communist regimes are alienated from the other governments in the region.

Another regional organization, sometimes pointed to as an embryo from which more elaborate and extensive international integration could develop, is the Organization of American States (OAS). Almost all the countries of the hemisphere belong to this twenty-six–member organization, except Canada, which has only observer status, and Cuba, which has been excluded from formal participation since 1962. In effect, the OAS is the institutional vehicle through which the United States can simultaneously interact with most of the Latin American countries. The hemispheric policies of the United States are often the focus of discussion in the OAS—United States policies of economic assistance and U.S. policies toward communist-oriented governments and movements. Motivated to maximize its influence in the hemisphere, to limit the growing economic competition from the European Community and Japan, and to limit the influence of Cuba and the Soviet Union, the United States usually attempts to gain OAS endorsement of its policies. The Latin members, motivated to restrain the United States from political (and military) intervention and from economically dominating them, are pleased to sustain the U.S. interest in OAS endorsements for this compels the United States to be more accountable to them than might otherwise be the case. Indeed, the main source of solidarity among the Latin Americans is their common resentment at U.S. tendencies to treat the hemisphere as a U.S. sphere of influence.

But even the common resentment of the "colossus to the North" is a flimsy basis for Latin American unity. The differences in domestic regime and ideology are so wide among the countries of Latin America (some are military dictatorships, some capitalist oligarchies, some representative democracies, some socialist autocracies) that their supposed solidarity rarely operates on matters of importance to any of them.

Within Latin America there are special groups of countries whose goals are to coordinate their commercial policies and to reduce barriers to trade among themselves—notable the four-member Central American Common Market (Costa Rica, El Salvador, Guatemala, and Nicaragua) and the five-member Andean Group in South America (Bolivia, Colombia, Ecuador, Peru, and Venezuela). But domestic turmoil and local rivalries are currently too pervasive in these regional subgroups to allow for any substantial progress even toward harmonizing their trading relationships.

In short, where a common regional front has been forged, as among the Third World oil producers or among the Arab antagonists of Israel, the regional coalition as often as not is held together by anti-American sentiments. United States officials in recent years have concluded that they usually can make more headway in obtaining cooperation with U.S. policies if they deal with individual countries rather than with any bloc of countries.

[*Issues in U.S. Foreign Policy*, 1984, pp. 187–190]

ALONE TOGETHER

Mahnaz Z. Ispahani

LAST OCTOBER the members of the Gulf Cooperation Council (GCC) in the Arabian Gulf region embarked on an unprecedented (and little remarked) event—their first major, three-week long combined military exercise, as part of their bid to create a local rapid deployment force. Earlier in 1983, the United States upgraded its diplomatic representation in Mozambique to ambassadorial level and it grew increasingly concerned about the outcome of the civil conflict in Angola, both African states being members of the Organization of Front Line States (OFLS) and both being vital to the successful resolution of the Namibian problem. These developments in different regions are not unrelated. The GCC and the OFLS represent a new phenomenon of micro-regional groups trying to assess, independently and within geographically circumscribed areas, a broad range of regional security concerns.

The past decade has seen the slow formation of a number of such cooperative ventures in developing countries. In 1976, the Association of South East Asian Nations (ASEAN) became a functional regional economic association which also assumed politico-diplomatic postures on local conflicts, such as that in Cambodia, and on a variety of regional security proposals. The same year, the OFLS emerged as a unified group with a common position, in an attempt to find a negotiated settlement for the transfer of power to a black majority government in Rhodesia. In 1981, the GCC was formed as a result of the Iran-Iraq war, to contend with the suddenly dramatic economic and security problems of the Gulf. An important new micro-regional organization is evolving, however inchoately, in South and Central America, in what is known as the Contadora group, which may become a critical player in the resolution of the Central American crisis. And the American invasion of Grenada focused attention on yet another regional group, the Organization of Eastern Caribbean States (OECS), which expressed its concern about the security situation in the area by inviting the Marines to alter the political picture in Grenada.

Four changes in international politics have contributed to the rise of such ventures. First, the inevitable disintegration of the massive and geographically diffuse pacts of the 1950s and 1960s, with their numerous members, obscure goals, and superpower leadership. Second, the growing divergence of perceptions on economic, political, and security issues between the developed and the developing world, which became evident in international fora during the late 1960s. Numerous regional economic associations, commodity cartels, and large political action communities such as the Organization of African Unity (OAU) emerged; these were the precursors of the new microregional organizations. Apart from the enviable success (now rather shaky) of the OPEC cartel, however, few of these movements proved resilient or efficacious. The OAU, for example, established a Defense Commission and laid down proposals for an African Intervention Force but, apart from a brief foray into Chad, little progress has been made. Third, with the departure of the colonial powers, the local states realized the need to fill the new vacuum of security and their ability to do so. Both the GCC and the OFLS emerged with the departure of the British and the Portuguese respectively from their former territories. Fourth, as the United States and the Soviet Union became mutual nuclear hostages, the venue for confrontation shifted from their territory and from the European theater to the Third World: to Asia, to Africa, to Central and South America. The effects of this deflected adversarial relationship have been twofold: countries which fear the impact of an East–West collision (and even of possible collusion) have sought means to keep the superpowers out of their areas and have banded together to do so; and, paradoxically, the "balance of terror" has provided these developing countries with a greater flexibility in their own affairs, as well as with the ability to manipulate the global interests of the superpowers in the service of their own security concerns.

What does the notion of regional security mean to states in such structures? It includes three elements: internal instability, interstate conflict, and superpower involvement. The new security ventures originate in a broader definition of security, one which differs from Western notions. Security in the developed democracies, where there exists greater coherence between government and society, is less a question of internal cohesion, of political and economic stability. It is more externally defined and more outward-looking. For most Third World countries, however, the security problems of the post-colonial era are different. They are the problems of intrinsic insecurity: an insecurity which stems as much, if not more, from domestic as from foreign sources, from economic as from military vulnerability. In these countries, nation and state do not often coincide, and the continued urge to self-determination constantly tests national sovereignty. There is a lack of internal cohesion and of regime legitimacy. Domestic factionalization is a prime cause of insecurity, therefore, because it sets the regime against internal rivals, and because such friction permits exploitation by other countries. It is essential that we understand more precisely the complex security predicament of such polities split sharply along ethnic or tribal or class lines. The legitimacy of ruling groups is perennially subject to dispute; the political pie is small and rarely shared; the economies are fragile and the civilian and military infrastructures weak; there is a heavy debt burden; money is always short, as is food; and there is a high reliance on imports for vital commodities. It is no wonder that states of such weakness have sought strength in numbers, and have attempted to compensate for common ills by a new framework for cooperation.

The creation of both the OFLS and the GCC was a result of regional crises which directly threatened internal stability and provided a potential opening for external intervention and for an escalation in regional insecurity. Both groups have worked towards purposeful integration. They have been attempts to redefine patterns of regional interaction. The GCC would appear to be more resilient, and perhaps slightly more effective, than the OFLS because the threat is more immediate, and the states that confront it have more in common: an offensive threat from Iran in particular remains an everpresent possibility, and the ideological and sectarian issues raised by Khomeini's Iran will continue to pose a direct threat to the Gulf monarchies and sheikhdoms. The GCC, moreover, has the financial resources necessary to purchase some of the requirements for security. Most important, the common character of the allied regimes will assist the GCC to advance in the area of internal security coordination, and in the attempt to mediate regional disputes.

In both the Gulf and southern Africa, however, the seeds of disintegration lie within the internal structures of member states. Regime change or revolution in any one of the GCC states will cause the organization to implode. In southern Africa, a UNITA victory in Angola or the ouster of the Machel government in Mozambique will drastically alter relations among the OFLS states. Currently the members of the OFLS are under severe economic and political strain. In this condition, it is difficult for them to pursue an active, joint policy on Namibia. There is a lack of harmony among the leaders; Zambia and Tanzania face economic crises born of recession, drought, and incompetent domestic economic policy; Mozambique and Angola are suffering not only hunger and economic dislocation but political assault on their regimes; and South Africa's arm-twisting is having greater impact daily. No one state is in any position to help another or to work with it in a common framework.

Finally, it may be said that regional arrangements such as the OFLS and the GCC can be successful in containing low-level regional threats, in suppressing interstate differences, in mediating some local disputes, and in allaying small-scale threats to their internal security. Their strength lies in their ability to diffuse local conflagrations and thus to avoid superpower interference, in their ability to project a strong, collective voice, and in their talent for gaining the support of major powers with compatible interests in the region. But the major threats to their areas—local powers or outside actors—will probably best such arrangements. They have not been able and will not be able to cope with them alone. In the near term, they will remain halfway houses on the road to security cooperation, dependent on the interest and support of outside powers, and absorbed, first and foremost, by their own political and economic instabilities.

["Alone Together: Regional Security Arrangements", 1984, pp. 152–75]

NUCLEAR NON-PROLIFER-ATION

REPORT ON
NON-PROLIFERATION

UNA-USA

THE SPREAD OF NUCLEAR TECHNOLOGY and weapons capability to an increasing number of countries is one of the most urgent problems facing the world today. Although past predictions that many countries would rapidly and openly acquire atomic weapons have failed to materialize, that good news is largely due to the vigilance of a number of countries, notably the US. Now, a dangerous complacency has developed. It is vitally important to recognize that nuclear proliferation still poses a grave threat to the security of the US, its allies, and the world. In making the recommendations in this report, we urge the US Government to recognize the urgency of the risk posed by nuclear proliferation and to assign a higher priority to curbing proliferation. We are aware that this may require choices that conflict with other foreign policy objectives or the interests of the domestic nuclear power industry. However, we are convinced that the dangers posed by proliferation are immediate and real.

In a proliferated world, conflicts that now are limited to conventional arms and local areas might not be containable. The world is riven by dozens of violent confrontations. Sooner or later, somewhere, nuclear weapons will be used. It is already clear that local conflicts between often uncontrollable client states are more likely to lead to confrontation between the superpowers than are any deliberate moves on the central front. With nuclear weapons available to local combatants the danger of escalation is infinitely greater.

Even local conflicts that do not threaten to drag in the superpowers still poison the political atmosphere and pose dangers for US interests. The fragility of the governments of some of the countries now close to acquiring nuclear weapons presents a danger. The world has been extraordinarily lucky thus far in that every country that has developed nuclear weapons has had a stable political system. Some of the countries now pursuing a weapons capability, such as Pakistan, South Africa, and Iraq, cannot be considered stable in the long run.[1]

The success of nonproliferation effforts to date has bought the world some time to do a more comprehensive job. And there are encouraging signs. Most of the world's states are party to the Non-Proliferation Treaty (NPT), (although the non-signatories include the countries most likely to acquire weapons capability) and none has ever withdrawn from the treaty. China is joining the International Atomic Energy Agency (IAEA), and the Soviets are negotiating to open some of their non-military nuclear facilities to IAEA inspection. The export policies of many supplier states, particularly France, have become considerably more cautious in the last several years. As technological and economic problems have clouded the bright promise of nuclear energy, many countries have cut back on their programs. And only one country, India, has indisputably tested nuclear explosives since the Chinese joined the nuclear club 20 years ago.

But this does not mean that the nonproliferation regime can afford to rest on its laurels. While the number of new members overtly joining the nuclear club has certainly been below expectations, the problem for nonproliferation policy now is increasingly one of how to deal with countries in the nuclear twilight zone, in which countries possess sophisticated nuclear technology but have not yet tested a weapon. A prime example is Argentina, whose recent announcement that it has mastered uranium enrichment technology indicates that access to materials directly usable in nuclear weapons continues to spread. Many experts think that a mysterious flash over the Indian Ocean detected by satellites in 1979 may have been a nuclear test, perhaps by South Africa. And Israel may have nuclear explosives partially or completely assembled that it has not tested, because the political costs of an overt test are so high, and because the technology is so well established that it feels no compelling need to test.

The IAEA safeguards system is clearly inadequate to monitor the quantities of separated plutonium that will exist as reprocessing becomes more common. Only small quantities of plutonium (the IAEA estimates 8 kilograms) are needed to make a bomb. Yet it is not even possible to estimate with precision the amount of plutonium contained in the spent fuel that goes into a reprocessing plant, much less to be sure exactly how much plutonium should come out. Nonetheless, the Europeans, Japanese, and Indians have not halted or even slowed their reprocessing programs, and other countries are pursuing the technology.

And there is little progress on other fronts. Despite strong US inducements, there are no indications that Pakistan has slowed its obvious pursuit of a nuclear weapons capability. The nuclear weapons states have pursued their arms race far more vigorously than they have pursued disarmament, contrary to their pledge under Article VI of the NPT.

In short, the world has been lucky to date. We cannot expect that luck to hold indefinitely. And no one country, even the US, has the power to hold back proliferation indefinitely. Moreover, while the framework of US laws dealing with proliferation is extensive, it contains loopholes that often do violence to the spirit of the legislation. Other nuclear supplier countries, furthermore, are not subject to the dictates of American export policy, and nuclear consumers are rapidly acquiring the capability to satisfy their own needs.

THE INTERNATIONAL ATOMIC ENERGY AGENCY

The IAEA has become the world's instrument for monitoring the peaceful uses of nuclear material. Nearly every non-weapons country that has significant nuclear activities has accepted IAEA safeguards on at least some of its nuclear facilities. The sole, but valuable, function of these safeguards is to raise the probability that diversion of a significant quantity of nuclear material from its specified peaceful purpose will be detected. The goals are to deter potential diverters by making it likely that they would be caught, and to permit countries to feel some assurance that their neighbors' safeguarded facilities are not being used to produce bombs. The Agency can do no more than to sound an alarm by notifying its Board of Governors if it detects anything suspicious. Nor can it compel countries to accept safeguards.

Nevertheless, the IAEA's limited mandate in safeguarding declared nuclear material in most of the world's peaceful nuclear activities is indispensable. If there were no IAEA, the alternatives would be either 1) a return to bilateral safeguards administered by supplier states as a condition of export, which might soon disappear as suppliers vied to make their exports more attractive, or 2) no safeguards at all, in which case states would have no assurance that any of their neighbors' activities were benign. The nonproliferation system depends on credible safeguards arrangements to assure the world that the vast majority of ostensibly peaceful nuclear activities are in fact peaceful, and to make exceptions conspicuous by contrast.

Unfortunately, the credibility of IAEA safeguards is low. Former American inspectors have testified to Congress and the Nuclear Regulatory Commission that safeguards as now conducted do not provide a high probability of detection of diversion. Some reports indicate that the IAEA carries out only half of its authorized inspections.

Part of the problem is the attitude of many IAEA member countries toward safeguards. Except for the nuclear supplier countries, most IAEA members are far more interested in the Agency's mandate to provide technical assistance for peaceful nuclear programs. Indeed, only one-third of the Agency's budget goes to safeguards. Safeguards are seen as an intrusive and irritating imposition required only of non-weapons states. The fact that the US, Britain, and France have opened their peaceful facilities to IAEA inspections and that the Soviets are negotiating to do so is an extremely important demonstration of weapons-state participation. Thus, many countries provide required reports to the Agency on their nuclear activities late and incomplete. Many countries in the 112-member Agency have no nuclear activity at all, but tend to vote with their fellow Group of 77 members on the Board of Governors and in the General Conference.

There are serious problems with inspections procedures. The number of inspectors (about 150) is pitifully small to inspect the more than 800 locations at which IAEA safeguards are applied. The geographical distribution requirements mean that many inspectors are chosen more for their place of origin than for their qualifications, and sometimes do not have the necessary technical training and ability. IAEA inspectors have to apply for visas and cannot make unannounced inspections, which may give countries time to hide evidence of efforts to divert nuclear material. And countries are free to reject any inspector on any grounds which led to the now-famous example of Iraq's Osirak reactor, inspected for a long period only by Soviet-bloc inspectors.

It may be that even with these handicaps, the IAEA safeguards are reasonably likely to detect diversions. The problem remains that they may not be perceived to be adequate. Since the ability of safeguards to inhibit proliferation depends largely on perceptions, lack of credibility is unacceptable.

There are several steps the IAEA can take to boost both the acceptability and the credibility of its safeguards. Sophisticated technical means of observation that do not require such frequent inspections have been developed and tested in a pilot program under the name Operation RECOVER (Remote Continual Verification). However, the technology is extremely expensive, and the program has not been widely implemented.

Surprise inspections might be more acceptable to countries if they were conducted by inspectors from small nations that were truly not aligned. A role model here is the Fijian contingent in UN peacekeeping missions. The Fijians see these contingents, whose neutrality is not suspect, as their contribution to world peace. The Swedes, who are both neutral and technically advanced, would be an appropriate example.

To resolve the credibility problem created by the right of countries to reject any inspector, IAEA inspectors might be sent in 2-person teams. At least one member of each team would be a national of a neutral country. Such an inspector would not be subject to rejection by any country.

The NPT Regime. In order to maintain the legitimacy and acceptability of the Non-Proliferation Treaty, the US must take steps to live up to its obligations to pursue disarmament and to facilitate the transfer of peaceful nuclear technology to NPT parties. By far the most important step would be to conclude a comprehensive test ban (CTB) treaty, which would restrain both horizontal and vertical proliferation. Other approaches to complement a CTB may be useful.

Nuclear-Weapons-Free Zones (NWFZs). Nuclear-weapons-free zones can provide an effective and non-discriminatory way for a region to reduce the risk of a regional arms race. At present, there are international treaties that declare Latin America, Antarctica, Outer space, and the seabed to be NWFZs. The Latin American treaty has been adhered to by most, though not all, countries in the region, and the terms of that treaty provide a useful example for other inhabited regions to follow.

Multilateral Fuel Cycle Centers. Multilateral facilities could overcome the inequities inherent in the existing regime that treats the facilities of different nations differently. By centralizing nuclear material, they could make safeguarding and physical protection of that material easier. A spent fuel facility would address an urgent problem facing many countries. In view of China's recent announcement that it might store other countries' spent fuel for a fee, it is urgent to move quickly to ensure that spent fuel facilities are put under safeguards. Reprocessing, enrichment, or plutonium centers, on the other hand, would spread sensitive technology while being unlikely to attract the participation of countries that pose the greatest proliferation risk.

[*Report on Non-Proliferation*, 1984, pp. 1–5]

IV

ESSENTIAL SERVICES AND MUTUAL DEPENDENCIES

IV. ESSENTIAL SERVICES AND MUTUAL DEPENDENCIES

THE BULK OF HUMAN INTERACTION AT THE "PEOPLE LEVEL" has little to do with guns, tanks, missiles and warships. The buzzword for the tightening network of ties between nations is "interdependence." But underneath that self-evident reality lies a profound question for the economic and technological "haves": how willing are they to cooperate with the world's majority of "have-nots" in ways that entail short-term costs in exchange for longer-range benefits? Will they remain fearful of being "taken," confident that their strength will continue to bring the economic security they seek?

Thomas W. Wilson, Jr. in his overview notes that international life since World War II has featured a steady expansion of international organizations, agreements and regulations that together have revised significantly the substance of world politics. Harlan Cleveland spells out the needful agenda for action at the greater-than-national level in a pluralistic world.

The concept of "functional cooperation" to international organization rather than the traditional constitutional approach was defined four decades ago by David Mitrany. This approach seeks, by linking peace to a specific activity, to break away from traditional links between authority and state territory (or, in the language of contemporary social science, to focus on "low politics" intead of "high politics"). The UNA-USA factual briefs report ways in which, despite wars and other global ills, the scourge of smallpox has been eradicated, radio frequencies allocated, mail delivered around the world, and international rescue vessels comfortingly located beneath Atlantic jet routes. Sections IVA and B thus set the stage.

In section IVC a Trilateral Commission report, reflecting US, European and Japanese expertise, explores the basic questions of global economic policy. Veteran economic analyst William Diebold, Jr. addresses the paradoxes of economic interdependence: people are increasingly uncomfortable with the technological pressures that increase dependencies, but nevertheless resist choosing between world-wide economic integration, and narrow nationalism that would reduce technology's productive advantages.

UN Secretary General Perez de Cuellar paints a mixed picture of the extent to which the UN has fulfilled its charge to promote social progress and better living standards. He feels it has successfully identified issues of importance, provided direct assistance, and helped to negotiate constructive agreements in the field of development. In an intriguing minority view, Prof. Kenneth N. Waltz contends that the very term "interdependence" obscures the fact that not all states are playing the same game since, while smaller states are interdependent by necessity, the superpowers can and do insulate themselves when they deem it expedient.

A series of experts then briefly explores several "sectoral" issue areas. On trade, Richard E. Feinberg of the Overseas Development Council observes that most Third World leaders, whether liberal or Marxist, are positively eager to take part in a world economy of integrated financial markets, multinational corporations, and cross-border trade flows, and look to the world economy for their own development in the absence of any realistic alternative. On the thorny monetary front, the Trilateral Commission argues that within a broad international framework there is wide scope for different exchange rate agreements by individual countries, given agreement among the relatively few dominant ones.

On energy, Edward A. Frieman, executive vice-president of Science Applications Inc., notes significant structural changes stemming from increases in energy efficiency by industrial users, as well as oil production increases among non-OPEC countries. In the field of communication, Prof. Seyom Brown sees dramatic advances in transportation and communications making of the world one community, yet still lacking adequate cooperative arrangements.

In the crucial food sector, the UN notes that estimates of world malnutrition range from 400 to 600 million in the developing countries, while average caloric intake in industrialized countries is around thirty three percent more than is healthful. The director of the UN Food and Agricultural Organization sees some progress in the search for a food security system, alongside growing difficulty, especially in Africa, to produce enough food for the growing population.

WORLD SECURITY AND THE GLOBAL AGENDA

Thomas W. Wilson, Jr.

The Gathering of Global Issues

PROBLEMS BEYOND THE REACH OF NATIONAL GOV-
ERNMENTS are, of course, not new. The International Postal
Union was established in the last century for the simple reason
that an internationally agreed system was needed to assure that
mail sent from one country would be delivered in another—just
as common rules were needed for maritime navigation to reduce
the likelihood of collisions at sea. Other international agreements and institutions came into being as needs arose to cope
with transnational problems: allocation of radio frequencies,
communicable disease control, weather reporting, and satellite
communication systems are familiar examples.

Indeed, the steady expansion of international organization
and agreements and regulations for dealing with a lengthening
list of transnational problems has been a distinguishing feature
of international life since the end of World War II. The whole
system of United Nations agencies stands in evidence—as does a
robust growth in nongovernmental organizations and the inau-
guration of major scientific research projects like the International Geophysical Year.

Some observers of this steady growth of international activities came to believe that a system of world governance eventually
must emerge from the ever growing practical need for technical
management of functional problems. In this view, such technical
arrangements would come to dominate political relations.

Functional cooperation, however, has been treated by governments of the traditional major powers as a minor appendage to the main body of international political relations, located somewhere on the outer periphery of day-to-day diplomacy. For them, the perceived mainstream of interstate relations remained the traditional political-military questions, plus the pursuit of other national interests, mainly economic, as these interests were defined—usually in competitive terms—in national capitals. Technical cooperation, in practice, does not seem to dampen political conflict; indeed, cooperative technical programs and projects can turn out to be among the first casualties of political crises, as we have just seen in the wake of the Soviet invasion of Afghanistan.

But what happened precisely in the 1970s is that the new agenda of global issues was gathered in from the fringes of diplomacy and injected into the mainstream of world politics. Many a matter once thought to be reserved for "domestic" attention was *internationalized*, and many a question once labeled "technical" was politicized within the UN system. In that process, the substance of day-to-day international politics was revised decisively. Issues bearing on the human condition and the state of the planet can no longer be relegated to the realm of functional problems, nor delegated to experts. And diplomacy will never be the same again.

Yet there should be no surprise in any of this. For these global issues are the direct political fall-out of the most conspicuous trends and events of contemporary times; indeed, they collectively describe a large part of the present global predicament.

On the one hand, the integrity of natural systems suddenly is an issue because expanded economic activity by a swollen population has increased exponentially the total human impact on global systems, and raised state-of-the-planet problems that are beyond the realm of national power or influence.

At the same time, the human condition has intruded upon international affairs because the collapse of the European system of empire brought a three-fold increase of accredited members— and a new majority—into the world political arena. The new majority is committed to sustained economic growth to escape the grip of pervasive poverty. And one thing all the new members can agree upon is that the international economic system, in which they are caught up inextricably, was not designed with their needs in mind and does not now function equitably from their point of view.

Small wonder, then, that modernization issues have been moved from the sidelines to center stage at the United Nations, and that a "North–South dialogue" has been opened on demands for the creation of an international economic order better designed for sustainable growth in an interdependent world. The wonder is that this has received such low political priority from governments in the industrialized world.

It is especially surprising because there is no chance whatever that the issues on the new global agenda will go away or diminish from benign neglect. The internal dynamics of the trends that brought some of these issues to the surface in the 1970s guarantee that things will get worse before they get better—hunger, unemployment, and soil erosion are examples—even if vigorous measures are taken now to reverse the trends. And from a political point of view, it is scarcely thinkable that the new majority in the world forum will lose its consuming interest in modernization in the immediate or mid-term future.

Of course, there is no way to force the United States or any other government to pay serious attention to the new agenda. We and other industrialized nations could keep our eyes fixed on the traditional agenda and adopt what is known in the trade as a "damage limiting posture" when forced into debate or negotiation on the new class of issues. This is roughly what has been happening. And this is to say that the world is becoming hungrier, dirtier, more crowded, more deprived, more incapacitated, more quarrelsome, and more prone to conflict from year to year.

["World Security and the Global Agenda," 1981, pp. 303–06]

GOVERNING A PLURALISTIC WORLD

Harlan Cleveland

IT HAS BEEN EASIER TO REACH INTERNATIONAL AGREEMENTS in the relatively "non-political" arenas where the U.N.'s specialized agencies do their work. Progress in one field of endeavor need not depend on simultaneous progress in the others. Yet the compelling reason for the creation of each specialized international agency—each adding another fragment to the pluralistic pattern—has been the advance of science and technology. Whenever scientists achieved a breakthrough in what can be done by man for man, it suddenly seemed outrageous not to be using for human purposes the new power that new knowledge brought in its train.

Before we knew that mosquitoes carried malaria, and before we knew how to murder mosquitoes with DDT, nobody thought about eradicating malaria from the face of the earth, because it could not be done. Now that we know it can be done, we keep trying to do it. We keep trying to do it even though DDT turned out to bring with it new dangers, even though the mosquitoes proved more resistant to our attempts to poison them than the scientists thought when they proudly swept every anopheles from the island of Sardinia just after World War II.

Before there was radio, we did not need to have a large standing international conference to divide up the frequency spectrum; now, the International Telecommunications Union's World Administrative Radio Conference is just that. Before there were airplanes flying across frontiers and oceans, we did not need an International Civil Aviation Organization. Today we have international agreements on aerial navigation because the alternative would be mayhem compounded.

Before we could take synoptic pictures of the world's

weather and sample from satellites the wind and temperature and pollution and air-sea interactions all around the globe (instead of operating from the earth's surface with only a tenth of the necessary coverage), there was no basis for complex human systems that tried to deal with the enormous sweep of the real atmosphere in the real sky. But these new technologies, plus the fast computer to make possible large-scale modeling and rapid combination of global data—fast enough to be analyzed before the weather itself has come and gone—have made a World Weather Watch suddenly feasible. From a standing start in the early 1960s it was only a decade before such a system was a working reality. We are now accustomed to watching the weather swirl across continents on the nightly televised satellite photographs.

Thus, each new scientific discovery, each technological innovation, seems to require the invention of new international arrangements to contain, channel and control it. A precept of American business is that necessity is the mother of invention. But in the business of international institution-building, the reverse is true as well: Invention is the mother of necessity.

Sometimes, this technological imperative is in curious contrast to the alarums and excursions of political rivalry among nations. Ever since the Bolshevik Revolution, the United States and the Soviet Union have been working together in the hunting of seals in the Bering Sea, simply because it makes sense to do so, Cold War or no. Ever since the early 1930s, the Turks and the Russians have maintained an annual joint cattle market, even while Stalin was claiming the very areas of Turkey where the cattle are raised and sold. Perhaps the clearest case of the technological imperative is the extraordinary cooperation among the scientists who explore the frozen continent of Antarctica.

Aristotle observed that physicians learn what health is by studying bodies from which health is absent. The observation is extendable to the conditions that may promote a world order. Since the existing architecture of world order has been built by analogy with the modern nation-state, perhaps the clue to building a New International Order that works is to make sure we know why the several national orders are falling down on the job of governance.

National Governments beyond their Depth

The evidence is now overwhelming that every national government is beyond its depth. This is certainly true of the industrial democracies, baffled by inflation, unemployment, pollution, insecurity and youthful crime. It is even more true of the Soviet system, unable to feed its people and afraid to let them escape. It is true of the "China model," whose new leaders now speak openly about "ten lost years" of Cultural Revolution and political infighting. It is true in most developing nations, unable to meet basic human needs or avoid the worst mistakes of the early Industrial Revolution.

Political leaders keep up a brave front, but their incapacity for decision-making becomes more and more visible. Central economic planning, popularized around the world partly by industrial democracies that do not practice it themselves, is nearly everywhere in disarray. Transnational companies, weathering the assaults of some sovereignties but welcomed by others, have adapted their outlook, policies and practices to life in an interdependent world far better than governments have. A "new proletariat" streams across international frontiers in enormous numbers. Ethnic and religious rivalries and subnational separatists threaten the integrity of long-established nations. South Africa, Nigeria, Ethiopia, Jordan, Lebanon, the United Kingdom and Canada are only the most current examples.

Part of the trouble is that the traditional institutions of national sovereignty are badly designed for the kind of problems they now face. In the real world, the agenda for action consists mostly of interdisciplinary, interdepartmental and interprofessional problems. Yet the traditional institutions of national sovereignty are not positioned accordingly. They tend to be bounded by artificial frontiers that survive from the history of rational thought (physics, biology, economics, anthropology), from the history of government activity in simpler times (mining, merchant marine, forestry, the regulation of commerce), and from the historic professions (law, medicine, engineering).

In direct consequence, national government agencies in the main still are not organized to handle problems that "cut across" disciplines, specialties and bureaucracies, to heighten awareness of the interconnectedness of things, and to encourage integrative training, staff work and decision making. Instead, every government is basically a collection of vertical ministries, in which recommendations travel "up" and orders travel "down." But everyone (including the inhabitants of these paper pyramids) knows that complex decisions that work are mostly the product of lateral negotiation—what we call committee work and the Japanese call consensus and the Communists call collective leadership.

A striking example of the resulting discontinuities has been evident in the U.S. effort to get hold of its energy problem. Before 1973, no part of the U.S. Government (and no international organization, either) was responsible for worrying about energy. The responsibilities for "oil" and "gas" and "coal" were scattered around as parts of the unstudied subject called "energy," which includes sunshine, cloud formations, ocean movements, industrial technology, trade, monetary stability, home insulation, housing patterns, transportation, the mobility of populations and much more. We obscured the fact that, in the end, the realm of "energy" is politics and the reach of "energy" is global.

Before 1973, everyone knew what the "policy" was: to help make abundant supplies of energy available at the cheapest prices in order to expand economic growth (for any purpose) and raise the productivity of labor. For this, the institutional arrangements were entirely adequate. But they were hopelessly unequipped to deal with, or even to think clearly about, the crisis that emerged after 1973.

From this crisis dawned a consciousness that energy was now going to be expensive, that very large international flows of investment capital would be thereby reversed, that the U.S. and its allies were dangerously dependent on Arab oil, that oil might be a dwindling asset in a generation, that exploiting coal and nuclear fission as the main short-term alternatives to oil raised scary environmental and security problems, that we were wasting energy and not developing fast enough the longer-term alternatives we would soon require. We have realized, all too gradually, that we could not solve any of these puzzles without a wholly new dimension in worldwide cooperation, including the invention, from scratch, of new international institutions.

THE NATIONAL ORDERS ARE LEAKING

If the earlier successes of nation-states resulted from their capacity to assemble power in the hands of the few, their current incapacity to govern stems from the inability of the few to deal with the expectations of the many, who increasingly will take charge of their own futures.

Power is, in fact, leaking out of the national orders in three directions at once. First, the vessel of national government leaks from the bottom, as the many get enough education to insist on participation in decisions affecting their newly understood rights and their dimly understood destinies. The advocacy of openness, student protests, consumer lobbies, public-interest law firms, the remarkable role of Common Cause, the California tax revolt, and the tendency of local communities to use planning and zoning authority to mold their futures—the evidence is piling up that, in the United States at least, the long history of accretion of power to Washington is beginning to be reversed.

Power leaks from the sides, too. Nongovernmental enterprise is typically faster on its feet, less constrained by national jurisdiction, and longer-range in its planning than are government agencies. This is why transnational business has managed to internalize so much of international commerce. (More than one-fifth of "international trade" are now the internal transactions of international companies.) This is why a growing range of functions, even those fully funded by government, are farmed out to nongovernment organizations—advanced research and development, legal services to the poor, educational and cultural exchanges with Asia, and the Post Office are only a few of many U.S. examples. Some of the power has even leaked out to universities, research institutes, think tanks and policy analysis groups, which each year provide a growing proportion of the strategic thinking and long-range planning used by the government. This trend is far advanced in the United States, but it has also been in evidence in Europe and Japan.

Because nongovernmental people are not "responsible," they are sometimes better able than government people (a) to work ahead of time on problems that are important but not yet urgent enough to command political attention; (b) to shake loose from conceptual confines and mix up disciplinary methodologies; (c) to think hard, write adventurously and speak freely about alternative futures and what they imply for public policy today; (d) to generate discussion among people in contending groups, different professional fields and separate sectors of society who might not otherwise be talking to each other, and (e) to organize "dialogue" across national frontiers on issues not yet ripe for official "negotiation."

Thirdly, national government leaks from the top. There is now a rapidly growing list of functions that only credibly international institutions can perform.

REQUIREMENTS FOR INTERNATIONAL COOPERATION

Since the creative burst of institution building after World War II, the requirement for international cooperation has been speeding up—while the pace of social invention has been slowing down. Lists of "naturally international" functions have been spread on the record in the North-South dialogue—timidly by the North, polemically by the South, and analytically by the RIO Report and parallel attempts to project the reshaping of international order. For our present purpose it will be enough to present them as topic sentences.

The biosphere

Systems are required to make sure that nations and their citizens, in the exercise of their sovereignties, do not transgress the ecological bounds of the biosphere we must all inhabit together. The needed systems are not yet in place, but the requirements are clear enough. The world community needs:

- a system that negotiates and monitors agreed standards of air and water quality and reviews national actions that pollute beyond national frontiers.
- a system that keeps watch on the damage and potential damage from human processes and blows the whistle on those that may affect people beyond national frontiers.
- a system that promotes exploration for, and keeps a world inventory of, nonrenewable resources that may be

needed by people outside the nations where the resources happen to be found.

- a system that keeps track of world production of food and fibers; seeks international agreement to limit overcropping, overgrazing, overcutting and overfishing; and provides for the exchange of timely information on national harvests and food requirements.

For all these functions, it will be necessary sooner or later to create an international system or systems for the use and protection of resource data generated by the constantly improving sensors operating from space vehicles.

Basic human needs

The global fairness revolution and the drive for universal human rights will bring into being a system for establishing and maintaining international standards for individual entitlement to food, health, education, employment and other agreed components of "basic human needs"; and for relating international economic cooperation, including aid, to progress toward these standards. Along with an internationally certified "poverty floor" may come a demand for international review and monitoring of national decisions about growth, affluence and waste in the more developed countries. Neither a "poverty floor" nor an "affluence ceiling" may be just around the corner. But concern with the distribution of wealth and income is unlikely to stop at any national frontiers, even those of the very rich.

The interdependent political economy

There is a growing requirement for international institutions to facilitate bargaining among nation-states on issues that are usually called "international economics" but reach deep into the "domestic" economic, social and financial policy—and therefore into the politics—of every nation. The most obvious systems waiting to be born are those needed:

- to hold, finance and manage buffer stocks of major world commodities, in order to assure continuity of supply and stability of prices for producers and consumers in relation to long-term market forces.

- to assure access by developing countries to markets in the industrial countries.
- to help manage constructive shifts in industrial geography and help nations plan investment in their own industries in the light of investment policies of other nations.
- to push agricultural productivity in the developing nations and meanwhile to make sure there is enough food for all through a world food reserve.
- to promote cooperation between oil producers and consumers, to help reduce energy waste in the industrial nations, to encourage international research and development of alternative energy sources, and to assist developing countries in devising sound energy strategies as a crucial part of their development planning.
- to resolve differences among transnational enterprises, host countries and home countries over such issues as taxation, employment, competitive practices and contributions to meeting basic human needs.
- to provide for effective international consultation on actions by international monetary authorities which substantially affect the money supply, and create international money in a manner and at a rate that is compatible with economic growth at reasonable rates of inflation—the definition of what is reasonable being itself the product of an international process.
- to regulate conflict, promote research, develop protein, conserve fisheries, and explore, exploit and share the revenues from the oceans, the continental margin and the deep seabed.
- to limit conflict by international conciliation and mediation, the development of international peacekeeping forces and (through arms control) the institutionalization of military uncertainty at the lowest possible cost.

["Governing A Pluralistic World," 1981, pp. 10–17]

A.

THE THEORY OF FUNCTIONALISM

A WORKING PEACE SYSTEM

David Mitrany

Introduction

WHEN THIS SHORT STUDY was first published in the summer of 1943 there was great confidence in the unity which had grown up during the war, and students of international organization were thinking mainly of how to consolidate that unity and expand it. Many of them felt that a definite constitutional framework was needed, within which the world society would grow of itself, and they naturally looked upon the ideas of this pamphlet as politically inadequate; others felt with the writer that a world society was more likely to grow through doing things together in workshop and marketplace than by signing pacts in chancelleries. Since then we have moved fast but not well. The structure of the United Nations has been erected in all its grandeur, but at the same time the practical unity of the war period threatens to fall to pieces. This uncertain situation has thrown us back again upon fundamentals. It seems best, therefore, in re-issuing this small study to leave the original argument as it stood, and in this new introduction to consider some of the ideas which have come up in the meantime.

For to prefer a functional to a constitutional approach is not to be timid, much less to be haphazard. The argument has grown out of a definite view of the historical problem of our time, the chief trait of which is the baffling division between the peoples of the world. All the great religions, as well as the lay creed of humanism, have preached world unity, in the sense of a common humanity, yet after centuries of such teaching we find ourselves with little sense of such unity left in our outlook and actions. That is all the more strange since in its material life the world has moved far toward a common unity. When the sense of unity was still alive, in the Middle Ages, social life was a mosaic of small and largely self-sufficient local units; now social life has a highly integrated organic unity, but politically our outlook is bound to a mosaic of separate national units. Much depends on our understanding of this paradox now that we stand at a historical turning point. How has it come about, what does it signify in terms of world politics? Very broadly, it was bequeathed us by the dynamic nineteenth century, which internationally moved on two separate and opposite lines. Politically it saw the rise of national states, a trend which was solemnly recognized when in 1919 the Paris conference took "national self-determination" as its guiding principle and which in the Middle East, the Far East, and possibly in Africa is yet far from spent. With a new social era before us we find national states a hindrance, but historically the trend was sound in itself. It had its roots in the same currents—the Renaissance, humanism, and anti-authoritarianism—which inculcated respect for the individual personality and so, by a natural extension, also for the group or national personality. And as the first led politically to the enfranchisement of the individual, the person becoming a citizen, in the wider society the second led to the enfranchisement of national groups through states of their own. Let us call that broadly the cultural side of Western civilization. But side by side with it the same period produced a rapid and growing division of labor. The economic self-sufficiency of the individual and of the local group was broken up by the development of communications, of new sources of power, of new materials, the opening up of new lands, and the rise of mass production—and these factors have bound peoples increasingly together. That is the material side of Western civilization, and national and world trends were the same.

To reconcile these two trends is the task which history is setting us. Both are legitimate; both must be satisfied. To ignore the deep-rooted loyalties of nationality in the search for material efficiency, or to deny the swelling cry for social betterment for the sake of a fictitious independence, is to perpetuate the unrest which is the spring of perennial conflict. It is in the light of this task—of how to achieve unity in diversity (and in the domestic sphere, too, the problem is how to have planning without breaking too many individual liberties)—that we must look at the various ideas for international organization. These have followed in the main three lines of thought: (1) An association of nations, like the League, which would leave the identity and policy of states almost untouched; though comprehensive, it would be a loose association merely suggesting the need for a measure of material integration. (2) A federal system, favored because it is thought it would provide the cohesion lacking in a league; but this would be so only within the limits of some new continental or regional group and so would tend to divide the world again into a number of potentially competing units. (3) The functional approach, which seeks, by linking authority to a specific activity, to break away from the traditional link between authority and a definite territory (perpetuated by either an association or a federation of nations). This approach resolves the dilemma of creating either too loose or too narrow an international organization by building up authorities which would be comprehensive and solid, in selected fields of common life.

Practical aspects of functional organization are discussed in the body of the pamphlet. The point that matters is that whatever the form and the manner, international organization must do the same things which national governments do in modern society, only with a difference in scale. It must do those things which cannot be done well, or without friction, except on an international scale. That would mean something very different from the scope of the League of Nations. It was in keeping with our former outlook that international law in general and the Covenant in particular were concerned primarily with defining the formal relationship of states, in a negative sense, and only vaguely with initiating positive common activities. The economic, financial, and other sections of the League were mere secretariats, and so in fact is the ILO. The functional bodies contemplated here would be executive agencies with autonomous tasks and powers; they would not merely discuss but would do things for the community, and that would be in keeping with the needs of the time. The trend at present is to enlarge and co-ordinate the social scope of authority, but national planning cannot work in harness with laissez-faire in the international field. The Charter of the United Nations has at least come near to recognizing the true nature of the problem. It has entrusted to the Security Council a first definite function of common government, that of law and order; while the Economic and Social Council, though not endowed with equally definite powers, does express by its mere existence a sense that the problem of our time is not how to keep the nations peacefully apart but how to bring them actively together.

This new approach toward the goal of international collaboration is free from dogma and avoids the cramping limitations of a more nicely designed but hard-and-fast system. It is an attempt, after looking squarely at the lessons of history, to offer a practical line of action that might overcome the deep-seated division between the needs of material unity and stubborn national loyalties—a division which explains why appeals to world unity have so far remained barren and why the task is essentially one of practical statesmanship. The two obvious tests for any step toward an international order are, first, the means by which we bring about the change, and, and, second, the fitness of the change for the communal needs of the time. Historically two ways have been known for adapting the range of government to changing needs and aspirations—conquest and consent. The Nazi "New Order" and the Japanese "Co-Prosperity sphere" were attempts of the first kind. For us the question is how far the peoples are ripe for consent, and the answer must largely determine our line of action. If the new international experiment is to be effective it must have real tasks of government entrusted to it. But at the same time it must in its makeup accept the present reality of a world that is divided into many national states. The most one could hope for during the period of transition is that national governments should act as willing agencies of the incipient international authority; for even if it were possible to deed formal authority in full to an international body, the elements which go to the making of power—raw materials and manpower, industrial potential and strategic positions—would in the nature of things, until national boundaries and authorities are done away with altogether, still remain in the grasp of particular national groups. Nothing could be more barren and confusing, therefore, than the habit of mind which, in the words of Dr. Reinhold Niebuhr, "thinks that we lack an international government only because no one has conceived a proper blueprint of it. Therefore they produce such blueprints in great profusion. These pure constitutionalists have a touching faith in the power of a formula over the raw stuff of history."

The ultimate ideal is simple and universal. But the prospect of the first steps toward it depends not a little on whether we struggle for a formal or constitutional idea—in regard to which there are many creeds—or work for a practical achievement toward which we might strive together. Some of the issues of constitutional principle and structure which have been discussed of late show how serious can be the difference if we choose one way or the other. There is no better illustration of this than the frequent plea for a "surrender of sovereignty," and no issue has strayed farther afield from practical needs and possibilities. Sovereignty is a legal concept, a status; it cannot be surrendered unless the units which form the political community, whether individuals or groups, abdicate their political rights. Individuals have not been asked by the national state to surrender their rights as citizens, except in totalitarian dictatorships; it has never been asked of the constituent members of a federation, which would not have come into being if that had been the price. The historical process has not moved that way at all. Abrupt changes in sovereignty have occurred, but by conquest or revolution, whereas the normal way has been a gradual transfer of sovereignty according to social needs and political developments. The proof of this is that the process has moved in both directions. British colonies acquired by conquest were gradually emancipated, parts of sovereignty being *pari passu* transferred to them. Internally too, sovereignty has usually been transferred by gradual steps from autocratic kings to popular parliaments, and administrative authority from lords and estates to elected local bodies. In all this the emphasis was on the political emancipation. But under the social pressures of our time the trend is now moving the opposite way, and authority is increasingly transferred from local bodies to central executives. Be that as it may, if a new world authority is to come into being by consent and not by conquest, its status will depend on how far the transfer of sovereignty from national groups is both willing and continuous.

To such willing transfers of sovereignty—or abridgment of national sovereignty—there is no limit except that set by our political maturity. But there is an effective minimum, which must include some essential functions now performed by national states. Security is first among them. There can be no real transfer of sovereignty until defense is entrusted to a common authority, because national means of defense are also means of offense and also of possible resistance to that common authority. The view that it is the function of the military arm to be the common keeper of law and order, and to that end must be under the control of a central authority, has now found a first international expression in the Security Council, and still more in the American proposals for the international control of atomic energy. Beyond this, many other tasks and activities could or should be made matters of common concern, and international society will grow precisely in the measure in which we do so join together. An editorial in *Nature* (December 1943) suggested that "functional co-operation may be a means of persuading the Powers ultimately to make the wide sacrifices in national sovereignty which the preservation of peace will demand." That is historically true and politically sound. In any normal evolution the change has been gradual—a gradual transfer of sovereignty from the ruler to the people, the people in their turn gradually entrusting its exercise to a central authority. Therefore the democratic tests have all along been expressed in a selection of policy and of ultimate control of its execution, and not in any grandiose juridical gesture. Sovereignty cannot in fact be transferred effectively through a formula, only through a function. By entrusting an authority with a certain task, carrying with it command over the requisite powers and means, a slice of sovereignty is transferred from the old authority to the new; and the accumulation of such partial transfers in time brings about a translation of the true seat of authority. If that has been the considered process in the domestic sphere, is it not still more relevant in the international sphere, where even the elements of unity have to be built up laboriously by this very process of patient change? It would indeed be sounder and wiser to speak not of the surrender but of a sharing of sovereignty. When ten or twenty national authorities, each of whom had performed a certain task for itself, can be induced to perform that task jointly, they will to that end quite naturally pool their sovereign authority insofar as the good performance of the task demands it.

This may seem a limping way toward world community. Yet eagerness for a finished constitution may actually hold up progress. It is too often overlooked that written constitutions have in the main served as a check to authority; and federal constitutions, while they serve to bind, also serve to divide. A federal system is by its nature both rigid and limiting. It arranges a few things to be done in common, but limits them strictly and also lays down the many things which must remain separate. The Indian experiment may break down on this very issue of power at the center. If that has been so in national federal states, the definition of spheres inevitably will be still more rigid at any first attempt to link up a number of states with differing political and social systems. But this is an age of potent social change. Who can foretell what the needs of social life will be a generation hence? Is it wise to open up an international era with a rigid division of tasks and authority? In the United States the effect of such constitutional division was so obstinate that in spite of a frantic crisis and the prestige of President Roosevelt the remedies of the New Deal could be set going only through political devices which bypassed the Constitution. The New Deal was a functional evolution all along the line, without any change in texts or forms, but the total effect has been to transform a loosely federal system into a highly centralized national government. The truth is that the federal idea goes in one sense too far and in another sense not far enough. Politically it is more than we can hope to obtain at present on a world scale; economically and socially it offers less than what is needed for a unified, peaceful development.

In America the functional method of change was followed not because it was easy, but because the constitutional method was well-nigh impracticable. Students of the problem realize how difficult it is to change written constitutions; they often suggested, therefore, that an international pact should provide for its periodical revision or for its amendment by a limited vote. That was the view which an American group circulated at the time of the United Nations Assembly in the spring of 1946. It proposed that the Assembly should be able to pass amendments by a two-thirds majority, the vote being weighted, and that these amendments should take effect when ratified by a majority of members of the United Nations. It is strange that such neat schemes should be put forward by American students who must know what a hard and ungrateful task it is to try to amend the Constitution in their own united country. It rarely succeeds, but it often brings up again issues and feelings which had lain dormant and so, if anthing, hardens the existing political division. Clearly it would be much more difficult in the case of an international constitution. The experience of the League and of the ILO has been that even when amendments are accepted by the international bodies they are rarely ratified by the governments concerned, not merely because they are sovereign states but because the very purpose of a formal constitution is as much to prevent change as it was to bring it about originally. Too many changes would alter the balance of power in a federal system, as all new functions allotted to the central authority would have a cumulative effect on its power; under a functional system that power would be distributed and dispersed. But this apart, most of the tasks before us are not formal issues, such as the rights of man, but practical tasks in the nature of social services. They need practical co-operation rather than formal submission to the will of a majority. When it is a matter of willing and active participation, formal amendment of established compacts is not the best way to make progress. . . .

Certain it is that power cannot be restrained except within an effective world system; and to be effective, indeed to come about at all, such a system will have to be built up not on tenets of formal equality but on such as would satisfy the one crucial question: How can we make this organization work and last? The transition from national to international control of power is bound to be stubborn. It is not an unprincipled or an unwise compromise to err, if need be, on the side of working democracy rather than of voting democracy.

[*A Working Peace System,* 1966, pp. 25–36]

B.

FUNCTIONAL AND TECHNICAL AGENCIES

UN SPECIALIZED AGENCIES

United Nations Association of the U.S.A.

UN SPECIALIZED AGENCIES AT A GLANCE

FAO—Food and Agriculture Organization (Headquarters: Rome)

Works to improve the quantity and quality of the world's food by developing low cost, high protein food, improving agricultural and fishing techniques, irrigation and pest control projects and more equitable distribution of agricultural products.

IAEA-International Atomic Energy Agency (Headquarters: Vienna)

Promotes peaceful use of atomic energy, applies safeguards to nuclear materials in more than 60 countries.

IBRD—International Bank for Reconstruction and Development (Headquarters: Washington, DC)

Known as the World Bank, with its affiliates the International Development Association (IDA) and the International Finance Corporation (IFC), supplies the largest quantity of development funds, in the form of low interest, long term loans for government and private enterprise in developing countries.

ICAO—International Civil Aviation Organization (Headquarters: Montreal)

Promotes safe and efficient civilian air travel by regulating aircraft operation, safety and navigation equipment, pilot training, the use of a common language (English) and noise levels over land areas; provides rescue and communication facilities and technical assistance to developing countries.

IFAD—International Fund for Agricultural Development
(Headquarters: Rome)

The newest of the UN's specialized agencies, will authorize grants and low-interest loans for increased agricultural development and improved nutritional levels in the developing countries, (The agreement to establish IFAD as a specialized agency was opened for signature in January 1977, following attainment of a target of one billion dollars.)

ILO—International Labor Organization
(Headquarters: Geneva)

Improves working conditions; sets international safety and employment standards; conducts manpower training and education programs to enable achievement of equal employment opportunities.

IMCO—Inter-Governmental Maritime Consultative
Organization (Headquarters: London)

Responsible for standards of ship design and safety and navigation procedures, this agency has sponsored a series of treaties to curb dumping of pollutants in the oceans, and one establishing liability for damage caused by oil spills.

IMF—International Monetary Fund
(Headquarters: Washington, DC)

Established to faciltiate international cooperation on economic problems, the agency is the major international mechanism for stabilizing currency exchange rates and for providing additional resources for countries with balance-of-payments problems.

ITU—Internatioanl Telecommunication Union
(Headquarters: Geneva)

Sets and regulates assignment of frequencies for all international radio, telephone, TV and satellite communications, acts as an international information and training center, and is now instituting a world-wide direct dialing system.

UNESCO—UN Educational, Scientific and Cultural
Organization (Headquarters: Paris)

Tries to stimulate and increase international cooperation and improve the quality of life through such efforts as literacy programs, basic and applied scientific research and the preservation and exchange of cultural and historic properties.

UPU—Universal Postal Union (Headquarters: Berne)

Standardizes postal rates, simplifies and assists in establishing or improving national postal services, accelerates customs treatment of mails and regulates international mail, ensuring that a letter mailed with a US stamp will be delivered anywhere in the world.

WHO—World Health Organization (Headquarters: Geneva)

Sets international regulations, conducts an epidemic warning system, assists in improving health education and public health facilities in developing countries, encourages and coordinates medical research.

WIPO—World Intellectual Property Organization
(Headquarters: Geneva)

Works to ensure administrative cooperation among nations in enforcing various international agreements on trademarks and patents, industrial desisng and the protection of copyrights.

WMO—World Meteorological Organization
(Headquarters: Geneva)

Act as as a clearing house for information, conducts research into weather patterns, coordinates an international network of meteorological stations as part of a world weather watch system.

Organizations Created By and Reporting
To the General Assembly:

Office of the United Nations Disaster Relief Coordinator (UNDRO) is a clearinghouse for information on relief needs and assistance, and mobilizes and coordinates emergency assistance.

Office of the United Nations High Commissioner for Refugees (UNHCR) extends international protection and material assistance to refugees, and negotiates with governments to resettle or repatriate refugees.

United Nations Center for Human Settlements (Habitat) deals with the housing problems of the urban and rural poor in developing countries. It provides technical assistance and training, organizes meetings, and disseminates information.

United Nations Children's Fund (UNICEF) provides technical and financial assistance to developing countries for programs benefiting children. It also provides emergency relief to mothers and children. It is financed by voluntary contributions.

United Nations Conference on Trade and Development (UNCTAD) works to establiish agreements on commodity price stabilization and to codify principles of international trade that are conducive to development.

United Nations Development Program (UNDP) coordinates the development work of all UN and related agencies. It is the world's largest multilateral technical assistance program, currently supporting more than 5,000 projects around the world, and is financed by voluntary contributions.

United Nations Environment Program (UNEP) monitors environmental conditions, implements environmental projects, develops recommended standards, promotes technical assistance and training, and supports the development of alternative energy sources.

United Nations Fund for Population Activities (UNFPA) helps countries to gather demographic information and to plan population projects. Its governing body is the Governing Council of UNDP, and it is financed by voluntary governmental contributions.

United Nations Industrial Development Organization (UNIDO) is an autonomous organization within the UN that promotes the industrialization of developing countries. It is in the process of being converted into a specialized agency.

United Nations Institute for Training and Research (UNITAR) is an autonomous organization within the UN that provides training to government and UN officials and conducts research on a variety of international issues.

United Nations Relief and Works Agency for Palestine Refugees in the Near East (UNRWA) provides education, health, and relief services to Palestinian refugees.

United Nations University (UNU) is an autonomous academic institution chartered by the General Assembly. It has a worldwide network of associated institutions, research units, individual scholars, and UNU fellows, coordinated through the UNU center in Tokyo. It has no faculty or degree students.

World Food Council (WFC) is a 36-nation body that meets annually at the ministerial level to review major issues affecting the world food situation.

World Food Program (WFP) is jointly sponsored by the UN and FAO. It supplies emergency food relief and provides food aid to support development projects.

["The United Nations at a Glance," pp. 2,15]

C.

INTERDEPENDENCIES: ECONOMIC, SOCIAL AND TECHNOLOGICAL

TOWARDS A RENOVATED INTERNATIONAL SYSTEM

The Trilateral Commission

II. THE NATURE OF THE PROBLEM

A. The Current Predicament

1. An Interdependent World

THE MANAGEMENT OF INTERDEPENCENCE has become indispensable for world order in the coming years. Its origins lie in the extraordinary expansion of interaction between modern states and societies. Although such interaction existed in earlier times, the development of modern technology and the evolution of the international economic and political system have brought a quantitative and qualitative change.

Interdependence has grown in various domains: psychological, social, economic, and political. In the psychological and social domain, the growth of communication, the flow of ideas, and the movement of persons as a result of modern transport and mass tourism have resulted in greater knowledge about other societies, in the wider impact of ideas, and in the formation of transnational links of interest and even action. From this interaction has come the rise of expectations in poor countries, matched in some degree by a growing feeling of compassion and sometimes of guilt among a number of people in the rich countries with respect to the poor countries, especially among youth. Yet misgivings over the limited results of many foreign aid programs—frustrated partially by rapid population growth—and the failure of some developing countries to undertake necessary internal reforms discourage larger resource transfers from the industrial countries.

In the economic and political domains, interdependence has grown to an unprecedented scale. The rapid growth of international trade and finance has led to an intense degree of mutual dependence. The vast amount of internationally owned and managed production provides a particularly important transnational link, as does mutual dependence on vital imports such as oil, food, and other raw materials. Economic events—and shocks—in one country are rapidly transmitted to other countries. In modern welfare states, national actions to meet the needs of their citizens often vitally affect economic life and political activity in other countries.

This state of affairs displays the dual character of interdependence: Intensive interaction between societies at various levels is essential for economic efficiency and improving the standard of living for individuals. On the other hand, it produces mutual interference across national frontiers which jeopardizes some of its advantages. Thus it requires steering mechanisms.

Among the negative aspects of interdependence are the threats of nuclear proliferation and harmful ecological change. Avoidance of nuclear war is rarely discussed as part of the problem of interdependence. Yet it is a condition for the solution of all other problems of world order, since nuclear war threatens the survival of mankind. Throughout the postwar era a stable nuclear balance, which affects the many states of the global system, has depended on the few nuclear powers, and primarily the United States and the Soviet Union.

Now, however, the worldwide resort to nuclear energy for power creates much wider risks of the spread of nuclear weapons. Effective measures against proliferation, therefore, can no longer be handled by a few; they require joint action by a large number of states with divergent outlooks and interests, and different economic status. Proliferation concerns no longer focus on countries like Germany and Japan—since they have ceased to be a problem in this respect, if they ever really were—but on unstable or adventurous countries in the developing world, especially in areas of conflict and violence, which could acquire a capacity to build nuclear weapons. In fact, unless the states of the world can cooperate in this field, a period of instability and violence could be opened, compared to which the past quarter century may appear as a *belle époque*.

Undesired ecological changes present a different problem. They may not be foreseen, and may already be serious or irreversible when their first symptoms appear. The environmental problem has its origins in industrialization, modern agricultural techniques and the expansion of population—through the perception of its wide-scale importance is recent. The problem is often international in that pollution in one country frequently affects the environment in others as well. Moreover, outsiders do not have the limited option to reduce the harm by cutting transnational links and interaction, as they can in many other types of interdependence—though at considerable cost.

The pressure of man on the environment has already caused many undesired changes, and could threaten partial breakdowns. A breakdown of the globe's biosphere is unlikely during this century, but there can be no certainty of its avoidance. Later, as the LDCs industrialize, the danger will increase. The prevention of ecological damage and breakdowns (and the repair of existing damage) ar major tasks for the globe as a whole.

Extreme poverty, especially in South Asia and parts of Africa, poses still another problem of interdependence. Poverty has been widespread throughout man's history, but it has now moved to the foreground of world politics with the revolution in expectations and concern. Despite two decades of international development efforts, it exists today on a massive scale and there is a general sense of failure. Though national incomes have grown considerably in the Third World, much of the advance has been absorbed by population growth and the remainder only partially passed on to the poor as a result of failures of internal reform. In terms of purchasing power, the average income in the Unitd States in 1972 was about thirteen times as high as in India. The total debt of the developing countries is now around 200 billion dollars. The number of those starving to death or dying from diseases related to malnutrition has to be counted in the millions annually.

The alleviation of poverty is a demand of the basic ethical principles of the West as well as of simple self-interest. In the long run an orderly world is unlikely if great affluence in one part coexists with abject poverty in another, while "one world" of communication, of mutual concern, and interdependence comes into being.

Interdependence varies considerably in kind and intensity in different regions, between particular states, and across different issue areas. It is highest among the countries of the trilateral area, due to intensive trade, investment, monetary interaction, security ties and other links. The general though varying dependence of the industrialized states on imports of raw materials from the Third World corresponds to mixed dependencies of the developing countries on capital goods and foodstuffs from industrialized countries. Among developing countries, interdependence is relatively low except for a general dependence on oil produced by some of them. In fact, the existing asymmetries of interdependence have themselves become a problem, one to which we shall return. And the communist nations have largely resisted close linkages with the non-communist world until the recent efforts to expand trade and technology transfers from the West.

2. Interdependence and the Welfare State

The interdependent world is made up of welfare states of various kinds. This inevitably poses problems for international cooperation.

The modern welfare state has developed in response to the rising expectations and demands of individual citizens who aspire not only to a minimum standard of living, but to social security in a broad sense, covering full employment, health services, security in old age, etc. To respond to these demands, all states conduct a wide range of policies to provide welfare for society and its groups, through overall economic management, employment policy, industrial and social policies and so forth. Even in the West, the "invisible hand" of the market is more and more directed or circumscribed by governments. The liberal premise of a separation between the political and economic realm is obsolete; issues related to economics are at the heart of modern politics. And in the rest of the world, governments intervene in society and economic life far more extensively, according to criteria and through instruments which vary widely from country to country.

Interdependence, despite its many benefits, complicates the management of the modern welfare state—it creates disturbances, interferes with national priorities and policies, and transmits problems from other systems. Conversely, conflicting national priorities of modern welfare states inevitably complicate the problem of managing a system of interdependence.

Interdependence among welfare states, therefore, inherently poses a sharp dilemma: Tariffs, export subsidies, industrial policy, privileged treatment and so forth, the very instruments used to implement social policy nationally, inherently threaten the systems of interaction and interdependence which are a source of prosperity in the industrial world and a precondition for meeting and surpassing minimum human needs in the developing countries.

Thus politicization of the international economy lies in the logic of modern welfare states. National intervention is inevitable in the name of a more just society, but it should be guided through international agreement and joint action in such a way as to preserve the advantages of interdependence.

3. Interdependence and National Roles

An international system must be able to accommodate shifts in power among nations and their desires for new roles. In the postwar period, the industrialized nations were able to adapt their decision-making structures to reflect the rise of the Federal Republic of Germany and later of Japan. Now the problem arises in two forms.

Certain developing countries have risen rapidly to positions of economic weight and political influence on the basis of the critical importance of certain raw materials (in particular, oil) or of successful development. Understandably, they demand a greater say in the decision-making of the international system commensurate with their newly acquired position.

But the issue also arises at a second and more difficult level as a result of shifts in perceptions. To many developing nations the hierarchy of power characteristic of the postwar world is no longer acceptable. They reject the central legitimizing concept of the liberal world economy, the maximization of global welfare through the market system, and assert that the formal equality of all participants has not been accompanied by a fair sharing of benefits from the division of labor in the present world economy.

For the weaker developing countries, interdependence appears as a system of dependence. Hence the appeal of theories which stress elements of *dependencia* in the world economy, including multinational corporations, and which underlie much of the rhetoric, if not the political strategy, of many developing countries. As they see it, their entire economy and external trade have been shaped according to priorities defined by stronger industrialized states and not by their own needs.

Some intellectuals, groups, and governments in the Third World increasingly advocate a strategy of disassociating North and South. Various suggestions at the 1976 Colombo conference of the nonaligned states and at the 1976 Mexico City conference on economic relations among developing countries clearly express such goals, e.g., proposals for a developing countries' payments union, the establishment of a joint development bank, preferential treatment, multinational corporations of their own, and so forth.

Such tendencies to "disassociate" need not necessarily be viewed with alarm. On the contrary, a healthy self-reliance may require some cutting of old links or dependencies, though it would have to overcome many obstacles before it could become a feasible strategy. The problem has to be taken seriously, however; for unless interdependence effectively serves the interests of the weaker states, the trend toward extreme disassociation is likely to grow, and to create disturbances damaging for the industrialized world, and probably even more harmful to the developing world.

B. The Need for Cooperation for World Order

The preceding analysis has brought into relief the most important tasks in striving for world order: keeping the peace; managing the global economy; controlling ecological damage; and meeting basic human needs. The specific requirements for these tasks will be examined later. Here the focus is on their common features.

These tasks all require extensive cooperation among some or most nations for effective handling. The separate states cannot cope with them.

Moreover, they call for joint action on two different time scales. The conditions of the contemporary world make it obvious that concerted efforts will be necessary to deal with current crises in order to contain violence and prevent breakdowns in the global economy or ecology. That is the minimum cooperation required for managing from day to day.

The effort to get at the roots of many of these problems will take a long time indeed. Thus deterrence and detente should be able to avoid major war between East and West, but it will take a very long period to remove the sources of conflict and rivalry. Similar is the goal of meeting basic human needs of the poorest billion or more people. Even with immediate and energetic efforts, it will take decades to achieve substantial progress on a large scale.

The requisite cooperation for both the short and long term must be based on the shared conviction that it maximizes overall gain and increases the welfare of all those involved. The philosophical roots of such a conviction go back to the 18th century notion of progress, that the human condition as a whole could be improved through human efforts to master parsimonious nature. Such thinking represented a revolutionary departure from the age-old notion that one man's gain must be another man's loss, or that one group could improve its condition only by robbing or exploiting other groups. Put in modern terms of game theory, the concept that the benefits for all can be enhanced by cooperation is known as positive-sum thinking, in contrast to zero-sum thinking. Although international cooperation continues to experience failures and setbacks, the conviction that positive-sum behavior is the most rational approach to international affairs has become the prevailing concept among Western political and intellectual elites.

A cooperative, positive-sum approach is a precondition for maintaining economic security in a situation of interdependence. Greater economic vulnerability can entail the risk of national social and economic breakdown as a result of actions by others. In the worst case, such actions may threaten the economic security of all those involved, although some countries may be more vulnerable than others due to economic weakness or dependence on specific products, such as oil or grain.

Within industrialized countries, a sense of community has been at the basis of policies to promote more equal opportunity and distribution of income, and more broadly it underlies the rise of the modern welfare state. Such an attitude has its roots in ethical and philosophical values of the West as well as in enlightened self-interest, since a minimum of social justice and reform will be necessary for stability in the long run. The same applies at the world level. Some global sense of community among human beings is important for a functioning world order. In particular, it is necessary in order to generate the energy and motivation for sacrifices, for transfer of resources, and for support of domestic socioeconomic changes to facilitate economic progress in poorer areas of the world.

Neither the widespread application of cooperative behavior nor the existence of a global sense of community implies that conflict and competition between states, groups, and different political creeds will disappear. In fact, a pluralistic world system is a creative asset to be preserved. But the presence and strength of a cooperative predisposition and of a global sense of community will decisively influence whether the ongoing change in world politics can take place without major disturbances or breakdowns.

Finally, such change will also depend upon effective international decision-making. The following criteria, as we shall examine in greater detail later, are crucial: First, decision-making should adequately involve those needed for solutions and take into account the views of others affected. Second, it should seek to reconcile national policies in interdependent relationships through a system of consultative procedures and mutual commitments. Third, decision-making arrangements should allow for flexible action in times of crisis and emergency. Fourth, these arrangements should secure an adequate distribution of gains from interdependence.

C. Obstacles to Cooperation

A realistic strategy of action must take into account the major obstacles to cooperative management of interdependence. Obstacles of particular importance are the desire for national autonomy, the impact of domestic politics, disparities in conditions among countries, political barriers, and sheer numbers of countries.

1. Desire for Autonomy

The desire for autonomy and the traditional concept of sovereignty aggravate the tension between national policies and transnational interaction. They tend to support attitudes and actions which disregard the effects of national measures on outside states or groups. They hinder the observation of the rules of international cooperation and impede the compromises and the day-to-day routines of consultation necessary for managing an interdependent world. These attitudes exist to some extent in all countries, often fluctuating over time in intensity.

The public and leaders of most countries continue to live in a mental universe which no longer exists—a world of separate nations—and have great difficulties thinking in terms of global perspectives and interdependence. Consequently, in the environmental field, for example, there is still a widespread belief that countries can in practice afford to pollute the biosphere across their own borders despite commitments to the contrary. In the rich democracies, it is extremely difficult to convince publics of the necessity for substantial aid to developing nations. The development aid lobby is weak, even though aid policy is partially employment policy for the rich countries, and remains imperative for reasons of enlightened self-interest, as well as ethics.

In developing countries, many of which have become independent so recently, the desire for autonomy poses special difficulties. Jealous of their independence, they often tend to regard the types of accommodation and consultation necessary in interdependent relationships as interference in their domestic affairs and an encroachment upon their sovereignty.

2. Impact of Domestic Politics

Although the social, economic, and political life of many modern states depends on functioning interaction with the outside world, the structure and issues of domestic politics continue to be shaped primarily by domestic concerns. Foreign issues remain secondary except in times of crisis. Political leaders rise or fall primarily on their performance on domestic issues. The concept of legitimacy remains confined to the territorial state, leaving aside the growing involvement of outside forces and the impact of national action on others. Values, traditions, institutions and habits are still heavily dominated by the concept of the traditional sovereign state.

The negative impact of domestic politics on the management of interdependence is two-fold. First, since domestic politics is inevitably more shaped by internal than external priorities, the political process produces varying degrees of parochialism which disregard the impact of national action on the outside world and show little understanding of the requirements of interdependence. The pressures for protectionist measures or export controls provide endless examples.

Second, the pressures of domestic politics encourage a short-term view of problems. The fact that politicians must present themselves to the voters every few years has the unfortunate effect of concentrating their attention on immediate issues which will secure their reelection and not on problems of the longer future. It rarely pays domestically to raise long-term problems, particularly if this means confronting voters with difficulties ahead and the need for sacrifices to master them. Thus long-term problems and strategies to solve them are not discussed as concrete political issues. The failure of American and European politics to respond adequately to the necessity to reduce oil consumption provides a telling example.

The nondemocratic systems show similar tendencies toward parochialism and short-term views. The theoretical advantage of a leader who does not have to go back to the electorate with its local, regional, or national priorities does not improve policy in practice. On the contrary, the policies of nondemocratic developed countries have usually been less globalist and less concerned for poorer countries than those of trilateral democracies.

The pluralism of democracy provides an important corrective to shortsightedness and parochialism which nondemocratic systems do not have, namely, open criticism and dissent, which ultimately have an impact on public debate and the election of politicians.

3. Disparities in Conditions

Disparities in conditions between political entities are natural; states inevitably differ in size, resources, population, geographic advantages and so on. Such disparities can, however, create obstacles for attempts to achieve a more effective world order. In particular, the wide disparity between rich and poor countries continues to be a serious impediment to the organization of relationships of interdependence which maximize welfare for all.

The disparity in income is associated with many other disparities. One is in vulnerability to outside forces, which make poorer states helpless victims of fluctuations of the world economy more often than wealthier states able to cushion the effects. Asymmetries in resources and economic wealth affect leverage in bargaining and disputes over the sharing of the world's resources. The disparity in economic prospects is equally striking: Even with very rapid economic growth, many countries can be sure that more than half of the benefit will be neutralized by popuation increase—a problem industrialized states no longer face.

Cooperation in a functioning world order presupposes national structures of decision-making capable of assembling information and implementing agreed decisions. Many states lack this requisite political and administrative infrastructure for cooperation. Many are weak either because they lack effective instruments of government or because of domestic instability, which may itself be closely associated with ineffective government or with unsolved social and economic problems. Such weakness makes it difficult for such states to protect their interests and fosters a sense of being exploited by more advanced nations.

Elites in some developing countries regard the present disparities between rich and poor countries as so extreme, with so little protection for the weak, that they tend to reject interdependence as a form of dependence and exploitation. Hence they may reject or resist collaboration with the advanced nations even though that may impede the alleviation of their problems.

4. Political Barriers

Antagonism between states is hardly conducive to collaboration for mutual benefit. It strengthens tendencies to disregard the effects of one's own actions on others. In undermining positive-sum behavior and cooperative action, interstate antagonism destroys an essential prerequisite for the effective management of interdependence. Indeed, interdependence may even provide an instrument for pressure, for example, by applying a boycott on the supply of oil or foodstuffs for specific political purposes.

The deep-seated antagonism in East-West relations illustrates the problem. While a common interest in survival forces both sides to cooperate in limited areas, there are fundamental barriers between them, notably in ideology, political structure, and foreign policy. The communist states still cling to the notion that they are engaged in a revolutionary struggle with the capitalist world, which they seek to defeat with all means short of war. Their autocratic systems are centrally directed and in relatively complete control of all interaction with the outside world; in contrast, in the pluralistic West a multitude of individuals, groups, institutions, and corporate actors interact with the outside world in ways Western governments can only partially control. This difference raises the danger that communist governments will exploit relationships of interdependence between East and West, submitting them to the priorities of a foreign policy which sees their own systems locked in a fundamental struggle with Western states.

Ideological differences of a less militant nature may also raise obstacles to a constructive approach to global problems. For example, ideological differences between free market and planned economy approaches have added difficulties to the search for solutions regarding commodity agreements and a new regime for the seabed.

5. Number of Countries

In this interdependent world, most countries have an interest in the management of many of its problems, even if that interest is sometimes strongly attenuated. Does this mean that nearly 150 nations should participate in all, or virtually all, matters of international discussion, negotiation, and collaboration?

If so, it would seriously impede the necessary cooperation. The mere presence of large numbers does inhibit the close discussion that is often essential for negotiation and agreement. Moreover, the low interest of many nations in specific issues of importance to others leads to their representation by nonexpert diplomats, often those at the local post where the discussions are being held. Since these representatives do not know the issues, they understandably hesitate to agree on technical points. The low material stake is also more likely to lead to politicization of the issue for the sake of hoped-for benefits in other, quite unrelated areas, or even for the sake of rhetorical effect, such as comments by communist countries on multinational corporations.

Is it feasible to meet this problem by a system of representation, as has been used in the International Monetary Fund for years and tried in the 27-nation Conference on International Economic Cooperation opened in Paris in December 1975 to discuss energy, raw materials, development, and financial problems?

In practice, representation modeled on the IMF has not effectively dealt with this problem. For instance, during the 1972–74 discussions by the Committee of Twenty on reform of the international monetary system, the number of participants was much larger than twenty, rarely in fact under 200, due to the presence of one and sometimes two national alternates to each "representative" at the table, not to mention central bank and finance ministry officials from each country, as well as international staff. Partly as a consequence of the unwieldiness of the group, the Committee stayed obstinately on the wrong track until major world financial events brought it back to reality during the last few months before it was to report and disband. The system of representation adopted by the CIEC scored somewhat better but did not produce conclusive proof that the method works. Few countries are willing to trust others to negotiate on their behalf, even within as cohesive a group as the European Community.

[*Towards A Renovated International System*, 1977, pp. 45–49]

THE US IN THE WORLD ECONOMY

William Diebold, Jr.

VERY FEW COUNTRIES CAN COPE with their so-called domestic economic problems without taking account of the international economy. They cannot safely assume that other countries will absorb whatever dislocation comes their way without reacting. Ironically, past success in cooperation has contributed to the present deterioration and that deterioration seems likely to continue. Barriers to trade and investment have come down, money moves freely around the world, the ability to insulate is limited and, regardless of a government's intentions, the effects of its actions may be felt abroad. Consequently, the gaps in the system of economic cooperation are more serious than they used to be.

At the same time, the troubles every country has with its domestic economy are harder to deal with because all economies are so exposed to one another. This is the paradox of interdependence. It is so well recognized, and so much written about these days, that there is no need to expand on the subject. It is necessary, though, to underline the basic challenge that interdependence poses. It was put clearly and forcefully by Ramsay Muir, a British Liberal, in *The Interdependent World and its Problems*, published in 1933:

> We have entered a new era, the era of world-interdependence; and this interdependent world is threatened with chaos because it has not learnt how to adjust its institutions and its traditions of government to the new conditions.

The situation has been familiar for many years: national politics and international economics. There are parallels in security. We are not about to see the end of the nation-state, so the tension will continue. There could be some pulling back from interdependence: some lines can be cut, some flows dammed, in the interests of gaining a freer hand to shape the national economy and meet domestic pressures. But for most countries, the area of maneuver is very limited; reducing interdependence is likely to mean reducing resources; the cost of extensive disturbances of established patterns of production, consumption and trade is likely to seem rather high. Some of these prices may have to be paid, if only because other countries will not cooperate to reduce them. Before asking what it might be reasonable to look for in new cooperative measures, it is worth asking whether there may not be other forces at play, pushing the world economy toward greater internationalization and further limiting the ability of governments to manage domestic affairs on a purely national basis.

Business is one possibility. Its internationalization is a complex process that has been gaining ground throughout the postwar period. This is not just a matter of the spread of multinational enterprises. The late Judd Polk argued long ago that we should focus on the characteristics of international production and its financing rather than on organizational forms. In many different ways, and through various kinds of financial links, the internationalization of business changes (and may conceal) who controls what and whose assets have to cover what obligations. It alters the meaning of national policies and the reach of national measures. Private business has to negotiate with governments but also has a certain freedom of action. Is it possible that, as entrepreneurs pursue their interests in flexible and ingenious ways, they will bring about a creative adaptation of the world economy to the new interdependence? It is, but that cannot be the whole answer. There has to be some means of asserting the public interest, and neither theory nor practice says that the invisible hand of the market will do so.

Moreover, there are many public interests and they have to be blended, compromised and offset. Present (and past) practice calls for all these interests to be balanced, fused or organized in the process of arriving at something called the national interest. This is not a very sensible procedure and becomes increasingly less so as economies are internationalized and their boundaries blurred. (Does anyone doubt that what happens to American companies abroad affects American as well as foreign interests?

In what sense are foreign-owned companies in the United States "American"?) Quite often, businessmen try to avoid bringing their "own" governments into disputes with other governments for fear that their own interests will be lost in the pursuit of other national aims. Surely we ought to make better use of the fact that most international economic issues involve clashes of interests within each country. Why have better ways not been invented to let private people make their cases to international bodies and foreign governments? Is it simply cultural lag? Or is it the inevitable consequence of the fact that the "consent of the governed" is asked and given entirely on a national level?

Along with business, technology has been a major force creating interdependence. The 50 years covered in this essay may have set a record in shrinking the globe. Perhaps the most dramatic economic effect has come from the almost instantaneous movement of money around the world. This technological marvel may not be all to the good. Years ago when my brother wrote one of the earliest papers on electronic banking, my wife said, "but I don't want the money taken out of my bank account as soon as I hand over my charge card." Governments may feel the same way, as they try to control their money supply.

What can you do, though, in the face of technological change? "Speed up the reaction time" is a common answer. But people are increasingly uncomfortable with the idea that they will be pushed around by machines or some disembodied force called Technology. What is the cost of resistance—to become Luddites, or laggards in a technological race all countries are forced to run? So far as one can see, most governments have opted for speeding up the race, but often get poor results. Can the race be run to the advantage of all—perhaps by increased internationalization of the effort, through private and public channels? Or do we ineluctably make it a zero-sum game if we all want the same thing—the lead?

As in the case of interdependence, we are back at a basic choice that wise men recognized long ago. In 1939, Eugene Staley wrote, in *World Economy in Transition:*

> Fundamental technological changes are pushing mankind in the direction of world-wide economic integration and interdependence, but . . . political tendencies . . . have strongly resisted that trend. . . . It would be unfortunate if

inability to solve the political problems connected with a world-wide economy should snatch away the productive advantages . . . offered by our technicians.

Many people, then and since, have accepted this proposition—but how much international action has been based on it?

["The U.S. in the World Economy," 1983, pp. 94–97]

REPORT OF THE
SECRETARY GENERAL
1983

Javier Perez de Cuellar

THE PREAMBLE OF THE CHARTER expresses the determination of the peoples of the United Nations "to promote social progress and better standards of life in larger freedom" and to this end "to employ international machinery for the promotion of the economic and social advancement of all peoples."

I am convinced that the impressive economic progress since the Second World War—in which almost all nations have shared—owes a great deal to multilateral co-operation which the United Nations has helped to bring about and develop. Recent trends and events, however, far from strengthening such co-operation, mark a clear retreat from these efforts. Indeed, while the effects of economic interdependence, due to growing integration in trade, finance and money, are widely acknowledged, obvious opportunities to address the major issues in these areas are being repeatedly missed. There can be no doubt that today more than ever many individual nations are affected—for good or ill—by trends elsewhere and by the decisions of others. Furthermore, there are categories of problems which can only be dealt with multilaterally or globally. All these developments intensify the need for international mechanisms to bring about greater harmonization of national policies.

Unilateral actions, taken without due regard for their effects on partner countries, would inevitably lead to the weakening of economic co-operation, thereby damaging world growth and development. They would lead to economic nationalism, the evil effects of which we witnessed during the '30s. Unresolved economic conflicts can be, and usually are, a breeding ground for dangerous political tensions.

A major economic imperative of our times is the accelerated development of the developing countries. The eradication of the poverty that continues to be widespread in several parts of the world must remain a collective responsibility. The needs of the least developed and other poor countries require particular attention. The total population of developing countries is projected to increase from around 3 billion to approximately 5 billion by the end of the century, that is, within less than two decades.

The slowing, and sometimes the halt, in the development process that has taken place in recent years should be seen as a temporary phenomenon that must be reversed in the coming years. In the mean time, every effort has to be made to reduce the vulnerability of developing countries to external shocks and to assist them in attaining greater autonomy and freedom of action, both by themselves and in co-operation with other countries—developed and developing.

At the same time, it is necessary to realize a higher level of growth in the industrialized countries. Thirty-two million people are unemployed in the Organization for Economic Cooperation and Development countries alone, and this figure is likely to rise in the immediate future. A burden of this magnitude cannot be economically or politically accepted as a permanent part of the realities of these countries. The need for investment in order to fight unemployment, to ensure structural adjustments and to deal with the needs of underprivileged areas and groups requires higher growth in that region. This would also encourage better prospects for increased trade and transfer of resources from the industrialized countries to the developing countries. Similar considerations call for high growth in socialist economies as well.

I have recently presented, in statements to intergovernmental bodies, my views on ways to revive the world economy and resume the process of development. There is a primary need for action at the national level to correct economic and social imbalances. Such efforts need to be supported by concerted action among nations and the assistance of multilateral institutions. In this connection I have emphasized the need to make additional finance available as part of concerted policies for world recovery and to examine basic reforms in international trade, money and finance. Economic co-operation among developing countries also needs strengthening.

Let me now turn to the role of the United Nations on economic issues. How effective is the United Nations in discharging the responsibilities with which it has been entrusted by its Charter? Contrary to the perceptions of some, the Organization has been successful in anticipating and identifying issues of importance, mobilizing public opinion, researching and analysing critical problems, providing direct assistance within its means and negotiating constructive agreements in various sectors of activity.

The record of performance and accomplishments of the United Nations system in the economic and social fields is varied and substantial. Through a vast network of technical co-operation activities, organizations of the United Nations system continue to assist developing countries in formulating and implementing a large number of specific projects, ranging from the establishment of primary health care centres to highly sophisticated institutions of agronomic research and training, and technology.

However, I am very much aware that much more needs to be done to improve the efficiency and effectiveness of the system and to ensure its responsiveness to changing needs. This requires efforts on the part of the Secretariat as well as of the Member States. . . .

As regards Governments, it is important to ensure greater cohesion and consistency in their positions in the different intergovernmental bodies. A greater sense of priority in the deliberations of the General Assembly and of the Economic and Social Council would encourage more effective consideration of issues. It would also strengthen the impact of resolutions. Frequently such resolutions lead to a proliferation of institutions. This can hamper efficiency and add substance to criticism of an ever-expanding bureaucracy. Improvement is also needed in the machinery and methods of negotiation.

Innovative measures should be considered to foster the habit of co-operation. In this connection, I wish to underline the need to strengthen the efforts of the United Nations system to support the initiatives of developing countries to promote co-operation among themselves through the implementation of specific and action-oriented measures.

It is incumbent on us to seize every opportunity to carry forward the development dialogue, setting aside, where necessary, traditional practices or methods which may be obsolete, and testing new means of strengthening the collective effort of Member States to attain their common objectives.

[*Report of the Secretary-General,* 1983, pp. 9–11]

THE MYTH OF NATIONAL INTERDEPENDENCE

Kenneth N. Waltz

THE AMERICAN RHETORIC OF INTERDEPENDENCE has taken on some of the qualities of an ideology. The word "interdependence" subtly obscures the inequalities of national capability, pleasingly points to a reciprocal dependence, and strongly suggests that all states are playing the same game.

If interdependence is really close, each state is constrained to treat other states' acts as though they were events within its own borders. A mutuality of dependence leads each state to watch others with wariness and suspicion. Near self-sufficiency and the possession of great capabilities, however, insulate a nation from the world by muting the effects of adverse movements that originate outside of the national arena. One who looks only at the activities of American firms and at their considerable stake in foreign countries, may then in one misdirected leap reach the conclusion that the size of this stake renders America vulnerable. At the level of the firm, it may be all right to dwell upon the extent of integration. At the level of international politics, it is grossly misleading to do so. It often seems that the approach of international economists would, if applied to domestic economics, cause it all to be written in terms of the firm and not at all in terms of the market. It is necessary to look at the matrix of action rather than simply at the discrete activities that fill it. One who does so reaches a different conclusion.

Someone who has a lot to lose can afford to lose quite a bit of it. This maxim is, of course, a common proposition of oligopolistic economics. That a large and well-placed firm can afford to run at a loss for some years is taken not as a sign of weakness and vulnerability but as being a considerable advantage. Where disparities are great, whether among firms or among states, the largest of them need worry least about the bothersome activities of others. Since in such situations interdependence does not reduce to zero, we can rightly say that all of the parties are vulnerable, but we should hasten to add that some are much less so. Some states, of course, are closely interdependent economically, but neither the United States nor the Soviet Union is among them. In economic terms and from their points of view, the world is loosely coupled.

Today, the myth of interdependence both obscures the realities of international politics and asserts a false belief about the conditions that may promote peace. The size of the two greatest powers gives them some capacity for control and at the same time insulates them to a considerable extent from the effects of other states' behavior. The inequality of nations produces a condition of equilibrium at a low level of interdependence. In the absence of a system of international regulation, loose coupling and a certain amount of control exerted by large states help to promote the desired stability.

["The Myth of National Interdependence," 1970, pp. 220–23]

TRADE

THE INTEMPERATE ZONE: THE THIRD WORLD CHALLENGE

Richard E. Feinberg

THE ONE-WORLD ECONOMY

WHETHER THEY ARE NEOLIBERALS, populists, social democrats, or Marxists, most Third-World leaders desperately want to participate in this new international system. They might like to alter it at the margin, or improve their own location within it; they cannot however, overthrow it. It is the only game in town. They are all locked into the one-world economy of integrated financial markets, multinational corporations, and international trade flows.

Neither rightist nationalists nor leftist socialists believe, as some once did, that autarky offers an alternative path to development. Everyone realizes that to rely solely on internal savings would require a prolonged and severe austerity. They also know that efforts to produce domestically all of the necessary goods for consumption and production would be both horrendously inefficient, and for many items, impossible. Their populations are accustomed to consumer goods that would require imported components and technology even if the goods could be produced locally. In fact, autarky is so costly and dislocating that it may even be unsustainable. For the increasing number of LDCs that are food importers, choosing autarky would invite mass starvation. To solve food shortages by "thinning the population" is crazy-quilt logic and any zealots wild enough to try imposing

351

such a harsh regime would face not only internal rebellion, but even external subversion or foreign invasion on humanitarian or ideological grounds.

With its massive population, diversified resources, and backwardness, China offered optimal conditions for autarky. Advances in agriculture and social services were realized during the Stalinist and Maoist periods of self-reliance, but the post-Mao leadership decided that broader advances in labor productivity, industry, science and technology, and national defense demanded an opening to the West. . . .

Far from desiring autarky, most LDCs would prefer to increase their imports. Their import levels are constrained not by ideological hostility to international trade, but by a very real lack of hard currency. Even Eastern Europe would increase its imports except for its scarcity of foreign exchange. Many LDCs have stretched successfully their capacity to import by borrowing heavily on international capital markets or by borrowing from official lending agencies that finance industrial-country exports.

LDCs do protect certain favored domestic producers against import competition. Assuming, however, that the lack of foreign exchange caps import levels, these trade barriers affect only the composition of imports and not the totals. It is true that during the postwar period many LDCs adopted economic policies that indirectly and inadvertently hampered exports, thereby slowing the growth of import capacity. Over the past decade, however, the pressures of the international economy and of the development process itself have caused many LDCs to dismantle some of these export disincentives, precisely to augment import capacity.

The pressures to improve export performance have been overwhelming. Economic development increases the demand for energy, food and high-technology products much faster than most LDCs can produce them domestically. The rising international prices of these terms swell already sizable import bills. When these imports have been purchased on credit, the resulting need to service the external debt makes the foreign-exchange requirements still larger. Caught on this treadmill of ever-rising pressures to augment imports and exports, many LDC economies have increasingly oriented themselves toward international trade—the reverse of an autarkic closure. For some countries, including trade-oriented South Korea, relatively closed India, and socialist Hungary, production devoted to exports grew even more rapidly than GNP in the decade of the Seventies.

LDCs also want to participate more actively in the international capital markets. Most LDCs would borrow even more than they do, if it weren't for the constraints imposed by future debt-service requirements. Even so, many LDCs have been borrowing at a pace that, if maintained, could exceed their means to repay, and the commercial banks or the Internatioanl Monetary Fund have imposed ceilings on their debt accumulation. Those fortunate enough to have surplus financial resources—from Venezuela to Libya—are pleased to deposit them in the large commercial banks of the West. Nowhere else can deposits so safely earn substantial returns.

Many LDCs have acquired debt service burdens that are eating up 25 percent and more of their export earnings. Nevertheless, none have repudiated these debts recently and those countries who once sinned—the Soviet Union, China, Cuba— are now major borrowers again. In fact, all nations must be concerned with maintaining their international credit ratings for fear of losing access to still higher levels of foreign indebtedness.

Developing countries have also learned to live with multinational corporations. LDCs now recognize that the multinationals offer technology, organizational skills, and information and marketing networks that are domestically unavailable. For example, the president of Mozambique, Samora Machel, told a *Time* correspondent:

> Foreign capital has experience working in socialist countries in Europe, Asia and Latin America. It will have the opportunity to find out that here, just as in those countries, it will be able to make profits at the same time that it is contributing to the construction of socialism. That is our view in today's world of independence and complementarity.

As the preceding sections have stressed, LDC governments have learned to use their leverage to alter the multinationals' behavior to suit national interests. Brazil, for example, has compelled multinational auto firms to establish local facilities that will produce a growing percentage of their automobiles domestically and then sell more of that production as exports. Mexico is now requiring the auto manufacturers to utilize a specified level of "local content" in their cars and to export enough of the finally assembled products to cover the costs of their imported contents. From China to Nigeria, governments have demanded that multinationals form joint ventures with either the government or with local capitalists.

Some critics of multinationals have argued that MNCs distort income distribution patterns in LDCs by making some workers more productive and by producing luxury items. In some instances, MNC activities may support and even strengthen inequalities. However, their activities in Eastern Europe and elsewhere suggest that MNCs can adapt to societies of more even wealth distribution. If circumstances demanded, they could presumably alter products and production techniques, and make the necessary outlays for research and development and for retooling. After all, many firms in the developed states began producing luxury items for a narrow segment of society and are now delivering consumer goods for the masses. And in many industries today, global competition is forcing a pace of new-product generation that is fiercer than ever.

Other critics have accused MNC subsidiaries of being relatively sluggish in exporting to other Third World countries. Understandably, subsidiaries might not wish to compete with siblings already operating in such markets. In some instances, the subsidiary still might be willing to engage in limited exporting and use its knowledge of global marketing opportunities to achieve export levels above the levels the LDC could gain alternatively. In other cases however, the LDC may decide that only a state-owned or a state-subsidized and nationally owned firm will aggressively promote exports. The trade-oriented Japanese and South Koreans have established many firms on this latter assumption.

Such decisions to support local ownership should not be confused with an intention to opt out of the one-world economy. Quite to the contrary, the objective is usually to increase the nation's participation in international commerce. Indeed, it may be the multinational which is inhibiting market mechanisms in favor of production patterns that benefit the oligopolistic firm. Ironically, in this instance, it is the aggressive LDC state that must overcome the interventions of the oligopolistic MNC to reassert the principle of comparative advantage.

No Other Options

One obvious reason for the LDCs' intense interest in joining the international economy is the lack of an alternative. Neither autarky, "South-South," or "collective self-reliance" are sufficient replacements. Nations may be able to reduce their dependence on certain imports, but, as China discovered, the very process of development creates demands for other imports. Nations can, to varying degrees, increase their trade with other developing states. Although such trade may be psychologically satisfying, the rules governing economic interchange among LDCs merely reproduce the strictures determining North-South relations. Nor is entrance into the socialist division of labor—the Council for Economic Cooperation (COMECON)—an attractive answer. COMECON markets offer opportunities for trade diversification, but they are not substitutes for the rest of the world. As the next chapter will discuss at greater length, the Soviet Union is leery of paying for "second Cubas"; that is, bankrolling the high costs of socialist transformations. Rather than absorbing new states, COMECON has been increasing its economic contracts with the West and socialist states of Eastern Europe are also becoming integrated into the one-world system.

Those LDC governments—such as Libya, Angola, Mozambique, Ethiopia, Nicaragua, and Grenada—that have recently adopted an "anti-imperialist" foreign-policy rhetoric have nonetheless continued to concentrate their economic ties with capitalist states.

Neither the radical rhetoric of these states, nor their security ties to the socialist bloc, have prevented them from selling their production to the West, or from remaining dependent upon imports from non-COMECON economies. Those with the requisite credit-worthiness are borrowing from international capital markets and are doing business with MNCs. The replacement of political elites or even the transformation of entire state structures within particular Third World nations does not alter the international economy. New elites face the same imperative to participate in the one-world system; they have no other choice.

[*The Intemperate Zone: The Third World Challenge to U.S. Foreign Policy,* 1983, pp. 109–14]

MONETARY

TOWARDS A RENOVATED INTERNATIONAL SYSTEM

The Trilateral Commission

A. INTERNATIONAL MONETARY ARRANGEMENTS

DURING THE PAST DECADE there has been much turmoil in international monetary relations. The monetary system laid down in the mid-1940s came under increasing strain, and the need for substantial adjustments in monetary arrangements became clear. But there was considerable disagreement—some technical in nature, some political in nature—on the magnitude and the character of the required revisions. So the process of adaptation to new circumstances was a prolonged one, and in the end new arrangements, notably the switch to flexible exchange rates, were forced by events rather than negotiated by governments. Belatedly, governments have accepted the situation as it evolved and have begun to build on it.

International agreement on the basic ground rules of monetary relations is highly desirable. Systems without overt cooperation can be imagined, but they would be stable only if implicit rules of behavior developed. We should be able to improve on that with a negotiated framework.

Several features of international monetary arrangements are worth noting: First, except when things go badly they are not a salient issue in domestic politics. Second, "monetary arrangements" is an esoteric subject, requiring a certain technical expertise. On both counts, domestic political considerations do not greatly complicate international negotiations, as they do

359

international trade negotiations. On the other hand, international monetary questions have sometimes taken on high symbolic value—President De Gaulle once referred to the "exorbitant privilege" of the reserve currency countries—and that symbolic aspect has occasionally made negotiations more difficult than in other arenas, which have not become involved in the high politics between nations.

The extent to which monetary arrangements are separable from other issues depends on the nature of the arrangements. Under fixed exchange rates, it was ultimately difficult to separate monetary questions from questions of trade and foreign investment. A persistently overvalued currency, for instance, led to pressures for protection against imports. The separability of monetary questions is greater with arrangements that do not permit prolonged over- or undervaluation of a country's currency. On the other hand, flexible exchange rates that in fact fluctuate widely and frequently can also create important problems outside the monetary area, especially for those engaged in foreign trade or in management of the domestic economy.

The monetary system is an area in which rule-making with decentralized management is eminently feasible; with general agreement on actions that should be avoided or occasionally those that should be taken, the actual execution of actions can be left largely to individual countries. The major exceptions to this generalization are international lending and creation of new international reserves. The latter is intrinsically collaborative if it is not to favor particular countries—those that produce gold or those whose currencies are used as international reserves. The former requires international cooperation if the scale of lending is such that it requires the spreading of risk and responsibility among a number of countries. And of course there are important advantages to the central collection and analysis of information, since the functioning of the system as a whole cannot usually be discovered from looking only at the individual parts.

Finally, a negotiated monetary framework needs to apply only to the five to ten leading countries in international trade and financial transactions. With an agreed framework among these "core" countries, other countries are likely to adopt similar arrangements; and if they find it preferable to adopt different arrangements, better suited to their individual circumstances, they can do so without jeopardizing the central framework. For example, many smaller countries could adopt flexible exchange rates without threatening a regime of fixed exchange rates among major currencies; or many smaller countries could fix the exchange rate of their currencies in one fashion or another without threatening a system of flexible exchange rates among major currencies. In *this* sense, the international monetary system is a question primarily for the major non-communist countries. Other countries, however, have a major interest in how it works. (Communist countries have by choice insulated themselves from the world's monetary arrangements through tight, occasionally brutally tight, exchange controls. Their influence is small, and is likely to remain small so long as they maintain these tight controls.)

The upshot of all this is that the major features of the core of the international financial system must be agreed and operated by the leading five to ten countries; a wide variety of arrangements is then possible for other countries around that central core. Widespread interest in the monetary system requires a mechanism for discussion of ongoing developments and of proposals for formal change in the system. These two requirements can be met under existing arrangments, with ongoing developments discussed within the nearly global International Monetary Fund and its various committees, and proposals for formal change discussed not only there but also by outside groups such as the Group of Ten. International institutions, by their nature, cannot be relied upon as sources for originating formal changes in the system, so such proposals generally must come from national or group initiative outside the IMF.

What about the content of monetary arrangements? Substantial changes have been made in the last decade. First, a new, man-made international money, the SDR, has been created for central banks. Related to this, the monetary role of gold in the international system has been diminished, just as it was diminished in domestic monetary systems decades before. Second, flexible exchange rates have been introduced among the major currencies. Most other currencies continue on an "adjustable peg" arrangement. That is, they are linked with a nearly fixed exchange rate to some major currency or to some group of currencies, such as the 16-currency composite SDR or the European "snake," but that exchange rate can be adjusted from time to time as economic conditions require.

These are major changes in international monetary arrangements, and they have not yet been fully digested. Central tasks for the next decade are to learn how to operate a system of flexible exchange rates and to assure that the SDR provides most if not all of the incremental reserves needed by the world economy. The first of these tasks involves developing practical guidelines to prevent large and erratic movements in exchange rates, which are damaging to foreign trade and other normal international economic transactions, and to prevent competitive manipulation of exchange rates, e.g. deliberate undervaluation of a currency to help create an export surplus and domestic employment. Collaboration is needed in this area since each exchange rate is inherently two-sided; without collaboration, countries could be working at cross-purposes. The responsibility here to provide a workable core falls mainly on the leading countries, partly because other currencies are typically attached to theirs, partly because of their sheer preponderance in international transactions. Failures of smaller countries in exchange rate management are not consequential for the system as a whole. As a result, they may enjoy greater freedom, and each can take responsibility for its own currency with respect to the core. Countries in the central core will change over time. During the past two decades Britain's relative importance has declined, while Japan, which was not consequential in this area twenty years ago, has become of central importance. Twenty years from now further significant changes will undoubtedly have taken place, and the system for collaboration must accommodate these gradual changes.

The second task is world reserve management. This involves wider cooperation, since the key to world reserve management is restraint in additions to central bank holdings of gold and of reserve currencies such as the U.S. dollar, the German mark, the British pound, and the French franc. So long as countries build up their international reserves with national currencies, the SDR will remain a secondary source of reserves. It will not be easy to switch habits to greater reliance on SDRs, and some observers even doubt the desirability of doing so. Thus the management of total world reserves will require further discussion and negotiation. It is not at the moment a matter of high priority, but it could once again become one, and that day should be anticipated through continuing surveillance of what is happening and continual discussion of possible alternative arrangements.

Such discussions should encompass not only official reserve holdings, but also the growth of international liquidity, some in official hands, some in private hands, that occurs annually through the medium of the international financial markets, and especially the Eurocurrency market. This market is only lightly regulated, and while it has been the source of much of the strength of international financial relations during the past decade, it also represents a source of potential vulnerability to the system's stability as well as a relatively uncontrolled source of international liquidity.

With respect to both tasks, it is desirable that the International Monetary Fund increasingly evolve into a central bank for national central banks. It already performs this function as a source of financial support, although it is not yet a true lender of last resort due to limitations on its resources. If SDRs become the principal reserve asset, the IMF will play a central role as a creator of international reserves. Moreover, under the Jamaica agreement of 1976 the IMF is charged with exercising close surveillance over currency interventions to influence exchange rates, with a view to assuring their consistency with agreed objectives and limitations on the use of exchange rates.

Beyond these tasks, the world economy requires much better coordination of macroeconomic policies than has been the case in the past. This again is a responsibility primarily of the major countries, especially the United States, West Germany, and Japan. These three countries are too large to ignore the rest of the world in framing their actions. They impose heavy costs on other countries, even under a regime of managed exchange rate flexibility, when they deflate their economies excessively or when they inflate their economies excessively. Some have done both in recent years. The international community should have a medium for making its views on economic management known to the responsible officials in the leading countries, and again the IMF in the future could provide the appropriate forum, if it were given that responsibility.

In terms of our general approach, in conclusion, international monetary arrangements illustrate several points: First, there is wide scope for different exchange rate arrangements by individual countries, but within a broad international framework. Second, the essential cooperation for maintaining that framework involves a relatively few countries, although all countries have an interest in it. Third, the failure of attempts to draw up a detailed blueprint applicable to all participating countries suggests the wisdom of a more pragmatic approach, concentrating on improvements on the arrangements we currently have.

[*Towards a Renovated International System*, 1977, pp. 45–49]

ENERGY

THE ENERGY SECTOR

Edward A. Frieman

THE WORLD TODAY is entering the second decade of a new energy regime following the Arab oil embargo of 1973 and the economic shock of the oil price explosion. Although a new state of equlibrium has not been attained, world wide changes have occurred; some of them of permanence and others perhaps illusory. The oil shocks created an economically paradoxical situation in which both inflation and recession occurred simultaneously and led to many of the oil importing nations accumulating financial debts which tend to place in jeopardy the world financial structure. The world wide recession is in large measure responsible for the present oil glut and the downturn in oil prices. The end result of this turmoil is a situation in which the price of energy absent the effects of inflation, has increased by about a factor of five over the decade.

There were sharp arguments among energy planners not too many years ago as to whether the energy/GNP ratio was rigid or flexible. Those arguments have now vanished as U.S. industry has improved its energy efficiency by about 33% in the time span from 1973 to 1982 and the energy/GNP ratio dropped by 19%. In the same time period, the world outside the centrally planned economies did almost as well at approximately 31%. One can say that there has been a significant structural change.

Yet another effect whose permanence is far from apparent is a lesser dependence on OPEC oil and its market pricing policies. Expansion of production in other areas, primarily the North Sea, Alaska and Mexico, have added 6 million barrels per day in non-OPEC production which it is hoped will lead to further freedom from the OPEC yoke. There are doubts on the part of some, as our earlier energy demand scenarios illustrated, that this situation can continue. Analysis of the drop in oil demand, crudely speaking, attributes about half to the recession and half to conservation. As we emerge from the recession on a world wide basis, it is argued that the other half will tend to reemerge while new energy efficiency measures cannot be adopted quickly enough to combat the increasing demand. More quantitatively, a demand increase of a million barrels per day, translates into a 5% increase in demand for OPEC's "oil of last resort." More worrisome is that this translates into a 20% increase from Persian Gulf supplies. It is in this sense, that one talks of a masking effect in which the market signals are in fact not truly reflecting a basic longer run serious issue.

There are other signs which also indicate that all is not well. The debt incurred by the developing countries in paying for their imports has seriously weakened their ability to continue economic growth. The broad "structural" unemployment which is stubbornly showing signs of remaining as the economy improves is thought in part to be a result of the increase in energy prices. The underlying reason is a shift to industries which consume less energy such as communications and services, displacing the heavier steel and other traditional "smoke-stack" industries. There has also been an inordinately slow growth in labor productivity and one speculation as to the cause involves the substitution of cheap labor for energy consuming devices.

The implications of the above for energy technology development are multi-fold. Resolution of the problem calls for a dual examination of policies which tend to limit the transition to newer sources of energy and for appropriate encouragement in the development of these technologies. The basic difficulty lies in the realization that there is an essential paradox at work, since the objectives of protecting the environment and public health, ensuring national security, promoting economic growth, and ensuring equity among nations and classes of people are in conflict.

Examination of energy supply and demand forecasts as well as the underlying technologies demonstrate what has now become widely accepted—we are not running out of energy, but we are running. To begin the transition over the next decades does not leave many options. The major steps appear to be:

1. Continue to press on energy efficiency and conservation technologies. The extension of the life of oil resulting from these actions is non-trivial. Although substantial progress has been made, impressive new opportunities

will be available over the next decades as existing capital stock is replaced. Confusing and conflicting market signals should not be interpreted by policy-makers as triggers to slow this development. The extent to which the energy/GNP ratio can be lowered without choking off economic development and producing other deleterious effects has been estimated to be a factor of two. This number is soft and argues for not relaxing efforts on the supply side.

2. Continue on efforts to enhance fluid fuel supply. This includes efforts at vigorous exploration for conventional oil and gas, pursuit of enhanced or tertiary recovery where applicable, fuel substitution (primarily coal for oil) in central station power generation and the initiation of development of a synthetic fuels industrial base. Associated with such a course of action are substantial policy issues, involving regulation, deregulation, tax policy, etc. as well as support for R&D.

3. Attempt to pursue a balanced coal and nuclear mix strategy. As fluid fuels phase down in the future, these two technologies, from our current perspective offer the only hope as economic alternatives for large scale electricity generation. Electricity demand growth projections have been notoriously wrong in the past. They are highly sensitive to assumed levels of energy efficiency and conservation measures, and to future price trajectories of electricity relative to other primary energy sources. The risks and problems attached to these technologies are, as noted earlier, considerable. A balanced strategy, at the least, offers future options for moving away from too premature a set of choices. The timing of the need for the breeder on the nuclear side of the equation is certainly not clear at this time. Some sort of technology base program or demonstration program appears to make sense.

The contribution of solar, geothermal, and hydroelectric power to the electricity generating sector appears, on all counts, to be small over the next few decades but is nevertheless of importance.

4. Pursue a vigorous investment policy in R&D both for the medium and long term. The sustainable technologies, namely, solar, the breeder, fusion and perhaps geothermal will be the workhorses of the future. The mid-term technologies discussed above all need continuing R&D for their improvement.

To carry out a program of the kind envisioned above requires detailed analysis of a number of domestic and foreign policy issues which are not in order here. Some of the more important are listed below.

One of the major lessons learned in the 70's was that tampering with the free flow of the market through mechanisms of regulation of price, through allocation of resources, through government subsidy to enforce market penetration, and other such measures, tends to worsen the problems the policy is supposed to correct. The market tendency toward equilibrating supply and demand has proven to be a powerful moderating force and barriers which prevent its natural action should be removed. Institutional barriers, such as building codes, which prevent the application of energy saving techniques or tax policies which require too short pay-back periods are trivial examples of such concerns.

As noted above further penetration of electricity is a major avenue for reduction in oil dependence. Because of uncertainties in electricity future demand, utilities are in a waiting mode on new investment. The regulatory regime for the utility sector has been at times capricious and ad hoc and in many instances tariff setting bodies have made it more difficult for the utilities to obtain adequate financing.

As we have repeatedly emphasized, coal, because of its low cost and abundance can become an effective substitute fuel. In fact, there are clear prospects for a more global international coal trade regime. For this to take place, a major investment in infrastructure related items will be needed, such as coal port facilities, coal slurry pipeline legislation, enhancing of inland transportation facilities, etc.

The acid rain issue is the one receiving the greatest amount of attention in the environmental, technological and political arenas. Significant reduction over the next decade must rely heavily on flue-gas desulfurization, commonly called "scrubbing." This option is now commercially available but is both costly and environmentally unattractive since it produces large amounts of sludge. Technical approaches involving burning coal in a cleaner and more efficient fashion at lower cost are clearly to be preferred. Fluidized-bed combustion in one form or another is a likely technology to come along rapidly. Serious attention should also be focussed on a possible large scale measurements program to understand the basic nature of the various components of the acid deposition process and to help in setting standards for mitigation.

Natural gas as a resource could be increased significantly before it too begins to wane. It is a desirable fuel in an oil displacement role but to encourage appropriate levels of market penetration requires detailed attention to pricing policies. In the past, tight controls have inhibited production and encouraged a trend toward oil. International arrangements for long distance gas pipelines may become more common in the future.

The pursuit of growth in the nuclear sector as we have noted previously is almost completely a policy rather than a technical issue. The U.S. has finally passed nuclear waste legislation with the result that a demonstration of technology under various geological conditions will take place. The policy questions involved are by now so well known that there is little benefit from further discussion here. For a complex of reasons, the current state of affairs resembles a nuclear moratorium in all but name. Utilizing this pause in a positive manner would seem to be a reasonable approach. For example, concepts are beginning to surface for ultrasafe reactors, and for schemes whose proliferation resistance is increased many fold. There is a tendency in the current climate to give such ideas short shrift, with the view that the very existence of new technology concepts somehow casts doubt on the old. The nuclear option might be better served by a relatively inexpensive R&D program focussed on innovative concepts and technology fixes. . . .

The energy supply and demand studies referred to above have tended to show that high gain breeders, which were once thought to be necessary shortly after the turn of the century will no longer be needed for that role. The likely course of development in the U.S. will be a technology base program for some time in the future.

It appears therefore that the major new requirements for reactors in the near term will all come from the military, for space, for submarine propulsion, and perhaps for materials production for the nuclear weapons complex.

For the very long range technologies, breeders, fusion, solar and perhaps geothermal, the R&D burden has essentially been borne by the interested governments or groups of governments. Under such arrangements, there should not be a loss of essential proprietary information due to the very long-term nature of the research. From the point of view of cost sharing, it is clear that serious international collaboration has many positive virtues. The United Kingdom has recently announced that it is joining a European based breeder development program. The European Economic Community has sponsored construction of the multi-national fusion device, JET. It is a challenge to the decision makers to enhance these collaborative ventures in an arena which is basic to humanity's future.

["The Energy Sector," 1984, pp. 165–90]

COMMUNICATION

NEW FORCES IN
WORLD POLITICS

Seyom Brown

MANY OF THE SCIENTIFIC ADVANCES and new technological applications of the twentieth century have had their most
dramatic cumulative or synergistic effects in the fields of transportation and communication, radically altering the role of
location, distance, and topographic barriers in human affairs.
From the standpoint of the physics of moving men, materials,
and ideas the whole earth is already a community. The degree to
which the earth community has been activated to form concrete
cooperative relationships, however, is infinitesimal compared to
what is now physically possible and rapidly becoming cost-
effective in economic terms. The reasons for this sluggish response are almost all political, not physical.

Despite energy shortages, intercontinental travel is becoming as easy and cheap as domestic intercity travel, sometimes
even easier. This does not mean, however, that individuals can
travel anywhere they want to or that men can ship any goods to
whatever destination they wish. For the sovereign state, loss of
control over who enters the realm or what is permitted in would
be in effect loss of control over fundamental social and economic
processes. The challenge of airline hijackings, narcotics smug-
gling, and other criminal uses of the global transportation
network has therefore not elicited vigorous and concerted international action. (As the Americans saw in 1789, the need to
regulate interstate commerce involves the enhancement of central law and order institutions.) Through standardization of air
traffic and international airport procedures already existing, the
means are technically at hand to develop effective international
policing mechanisms. For such a development, however, the
separate nations would be required to countenance a degree of

supranational jurisdiction which some still consider threatening to their sovereign prerogatives.

Similarly, as more and more communications are handled by earth-orbiting satellites, there will be few if any purely technological barriers to linking the entire world in one comprehensive communications system. Such a system would probably be most efficient, costing consumers less and handling more traffic without message interference. But the political-economic questions are far from being solved, even in principle. The provision and maintenance of equipment for a global communications system involves very lucrative contracts. Who is to get these contracts? Who will let them? And by what criteria? As experience with the U.S.-dominated INTELSAT consortium shows, now that international satellite communications are no longer experimental, a pure efficiency standard for letting contracts is unacceptable to most nations since it would perpetuate U.S. dominance. A related set of questions concerns the allocation of preferred orbital positions and bands on the frequency spectrum. Should those who get up there first have the first claim to the preferred positions?

Probably the knottiest of all the political issues in the new era of communications is over the degree of freedom to broadcast directly to foreign populations. . . . Once this technology exists, should there by any legal regime to regulate program content? At one extreme is the United States, which now champions maximum freedom of international broadcasting; at the other extreme is the Soviet Union, which insists that each country have a veto on the programs beamed to it, and that the right to jam broadcasts or shoot down offending satellites be legitimized.

Another challenge to the meaning of national borders derives from the development of photographic and remote sensing systems, carried by spacecraft, which survey earth resources and activities on a contininuing and global basis. The information gained from the observations of earth from space will facilitate the development of global models of the earth's natural ecosystems, climatic patterns, resources, and man-made alterations of the environment. This will make possible more effective local planning and, to the extent that it becomes feasible politically, global planning for the use of resources. This is the positive side of the coin. From the standpoint of some countries that expect to be technically ill-equipped for optimum use of the new information, the negative side is the loss of control over what some nations previously considered proprietary data important in negotiating terms of access to their resources by foreign entrepreneurs. In this field too the questions of who owns, manufactures, maintains, and provides the various technical services are still handled essentially on the basis that capability makes right. If they continue to be handled unilaterally, however, optimal use of the technology is unlikely since fully elaborated and cooperating global networks, including ground stations, will be important for worldwide monitoring. Multilateral decision making and management of the technology, as already indicated, would require a considerable reorientation toward international as opposed to purely national control on the part of the technologically advanced nations, particularly the United States.

[*New Forces in World Politics*, 1974, pp. 140–43]

FOOD

HUNGER

United Nations

ESTIMATES OF THE NUMBER OF malnourished in the world vary. The most conservative estimates are those of FAO. These are based on the numbers of people thought to be consuming 20 per cent below the level needed to sustain life and a light amount of activity. This cut-off point corresponds to 1.2 times the Basal Metabolic Rate—the level for life sustenance. Estimates based on this measure must be considered the lowest probable limit of malnutrition.

Using this measure, FAO reported that in 1969–71 there were some 401 million people, 24 per cent of the surveyed population, who were malnourished. In 1972–74, when poor harvests in Africa and the Far East affected the situation, the total rose to 455 million. By 1974–76, the numbers had fallen, but only slightly, to 435 million, or 23 percent of the population to the developing market economies.

The World Bank estimates use of a higher calorie level as the threshold of malnutrition, based on the average level recommended for each country by the expert committee of FAO and the World Health Organization. On this basis World Bank economists estimated that in 1973 no less than 808 million people had a calorie intake lower than the recommended level, or 61 per cent of the total population of the countries surveyed. Of these people, almost 600 million were consuming less than 90 per cent of the recommended intake.

No more recent global estimates are available, but the total number is unlikely to have declined. In 1978–80, out of 119 developing countries, no less than 56, or almost half, had averaged *per capita* calorie supplies below their recommended needs. The population of these countries was more than one and a quarter billion. More than a billion people lived in countries where *per capita* calorie supplies in 1978–80 were lower than, or the same as, they had been in 1969–71. Twenty-four countries, or one in five, had average intakes in 1978–80 of 90 per cent or less of their recommended levels.

Poverty, in its various aspects, is the major cause of malnutrition. At both the country and individual levels, inadequate food supplies are the result of insufficient land or other resources to grow enough food, or insufficient funds to purchase these.

The calorie intake of the average person in a developing country has improved significantly over past decades. In 1961–63 it was only 89 per cent of recommended levels. By 1974–76 it had risen to 96 per cent and, four years later, reached one per cent above requirements. At the same time the average inhabitant of the wealthier developed countries was consuming 33 per cent more calories than recommended, resulting in increased risk of heart disease and obesity.

But the satisfactory average, when all developing countries are considered as a whole, conceals wide inequalities. The wealthier regions were in excess of their recommended levels—West Asia by 11 per cent and Latin America by 9 per cent in 1978–80. The Asian centrally planned economies reached 104 per cent of their recommended levels—back in 1961–63 they had been 17 per cent below. In contrast, the average intake in East Asia in 1978–80 was still only 96 per cent of recommended levels, while Africa's was only 94 per cent.

Africa's *per capita* calorie supply was virtually stagnant over the 1970s. And the 31 least-developed countries, generally the poorest and most vulnerable economies, registered an actual decline, from 88 per cent of recommended levels in 1969–71 to only 84 per cent in 1978–80. Over this same period calorie availability fell or stagnated in no less than 40 developing countries out of 119.

These national averages conceal wide inequalities within countries: even in countries with average intakes above the recommended level, large numbers of people may be getting far less food than required.

High-income groups invariably have higher calorie intakes than low income groups, and the quality of their diet is usually also better in terms of protein, vitamins and minerals, because they spend proportionately more on fish, meat and dairy products and fruit and vegetables. Smallholders and the landless are more likely to be malnourished than those with larger holdings of land. Pronounced inequalities may exist within individual families: the adult men often take priority over women and children in the share-out of the family's food. Children under five and pregnant and lactating women, are the most vulnerable groups. This pattern of food distribution in the family poses a continuing threat to the physical and mental health and capabilities of future generations.

[*UN Chronicle,* Jan. 1983, p. 77]

MIXED PICTURE ON FOOD

United Nations Food and Agricultural Organization

SPEAKING AT THE OPENING of the seventh annual session of the 89-member Committee on World Food Security, Edouard Saouma, the Director-General of FAO, said that the time had come to "review and redefine all the various components of food security in order to establish some new approaches towards solving the apparently insoluble problem." He said that "some progress" had been made in the search for a food security system in the past seven years, but there had also been failures and disappointments.

Reviewing the food security situation since the 1974 World Food Conference in Rome, Mr. Saouma urged an evaluation of the whole pattern and effectiveness of the food security institutions set up by the Conference, noting that its minimum food aid target of 10 million tons had never been reached.

He said the recent improvement in cereal harvests, together with the impasse in international negotiations on a grains agreement, provided "a breathing space" for a general review of the whole concept of world food security, including the role of the Committee on World Food Security.

He noted the Committee had been created during the 1975 food crisis as one of the first follow-up actions to the World Food Conference, but he doubted whether it had fulfilled the hopes of its founders.

CEREAL PRODUCTION UP

Mr. Saouma welcomed the fact that, after two poor seasons, world production of cereals had risen last year by 95 million tons, which should permit a substantial replenishing of global stocks. He added, however, that those global figures must not be used to conceal or ignore the growing difficulties of many low-income countries, especially in Africa. Some 37 food-deficit developing countries had recorded negative rates of growth in their cereals output on a *per capita* basis over the past decade and 19 of those had had an actual decline in output. "Far from moving closer towards self-reliance, they are now facing their widest food gap on record," he said.

Food Insecurity

Mr. Saouma cited various problems as contributing to food insecurity, including the growing dependence of developing countries, particularly the low-income nations, on cereal imports, which had doubled in the past 10 years. Other contributing factors were price instability, which affected producers and consumers alike, decreasing food aid allocations, faltering assistance to developing countries in building up national food security reserves, and protectionist policies.

"It is paradoxical that at a time when stocks are being built up and acreage is reduced in developed exporting countries, total food aid allocations of cereals are falling," Mr. Saouma said. "Also, international assistance to developing countries for building up national food security reserves falters and stagnates."

The Director-General noted the FAO Committee on Food Aid Policies and Programmes had agreed at its last session on a joint pledging conference for the regular resources of both the WFP and the International Emergency Food Reserve (IEFR), and added: "It remains to be seen how effective this device will be. The IEFR is not as yet placed on a fully multilateral basis, freely available at the disposal of WFP. Nor has serious consideration been given to proposals for prepositioning food reserves in strategic locations for quick use at times of urgent need."

[*UN Chronicle*, June 1982, pp. 95, 98]

V

THE "GLOBAL COMMONS"

V. THE "GLOBAL COMMONS"

THE NOTION OF "COMMONS" stems from traditional law and practice, in which the high seas, seabeds, and outer space, no less than the grassy town common in the heart of the small New England village, are considered to be owned by no one, and thus the possession of all in the "community" at whatever level. Competing philosophies of governance and economic policy among the nations of the world are in direct collision concerning the philosophical as well as practical implications of national and international activity in both the deep seabed of the oceans and in outer space. In both environments there is already much national and international activity. While the current "might makes right attitude of the superpowers may work for a while, logic suggests that for the longer term some effective structures of cooperative international action will be the only alternative to international anarchy. The authors in Part V sketch out the limited fragments of cooperation that do exist.

Prof. Donald J. Puchala sets the stage by asserting that technically advanced countries, while doubtless benefiting from a short-run scramble to close off the "global commons" and parcel it into national jurisdictions, would benefit in the long run from a legal regime that provides an equitable division of benefits between present and future generations. Per Magnus Wijkman of the Swedish Board of Commerce spells out the moves by nations to enclose portions of the global commons, transferring the "heritage of mankind" into a national inheritance. He concludes that each case should be judged on its merits.

Five cases in point are then briefly explored. The first two selections report on the formidable—and contentious—effort by 150 nations over a nine-year period to draft a definitive

Law of the Sea treaty containing provisions for equitable and strategically acceptable rules for three fourths of the world's surface. The effort was recently put in question by US objections to provisions for international regulation of deep seabed mining of hard minerals. A second major issue area, briefed here in a UN publication, is outer space, where the 1967 treaty on Peaceful Uses contends with growing superpower militarization.

The overall "environment" issue has come to include multiple sets of issues, summed up by World Resource Institute president James Gustavus Speth in a selection from a 1985 report from the Center for National Policy. Among the issues he identifies are the immensely important roles tropical forests play, not only as a source of raw materials, but also as the planet's largest net producer of oxygen. Yet tropical forests are in process of being destroyed, which could have irrevocable consequences unless checked. He also deals with the ways in which human activity will soon play a major role in changing the world climate, particularly given the so-called "greenhouse effect" that could gravely affect world food production. International organizations expert A. Leroy Bennett describes international concern about pollution that threatens the global biosphere, and reviews national attitudes toward environmental practices that continue to inhibit international cooperation.

At the close of this section Harlan Cleveland and Club of Rome president Alexander King explain why troubling questions are asked about traditional approaches to growth. In counterpoint, economist Julian Simon takes the optimistic side of the debate between those who feel that nonrenewable resources are becoming irrevocably squandered and demand corrective cooperation, versus those who think the problem has been vastly overstated, and that the ultimate resource is skilled people who extend their will and imagination for their own benefit and, in the end, the common benefit.

A.

THE
CHALLENGE

AMERICAN INTERESTS AND THE U.N.

Donald J. Puchala

PRESERVATION OF THE EARTH'S RESOURCES

INCREASINGLY DURING THE LAST DECADE, the United Nations has been led by its members into issues concerning the disposition of the global commons. The commons are those domains possessed by no nation but used by many or all. These include the high seas, regional seas, the seabed, international river basins, the atmosphere, the ionosphere, and outer space. A generation ago the exploitation of many of these common domains was technologically unfeasible, and their despoilation was unimaginable. Yet today we can mine the oceans and the moon, direct electronic signals and laser beams through the ionosphere, and travel in outer space. We can also pollute the oceans, change the rains to acid, destroy the earth's ozone layer, squander reserves of fresh water, contaminate the atmosphere with radioactivity, and station nuclear weapons on the floor of the sea and on platforms orbiting in outer space. Moreover, because some countries are more technologically able to accomplish these feats than others, there is danger that the exploitable commons will disappear as the pioneers scramble to extend their national jurisdictions. There is also danger that present-day polluters will pass on a highly contaminated earth to future generations.

The thrust of U.N. efforts on issues of global commons has been to attempt to regulate these domains under international law. Some law-making via treaty, convention, and code has been directed toward forestalling the closure of the commons by guaranteeing access to all countries regardless of present power positions or technological prowess. This, for example, has been a major element in U.N. efforts to draft a new treaty codifying the Law of the Sea and in institutionalizing the principle that the oceans are the "common heritage of mankind." Forestalling closure is also a key element in negotiations concerning the allocation of radio and television frequencies, considered at the World Administrative Radio Conference in 1979. A similar issue has been the parceling of satellite space in the earth's geostationary orbit. In 1980, U.N. members concluded the Agreement Concerning the Activities of States on the Moon and Other Celestial Bodies, stipulating that neither the moon's surface nor its subsurface shall become the national property of any state. Outer space as well as the seabeds were previously demilitarized by U.N.-sponsored treaties in 1967 and 1971. As esoteric as some of these matters may appear, they are but hints of the world affairs of the future fashioned by advancing technology. Current efforts to establish legal regimes are attempts to provide means for future conflict resolution by adjudication rather than by force.

Legislation concerning environmental matters in the United Nations is designed to elicit commitments from states either to refrain from polluting or to cooperate in clean-up efforts. By U.N. agreement, for example, ocean-going oil tankers are regulated by international law, and owners are held responsible for pollution their ships may unleash. A major U.N. treaty, the Treaty Banning Nuclear Tests in the Atmosphere, in Outer Space and Under Water, attempts to slow the nuclear arms race, but also stems contamination by radioactivity in the atmosphere and the oceans. Ocean contamination is also the target of the U.N. Environmental Program's emphasis on regional seas, where activities are underway to combat pollution in the Mediterranean, the Caribbean Sea, the Red Sea, the Persian Gulf, the Gulf of Guinea, and other areas of the Pacific. All of these programs involve commitments to common action by littoral states, and all are funded by international trusts established to finance U.N. environmental activities. In 1977 the United Nations also adopted a Plan of Action to Combat Desertification at the perimeters of the Sahara, as well as a global plan to preserve the earth's fresh water resources.

American interest in the global commons is consistent with the intent and direction of U.N. efforts. Americans use the global commons much more than other peoples. The United States would probably benefit from a short-run scramble to close off the commons and parcel it into national jurisdictions. Since our technology permits us to exploit now what others can only hope to exploit in the future, we would for a time command the lion's share of the parcelled commons. But there should be no doubt that such a policy would invite challenge and conflict in the future—much as colonizers' territorial conquests in the past invited later decolonization. A commons regulated by law, protected from contamination, and exploited under a regime which allocates shares among users, including the United States and other industrialized countries, promises greater international tranquility by providing an equitable division of benefits between present and future generations. Far from contradicting American beliefs in free market behavior (since abusive exploitation is regulated even in our own country), U.N. programs concerning the global commons affirm the fundamental American belief that law and not force must be the basis of public order.

["American Interests and the UN," 1984, pp. 440–41]

MANAGING THE GLOBAL COMMONS

Per Magnus Wijkman

THE CURRENT TENDENCY AT MANY UNITED NA-
TIONS CONFERENCES is to subdivide internationally shared
resources, placing the parts under exclusive national control.
Although contrary to the publicly proclaimed common heritage
philosophy, this nationalistic development is not surprising.
Income and population growth have raised the prices of natural
resources relative to other goods. Stimulated by this, technical
progress has opened previously inaccessible resources for exploitation. As the exploitation of marginal resources becomes
worthwhile, prime resources generate more rents. Distrustful of
international organizations, nations strive to enclose the resources and to appropriate the rents. The common heritage is
thus transformed into national inheritances.

Whether national enclosure is more efficient than managing
these resources through a supranational resource regime, and
whether it is as fair, must be judged from case to case. It depends
on the answers to three questions. First, does the resource
possess such common property characteristics that coordination
of use provides benefits sufficiently large to offset the management costs? Second, can the voluntary cooperation of co-owners
achieve coordinated use more cheaply than a centralized decision-making authority? Third, how do awards of new property
rights and the loss of historical rights affect the distribution of
wealth?

This section evaluates the resource regimes currently being
proposed in various international forums for fisheries, for the
resources of the continental shelf and of the deep seabed, for
Antarctica and the Southern Ocean, and for the orbit-frequency
spectrum. It illustrates the practical problems of negotiating
regimes that involve many governments.

Fisheries and Antarctic living resources fall in the category of resources that are costly to subdivide. The amount harvested must be limited and harvesting rights allocated. The difficulties of the distributional issue are compounded by efficiency considerations. The resources of the deep seabed and the continental margin constitute a commons that can be partitioned, and its parts individually exploited, without much extra cost. Subdivision poses mainly a question of equity, and the primary function of an international authority should be to negotiate an acceptable initial distribution of private property rights. The orbit-spectrum resource provides an intermediate case, with characteristics of both of the above categories.

Fishing stocks are a classic example of a common property resource. Early in the Third United Nations Conference on the Law of the Sea delegates agreed on the principle of an exclusive economic zone (EEZ), whereby each coastal state would be granted exclusive management and fishing rights within two hundred nautical miles of its coastline. In most cases, this border includes the continental shelf, in whose shallow waters are located the richest fishing grounds. The world's annual fish catch was worth close to $20 billion in the late seventies, and virtually all of this is caught in the proposed EEZs. Thus, UNCLOS III proposes in effect that eighty coastal states enclose the world's major fishing grounds.

For the purpose of conserving fishing stocks, two hundred-mile EEZs are superior to the current regime of nonexistent or voluntary management, but they probably are inferior to a supranational management regime. National management will result in efficient management of stocks only if the extension of fishing limits brings the fishing stock, and sometimes also the fish it preys upon and those that prey upon it, entirely within the coastal state's jurisdiction. The key question therefore is how often this occurs. Many stocks that migrate along coasts remain transboundary resources even after the outward extension of fishing limits. In Africa, where coastlines tend to be short, fishing stocks pass through the waters of several countries in their seasonal or life-cycle migrations. The waters of both Chile and Peru contain the Pacific anchovy stock; the North Sea remains a common fishing ground for five European countries. Georges Bank is shared by Canada and the United States, even with limits of two hundred nautical miles. With some exceptions—Icelandic cod is notable—major fishing stocks will remain common property resources, though common now to fewer states than before.

The fewer the states, the more willing each government will be to limit the catch in its EEZ and to rely on other governments' promises to do likewise. Will this extension of fishing limits reduce the number of co-owners of fishing stocks sufficiently to induce effective voluntary cooperation? The answer to this requires a detailed study stock by stock, but no such studies were made prior to UNCLOS III. Thus, its Draft Convention proposes dispensing management rights to coastal states without any assurances that management will be effective.

In addition to imperfectly managing stocks, governments will be tempted to follow protectionist policies. The political difficulties encountered by a government that attempts to introduce effective management programs should not be underestimated. Programs to control harvesting are unpopular with fishermen, who see extended fishing limits as a means to protect domestic fishermen rather than fishing stocks. The Draft Convention produced by UNCLOS III condones protectionist use of extended fishing limits. It does not require that entry to fishing grounds be controlled in a nondiscriminatory way, for example by requiring domestic and foreign fishermen to pay the same price for fishing licenses. In many of the eighty countries that now claim two hundred nautical mile fishing limits, domestic fishermen have replaced foreign fishermen and domestic political opposition has postponed the introduction of effective controls on total catch. The effect of protectionist policies is to reduce the efficiency of the world's fishing fleet by forcing parts of it to move to new waters and to convert to new types of fishing.

The Draft Convention proposals would also have significant income redistribution effects. The creation of EEZs permits the coastal state to appropriate all the rents from fishing grounds should it wish to. These rents have been estimated to be at least $2 billion annually. Compared with the existing situation, this would redistribute income from nations with long-distance fishing fleets to states with long coasts bordering on rich fishing grounds. Since the richest fishing grounds, like the richest countries, are located in the temperate zones, the benefits go mainly to developed coastal states. One may debate the fairness of this redistribution, but one cannot deny either that it fails to compensate those who lose historical fishing rights or that it favors rich countries more than poor countries.

HYDROCARBON RESOURCES AND MANGANESE NODULES

The continental margin and the deep seabed traditionally have been international commons under the doctrine of the freedom of the high seas. However, since the Truman proclamation in 1945 an increasing number of coastal states have extended their resource jurisdiction over the adjoining continental shelf. UNCLOS III proposes to place the resources of the continental margin and those of the deep seabed under separate regimes. It would confirm the coastal states' jurisdiction over most of the continental margin while placing the remaining area of the seabed under an International Seabed Authority. Do the resource characteristics of these areas justify these different assignments?

The main resources of the deep seabed are currently believed to be manganese nodules, containing most notably manganese, nickel, cobalt, and copper. Deep-seabed mining holds out the prospect of commercial success, especially for prime mine sites in the Pacific. In the absence of limits on production the seabed might provide the major part of world consumption of these minerals in twenty or thirty years.

Hydrocarbons are the main resource of the continental margin. Currently, offshore oil and gas come entirely from the continental shelf (e.g., from the North Sea and the Gulf of Mexico); large areas remain to be exploited—Georges Bank, the Arctic Sea, and the China Sea. The average water depth of the shelf is two hundred meters. Recently, however, deposits have been discovered on the continental slope, which descends down to about two thousand meters. Recovering hydrocarbons from these water depths is already technically possible, and will become commercially feasible as the relative price of oil increases. Today offshore reserves account for about 20 percent of the world's total oil and gas production, a share that may double by the year 2000.

Efficiency considerations do not justify regulating the exploitation of manganese nodules or of hydrocarbons, except in rare cases.

Manganese nodules present none of the characteristics of common property resources that make private ownership or national jurisdiction inefficient. On the contrary, efficient mining requires exclusive rights to mine a well-defined site. The seabed regime proposed by UNCLOS III provides exclusive mining rights, but it also proposes to limit the volume of seabed mineral production. Pollution aside, seabed mining does not exhibit the external economies that require coordination of mining activities. Production limitation, therefore, reduces the economic efficiency of mining.

Hydrcarbon exploitation on the continental margin may provide examples of common pools, which would benefit from coordinated management. Common pools occur in the North Sea and elsewhere (e.g., fields off Newfoundland and the Aleutian Islands). However, it is unlikely that more than two governments, or one government and the International Seabed Authority, will share a pool. This increases the likelihood that the involved parties will be able to negotiate a solution to the common-pool problem on their own. Even if they cannot, this problem is likely to remain no matter where the boundary between national and international jurisdiction over resources is drawn.

In the case of the continental margin and the deep seabed, in contrast to international fisheries, efficiency considerations argue for allowing private property rights but not for imposing central production control. The primary function of an international authority should be to distribute resource rents and consumer surplus, not to regulate production. National enclosure of the deep seabed would award its rents to the new owners unless they paid a market price for seabed real estate. However, auctioning off large tracts of the seabed would favor large countries and those rich in capital, while allowing coastal states alone to enclose the deep seabed would preclude the possibility of extracting a market price. Consequently, distributional considerations argue against national enclosure of the seabed and in favor of allowing an International Seabed Authority to sell or lease mine sites at market prices and to distribute the resulting revenues among governments.

THE ANTARCTIC

The Antarctic is a disputed commons. Seven countries claim sovereignty over parts of the continent. The claims of Argentina, Chile, and the United Kingdom partially overlap; Australia, France, New Zealand, Norway, and the United Kingdom recognize one another's claims. These seven, together with six nonclaimant states, are parties to the Antarctic Treaty of 1959.

The treaty is designed to ensure the exclusively peaceful use of the continent—one-tenth of the globe's land surface—and to facilitate scientific research by allowing scientists access to the whole area. It sidesteps the issue of territorial claims by freezing existing claims and prohibiting new ones. It does not deal with the issue of the exploitation of Antarctic resources.

The natural resources of the Antarctic consist of onshore and offshore oil and gas reserves estimated to be about one-half of Alaskan offshore reserves. There are also large but currently inaccessible coal and iron ore deposits. The living resources include fur seals, crabs, lobsters, fish, and krill; the last may be the most important. The annual sustainable catch of krill has been estimated at between 50 and 150 million tons, and thus perhaps equivalent to the current annual world catch of all other seafoods.

The Treaty's tenth consultative meeting (1979) initiated negotiation of a convention to regulate the exploitation of living marine animals other than whales and fur seals (which are covered by separate conventions). The treaty, signed by the parties in December 1980, adopts a comprehensive ecosystem management approach. Krill is the base of a complex food web in the Antarctic ecosystem. The amount of krill harvested annually affects the stocks of animals that prey upon it and, in particular, affects the already severely decimated population of Antarctic baleen whales. During the Antarctic winter, these whales migrate toward the equator and are caught by countries other than Antarctic claimant states. The amount of krill harvested thus affects a group of countries and interests wider than just the krill fishing nations (USSR, Japan, West Germany) or even the thirteen nations party to the Antarctic Treaty.

Furthermore, the circular flow of ocean currents around the Antarctic continent makes the planktonic krill a common property resource. No single claimant state can by itself control the size of the stocks of krill under its jurisdiction. The governments must agree upon and enforce a common management policy and extend their jurisdiction beyond two hundred nautical miles if they are to manage all krill stocks.

Comprehensive management of the Antarctic's living resources is thus essential, and must cover the major animal groups of the food web and their habitats. It is therefore unfortunate that the harvesting of whales and seals is regulated by separate conventions. Another weakness is that the convention, while establishing a scientific committee, provides no financial supports to make it independent of the treaty members; nor does it empower the committee to determine the annual harvesting capacity of the resource. There is no political mechanism to allocate national quotas, since this might prejudge the issue of territorial claims, and consequently there is no enforcement mechanism to ensure that the actual harvest does not exceed the allowable catch. Given the large number of countries involved either as claimant states or as exploiters of the resource, management based on voluntary observance may well prove ineffective. Interests not represented in the decision-making process may be especially reluctant to comply with the committee's recommendations.

The lack of a supranational enforcement mechanism, a serious shortcoming of the convention, may be due to a desire to avoid creating a precedent for the convention on mineral resources on which negotiations started in 1981. These resources also provide examples of external economies. Some oil pools may be common to several Antarctic claims, and the exploitation of offshore oil reserves may affect the living resources of the Southern Ocean. Comprehensive management with supranational enforcement is appropriate here as well. However, enforcement presupposes representation of the interested parties in the decision-making process, and identifying the parties interested in the exploitation of Antarctic resources broaches the question of who owns Antarctica. Rising prices of raw materials, and especially of hydrocarbons, increase the value of territorial claims to the continent and of membership in the Antarctic club. This encourages the members to retain for themselves the right to exploit and otherwise to benefit from Antarctic resources. Not surprisingly, developing countries have suggested that these benefits be shared with a larger group of countries.

ORBIT-SPECTRUM RESOURCE

The orbit-spectrum resource consists of the electromagnetic spectrum through which radio waves are transmitted and the orbits in space in which satellites and space platforms are placed. It has traditionally been viewed as a common resource that no single country may appropriate. Rights to use these resources are awarded by the International Telecommunications Union, a United Nations agency. A country requiring frequencies informs the Union, which assigns them so as to minimize interference. User rights are awarded on a first-come, first-served basis and are free of charge.

As long as the electromagnetic spectrum was a plentiful resource, zero user fees were appropriate. Now, however, the spectrum is congested, as soon the geostationary orbit for parking satellites will be. This common resource has become scarce and consequently valuable, and national governments strive to enclose it. The equatorial countries, for example, have claimed sovereignty over those parts of the geostationary tube that lie above their respective territories.

Since telecommunications technology developed in the industrial countries first, 90 percent of existing user rights have been allocated to the richest 10 percent of the world's countries. Fearing that the electromagnetic spectrum will be occupied before they are ready to use their "share," the developing countries in 1979 claimed an allocation of user rights based on their future rather than on their current needs at the World Administrative Radio Conference. Since allocations are held for twenty years, this would result in an inefficient hoarding of frequencies and orbits.

A more efficient alternative would be to assign frequencies and permit their subleasing. This would enable a country to benefit from an assignment without itself having to use the frequency. This would effectively award ownership of orbit-spectrum resources to national governments. The fairness of any particular initial distribution of rights is a matter of opinion. However, carving up the orbit-spectrum in national or private segments and allowing subleasing rights may be inefficient if there are important external economies in its use. Transmissions on one frequency often interfere with transmissions on neighboring frequencies using the same time and place. Satellites wander around their orbital slots and can collide with other satellites.

It is not clear whether private markets or international regulation would prevent unwanted interference more cheaply; factors work both ways. Interference is usually two-directional: sender A interferes with sender B, which in turn interferes with A. Satellite A cannot collide with satellite B without being harmed itself. This interdependence gives both parties strong incentives to agree on measures to keep interference at a mutually acceptable level. On the other hand, each transmitter or satellite may mutually interfere with a large number of other transmitters or satellites. With many parties involved, the costs of contracting a liability system and enforcing it in the courts may be high. If this is the case, public management of the common property resource may be more efficient than the allotment of private property rights. With many nations claiming user rights, an intergovernmental agency would need coercive powers.

The appropriate organization for managing a commons depends on a variety of factors, the most important being why communal ownership is maintained to begin with and how many co-owners are involved.

When the resource is held as a commons simply because the parties cannot agree on how to subdivide it, the organization serves primarily to pool risks, distributing to co-owners the revenues that result from auctioning user rights.

If communal ownership is maintained because external

diseconomies in resource use are significant, the organization in addition must limit production to a level that is socially optimal. When several governments share jurisdiction over the resource, interdependence between the firms exploiting it results in policy interdependence of the governments. In some countries politicians may resent this interdependence, but refusal to recognize it will result in less efficient use of the resource.

When few governments share jurisdiction over the resource, strong economic incentives exist for them to cooperate voluntarily in managing the commons in order to avoid inefficiency. They are more likely to do this if their respective national interests in the resource are roughly equal and if they share common values. On the other hand, when many governments share jurisdiction over the resource, experience shows that effective management requires that the organization have coercive powers, that is, the power to make decisions binding on members and to monitor and enforce compliance.

Sovereign governments are normally reluctant to surrender jurisdiction, although their reluctance may be less in regional organizations than in international organizations with more heterogeneous membership. It is easy to despair, therefore, about the ability of international organizations to deal effectively with the problems posed by transborder fisheries, ozone layer depletion, and atmospheric carbon dioxide accumulation.

Nevertheless, let us hope that governments will be persuaded to pool modest jurisdictional powers before the global commons suffer large and irreversible damage. They may do this if they recognize that the unique physical characteristics of common property resources require governments to coordinate their management powers regardless of any distributional considerations; that distributional goals can be achieved independently of resource use given political willingness to effectuate income transfers; and that the price mechanism can be an effective facilitator of compromise for conflicts over resource use.

["Managing the Global Commons," 1982, pp. 526–36]

B.

ISSUE AREAS

LAW OF THE SEA

SUMMARY OF PROVISIONS

Law of the Sea Treaty

LAW OF THE SEA PROVISIONS

Following are the main provisions of the Law of the Sea Treaty, which was signed yesterday in Montego Bay, Jamaica:

Territorial Waters—Each nation's sovereign territory extends 12 miles beyond its coast. In this zone, however, all foreign vessels must be allowed the right of innocent passage, that is, passage that does not threaten the nation's security.

Free Passage—Beyond 12 miles, all ships and planes, military and commercial, can move freely. Submarines can travel underwater.

Exclusive Economic Zone—Every coastal nation has exclusive rights to the fish and other marine life in the waters extending 200 miles beyond its shores. When nations are separated by a body of water less than 400 miles, they must establish dividing lines for the zones.

Straits—More than 100 straits or choke points are 24 miles wide or less but do not become territorial waters. All ships and planes shall have a right of "transit passage" through the straits, such as Gibraltar and Hormuz.

Continental Shelf—The most critical economic portion of the treaty deals with the continental shelf extending from a nation's shores and under the seas. Each nation is given exlusive rights to the oil, gas and any other resource in the shelf for 350 miles beyond the coast.

Seabed Mining—The nodules of copper, nickel, cobalt and zinc lying on the Pacific Ocean floor under the high seas are "the common heritage of mankind." To mine these metals, a complex global authority is established, but priority contracts shall be awarded to four groups of companies led by American mining concerns, a French consortium and ventures controlled by Japan, the Soviet Union and India. A global mining enterprise shall be given one site equal in size or value to any mined by a national or private company. The treaty fixes a production ceiling to support present prices of the metals and insure that they are not reduced by seabed yields. Private mining concerns must sell their technical knowledge to the global enterprise. The whole arrangement can be amended by agreement among three-fourths of the treaty signers.

Disputes—Virtually all quarrels involving nations or individuals over the convention must be settled either by a new International Tribunal for the Law of the Sea, arbitration or the International Court of Justice at The Hague.

Ratification—The treaty will come into force one year after 60 nations have ratified it.

[*New York Times,* Dec. 11, 1982]

ISSUES BEFORE THE 38th UNGA

United Nations Association of the U.S.A.

THE 1982 LAW OF THE SEA CONVENTION was signed by
an overwhelming majority of states on December 10, 1982 in
Jamaica. By July 1983, it had been ratified by Fiji, Ghana,
Jamaica, Mexico, Zambia and the United Nations Council for
Namibia. One year after 60 nations have ratified it, it will enter
into force [art. 308].

Yet the future of the Convention is by no means clear. The
determination of the United States Government to reject the
Convention because of its provisions concerning **deep-seabed
mining** has placed most of the other pioneer mining nations in a
quandary. They find the mining provisions equally objectionable, but they approve of most of the rest of the treaty. These
countries also remain committed to the treaty process and are
hoping that problems in the seabed mining area can be resolved.
At the same time, they are not certain that this can be achieved.

Signature of the Law of the Sea Convention by well over the
requisite 50 nations in December triggered the establishment of
the Preparatory Commission envisaged by Conference Resolution I [PR SEA/517]. Its task is to lay the groundwork for the
International Seabed Authority that will regulate mining in the
seabed beyond national jurisdiction. The Commission will also
set up the Enterprise, which will be the Authority's operational
mining arm and the International Tribunal for the Law of the
Sea. In addition, the Commission will draft the critical implementing rules for the mining portions of the treaty. A delay in
prospects for commercial deep-seabed mining operations is
presently reducing the pressures on governments and industry
to produce an acceptable and workable mining regime in the
immediate future. On the other hand, any delay in preparing

the implementing rules in the Preparatory Commission, which will clarify and refine treaty mining provisions, will also postpone signature and/or ratification by the mining states. This would argue for early work by the Commission on those procedural rules and standards that would be critical to mining states' decisions about the treaty.

Thus, prospects for Convention entry into force are neither bleak, given the universal support for its non-seabeds portions, nor are they entirely favorable. The work of the Preparatory Commission holds the key to the endorsement of the Convention by the major industrialized countries and the developing nations.

The US Government is actively pursuing initiatives to secure national ocean interests through alternative bilateral and multilateral ocean agreements. On March 10, 1983, President Ronald Reagan proclaimed a 200-nautical-mile **exclusive economic zone** (EEZ) off US shores and issued an oceans policy statement that sets forth a summary interpretation of US ocean rights and obligations on the basis of customary international law. While not inconsistent with the Law of the Sea Convention in nonseabed areas, it ignores revenue-sharing obligations from minerals development on the continental shelf beyond the EEZ and refrains from claiming a US 12-nautical-mile territorial sea or jurisdiction over scientific research within the EEZ. Nor does it recognize national jurisdiction over tuna, a highly migratory species. Nevertheless, with the exception of its failure to acknowledge jurisdiction over tuna, it acknowledges foreign state jursidiction in these areas as reflected in the Convention "so long as the rights and freedoms of the United States and others under international law are recognized by such states" [White House press release, 3/10/83].

The US proclamation met with critical reactions from the Group of 77, the third world's negotiating bloc, and from the Soviet Union because it reflects a US "pick and choose" approach to the provisions of the Law of the Sea Convention, which was understood to be a single package by particpants at the Third United Nations Conference on the Law of the Sea. To date, there have been no serious challenges to US exercise of its claimed ocean rights. For one thing, most states still hold out hope that the United States will adhere to the Convention.

Second, the Convention is not yet in force, and it is difficult to single out the United States at this time for retaliation. Third, there are a number of states that have national laws that are at variance with the Convention's provisions. Until they bring these laws into conformity with the 1982 treaty, it is difficult for them to openly question US actions.

["Issues Before the 38th UN General Assembly," 1983, pp. 103–05]

OUTER SPACE

THE UN ROLE
IN SPACE

United Nations

SPACE ACTIVITIES may be classed in four categories: *science, communications, Earth observations, and in–space industry,* plus the *technology development* needed to pursue them. Several of these activities have already made considerable impact on the quality of life on Earth. It is possible that there will be a truly dramatic growth in that impact during the next few decades, for though the developed nations have led humanity's move into space, for various reasons, the bulk of the need for solutions provided by space activities lies in the developing world. One of the chief purposes of UNISPACE 82 is to explore the pathways by which this transition can be effected, to the ultimate benefit of all the peoples of the world.

SCIENCE

Scientific discovery has been a major goal of spaceflight from the very beginning. By far the most important result of the International Geophysical Year, which inspired the birth of the Space Age in 1957, was the discovery by the United States Explorer I satellite of the van Allen radiation belts circling the globe, which dominate our radio communications and much of our weather. Scarcely two years later, the Soviet Lunik II detected the solar wind, that never-ending and all-important stream of charged atoms and electrons blasted out from the Sun that dictates the shape of the van Allen belts and thereby the behaviour of the Earth's atmosphere.

Since then we have observed the Earth's biosphere (land, oceans, and atmosphere) in great detail; we have studied the

Moon both from orbiting spacecraft and first-hand by people and robot explorers; we have examined the planets Mercury, Venus, Mars, Jupiter, and Saturn using ultra-sensitive robot spacecraft to fly by them, orbit them, and in some cases even land on their surfaces; and we have used elaborate orbiting observations high above the obscuring atmosphere to study the stars, the galaxies, and intergalactic space. Pulsars, quasars, x-ray stars, and evidence indicating the existence of black holes were first detected by space-based instruments. The new science of bioastronautics was founded by orbiting manned spacecraft which exposed people to the space environment for as long as six months at a time, demonstrating clearly not only man's ability to live and work in space effectively, but also revealing much about the effects of gravity on all biological organisms.

The next 10 years will see a continuation of all these activities using much more sophisticated instruments: for example, the 2.4 meter space telescope to be launched by the United States in 1985; the Salyut 7 and even larger multi-person space stations to be orbited by the Soviet Union in the mid-1980s; the United States Galileo spacecraft which will send probes down into Jupiter's atmosphere in 1988; the European International Solar Polar spacecraft whose mission is to map the Sun's poles in 1985; spacecraft launched by the USSR, by Europe and by Japan to observe at close hand the literally once-in-a-lifetime visit of Halley's comet in 1986; and a host of others.

COMMUNICATIONS

True global contact among the Earth's peoples became possible only with the advent of satellite communications. Today there is an existing world network: INTELSAT, owned by 106 nations and used by several dozen more; regional networks in western Europe, eastern Europe, and Indonesia; and many domestic systems around the globe. These satellite systems link people together by telephone, by radio, and by television and transmit vital data on weather, crop conditions, financial matters, and business operations. Several nations use dedicated satellite communications systems for defense related purposes. Satellites are used effectively to warn people of impending disasters—floods, hurricanes or typhoons, ice-cover changes, and blizzards; for search and rescue purposes; and have been shown to be particularly effective for mass educational programmes in both developed and developing nations.

A global maritime communication satellite system, INMARSAT, has recently begun to supplement national systems launched for military purposes but utilized broadly for civil needs. Future prospects include communication systems not only for ships, but also for aircraft, mobile land vehicles, and eventually even for individuals.

EARTH OBSERVATIONS

Data from meteoerological satellites both in polar orbits and in the geostationary orbit have been integrated by the World Meteorological Organization (WMO) into a global weather forecasting system. This system is one of the diadems in the crown of international space cooperation, providing much-needed services upon request to all users. It will continue to grow and improve, aiming for better and faster dissemination of processed data, longer-range forecasts, and more comprehensive weather-disaster warnings.

Military surveillance and reconnaissance satellites have extremely high resolution, so analysis of their data is both expensive and time-consuming. Such systems are therefore very different from civil-oriented Earth-observation satellites; they are, however, essential for monitoring disarmament treaties, whether operated unilaterally by the major space powers, as they are today, or by an international treaty-monitoring agency, as has been proposed. The greatest potential benefits from remote-sensing satellites will undoubtedly be derived from those that observe the land surfaces of the Earth.

There is little doubt that the future will see the integration of national remote sensing systems into a globally coordinated and compatible network, comparable to that of INMARSAT or the WMO weather satellite system. The problems are not technological, but rather economic, institutional, and political (e.g., who has priority to data from a sensed nation and who has access to possibly sensitive or defense-oriented data). An important prospect is the combination of such a global remote-sensing network with a satellite communications network to create a Global Resource Information System, possibly utilizing the above-mentioned large, multipurpose geostationary-orbit platforms.

In-Space Industry

Industrial operations in space are different from the other activities mentioned heretofore in that they utilize the unique character of the space environment itself rather than the vantage point offered by an orbit high over the Earth. That environment provides, for the first time in mankind's history, continuous microgravity (often called "zero-g"), a "vacuum pump" of virtually infinite capacity, and a wide range of available temperatures available continuously and at no cost from the Sun.

Preliminary studies of space processing potentials in this new environment were conducted during the United States Apollo and Skylab programmes, the Soviet Soyuz and Salyut orbital flights, the joint United States/Soviet Apollo/Soyuz project, and during brief sounding-rocket flights by many nations. Particularly promising product lines for future space manufacturing operations, that is, products which can be made far better and more cheaply in the space environment than on Earth, include pharmaceuticals, microelectronic circuit substrates (chips), optical-quality glass (especially for lasers), special alloys, and catalysts for manufacturing chemicals. Note that none of these products require massive payloads to be carried to and from orbit.

One highly promising but presently dormant prospect is the space-based satellite power system for collecting solar energy in space, where the continuous sunshine is unobstructed by nightfall or clouds, and beaming it to the Earth's surface by electromagnetic waves for use in terrestrial power grids. A mix of such central-station generators with dispersed Earth-based solar power plants was analyzed recently by the French, and found to be quite suitable as a global power system concept. The high cost of development of satellite power systems has stalled their evaluation at present; however it is clear that the future will eventually see these studies resurrected.

One fascinating prospect, dictated by the economics of producing space power stations should they eventually be deemed viable, is the utilization of nonterrestrial raw materials for their construction. Lunar materials are already known (from United States Apollo and Soviet Lunokhod samples) to contain nearly all the elements needed to build power stations, and the asteroids represent a virtually inexhaustible future resource. Here again, as in space manufacturing, the pace of development will be governed by economic demand, but there is little question that such development will eventually take place. Its implications are indeed profound: people will be living in space cities, just as they live here on Earth today, supported by their eminently profitable and socially useful industry.

TECHNOLOGIES

In order for space development to proceed actively and vigorously, a number of technologies must be pursued. The present rapid progress in computerized data processing, data analysis, electromagnetic transmission, and electromagnetic system operations will help ensure the growth of satellite communications and remote-sensing applications.

Considerable effort is still required, however, in rocket propulsion, large space structures and their control, materials, symbiotic operations of people and robots, and particularly in the development of cheap, reliable space transportation systems, not only for launching payloads (and peoples) from the Earth into orbit, but also for transferring payloads from one orbit to another.

The United Nations system provides support to Member States wishing to develop space technology in a number of ways through many of the agencies of the United Nations family. United Nations assistance activities can be divided, based on how they are administered, into three categories: **funding; project support; and co-ordination.**

FUNDING

Funding for space activities, as for other assistance activities, comes primarily from the United Nations Development Programme (UNDP) and from the World Bank, the UNDP granting money for technical assistance and pre-investment projects, while the World Bank lends money for investment in economic production.

Currently, about 85 per cent of UNDP funding goes to national projects, while 12 per cent goes to regional projects and 3 per cent to interregional and global projects. Once the project is funded, it is managed by an appropriate technical agency, most commonly a United Nations specialized agency or a technical department of the United Nations Secretariat.

PROJECT SUPPORT

United Nations projects for development of space science and technology, once they are funded, are implemented by the appropriate United Nations technical agency. The agency will provide technical experts to assist the country in planning the project, acquiring equipment, organizing education and training, and managing project activities. The agencies that are most active in project support are the International Telecommunication Union (ITU) (telecommunications), the World Meteorological Organization (WMO) (meteorology), the Food and Agriculture Organization of the United Nations (FAO) (agriculture, forestry, fisheries), the United Nations Environment Programme (UNEP) (environmental monitoring), the United Nations Educational, Scientific and Cultural Organization (UNESCO) (science and education) and the Department of Technical Cooperation for Development of the United Nations Secretariat (geology, cartography, water resources).

CO-ORDINATION

The United Nations Committee on the Peaceful Uses of Outer Space is the body concerned with the general co-ordination of space activities. The Committee is responsible for the Space Applications Programme, and has, through its Legal Sub-Committee, produced a series of international space law agreements.

[*UN Chronicle*, July 1982, pp. 59–64]

ENVIRONMENT

ENVIRONMENT, ECONOMY, SECURITY: THE EMERGING AGENDA

James G. Speth

TODAY A NEW ENVIRONMENTAL AGENDA is emerging. It is just now forcing itself on the attention of policymakers and the public at large. Once fully visible, this agenda will scarcely resemble the environmental agenda of a decade ago. Its concerns are both practical and urgent; they address the survival of human, animal, and plant populations over vast sections of our globe.

These emerging concerns encompass the great life-supporting systems of the planet's biosphere—the atmosphere, oceans, climate, soil, and forests. Today's issues are arising from the spread of deserts, the loss of forests, the erosion of soils, the growth of human populations, the exhaustion of ecological communities, the accumulation of wastes, and the alteration of the biogeochemical cycles of the planet. *Today's environmental concerns transcend borders, national laws, and local customs. As a result, the politics needed to meet present and future challenges require a new vision and a new diplomacy, new leaders and new policies.*

Of course, the old, predominately domestic agenda will not disappear. It is still important, still much in need of attention. The efforts launched in the 1970s to control local pollution; regulate hazardous substances; curb stripmining and clearcutting; and protect our parks, wilderness, wetlands, and wildlife have been only partially successful. Much more needs to be done to achieve the goals set in a score of major federal environmental laws passed in the 1970s. Nor have we made enough progress

429

toward harmonizing, simplifying, and improving the economic efficiency of environmental regulations.

But we must also make room for the emerging agenda. There are many compelling reasons for a high level of concern and response: reasons of humanity, of environment, of science. But increasingly we are seeing that the way in which the new agenda is addressed will profoundly affect U.S. economic and security interests. The new agenda will demand attention in the 1980s and 1990s in part because its concerns are inextricably linked to other pressing international goals:

- expanding international trade and markets,
- improving North-South relations,
- promoting sustainable economic development,
- managing the pressures of population increases, and
- ensuring long-term political stability in the Third World.

In a world that is daily more complex and interdependent economically, the economic and security interests of the U.S. must be understood in a broad global context. Economic problems elsewhere in the world—for example, those stemming from food, resource, and population pressures—can affect such U.S. national concerns as economic growth, hemispheric security, and international political stability. Private and public decision-makers in the U.S. must together attend to these emerging issues.

Starting about 15 years ago, U.S. leaders in Congress and elsewhere began to respond vigorously to the environmental concerns emerging then. Today, we face a new agenda of environmental, resource, and development issues that, if anything, are even more important to our basic values and long-term interests than the concerns of the 1970s. Granted, these newer concerns are less "in our own back yard" and thus are harder to grapple with politically. Still, the emergence of this new set of critical issues presents U.S. leaders, both in government and in the private sector, with a special opportunity and responsibility.

A New Agenda

Consensus seems to be developing, within the international scientific community and among other experts, on exactly what

are the priority environmental, resource, and population problems, at least given the current state of our information and
understanding.

In 1982, the Royal Swedish Academy of Sciences convened
a week-long international gathering of scientists to look at
environmental priorities for the 1980s. At least 40 issues had
been targeted ahead of time for serious consideration, and one
goal of the meeting was to trim this to a short list of front-ranked
items.

More recently, 75 leaders from science, business, government, and environmental affairs representing 20 countries were
brought together for several days by the World Resources Institute for a conference entitled "The Global Possible: Resources,
Development, and the New Century." Again, a goal was to
identify key concerns of global scope and what to do about
them.

These two exercises produced very similar results regarding priority concerns—results that have been reached by others
as well. Both efforts identified the following problems as truly
serious and deserving of wide international attention:

1. *loss of crop and grazing land* due to desertification,
   erosion, conversion of land to non-farm uses, and
   other factors. The United Nations reports that, globally, farm and grazing land is being reduced to zero
   productivity at the rate of about 20 million hectares a
   year. (One hectare equals about 2.5 acres.)
2. *depletion of the world's tropical forests,* which is leading to
   loss of forest resources, serious watershed damage
   (erosion, flooding, and siltation), and other adverse
   consequences. Deforestation is projected to claim a
   further 100 million hectares of tropical forests by the
   end of this century.
3. *mass extinction of species,* principally from the global loss
   of wildlife habitat, and the associated loss of genetic
   resources. One estimate is that more than 1,000 plant
   and animal species become extinct each year, a rate
   that is expected to increase.
4. *rapid population growth,* burgeoning Third World cities,
   and ecological refugees. World population will most
   likely double by the early decades of the next century,

and almost half the inhabitants of developing countries will live in cities—many of unmanageable proportions.

5. *mismanagement and shortages of fresh water resources.* It now seems possible to many researchers that water will be to the 1990s what energy was to the 1970s.

6. *overfishing, habitat destruction, and pollution in the marine environment.* Twenty-five of the world's most valuable fisheries are seriously depleted today due to overfishing.

7. *threats to human health* from mismanagement of pesticides and hazardous substances and from waterborne pathogens. Waterborne diseases are responsible for about 80 percent of all illness in the world today.

8. *climate change* due to the increase in "greenhouse gases" in the atmosphere. The steady build-up of carbon dioxide and other gases in the atmosphere, due principally to fossil fuel burning, is predicted to create a "greenhouse effect" of rising temperatures and local climate change—the question increasingly is not "if?" but "how much?"

9. *acid rain* and, more generally, the effects of a complex mix of air pollutants on fisheries, forests, and crops. The "export" of acid rain harms not only natural resources but also constructive relationships among neighboring states in political and economic affairs.

10. *mismanagement of energy fuels and pressures on energy resources,* including shortages of fuelwood, the poor person's oil. Although market forces and government actions have eased pressures, these vital resources are, undeniably, finite in quantity and disparate in locale. Our energy problems may be forgotton, but they have not gone.

It is instructive to reflect on this list. Taken together, these ten problems mainly stem from either excessive poverty and population growth in the developing countries or from the careless and excessive use of certain technologies and resources in the developed countries. While the U.S. and other developed countries are affected by most of these problems, the cumulative impact of these threats is far more serious in the poor countries than in the rich. Yet, because of their wealth, technology, and an ability to exercise international leadership, the rich countries are far more able to do something about them.

Another point to note is that these ten problems are not, by and large, the environmental concerns to which the U.S. and other industrial countries turned priority attention in the early 1970s. While many of these problems have been recognized for some time, they represent a new policy agenda for the United States, one that has emerged since the early 1970s, one that is more international and global in its scope and implications and is concerned more with management of economically important resources than with traditional pollution control.

COMMON GROUND: A NEW POLITICS

The politics of this new agenda are different from the environmental politics of the past deacde. The predominantly domestic environmental causes of the 1970s had little going for them but the people. The environmental movement handed the business community a long string of defeats; it left the scientists anxious in their efforts to keep up. Economists were aghast; ecologists, even lawyers, were lionized. Citizens took on government at all levels, and won. Large minorities of the public were strongly pro-environment—and they still are, as the Reagan Administration learned the hard way.

The politics of the new agenda, on the contrary, must be a search for common ground. Popular support for the new agenda is now weaker than for the old: the issues are more remote, more distant in space and time. Although there are conspicuous exceptions (like acid rain), the new agenda addresses the relationship of environment and development in the Third World, the health of the global commons, and a series of resource and environmental threats that, while serious, are less visible, often slow to develop, or affect the U.S. only indirectly. But, as if to compensate, the new agenda invites strangers and even old antagonists to work together. Economic growth is needed to attack poverty, the worst destroyer of the environment worldwide, so business and labor leaders and environmentalists must make common cause in promoting sustainable growth. Economists and ecologists must cooperate if development strategies are to promote this goal. The development, population, and environmental communities now face the same set of problems. The relevant bureaucracy in national and international agencies—now almost immune from litigation and able to cloak itself in the mysteries of foreign policy and national security—must be wooed on its own terms. Yet, the bureaucracy too will not succeed unless it comes to terms with global-scale resource, environmental and population issues.

THE NEW AGENDA AND THE U.S. ECONOMY

The emergence of the new agenda has been accompanied by a growing realization that the goals of environmental conservation and economic growth in both developing and industrial countries are more complementary than often depicted. Most of the resources under stress today are vital to healthy, long-term economic development and growth. A. W. Clausen, president of the World Bank, has stressed these relationships:

> There is increasing awareness that environmental precautions are essential for continued economic development over the long run. Conservation, in its broadest sense, is not a luxury for people rich enough to vacation in scenic parks. It is not just a "motherhood" issue. Rather the goal of economic growth itself dictates a serious and abiding concern for resource management.

Similarly, the conservation community is increasingly aware that resource pressures in developing countries will not be alleviated without the economic growth necessary to provide people with non-destructive livelihoods. Some of the worst environmental destruction occurring today stems from the impact of poverty on the land.

One important way the U.S. economic future is linked to global resource, population, and environmental problems is through the effects that these problems have on economic development in the Third World. To state the matter simply, the better resource and population challenges are managed in the developing countries, the greater the prospects for sustainable economic development in those countries. And sustainable development means a greater boost for developed economies. . . .

In light of these growing economic ties, resource and environmental degradation in developing countries—including the failure to find attractive substitutes for high-cost energy imports, to manage renewable natural resources for sustainable production, and to protect public health from environmental diseases—can affect U.S. economic performance adversely. . . .

An especially bleak developing world scenario depicts a future in which resource, environmental and population problems are not addressed and economic development lags. In this scenario a vicious cycle involving people, poverty and resources is prevalent. Poverty grows, as does the gap in per capita income between rich and poor. Frustration, resentment and even civil strife mount. In such an atmosphere, the United States finds itself buffeted in many ways: pressures for U.S. foreign assistance and humanitarian concessional aid increase, as do the expenditures needed to sustain military readiness in many parts of the world; the U.S. is faced with a variety of hostile economic acts, including nationalization, debt cancellation, cartels, boycotts, and closing of markets. Destabilization and civil turmoil make trade and successful economic ventures impossible or less likely, and the "Western model" and free institutions come under increasing pressures as authoritarian measures become more attractive to governments struggling to cope.

Growth cannot flourish in an atmosphere of political instability. Whether a future that is hospitable and favorable to investment and trade emerges depends in part on the seriousness and concern with which global-scale resources, environmental, and population problems are addressed.

Beyond a general interest in the global sustainability of natural resources and the development which depends on them, business has both direct and indirect reasons to care about specific environmental and resource-management issues. There, are, of course, direct economic consequences for certain sectors of domestic and international commerce: the price and availability of oil, for example, or the marketability of food sprayed by certain pesticides. But indirect consequences are also important: the geopolitical effects of irrigation and fishing practices, for example, or the effects on agriculture of climate change caused by the buildup of carbon dioxide (CO_2) in the atmosphere.

In several ways, global-scale resource depletion and environmental degradation can create significant costs or risks for the U.S. economy and particular commercial sectors. In the food sector, for example, conditions of climate, the genetic base, and basic water and land resources all affect productivity.

CLIMATIC RESOURCES

The most troubling aspect of the global warming that may already be occurring as a result of the buildup of CO_2 and other "greenhouse gases" in the atmosphere is not the warming *per se* but the large-scale disruption of the global weather machine. This disruption stems from the differential warming that could occur: very slight at the equator, very significant at the poles. The change in weather patterns in the agricultural regions in the Midwest could be significant if, for example, the concentration of CO_2 in the atmosphere rose to twice the pre-industrial level by the early decades of the next century. No region of the world has more at stake in the "greenhouse issue" than the U.S. breadbasket.

The "greenhouse" theory and models were once thought to be speculative, even after the steady increase in atmospheric CO_2 had been well documented. But recent scientific reviews have found no reason to doubt the theory, and some evidence suggests that a warming is already under way. The consequences are still thought of as occurring in the distant future. The problem with that view, however, is that the leadtime needed to plan and execute a response, whether prevention or adaptation or both, is necessarily long. Clearly, we should be coming to grips with this problem now, while we can do something about it.

Fishery Resources

Much of the world's population depends on fish for food and protein, and the global fisheries support a large industry in both food and industrial products. Thirty-two countries receive one-third or more of ther animal protein from seafood, according to the United Nations Environment Programme, and another 11 consume twice the world per capita average.

The harvesting of fish has increased dramatically in this century. Between 1900 and 1962, the total catch from marine and fresh waters rose by a factor of eight. Between 1948 and 1967, production from marine fisheries tripled, to about 65 million tonnes (metric tons). This growth then slowed remarkably in the 1970s, and the yields of some fish have declined, principally because of overfishing and environmental factors. Also, such locally important fisheries as the Chesapeake Bay are showing signs of serious stress. Many observers believe that the harvests of traditional fisheries are not likely to increase greatly on a sustainable basis, and some catches may already exceed the sustainable yield.

It seems clear that we have reached the point where preserving this major food source and the industries that depend on it requires careful national and international supervision and improved protection of the marine and fresh water environments. Natural environmental threats, such as shifts in the Humboldt Current, are seriously compounded by inadequate management and overfishing, man-made pollution, and changes in fish habitat created by land development and other factors. Meeting world food needs and satisfying our demand for seafood will require careful attention to these problems.

Genetic Resources

Scientists estimate that between five million and ten million plant and animal species now live on earth, and there is wide agreement that the extinction rate for these species is both high today (perhaps 1,000 species a year) and rising. Wild species are commonly thought to be important for their aesthetic and scientific value—evidence of a diverse and creative nature. But species are also important economically. Species and genetic resources provide new sources of food, materials for energy and construction, chemicals for pharmaceuticals and industry, and natural pest controls, as well as the basis for adapting to climatic variability and other broad environmental changes.

According to Norman Myers, an ecologist who has studied the monetary significance of wild species, the routine infusion of wild germplasm into agricultural crops increases productivity value by as much as $1 billion a year in the United States, and similar gains are common in Canada and the Soviet Union.

Human health is also benefited. In four specific examples, sea urchins produce holothurin, which may save thousands of lives by correcting coronary disorders; octopi secrete an extract that relieves hypertension; Caribbean sponges produce an antiviral compound; and shellfish skeletons are the source of an enzyme that protects medicine from fungal infections.

Myers estimates that the U.S. market value of drugs and pharmaceuticals derived from plants is $20 billion a year. Conversely, loss of species with potential for medical products might be costing humanity more than $200 billion a year in unrealized healing. He considers this calculation conservative, since it rests on the assumption that species loss will continue at current levels, whereas it may be accelerating.

Ironically, the current loss of species is occurring just as the techniques of genetic engineering make it easier to utilize genetic resources for the benefit of mankind.

Agriculture

The lands used to produce food and fiber crops in the United States and elsewhere are now under many pressures: conversion to non-agricultural uses, soil erosion, salinization, compaction and water-logging, declining groundwater tables, and the spread of deserts. One recent estimate put the average annual loss of agricultural land globally at 8 million hectares from non-agricultural conversion, 3 million hectares from erosion, 2 million hectares from desertification and 2 million hectares from toxification. U.S. agriculture is certainly not immune from these disturbing trends, although continued domestic productivity increases can compensate, at least for a period, for problems that are more apparent elsewhere in the world.

Another environmental problem, airborne pollution, can harm crops and forests in addition to posing health hazards. Ozone is formed by photochemical reactions with the exhaust from fossil-fuel combustion. A recent survey of four U.S. crops by the Congressional Office of Technology Assessment estimated annual losses from ozone damage at perhaps $3 billion. This survey showed a loss of about 5 percent in wheat, corn, soybean, and peanut harvests.

Commercial forests in many areas in the Northern Hemisphere are believed to have been damaged by air pollutants, including acid rain. In West Germany, for example, one-third of the forests have been adversely affected by air pollutants, according to a 1983 Ministry of Agriculture survey. As a result of this evidence, acid rain politics in West Germany have changed dramatically. Data on damage to U.S. eastern forests is also beginning to accumulate.

These examples could be supplemented by many others. Cumulatively, they suggest that major sectors of the U.S. economy have a significant stake in the protection of the planet's increasingly pressured renewable resource base. In each of these areas, there are remedial actions that should be carefully considered, and both public and private sectors have major roles in finding appropriate answers.

These resource issues present U.S. business and labor with both opportunities and challenges. One opportunity is to address this new set of more global resource questions as active leaders, thus avoiding the confrontation and adversary style that often was the hallmark of our domestic environmental politics in the 1970s. Global environmental issues can be handled in a way that allows both practical commercial considerations and good citizenship to motivate a greater leadership role for U.S. business and labor.

In fact, these large-scale resource issues will probably not be successfully addressed *without* the support and cooperation of American industry. Not only are U.S. companies major actors on the international scene, offering employment and economic stimulation, but they also have the technology and management expertise for successful environmental and resource management.

["Environment, Economy, Security: The Emerging Agenda," 1985, pp. 11–15]

INTERNATIONAL ORGANIZATIONS

A. Leroy Bennett

WIDESPREAD CONCERN THAT THE HUMAN RACE may be potentially as threatened by pollution as it is by nuclear holocaust is a relatively recent phenomenon. The possibility of nuclear contamination of air, water, and soil in a large-scale nuclear war has been realized since Hiroshima and was reemphasized when Japanese fishermen were affected by nuclear fallout in the Bikini test of March 1, 1954. The ultimate peril is dramatized by such a novel as Nevil Shute's *On the Beach*. Localized threats to health from air pollution have existed for many years in such places as Los Angeles and London (before the latter city imposed regulations to reduce the threat), and from water pollution in myriad rivers and lakes, and oil pollution on numerous beaches. But gradually the realization has spread that major environmental problems require international attention, in addition to national and local concern, in order to foresee and forestall the various forms of eco-catastrophe that could overtake humankind.

Attention has recently focused on a wide range of pollutants that threaten the natural balance of the biosphere necessary to sustain healthy human life. A study sponsored by the Massachusetts Institute of Technology identified the following pollutants as worthy of special attention—carbon dioxide; particulate matter; sulfur dioxide; oxides of nitrogen; mercury and other toxic heavy metals; oil; DDT and other hydrocarbons; radionuclides; heat; and nutrients, especially phosphates. Severe problems may exist locally with other pollutants but this list represents the residuals that have global effects on the climate or on ocean or terrestrial ecology, or that create major problems in many countries.

International agencies have given limited attention to prob-

440

lems of the human environment for many years, but the programs have been selective, low-scale, and often incidental to the main thrust of the efforts of these agencies. The pressure for a comprehensive and better-coordinated effort is of recent origin. A perusal of the activities of the specialized agencies affiliated with the United Nations reveals that the agencies giving the greatest attention to environmental problems are the World Meteorological Organization (WMO), which is concerned with air pollution and the climatic effects of pollutants; the World Health Organization (WHO), which is involved in a wide range of projects in environmental health; UNESCO, which has sponsored several studies and conferences of experts; the Food and Agriculture Organization (FAO), whose interests include pesticide accumulation and misuse of the environment; the International Atomic Energy Agency (IAEA), which is concerned with nuclear wastes; the Inter-Governmental Maritime Consulatative Organization (IMCO), which has a special interest in oil pollution of the oceans; and the International Labor Organization (ILO), whose concerns include atmospheric pollution in the working environment.

The United Nations Conference on the Human Environment (UNCHE) approved as its theme "Only One Earth" to emphasize the essential unity and interdependence on the global life-support system. The conference adopted a 26-point Declaration on the Human Environment and a 109-point Action Plan for the guidance of governments and international organizations in implementing a program of environmental protection. The conference also proposed the settling up of permanent international machinery within a United Nations Environment Program (UNEP).

One major focus of the action program adopted at Stockholm is an "Earthwatch" network to assess current environmental conditions in all parts of the globe and to monitor changes that presage danger. Atmospheric conditions will be monitored for pollutants that threaten health or climatic modification. Marine pollution and the release of toxic substances into the life-support system will be checked, and any threatening changes will be publicized. Earthwatch activities include an International Referral System connecting national information centers to a central data bank in Geneva, an International Register of Potentially Toxic Chemicals, and a Global Environmental Monitoring

Service (GEMS) with a projected 110 monitoring stations throughout the world. Another UNEP concern is for endangered species with imperative attention to the extinction of whales. Other topics assigned high priority include human settlements, education, information, transfer of technology, conservation of natural and genetic resources, and energy.

The pace of UNEP activities gradually accelerated after a slow start. In 1976 the Environment Fund dispensed approximately 30 million dollars for a variety of projects. Among those instigated by that date was an early warning system for typhoons in the Bay of Bengal. In May, 1976 an agreement was signed at Barcelona to combat pollution and other environmental problems in the Mediterranean and its coastal states. A regional center was established in Malta to handle oil spills and pollution emergencies. Dumping of certain highly toxic substances into the Mediterranean was prohibited. For another list of substances, dumping was severely restricted. In April, 1978 a similar agreement was drawn up for the Persian Gulf region by eight major oil-producing states. The threat of oil and industrial pollution is especially severe in this area. In October, 1977 a conference sponsored jointly by UNESCO and UNEP in Tbilisi, USSR issued a declaration stressing the importance of environmental education for all ages and through the mass media. These projects represent only a sampling of the varied activities of the UNEP.

The chances for dramatic results in checking the environmental threats are mixed. The impetus toward effective action was provided by the Stockholm conference and by the setting up of special machinery to implement the approved Action Plan. National attitudes toward environmental protection include many negative factors. References have been previously made to the doubts and reservations of the developing countries. In the industrialized countries the energy crisis that developed in 1973 resulted in a possibly temporary but significant deemphasis of environmental concerns. There is danger that, in spite of warnings of impending environmental global catastrophe, higher national priorities will be assigned to rapid economic development and to maintaining the upward spiral of energy consumption than to environmental protection.

[*International Organizations*, 1980, pp. 311–16]

NON-RENEWABLE RESOURCES

THE RENEWABLE WAY
OF LIFE

Harlan Cleveland and Alexander King

AT THE BEGINNING OF THE 1970s, people in very large numbers in many parts of the world were questioning both the possibility and the desirability of continuing to stimulate "growth" in the directions that had become traditional—growth of the economic product, human populations, urban development, numbers of automobiles, and size of bureaucracies. The environmental risks and the threat of resource depletion were only part—an important part—of this disillusion with material growth. The doubts about growth were intensified by the petroleum crisis with its sudden and massive increase in the cost of energy, its wholesale shift in the world balance of payments and pattern of investment, and its demonstration of the vulnerability of industrialized, oil-importing countries to disruption of supplies that could threaten their economic health and styles of life. Most of the less developed countries likewise suffered from the greatly increased cost of the fuels and fertilizers they needed if their exploding populations were to be adequately fed. In both "developed" and "developing" countries the realization was coming in a rush: that oil resources could run out, and that new energy sources had to be found or invented, and developed, before the oil wells dried up.

The natural conclusion of this line of thinking was to reassess economic needs and the ways of meeting them in such a way as to reduce reliance on resources that might be near exhaustion, or at least would predictably become more and more costly during the generations to come. On the positive side, the same reasoning led naturally to working *with* nature. Maybe humanity should modify its economic practices so as to use much better the bioresources provided, and continuously

445

regenerated, by a bountiful nature. Maybe the bioproductivity of the planet could be preserved, and indeed enhanced, to ensure this eternal renewal.

The arguments supporting such an approach seemed clear enough:

- Present and foreseeable increases in world population will call for increases in materials and energy that are unlikely to be met if present practices, policies, and lifestyles persist.
- Provision of basic physical needs (especially of food, clothing, shelter) of existing and foreseeable populations is politically and humanly urgent; so is a fairer chance for deprived peoples to participate in a life of modest prosperity and human dignity.
- The limits to the carrying capacity of the planet, and its toleration of human intervention and waste, are at best uncertain.
- The interest of future generations—and perhaps even of our own—requires us to reduce our reliance on nonrenewable resources such as minerals and fossil fuels, to adopt conservationist and recycling practices, and to encourage a much more effective use of the continuous inflow of solar radiation, notably the photosynthetic mechanism of the green plant.
- Humanity will need to maintain and increase the bioproductivity of the planetary soil, and mould agricultural policies and practices so as to ensure a full and regenerative use of the biomass available to man, recycling "wastes" as a new form of raw material.

["The Renewable Way of Life," 1980, pp. 49–50]

THE ULTIMATE RESOURCE

Julian Simon

RESOURCES IN THEIR RAW FORM are useful and valuable only when found, understood, gathered together, and harnessed for human needs. The basic ingredient in the process, along with the raw elements, is human knowledge. And we develop knowledge about how to use raw elements for our benefit only in response to our needs. This includes knowledge for finding new sources of raw materials such as copper, for growing new resources such as timber, for creating new quantities of capital such as farmland, and for finding new and better ways to satisfy old needs, such as successively using iron or aluminum or plastic in place of clay or copper. Such knowledge has a special property: It yields benefits to people other than the ones who develop it, apply it, and try to capture its benefits for themselves. Taken in the large, an increased need for resources usually leaves us with a permanently greater capacity to get them, because we gain knowledge in the process. And there is no meaningful physical limit—even the commonly mentioned weight of the earth—to our capacity to keep growing forever.

Perhaps the most general matter at issue here is what Gerald Holton calls a "thema." The thema underlying the thinking of most writers who have a point of view different from mine is the concept of fixity or finiteness of resources in the relevant system of discourse. This is found in Malthus, of course. But the idea probably has always been a staple of human thinking because so much of our situation must sensibly be regarded as fixed in the short run—the bottles of beer in the refrigerator, our paycheck, the amount of energy parents have to play basketball with their kids. But the thema underlying my thinking about resources (and the thinking of a minority of others) is that the relevant system of discourse has a long enough horizon that it makes sense to treat the system as not fixed, rather than finite in any operational sense. We see the resource system as being as unlimited as the number of thoughts a person might have, or the number of variations that might ultimately be produced by biological evolution. That is, a key difference between the thinking of those who worry about impending doom, and those who see the prospects of a better life for more people in the future, apparently is whether one thinks in closed-system or open-system terms. For example, those who worry that the second law of thermodynamics dooms us to eventual decline necessarily see our world as a closed system with respect to energy and entropy; those who view the relevant universe as unbounded view the second law of thermodynamics as irrelevant to this discussion. I am among those who view the relevant part of the physical and social universe as open for most purposes. Which thema is better for thinking about resources and population is not subject to scientific test. Yet it profoundly affects our thinking. I believe that here lies the root of the key difference in thinking about population and resources.

Why do so many people think in closed-system terms? There are a variety of reasons. (1) Malthusian fixed-resources reasoning is simple and fits the isolated facts of our everyday lives, whereas the expansion of resources is complex and indirect and includes all creative human activity—it cannot be likened to our own larders or wallets. (2) There are always immediate negative effects from an increased pressure on resources, whereas the benefits only come later. It is natural to pay more attention to the present and the near future compared with the more distant future. (3) There are often special-interest groups that alert us to impending shortages of particular resources such as timber or clean air. But no one has the same stake in trying to convince us that the long-run prospects for a resource are better than we think. (4) It is easier to get people's attention (and television time and printer's ink) with frightening forecasts than with soothing forecasts. (5) Organizations that form in response to temporary or non-existent dangers, and develop the capacity to raise funds from public-spirited citizens and governments that are aroused to fight the danger, do not always disband when the danger evaporates or the problem is solved. (6) Ambition and the urge for profit are powerful elements in our successful struggle to satisfy our needs. These motives, and the markets in which they work, often are not pretty, and many people would prefer not to depend on a social system that employs these forces to make us better off. (7) Associating oneself with environmental causes is one of the quickest and easiest ways to get a wide reputation for high-minded concern; it requires no deep thinking and steps on almost no one's toes.

The apparently obvious way to deal with resource problems—have the government control the amounts and prices of what consumers consume and suppliers supply—is inevitably counter-productive in the long run because the controls and the price fixing prevent us from making the cost-efficient adjustments that we would make in response to the increased short-run costs, adjustments that eventually would more than alleviate the problem. Sometimes governments must play a crucial role to avoid short-run disruptions and disaster, and to ensure that no group consumes public goods without paying the real social cost. But the appropriate times for governments to play such roles are far fewer than the times they are called upon to do so by those inclined to turn to authority to tell others what to do, rather than allow each of us to respond with self-interest and imagination.

I do not say that all is well. Children are hungry and sick; people live out lives of physical and intellectual poverty, and lack of opportunity; war or some new pollution may do us all in. What I *am* saying is that for most of the relevant economic matters I have checked, the *trends* are positive rather than negative. And I doubt that it does the troubled people of the world any good to say that things are getting worse though they are really getting better. And false prophecies of doom can damage us in many ways.

Is a rosy future guaranteed? Of course not. There always will be temporary shortages and resource problems where there are strife, political blundering, and natural calamities—that is, where there are people. But the natural world allows, and the developed world promotes through the marketplace, responses to human needs and shortages in such manner that one backward step leads to 1.0001 steps forward, or thereabouts. That's enough to keep us headed in a life-sustaining direction. The main fuel to speed our progress is our stock of knowledge, and the brake is our lack of imagination. The ultimate resource is people—skilled, spirited, and hopeful people who will exert their wills and imaginations for their own benefit, and so, inevitably, for the benefit of us all.

[*The Ultimate Resource,* 1981, pp. 346–48]

VI.
"INTERNATIONAL ENTITLEMENTS": CLAIMS AND CLAIMANTS

THIS IS PERHAPS THE MOST CONTROVERSIAL of the global debates today. For over a decade the majority of developing countries (LDCs) has established as a goal for the international system the "New International Economic Order," or NIEO, which since 1974 has dominated UN debates on economic and social policy (and is briefly summarized in a UN publication in section VIA).

The wealthier countries of the world (including some of the oil-producing states and newly industrialized LDCs reject the notion of an integrated program involving massive transfers of wealth and resources from rich to poor. Some practical, if modest, remedies such as access to Western markets for LDC manufacturered goods and some debt restructuring, have been advanced on an ad hoc basis. But Ivan L. Head, president of the Canadian International Development Research Centre, contends that the industrial countries of the "North" are far more dependent on the underdeveloped "South" than they admit, with more of their exports going to developing countries than to each other, though without adequate means of payment.

The drive for structural reform of the economic and social system has spilled over into a parallel quest for a "New World Information Order," interpreted by some LDCs as part of their claim for greater fairness, but by virtually all Western countries as an unacceptable assault on journalistic freedom. Brief documentation from both the UN Association and State Department sources elaborates demands of the LDCs for a more "balanced" flow of news through licensing of journalists, codes of ethics imposed on reporters, curbing of advertising, and extending governmental control over the press. The West has so far successfully opposed proposals aimed at restricting freedom of the press, while supporting a practical approach to communications development.

Human rights as a set of international standards is defined by the text of the Universal Declaration of Human Rights, the first selection in section VIC. There follows a brief selection of my own identifying three kinds of rights, one concerning the integrity of the person, the second civil and political rights familiar to the West, and the third the more controversial assertion of legal "rights" in the economic and social realm. Nigel S. Rodley, legal adviser to Amnesty International, observes that nations are more willing to enunciate desirable standards than to assume direct legal obligations, and tracks the covenants and treaties drafted by the UN, initially at US initiative but subsequently with less American support as rights came increasingly to connote socioeconomic as well as political and civil.

A.

A NEW INTERNATIONAL ECONOMIC ORDER?

NEW INTERNATIONAL ECONOMIC ORDER

United Nations

THE NEW INTERNATIONAL ECONOMIC ORDER called for by the United Nations General Assembly in 1974 would have certain essential characteristics.

1. It would support the development effort of poor countries in all areas by changing unfair and inadequate rules and regulations that now exist. Such changes would be particularly important in trade and monetary affairs where developing countries say that existing rules and regulations either actively discriminate against them or do so by not making any allowance for their weakness.

2. It would increase the share of developing countries in world industrial and agricultural production, including food, as well as in such areas as trade, transport and communications.

3. It would change the patterns of trade, technology flow, transport and communications from a primarily North-South orientation to one of more equal interchanges. One-sided dependence would be replaced by genuine interdependence.

4. It would require States to behave according to an agreed code in international economic relations. The norms of such behaviour have been set out in the Charter of Economic Rights and Duties of States, a seminal document of the North-South encounter. The aim of the Charter is to ensure that small countries are not bullied out of their natural resources and that in decisions affecting them their views are considered.

455

NORTH AND SOUTH

The demand for the New International Economic Order originated from a group of developing countries in Africa, Asia and Latin America. They have been collectively dubbed the "South" of the world in relation to the developed countries of Europe and North America. The discussion of global economic change between the rich and the poor has thus come to be known as the "north-South" dialogue. The expression is imprecise, for Japan is in Asia and Australia and New Zealand are in the southern hemisphere. Also, the socialist countries of Eastern Europe object to being lumped with market economy countries in the "North." But the phrase has been too convenient to fall into disuse. In the years since the call for a new world order, the dialogue has settled into negotiations on a number of subjects and it would be more correct today to speak of North-South negotiations rather than of dialogue.

When the United Nations General Assembly called for the New International Economic Order it did so by consensus. But this consensus hid serious differences between the developing country group and several of the richest countries. In essence, their differences turned on the issue of whether the existing order of the world economy could be reformed or whether it needed to be structurally changed. Developed countries which had benefited most from the post-war economic system were loath to support basic changes. Developing countries, many of whom had not participated in the creation of this system and few of whom had benefited from it, see no reason why a new order should not be negotiated from the basics.

Since 1974 the dialogue and the negotiations between the developed and developing countries have been almost continuous. In a number of forums they have dealt with all the major issues involved in changing the world's economy. This includes trade, money, food, industry, science and technology, transport and communications.

The process has involved Governments in major world conferences. It has brought countless panels of experts to study specific aspects of the subject. It has involved reports from eminent commissions such as those led by Willy Brandt of the Federal Republic of Germany and Sean McBride of Ireland.

Non-governmental organizations have participated, as have journalists in influential sections of the media.

In recent years North-South negotiations have been in the doldrums. Important advances in several areas had been made, but the urgent and comprehensive action that was asked for by the General Assembly has not been taken.

[*UN Chronicle*, Oct. 1982, pp. 37–38]

NORTH-SOUTH INTERDEPENDENCE

Ivan L. Head

IN THE INDUSTRIALIZED COUNTRIES there is under-standable resistance to the concept of dependence on others, unwillingness to accept that a nation's fate or health or freedom of movement is held hostage beyond its shores. Yet when last did the nations of the North, individually or in unison, undertake successfully a major foreign policy initiative that was not a reaction to events elsewhere, most often in the South, sometimes in the East?

Notwithstanding this pattern of reaction, the Northern nations appear incapable of proposing changes in global rela-tionships which would at once acknowledge that dependence—or, better, interdependence—and move toward easing the struc-tural inequities which, unattended, guarantee an ever worsening sequence of events.

What is the evidence of dependence that Northern leaders choose to reject? The Brandt Commission, reporting on North-South relations, as was its mandate, concluded: "At the begin-nings of the 1980s the world community faces much greater dangers than at any time since the Second World War." The Global 2000 Report warned that unless steps are taken to reduce worldwide pressures on cropland, pastures, forests, mineral and water resources, the world will become even "more crowded, more polluted, less ecologically stable and more vulnerable to disruption than the world we live in now."

Of dependence, the evidence is clear. World Bank figures reveal that in 1979, 43 percent of Japanese merchandise exports were sold in the non-oil-exporting developing countries; 36 percent of U.S. merchandise exports that year went to the same markets, as did 32 percent of Australian merchandise exports.

458

What this means for the United States is that one U.S. worker out of 20 is producing exports for the Third World.

These imports by the less developed countries in the 1970s grew at a pace more than 50 percent faster than merchandise trade among the industrialized countries. Thus, the European Economic Community and the United States send more than one-third of all their exports to the developing countries. In comparative terms this means that the United States exports twice as much to the developing countries as to the nations of the European Economic Community, and the community exports three times as much to the developing countries as to the United States.

Even these figures do not reveal the comparative trade advantage enjoyed by the Organization for European Cooperation and Development. A recent report to the Trilateral Commission shows that in 1979 Japan's export-import ratio in trade of manufactured goods with the South was seven-to-one; that of Europe four-to-one; that of North America two-to-one. This overwhelming advantage in value-added goods explains why, between 1973 and 1977, exports to the South created five million new jobs in Organization countries.

Agricultural products are part of this export trade as well, and in immense quantities. U.N. Food and Agricultural Organization statistics reveal that developing countries imported food in 1979 to the value of $38 billion, most of it from the industrialized North.

To sustain or to improve this purchasing pattern, the developing countries must have the means to pay. It is to insure such means that they seek reforms in the international financial institutions. Such reforms are blocked by the industrialized countries on the grounds that their own stagnant economies must first be put in order. Yet such blockage refuses to accept that economies North and South are trapped inexorably in the turbulence of the post-Keynesian period. If either is to emerge, it must be in cooperation with the other. . . .

The North-South dialogue is very much more than a simple matter of transfer of resources. What it comes down to is a sharing of power and of responsibility among the countries of the world. When the South speaks in terms of a new international economic order, it asks that the international system be one that is not tilted permanently against it in terms of commodity prices, access to credit, flows of technology and the control of markets and decisions, most of which are determined in the North. When we tell the South to raise itself by its own bootstraps, we must be very sure that we are not standing on those bootstraps.

["North-South Interdependence," 1984, pp. 96–100]

B.

AN "INFORMATION ORDER"?

ISSUES BEFORE THE 38th UNGA

United Nations Association of the U.S.A.

AT THE NONALIGNED MOVEMENT'S SUMMIT CONFERENCE in Algiers in 1973, an agreement was reached to enhance information flows between the developing countries, and the development of national communications systems and policies was accepted as fundamental to economic self-reliance. Since then, the "decolonization" of communications has grown into a highly controversial issue, culminating in calls for the establishment of a **New World Information and Communication Order** (NWICO). It has been discussed in various forums, including the United Nations Educational, Scientific and Cultural Organization (UNESCO), the United Nations Committee on Information, the International Telecommunication Union (ITU) and the nonaligned movement.

Communications issues have occupied center stage at the UNESCO biennial general conferences since 1974, during which a controversial "Draft Declaration on the Role of Mass Media" [UNESCO 18 C/35] was introduced by the Soviet Union. The declaration became a divisive issue, and Western members asked the UNESCO Director-General to prepare a revised draft for the 19th General Conference in Nairobi, Kenya in 1976. At the Nairobi conference, the differences could still not be resolved, and a vote on the declaration was postponed further till 1978. Also, at the Nairobi meeting it was agreed by consensus that a review be undertaken "of the totality of the problems of communications in modern society," on the basis of which an International Commission for the Study of Communication Problems was appointed under the chairmanship of former Irish Foreign Minister Sean MacBride. The final report of the Commission was published in 1980 under the title "Many Voices,

One World," the first study on modern communications ever undertaken on such a global scale [unesco icscp (063.2)c6]

At the General Conference of UNESCO held in Paris in 1978, attention began to focus on the more pragmatic and concrete approaches to the perceived international imbalance in information flows and infrastructures, out of which emerged a proposal to establish an **International Programme for the Development of Communications** (IPDC). The Programme was approved by consensus at the 1980 UNESCO Conference in Belgrade, Yugoslavia. It is intended to serve as a vehicle for channeling resources for technical training and advice and for providing equipment to accelerate the development of communications infrastructures in the third world.

The question of an NWICO came before the 33rd General Assembly, leading to a resolution that linked the establishment of a new information order with the search for a New International Economic Order (NIEO) [A/Res/33/115]. At the same meeting, an item entitled "Questions relating to information" was included on the Assembly agenda, and a Committee to Review United Nations Public Information Policies and Activities, consisting of 41 member states, was established. It was subsequently renamed (at the 34th Session) the Committee on Information, and its membership was increased to 67.

The debate on the NWICO has so far concentrated on a great variety of issues, including the structure and flows of international news, access to telecommunications infrastructures and prevailing allocation procedures. The developing countries' concern with these issues reflects a growing awareness on their part of the political, economic, social and cultural significance of information systems in assisting their efforts at development. These countries' demands can be generally grouped under two categories: first, they are requesting a "more balanced" flow of news between the developed and developing worlds. In this context, it is argued that the four major Western-based international news agencies (United Press International, The Associated Press, Reuters and Agence France-Press) monopolize the world news "market" [The Inter Dependent, Sept./Oct. 1981]. It is also claimed that the news gathered, selected and disseminated by these agencies when covering the third world lacks impartiality and objectivity, and such reporting is seen as one-sided and sensationalistic. Secondly, supporters of the NWICO are asserting a "right to communicate" for those nations lacking in the means of communications, and toward this aim they are requesting financial and technical assistance from the industrialized countries. Western spokesmen, on the other hand, while admitting the existence of imbalances in international news flows, are voicing unease over perceived threats of news control and over attempts to limit access of journalists to nonofficial news sources by governments too ready to protect and legitimize their political power.

The recent integration of satellite and computer technologies has led to a rapid expansion in the applications of satellite communications. The emerging systems include direct satellite broadcasting, remote sensing of the earth's surface and transborder data transmissions. These revolutionary breakthroughs have introduced complex and controversial legal and political issues. The principle of "unrestricted free-flow" has at times conflicted with principles of national sovereignty and of privacy, resulting in the gradual spread of the information issue into the more specialized and technical agencies of the UN. For example, the United Nations Commission on Transnational Corporations has been considering the legal and economic implications of transborder data flows and the question of equal access to processed and nonprocessed information. Similarly, the United Nations Committee on the Peaceful Uses of Outer Space has been debating issues of priority of access to nonprocessed data and the implications of direct satellite broadcasting on the national sovereignty of states.

Also, as a result of an increased international demand for geostationary orbital slots and radio frequencies—especially due to the requests of the developing countries for equal access to these scarce resources—the ITU has become a central forum of debate.

These argumentative and important issues will remain on the agendas of the relevant UN agencies as the search for greater international cooperation and agreement in world communications issues continues.

[Issues Before the 38th General Assembly, 1983, pp. 132–35]

NEW WORLD INFORMATION ORDER

U.S. State Department

BACKGROUND

ESTABLISHMENT OF A NEW WORLD information order (NWIO), by which the developing countries would acquire information and communications facilities approaching those enjoyed by the developed countries, has been discussed in UNESCO and other UN bodies over the past decade. The discussion has generated much controversy because of the important philosophical, developmental, and commercial issues involved. An NWIO has never been codified and probably cannot be codified in a way that reconciles the diverse views of the international community. It remains a vague concept with little program content and no timetables.

THIRD WORLD POSITION

Advocates of an NWIO among the developing countries point out that a small number of developed countries provide most of the world's news coverage, entertainment, and advertising. Much of the news coverage is controlled by a few multinational news agencies. According to NWIO advocates, this is unacceptable because the agencies devote too little attention to the domestic affairs of the developing countries and foster a negative image of those countries by focusing on sensational and disastrous events while ignoring positive ones, particularly development issues. In addition, NWIO proponents view commercial advertising as fostering biases in favor of the industrialized

466

world and multinational corporations and as a threat to their cultural heritage.

For some of the more radical NWIO advocates, the remedy is to restrict the free international flow of information, particularly by curbing the power of the multinational news agencies. Specifically, they seek to license journalists, impose international codes of journalistic ethics, inhibit advertising, and extend government control over the press. In this way, they hope to limit outside influences and keep a tighter control over the information coming in and out of their countries. The Soviets assiduously support all of these proposals for restricting press freedoms.

Not all developing countries see an NWIO in such negative terms. Many believe that the gaps in information and communications capacity are real and should be filled by practical development efforts, including more assistance from the developed countries. They seek cooperation with the developed countries, not confrontation.

US POSITION

The US recognizes the existence of an information and communications imbalance and supports a practical approach to communications development. As the result of a US initiative in late 1980, UNESCO established the International Program of the Development of Communications (IPDC). The US hopes that the IPDC will bring a greater degree of coordination to international communications development efforts and that it will raise the priority assigned to communications by national and international development experts. At the same time, our fundamental commitment to First Amendment and free market values causes us to reject efforts to restrict the free international flow of information under cover of a new world information order.

The Universal Declaration of Human Rights and UNESCO's constitution protect the free flow of information. It is inappropriate that organizations of the UN should be used for, or should lend themselves to, the promotion of restrictions on the press. Article 19 of the Universal Declaration states: "Everyone has the right to freedom of opinion and expression; this right includes the freedom to hold opinions without interference and to seek, receive and impart information and ideas through any media and regardless of frontiers."

The US concurs in the views expressed in the May 1981 Talloires Declaration (France), a statement by 62 members of the private media from 21 developed and developing countries. The declaration, among other things, decries censorship and other press restrictions as a violation of every individual's right to be informed. It sees the licensing of journalists as inconsistent with a free press and an international code of ethics for journalists as damaging and impractical in a world of diverse views and communication policies. It recognizes advertising as an important source of information and as a source of financial support that is fundamental to an independent press.

At a time of rapid technological change in the communications field, the US looks forward to expanded information horizons for all individuals and peoples and is prepared to work constructively with others to reach this goal.

["New World Information Order," 1981]

C.

HUMAN RIGHTS

UNIVERSAL DECLARATION OF HUMAN RIGHTS

United Nations

THE DECLARATION was the work of the UN Commission on Human Rights which met in January 1947 under the chairmanship of Mrs. Franklin D. Roosevelt. The Universal Declaration of Human Rights they drew up was adopted and proclaimed by the General Assembly on December 10, 1948. It was the first effort to set common standards of achievement in human rights for all peoples of all nations.

PREAMBLE

Whereas recognition of the inherent dignity and of the equal and inalienable rights of all members of the human family is the foundation of freedom, justice and peace in the world,

Whereas disregard and contempt for human rights have resulted in barbarous acts which have outraged the conscience of mankind, and the advent of a world in which human beings shall enjoy freedom of speech and belief and freedom from fear and want has been proclaimed as the highest aspiration of the common people,

Whereas it is essential, if man is not to be compelled to have recourse, as a last resort, to rebellion against tyranny and oppression, that human rights should be protected by the rule of law,

Whereas it is essential to promote the development of friendly relations between nations,

Whereas the peoples of the United Nations have in the Charter reaffirmed their faith in fundamental human rights, in the dignity and worth of the human person and in the equal rights of men and women and have determined to promote social progress and better standards of life in larger freedom,

Whereas Member States have pledged themselves to achieve, in co-operation with the United Nations, the promotion of universal respect for and observance of human rights and fundamental freedoms,

Whereas a common understanding of these rights and freedoms is of the greatest importance for the full realization of this pledge,

Now, therefore,

The General Assembly

Proclaims this Universal Declaration of Human Rights as a common standard of achievement for all peoples and all nations, to the end that every individual and every organ of society, keeping this Declaration constantly in mind, shall strive by teaching and education to promote respect for these rights and freedoms and by progressive measures, national and international to secure their universal and effective recognition and observance, both among the peoples of Member States themselves and among the peoples of territories under their jurisdiction.

Article 1

All human beings are born free and equal in dignity and rights. They are endowed with reason and conscience and should act towards one another in a spirit of brotherhood.

Article 2

Everyone is entitled to all the rights and freedoms set forth in this Declaration, without distinction of any kind, such as race, colour, sex, language, religion, political or other opinion, national or social origin, property, birth or other status.

Furthermore, no distinction shall be made on the basis of the political, jurisdictional or international status of the country or territory to which a person belongs, whether it be independent, trust, non-self-governing or under any other limitation of sovereignty.

Article 3

Everyone has the right to life, liberty and the security of person.

Article 4

No one shall be held in slavery or servitude; slavery and the slave trade shall be prohibited in all their forms.

Article 5

No one shall be subjected to torture or to cruel, inhuman or degrading treatment or punishment.

Article 6

Everyone has the right to recognition everywhere as a person before the law.

Article 7

All are equal before the law and are entitled without any discrimination to equal protection of the law. All are entitled to equal protection against any discrimination in violation of this Declaration and against any incitement to such discrimination.

Article 8

Everyone has the right to an effective remedy by the competent national tribunals for acts violating the fundamental rights granted him by the constitution or by law.

Article 9

No one shall be subjected to arbitrary arrest, detention or exile.

Article 10

Everyone is entitled in full equality to a fair and public hearing by an independent and impartial tribunal, in the determination of his rights and obligations and of any criminal charge against him.

Article 11

1. Everyone charged with a penal offence has the right to be presumed innocent until proved guilty according to law in a public trial at which he has had all the guarantees necessary for his defence.
2. No one shall be held guilty of any penal offence on account of any act or omission which did not constitute a penal offence, under national or international law, at the time when it was committed. Nor shall a heavier penalty be imposed than the one that was applicable at the time the penal offence was comitted.

Article 12

No one shall be subjected to arbitrary interference with his privacy, family, home or correspondence, nor to attacks upon his honour and reputation. Everyone has the right to the protection of the law against such interference or attacks.

Article 13

1. Everyone has the right to freedom of movement and residence within the borders of each State.
2. Everyone has the right to leave any country, including his own, and to return to his country.

Article 14

1. Everyone has the right to seek and to enjoy in other countries asylum from persecution.
2. This right may not be invoked in the case of prosecutions genuinely arising from non-political crimes or from acts

contrary to the purposes and principles of the United Nations.

Article 15

1. Everyone has the right to a nationality.
2. No one shall be arbitrarily deprived of his nationality nor denied the right to change his nationality.

Article 16

1. Men and women of full age, without any limitation due to race, nationality or religion, have the right to marry and to found a family. They are entitled to equal rights as to marriage, during marriage and at its dissolution.
2. Marriage shall be entered into only with the free and full consent of the intending spouses.
3. The family is the natural and fundamental group unit of society and is entitled to protection by society and the State.

Article 17

1. Everyone has the right to own property alone as well as in association with others.
2. No one shall be arbitrarily deprived of his property.

Article 18

Everyone has the right to freedom of thought, conscience and religion; this right includes freedom to change his religion or belief, and freedom, either alone or in community with others and in public or private, to manifest his religion or belief in teaching, practice, worship and observance.

Article 19

Everyone has the right to freedom of opinion and expression; this right includes freedom to hold opinions without interference and to seek, receive and impart information and ideas through any media and regardless of frontiers.

Article 20

1. Everyone has the right to freedom of peaceful assembly and association.
2. No one may be compelled to belong to an association.

Article 21

1. Everyone has the right to take part in the government of his country, directly or through freely chosen representatives.
2. Everyone has the right of equal access to public service in his country.
3. The will of the people shall be the basis of the authority of government; this will shall be expressed in periodic and genuine elections which shall be by universal and equal suffrage and shall be held by secret vote or by equivalent free voting procedures.

Article 22

Everyone, as a member of society, has the right to social security and is entitled to realization, through national effort and international co-operation and in accordance with the organization and resources of each State, of the economic, social and cultural rights indispensable for his dignity and the free development of his personality.

Article 23

1. Everyone has the right to work, to free choice of employment, to just and favourable conditions of work and to protection against unemployment.
2. Everyone, without any discrimination, has the right to equal pay for equal work.
3. Everyone who works has the right to just and favourable remuneration ensuring for himself and his family an existence worthy of human dignity, and supplemented, if necessary, by other means of social protection.
4. Everyone has the right to form and to join trade unions for the protection of his interests.

Article 24

Everyone has the right to rest and leisure, including reasonable limitation of working hours and periodic holidays with pay.

Article 25

1. Everyone has the right to a standard of living adequate for the health and well-being of himself and of his family, including food, clothing, housing and medical care and necessary social services, and the right to security in the event of unemployment, sickness, disability, widowhood, old age or other lack of livelihood in circumstances beyond his control.
2. Motherhood and childhood are entitled to special care and assistance. All children, whether born in or out of wedlock, shall enjoy the same social protection.

Article 26

1. Everyone has the right to education. Education shall be free, at least in the elementary and fundamental stages. Elementary education shall be compulsory. Technical and professional education shall be made generally available and higher education shall be equally accessible to all on the basis of merit.
2. Education shall be directed to the full development of the human personality and to the strengthening of respect for human rights and fundamental freedoms. It shall promote understanding, tolerance and friendship among all nations, racial or religious groups, and shall further the activities of the United Nations for the maintenance of peace.
3. Parents have a prior right to choose the kind of education that shall be given to their children.

Article 27

1. Everyone has the right freely to participate in the cultural life of the community, to enjoy the arts and to share in scientific advancement and its benefits.

2.   Everyone has the right to the protection of the moral and material interests resulting from any scientific, literary or artistic production of which he is the author.

Article 28

Everyone is entitled to a social and international order in which the rights and freedoms set forth in this Declaration can be fully realized.

Article 29

1.   Everyone has duties to the community in which alone the free and full development of his personality is possible.
2.   In the exercise of his rights and freedoms, everyone shall be subject only to such limitations as are determined by law solely for the purpose of securing due recognition and respect for the rights and freedoms of others and of meeting the just requirements of morality, public order and the general welfare in a democratic society.
3.   These rights and freedoms may in no case be exercised contrary to the purposes and principles of the United Nations.

Article 30

Nothing in this Declaration may be interpreted as implying for any State, group or person any right to engage in any activity or to perform any act aimed at the destruction of any of the rights and freedoms set forth herein.

FROM IDEOLOGY TO PROGRAM TO POLICY

Lincoln P. Bloomfield

POLICIES REGARDING HUMAN RIGHTS are of course as old as the Republic itself. But the U.S. position with regard to human rights varies from one administration to the next. Part of the variation appears in the degree of agressiveness with which human rights elsewhere are supported. Part, however, is found in the kind of human rights on which emphasis is placed.

Those rights most prominently featured in the Carter years were rights involving the "integrity of the person," including the right not to be subjected to arbitrary arrest and imprisonment, summary executions, torture, disappearance, or acts of genocide. A second group of rights, however, is embodied in traditional American and western concepts of "civil and political" rights: freedom of thought, assembly, religion, speech, and press, as well as freedom of movement and freedom to take part in government. Still a third group of rights, markedly different in character, increasingly dominates U.N. debates, asserting the entitlement of individuals everywhere to fulfillment of "basic human needs" such as food, shelter, health care, and education.

In countries grounded in the western constitutional and economic tradition, profound legal and philosophical problems arise from attempting to give the same emphasis to all three groups of rights. The first group, emphasized by Carter, offers no difficulties. The second group, traditionally enshrined in the organic instruments of western political freedom, also presents no philosophical problems; what is at issue is the calculus of costs and benefits in seeking to impose such concepts on other governments. The third group, however, presents real difficulties for American governments, difficulties that vary in intensity from one administration to the next.

More precisely, the American political–philosophical tradition rests on the notion of explicit limitations on the powers of government. But emphasis on the right to jobs, food, health care, and other basic needs connotes the exact reverse—empowering governments to provide for the individual. This contradiction creates deep conceptual difficulties for our own system of governance, whose federal powers are explicitly limited and whose central philosophy supports the right to a fair chance rather than a fair share.

The ideological split among Americans toward human rights policy stems historically from the country's curious mix of Jeffersonian idealism and Hamiltonian pragmatism. The Jefferson commitment is to the principle of governance with the consent of the governed, accompanied by a positive distaste for tyrannies, dictatorships, and other repressive forms of political rule. The Hamiltonian approach rests on an expedient assessment of the national interest that takes the world as it is, rather than as personal ethic writ large. This attitude accepts moral compromises in order to protect the nation's security as its leaders conceive the latter.

["From Ideology to Program to Policy: Tracking the Carter Human Rights Policy," 1982, pp. 2,3]

THE UN SYSTEM AND HUMAN RIGHTS

Nigel S. Rodley

DURING THE PAST THREE DECADES the intensity of United Nations activity in getting states to agree to international standards on human rights, then in taking action against violations of the standards, has increased. In general, the UN has been more active and effective in "promoting" human rights (its norm-creation function) than in "protecting" these rights (i.e., in implementing the norms). Nongovernmental organizations (NGOs) have been active from the beginnings of the UN both in the attempt to develop an internationally agreed code of behavior constraining governments in the treatment of their citizens and in urging the UN itself to help enforce respect for the code. . . .

Proclaimed on December 10, 1948, the Universal Declaration of Human Rights remains, and may be expected to remain, the moral touchstone for all claims at the international level that justice has not been done at the national level. Its broad scope, ranging from its guarantees of a fair trial to those of a right to adequate housing, health care, and education, enables its provisions to be invoked explicitly or by implication to virtually any unfair overreaching or negligence of governments toward the governed.

At the time of the Declaration's adoption it held itself to be "a standard of achievement for peoples and all nations." Accordingly, governments did not consider themselves to be undertaking legally binding obligations when voting for it. It is not by accident that the Universal Declaration contains no instrument for its enforcement and that the Commission that drafted it had already decided in 1946 that it had no power to take action on complaints of human rights violations, a position subsequently ratified by ECOSOC. This was the beginning of the emergence of the practice whereby states were to prove themselves more willing to enunciate desirable standards as long as this did not involve direct legal obligation or multilateral implementation of the standards than they were when their commitment involved legal obligations to implement defined norms.

It was not until December 16, 1966 that the General Assembly adopted the other components of the International Bill of Human Rights: the International Covenant on Economic, Social and Cultural Rights; the International Covenant on Civil and Political Rights; and the Optional Protocol to the latter Covenant. (The former Covenant only came into force on January 3, 1976, and the latter one and the Optional Protocol came into force on March 23, 1976.) By the end of 1981, 71 countries had ratified or acceded to the International Covenant on Economic, Social and Cultural Rights, 69 countries had ratified or acceded to the International Covenant on Civil and Political Rights, and 27 countries had become parties to the Optional Protocol.

The caution evinced by the low incidence of ratification of these instruments is paralleled by the careful, confined definitions in their provisions. Thus, the articles guaranteeing the so-called fundamental freedoms (movement, conscience, expression, assembly, and association) are hedged about with provisos permitting restrictions on their exercise on such grounds as national security, territorial integrity, public policy, public morality, and protection of the rights and reputation of others (Articles 12, 18, 19, 21, and 22). The scope of these concepts remains to be defined at the international level. (The restrictive approach of the regional-level organs of the European Convention on Human Rights is not encouraging.)

Given the practice of some countries to justify the suppression of any activity against the officially approved policy on the basis of these exceptions, it would certainly appear that many parties to the Covenant may not feel that its obligations are unduly onerous. The same observation may be made about the provisions of the International Covenant on Economic, Social and Cultural Rights, most of whose obligations are framed in terms of recognition of a need to work to achieve progressively the full realization of the rights recognized in the Covenant. The essentially programmatic nature of the rights makes such an approach essential. But so does the fact that there is no international consensus on what national economic and social systems are best suited to the attainment of objectives that, inter alia, guarantee the right to work, to social security, to an adequate standard of living, to the highest attainable standards of physical and mental health, and to education.

The system of implementation of the Covenants may also be characterized as prudent, given the restricted degree of international scrutiny to which parties submit themselves. Under the International Covenant on Civil and Political Rights, the only automatic monitoring is provided for by Article 40, which obliges states parties to submit periodic reports to the Human Rights Committee, an 18-member group of experts elected by the states parties to the Covenant. In 1981–82 the Committee was still in the process of examining the first reports of states parties; it is thus far difficult to see how the Committee will use its power to induce states to comply with their obligations. Individual Committee members characteristically pose questions on generally self-serving reports to government representatives. The responses frequently increase in vagueness in direct proportion to the specificity of the question, and the Committee has not shown itself disposed to insist on adequate factual answers to its members' questions. Indeed, despite sending several "reminders," as of the end of 1981 it had not even been able to elicit the first report of one state party—Uruguay. Nevertheless, at this early stage, the potential of the Committee's review of states' reports cannot be dismissed. The mere fact that representatives of states are called to appear before and respond (however inadequately) to questions from members of an intergovernmentally established body on matters of the most extreme sensitivity for most governments is a development of some magnitude in a field that international law used to consign to the realm of domestic jurisdiction.

A further, so far untested, power is granted to the Human Rights Committee under Article 41 of the Covenant, which provides for states to make declarations whereby the Committee can receive complaints of violations by them of the rights contained in the Covenant from other states that have made a similar declaration. Since the tenth declaration required to bring the Article 41 procedure into force was only deposited with the

UN Secretary-General on December 28, 1978, and, given the relative homogeneity of the 14 states that have now made such declarations, it will probably be some time before the Committee's powers to reconcile interstate disputes will be exercised.

The most radical aspects of the Covenant system of protection is that contained in the Optional Protocol to the International Covenant on Civil and Political Rights. Under this protocol individuals residing in states that have ratified it can lodge complaints ("communications" addressed to the UN Secretary-General) alleging violations by ratifying governments of the rights guaranteed them under the Covenant. As of its 1981 report to the General Assembly, the Human Rights Committee had had 102 complaints from 13 countries placed before it. The Committee reported to the General Assembly that it found violations by Uruguay in respect of 14 "communications." In one case, it concluded coyly that it could not find that there had *not* been a violation by Uruguay. Only the first finding of a violation was before the General Assembly at its 34th session (1979). The next five findings were before it at its 35th session (1980) and another eight at its 36th session in 1981. Uruguay ignored these findings and the Assembly did not address itself to the matter at either session. This is a serious challenge to the authority of the only UN body formally and explicitly mandated to deal with individual complaints of human rights violations. Even though the Committee, not being a judicial body, has no power to give binding decisions, it will be regrettable if the flouting of its findings entails no formal political costs within the UN. Whatever the outcome, the very fact of these findings will reinforce the work of NGOs on behalf of specific individuals and groups, in terms of the legitimacy and accuracy of their own denunciations.

The system for monitoring implementation of the International Covenant on Economic, Social and Cultural Rights is even weaker than that of the International Covenant on Civil and Political Rights, for the monitoring body is the Economic and Social Council of the United Nations (ECOSOC), an intergovernmental body, and not a group of individual experts invested with international status and called upon to act impartially. Despite the nonperemptory nature of most of the obligations contained in the Covenant, ECOSOC's powers are confined to the examination of reports submitted by states parties under Article 16 of the Covenant. It took ECOSOC until 1979 to establish a procedure for dealing with the reports (a sessional working group composed of 15 ECOSOC representatives of governments that are also parties to the Covenant studies the reports). The working group started considering reports of states for the first time at ECOSOC's Spring 1980 session.

In view of the none-too-demanding nature of many of the substantive obligations of both Covenants, the inherent weakness of the basic system of monitoring compliance through consideration of reports submitted by states parties, and the limited number of states accepting stronger (and still not fully effective) measures of implementation under the International Covenant on Civil and Political Rights, it may be wondered why NGOs are committed to working for the widest possible ratification of the Covenants and the Optional Protocol. The following factors are relevant. First, some substantive obligations (for example, the right not to be subjected to torture) are reasonably unambiguous and may not even be suspended even in time of emergency. Although states may nevertheless fail to comply with them, as illustrated by the findings of the Human Rights Committee on the situation in Uruguay, the mere existence of these legally binding standards may serve both to inhibit flagrant state disregard for their provisions and strengthen the legitimacy of the work of NGOs as they campaign to hold governments to their international promises. Second, the weakness of the basic monitoring mechanism and even of the voluntary improvement on it contained in the Optional Protocol must be seen as part of a process. Campaigning for respect for human rights is essentially a technique of step-by-step application of the pressure of international public opinion. The more steps that can be brought into play, however modestly, the greater are the chances of some kind of success.

In addition to the general human rights documents contained in the International Bill of Human Rights, the UN has promoted the adoption of a large number of instruments, both legally binding treaties and resolutions of debatable and varying legal force on specific areas of human rights. These have dealt with such areas as women's rights, children's rights, workers' rights, rights of the disabled and of the mentally retarded, educational rights, and religious rights. Some, such as those relating to the rights of aliens and migrant workers, are still in the process of being drafted. The first of these was the Convention on the Prevention and Punishment of the Crime of Genocide adopted on December 9, 1948. It basically singled out the major crime against humanity as defined at Nuremberg and made it susceptible of national jurisdiction in the territory where the crime was committed and of international jurisdiction before any competent future international tribunal.

It took a significant change in the composition of the UN before serious attention was given to a less sensational but related area of human rights violation, namely, racial discrimination. It was not until 1965 that the Convention on the Elimination of All Forms of Racial Discrimination was adopted. This followed the adoption on November 20, 1963 of the United Nations Declaration on the Elimination of All Forms of Racial Discrimination (General Assembly Resolution 1904 [XVIII]). The Convention, which defines and prohibits discrimination on the ground of racial origin, established an 18-member Committee on the Elimination of Racial Discrimination (CERD) empowered to examine periodic reports submitted by states parties. It can also receive interstate complaints under Article II, although none has been made since the Convention entered into force on January 4, 1969. Under Article 14, it may also receive complaints of violations from individuals in countries whose governments have deposited a separate declaration with the UN Secretary-General. As of the end of 1981 this procedure was not yet in force, the Secretary-General now having received only eight of the required ten declarations. . . .

Attempts by the United Nations to define its human rights role in programmatic terms have tended to cause gloom in human rights circles in the West. This is because a majority of UN members prefer to put the accent on economic and social development rather than on how much civil and political freedom they grant their citizenry. In 1968 the UN proclaimed:

> Since human rights and fundamental freedoms are indivisible, the full realization of civil and political rights without the enjoyment of economic, social and cultural rights is impossible. The achievement of lasting progress in the implementation of human rights is dependent upon sound

and effective national and international policies of economic and social development.

At the time this statement was made, it could have been interpreted as providing balance to an earlier paragraph of the same Proclamation:

> The primary aim of the United Nations in the sphere of human rights is the achievement by each individual of the maximum freedom and dignity. For the realization of this objective, the laws of every country should grant each individual, irrespective of race, language or political belief, freedom of expression, of information, of conscience and of religion, as well as the right to participate in the political, economic, cultural and social life of his country.

By 1977, however, the General Assembly was reaffirming the first of the paragraphs just quoted, but not the second. In resolution 32/130 of December 16, 1977, for example, the Assembly put the accent on massive violations of collective rights and spoke of according priority to the realization of the new international economic order, since this was "an essential element for the effective promotion of human rights and fundamental freedoms." Fifteen countries, mainly Western, abstained in the vote.

["The UN System and Human Rights," 1983, pp. 265–78]

VII

CREATING A COMMONSENSE —AND HUMANE— INTERNATIONAL ORDER

VII. CREATING A COMMONSENSE— AND HUMANE— INTERNATIONAL ORDER

WITH HUMILITY AT APPEARING IN THE COMPANY OF ALEXANDER HAMILTON, I assert in VIIA that moving toward a more effective community does not call for world government, but rather a society of independent states that in their own enlightened self-interest agree in advance to submit on some issues to the will of a highly qualified majority, with some form of national veto in extreme circumstances. In a quest for more effective structures of cooperative action in a diverse and pluralistic world, it helps to keep in mind the American constitutional concept of "reserved powers." The Hamilton selection (from Federalist Paper No. 17) concerns factors that shield the parts of a political system from unwarranted encroachments by a central authority.

In VIIB Harlan Cleveland rejects the argument that a world order must evolve along the lines of American experience, while identifying the objective trends toward a modest form of "pluralistic governance." An Atlantic Council of the US study group (for which I acted as rapporteur) prescribes a mixed strategy that distinguishes issues where the UN system should take the initiative from action items that may be more likely to be implemented by groupings with partial rather than universal membership.

In the final selection in the volume, I urge that Americans try hard to combine sober realism with practical idealism, in recognition of the reality that "though major forces affecting

491

human life are increasingly transnational, only states can undertake the diplomacy essential for coping with them." My conclusion is that the development of genuinely effective multilateral instruments and agencies has become for the first time in history a sheer necessity instead of a luxury.

A.

"RESERVED POWERS" ON A GLOBAL SCALE

THE UN AND US FOREIGN POLICY

Lincoln P. Bloomfield

THE OBJECTIVE is not necessarily to form a larger polity, anticipating the end of smaller national units. This age of neonationalism does not yet look like fertile soil for drastic supranationalism. Nor is world government necessarily desirable. It is, for example, by no means clear that world-government enthusiasts have sufficiently examined the implications of tyranny on a global scale. Here, more than anywhere else, the perfect is the enemy of the good, and the good is desperately needed. Nationalism can be even a positive good. The vices of extreme nationalism are mirror images of its virtues, virtues that are creating the beginnings of a new and freer pattern for the Eastern European states.

In the middle run of time and planning, then, barring a great catastrophe, the goal should not be the utopia of world government. But having said that, one can establish reasonable and even exciting goals of community building that, in recognizing the growing web of interconnected purposes and activities in which all mankind is bound, offer creative political substitutes for historically destructive nationalism of the virulent and exclusive type.

A more reasonable picture of a middle-range political future would appear to be a society of independent states that would have agreed in advance to submit on some issues to the will of a highly qualified majority, but with some form of national veto retained *in extremis*. Universal collective security remains a rational ideal, but in this age it has to be—and has been—modified. In the realm of cooperation the American goal should be, first, to create the consensus without which there can be no community, and then to encourage the formation of the community institutions, regional and global, that give political life to the consensus. This is a broad-spectrum goal applicable to regional organizations for Western Europe, Central America, or Africa, or to those organizations embodying worldwide programs polarized not around abstractions, but around concrete international tasks based on shared interests, whether they be trade, science, space, or the control of armaments.

[*The United Nations and U.S. Foreign Policy*, 1967, pp. 38,39]

THE FEDERALIST NO. XVII

Alexander Hamiltion

THE ADMINISTRATION OF PRIVATE JUSTICE between
the citizens of the same State, the supervision of agriculture and
of other concerns of a similar nature, all those things, in short,
which are proper to be provided for by local legislation, can
never be desirable cares of a general jurisdiction. It is therefore
improbable that there should exist a disposition in the federal
councils to usurp the powers with which they are connected;
because the attempt to exercise those powers would be as
troublesome as it would be nugatory; and the possession of
them, for that reason, would contribute nothing to the dignity,
to the importance, or to the splendour of the national government.

But let it be admitted, for argument's sake, that mere
wantonness and lust of domination would be sufficient to beget
that disposition; still it may be safely affirmed, that the sense of
the constituent body of the national representatives, or, in other
words, the people of the several States, would control the
indulgence of so extravagant an appetite. It will always be far
more easy for the State governments to encroach upon the
national authorities, than for the national government to encroach upon the State authorities. The proof of this proposition
turns upon the greater degree of influence which the State
governments, if they administer their affairs with uprightness
and prudence, will generally possess over the people; a circumstance which at the same time teaches us that there is an inherent
and intrinsic weakness in all federal constitutions; and that too
much pains cannot be taken in their organisation, to give them
all the force which is compatible with the principles of liberty.

The superiority of influence in favour of the particular

governments would result partly from the diffusive construction of the national government, but chiefly from the nature of the objects to which the attention of the State administrations would be directed.

It is a known fact in human nature, that its affections are commonly weak in proportion to the distance or diffusiveness of the object. Upon the same principle that a man is more attached to his family than to his neighbourhood, to his neighbourhood than to the community at large, the people of each State would be apt to feel a stronger bias towards their local governments than towards the government of the Union; unless the force of that principle should be destroyed by a much better administration of the latter.

The separate governments in a confederacy may aptly be compared with the feudal baronies; with this advantage in their favour, that from the reasons already explained, they will generally possess the confidence and good-will of the people, and with so important a support, will be able effectually to oppose all encroachments of the national government. It will be well if they are not able to counteract its legitimate and necessary authority. The points of similitude consist in the rivalship of power, applicable to both, and in the CONCENTRATION of large portions of the strength of the community into particular DEPOSITS, in one case at the disposal of individuals, in the other case at the disposal of political bodies.

[*The Federalist* No. 17, 1787, pp. 79–82]

B.

"GOVERNANCE" REDEFINED

GOVERNING A PLURALISTIC WORLD

Harlan Cleveland

LIFE SIGNS OF A NEW INTERNATIONAL ORDER

FIVE YEARS AGO, an international working group assembled by the Aspen Institute studied the political economy of this new kind of world order and called it a "planetary bargain." A report of the working group observed in part:

> The complexity of the issues and the congestion of interest-groups involved (195 nation-states, a hundred major transnational corporations, dozens of nonprofit multinationals, all meeting in 700 intergovernmental conferences and more than 3,000 international association meetings a year) make nonsense of the notion that with one great political act a New International Economic Order might be created. The process, if it works, will be more like a global bazaar, in which negotiators are continuously engaged in parallel negotiations about strategically related but tactically separable matters. Yet the environment for constructive bargaining has to be created by a shared sense that bargains can be struck which advance the interests of all, that a political consensus can be formed by widespread realization that peoples of every race and nation are in dangerous passage together in a world of finite resources, ultimate weapons and unmet requirements.

We are still very far from such a political consensus; the distance to be traversed is obvious from the stridency of the rhetoric and the emptiness of the dialogue between "North" and "South." Yet there is evidence of trends which might in time add up to the political underpinning for institutions as wide and deep as the "naturally international" functions that are somehow going to have to be performed.

One trend is the growing awareness of a shared human predicament. Science and technology have brought us close to the ultimate in military weaponry and close to the margins of biospheric damage. The need for a farseeing collective prudence is now widely understood—even if it has not yet filtered into the chancelleries where short-term politics often wins the arguments about long-term destiny.

Science and technology have also made possible—and therefore necessary—the meeting of human needs at a level that nearly everybody would agree is a human right. The requirements side of the human-needs equation is already global. The supply side—meeting the needs—is still mostly regarded as a national responsibility. But the rapid spread of a basic-needs ideology—centering on the notion that the meeting of basic needs should be a first charge on world resources—may provide a basis for "next steps" at the international level.

At the same time, in the existing international agencies, there are signs of common sense about procedures for cooperation. One sign is the increasing tendency in international organizations to eschew two-sided adversary proceedings and avoid voting procedures—moving instead toward action by consensus. People and even diplomats have noticed that voting leads to rapid and acrimonious disagreement about general principles, whereas consensus procedures can lead (often at tedious length) to quiet agreement about collective action to be taken on particulars.

Another sign is the invention of new kinds of international organizations—short of the "supranational" institutions described by theorists of world government, but an improvement on arrangements that are bounded by what can be agreed from day to day in a committee of instructed national representatives. One such "extranational" organization is the European Commission, whose Cabinet-level members are appointed by but cannot be removed by their own governments, and which (under the Treaty of Rome) exercises the initiative on some classes of actions on which national governments have agreed not to make national policy. Another is the World Bank, which has escaped some of the sand in the gears of other "committees of sovereigns" by the leadership of a series of strong-minded central executives—making it more like a multinational company than, say, like UNESCO. . . .

There is a place for extranational institutions—with a wider reach and stronger powers than a U.N.-style committee of governments, yet not a world government from which there is no earthly appeal. Most of the institutions will not need to be global: The interests of people and nations vary greatly according to size and structure, geography and geology, priorities and purposes. A pluralistic world order will be made up of regional and functional communities of the concerned. But it will nearly always be important for the community-of-the-concerned to keep in touch with a wider circle-of-the-consulted—through a broad political body such as the United Nations General Assembly or an *ad hoc* world conference such as Stockholm 1972 and its successors or a special-purpose standing assembly such as the one established for Intelsat.

The priceless ingredient of pluralistic governance is a common feel for shared problems, as a basis for that "shared sense that bargains can be struck which advance the interests of all." To produce and project the analysis on which such a common feel can be rationally and emotionally based is the primary task for international political leadership. Only thus will the national "representatives" and the international specialists be enabled to face the most puzzling dilemma of all: that in a pluralistic system, each "faction" has to think hard about strategies for dealing with the whole predicament in order to deal relevantly with the parcel that especially touches its own interest.

There is nothing in the United Nations Charter that prevents the development of policy planning staffs and extranational institutions to organize the kind of practical bargaining that is already overdue. The corrosive sludge of procedure admittedly stands in the way, even though most of it is not required by the Charter. (The Charter describes voting arrangements, for example, but does not require them in preference to consensus procedure.) But the primary obstacle to next steps is the still widespread illusion that the mutation of international institutions must be modelled on the increasing centralization of the modern nation-state.

The crisis of national governance provides the occasion—

for theorists of a New International Order, the opportunity—for a breakthrough in the evolution of international institutions. The way to start is clearly not to replicate at the global level the formulas for centralized power and central planning that are failing to handle complexity even at the national level.

Real "world order" is likely to mean a more Madisonian world, a world of bargains and accommodations among national and functional "factions," a world in which peoples are able to agree on what to do next together without feeling the need (or being forced by global government) to agree on religious creed or political credo. A practical pluralism, not a unitary universalism, is the likely destiny of the human race.

["Governing A Pluralistic World," 1981, pp. 18–22]

WHAT FUTURE FOR THE UN?

Atlantic Council of the U.S.

Toward a Strategy of World Order

WE BELIEVE THAT THE INTERESTS of the United States and of all nations require that a more effective system of international organizations be put in place to deal with the management of three areas that traditional bilateral relations can no longer handle: the economic issues dividing the "have" and "have-not" nations: the undiminished agenda of international disputes threatening the peace; and the complex network of functional interdependencies.

We are convinced of the urgent necessity, today as never before, of multilateral instruments of discussion, bargaining, and action across a wide spectrum to cope with these clusters of issues. Where such issues have a global character, there is no substitute for a system of agencies with near-universal membership and acknowledged jurisdiction, to deal with problems no nation can tackle alone.

The UN system as a central organization with almost universal membership, can and should take the initiative on global issues, as it has done usefully in the past on food, population, drugs, peacekeeping, disaster relief, status of women, arms control, human rights and law of the sea. But *international organizations with partial membership, whether based on regional location or on functional necessity, should, where possible, take on more of the action items on the new international agenda.*

The main emphasis must be on getting the job done, rather than dogmatically working within any particular institutional framework.

We recommend a *"mixed strategy"* that envisages the international organization system of the future as *pluralistic* rather than strongly centralized, though with such coordination as is feasible.

The United Nations, with all its weaknesses, is currently the prime place of contact with Third World forces. It is in this sense irreplaceable, and US national interests require that we continue to play a fully constructive part, proposing reforms when necessary.

In our view the United Nations can be only marginally helpful in bridging East-West differences. On crucial issues such as strategic nuclear arms control, mutual force reductions in Europe, détente ground rules, East-West trade, emigration, or most-favored-nation treatment, the United Nations does not provide a useful instrumentality. There are sound reasons for continuing to minimize US-Soviet confrontations in international organizations and to continue what is, in effect, their "second-order agreement" to disagree profoundly on basic philosophy, but to work together in the UN on specifics such as Middle East peacekeeping.

The United Nations is, however, valuable as a means of "legitimizing" East-West arms control agreements. Where US and Soviet power come into conflict in areas such as the Middle East or southern Africa, the United Nations could be far more helpful by devising agreed ground rules between the two that minimize their intervention, along the lines of the proposed Indian Ocean "zone of Peace." When, despite bilateral efforts, a local issue becomes globalized, world-level machinery can be useful to assist the process of tranquilizing the dispute and minimizing the possibilities of superpower intervention.

So far as relations between the democratic industrialized nations (DINs) are concerned, other organizations (such as the OECD) exist to regulate their economic interactions. At the same time a more forthcoming "DIN diplomacy" in the UN system could in our view be a force for constructive global problem-solving.

In appraising international institutions for cooperation, a sharp distinction must be recognized between multilateral bodies in which all the world's nations *debate* their views, and global or regional bodies which take *action*.

Global Debates: The General Assembly

Much of the American crisis of confidence centers on actions taken in the General Assembly.

The General Assembly has of course only the power to recommend. Its one-state-one-vote does not accurately reflect the world distribution of power or population. But its majority may represent two-thirds of the world's population and the majority of its resources and land. Its recommendations thus can often have significant political consequences, even to be taken as "victories" by the majority and "defeats" by the often grossly outnumbered Western powers.

Some Americans accept that the Western powers in an earlier period used *their* numerical majority to vote through resolutions that were objectionable to the minority (at that time, the Soviet Bloc).

Other Americans would argue that the situations are dissimilar, and that, at all events, present trends could be destructive for the system by driving away the United States, whose support is crucial for the UN.

Where the primary aim is to air grievances and exchange views, or to design and launch programs at the global level, the General Assembly is in our judgment the appropriate forum. There, all nations have an equal voice, and an equal right to be heard. The General Assembly is needed precisely *because* of great differences between those who favor political democracy and rights and those emphasizing greater economic equality. The great differences between nations and systems should not be taken as implying an unbridgeable moral gulf. Each has something of value to say to the other, and neither can comfortably survive an all-out conflict with the other. Global organizations have their highest value as places for continuous bargaining to achieve the objective of an improved world order in which *all* systems can coexist with a minimum of dangerous frictions and wars, and in which reconciliation replaces confrontation. On occasions when the Assembly renders important judgments of which the United States is critical, we should first ask ourselves—as we used to tell the Russians to do when they were in the minority—whether everyone is really out of step but Johnny.

In addition *the United States should use the General Assembly more actively to explain its positions, refute unfair allegations, and seek support on important programs.* We would like to see the *US resume the lead as "number one,"* not merely in raw economic and military power, but as the respected voice of conscience and supporter of human rights and democracy.

The habit of voting on virtually every question dealt with by the UN has in our judgment magnified the UN problem. *The United States should work with other members to de-emphasize the voting process as an invariable way of terminating international discussions. We recommend much greater use of the consensus process in international debating bodies, instead of formal votes for recording the sentiment of countries.* Sometimes this may only blur differences. But growing experience suggests that it is often preferable to voting.

In the worst case, *in the face of proposals by the Assembly that are patently outrageous, destructive of compromise solutions, or contrary to the UN Charter, the United States should consider a range of forms of selective participation as a way of expressing its profound disapproval.* Normally the United States should be present to argue vigorously for its positions and, when voting takes place, to muster what support it can. But when *Assembly procedures are flagrantly abused, the United States should consider the possibility of refraining from voting, and asking to be recorded as "refusing to participate."*

In the face of extremely tendentious or calumnious resolutions, when it has good reason to believe that its voice will be totally disregarded, the United States should feel free to absent itself from the debate entirely. In such case a clear public statement should be made of the reasons for the action. Of course, the action in such exceptional circumstances will have far greater impact if the United States can persuade others to join it.

A Pragmatic Approach to Action Programs

Where concrete international *action* on economics, financial, or technical policy is required, smaller bodies can often be more effective. Such smaller groupings can exist inside or outside the United Nations. In many cases, *peripheral organizations with partial membership based on regional location or on functional necessity should take on more substantial portions of the international agenda.*

The goal is to have in place a range of greater-than-national "regimes" which institutionalize agreed ground rules for a wide spectrum of human affairs that cannot be effectively dealt with by any nation or pair of nations—or perhaps even by presently constituted international machinery and procedures. In doing so *we recommend a spirit that might be called "the new pragmatism."*

High priority should now be given to blueprinting the framework, rules, and instruments for international steering and management of common problems in the realms of trade, commodity pricing and stocks, fair sharing and pricing of non-renewable resources, monetary management, development and population control, energy sources, food, pollution, conventional arms trade, conflict prevention, peacekeeping, the seas and seabed, and outer space. Looking into the middle-range future, we should add weather-modification prevention, nuclear terrorism, and development of exotic weaponry and other lethal technology. Some problems of control simply cannot wait; for instance, the rapid proliferation of nuclear fuel-cycle technologies.

The UN system can furnish some, though by no means all, of the machinery for coping with the interdependence agenda. Fixed doctrine about "working within the UN system" (or "avoiding the UN") should not stand in the way of practical movement toward solutions. *But neither should* ad hoc *activity in one sector or another furnish additional excuses to make an empty shell of the United Nations.*

We should avoid multiplying the number of "plenary" bodies of a universal, one-nation-one-vote character, and should rather focus institution-building on small, flexible, task-oriented structures. We would like to see renewed momentum in following through on the constructive recommendations along the lines contained in the recent UN Ad Hoc Committee of Experts report.

In the process of setting up new organizations and agencies *the governing principle should be one of representational and voting arrangements that take into account the relative power and capacity of the states without whose cooperation decisions are meaningless.* No formal change is contemplated in the one-nation-one-vote General Assembly, where all nations should have an equal voice in airing their general policies. But in one fashion or another, collective decisions on action programs must reflect far more concretely than they do now the responsibilities and the capacities of various member states to deal with the specific problems at issue. This is already the case in several important multilateral action programs.

Where decision-making is realistically weighted, the United States and others who share its aspirations for a more effective multilateral system should agree to give substantially greater weight to certain resolutions passed in that fashion by multilateral assemblies.

Peace and Security Problems

The Security Council has a mixed record that includes a number of successes, and a number of failures—including failure even to discuss major breaches of the peace, whether in Hungary or Vietnam, Ethiopia or Angola.

The Council, under the Charter, should be the place of last rather than first resort. But in the light of recent history, the multilateral route may prove in retrospect to be less costly than the unilateral route, and deserves more serious consideration by the US than it has had. Indeed, if the United States had turned to the United Nations about Indochina in 1953–54 instead of defining the threat as "Chinese" and shouldering the role in which French colonialism had already failed, our national interests would surely not have been served any worse than they were in the tragedy that ensued.

We thus believe that *the United States and other countries would better serve their own interests by making more effective use of the UN Security Council, particularly in those cases in which direct intervention would pose an unacceptable risk.*

More use should be made of the Security Council's potential for "spotlighting" external meddling in local conflicts. The best policy for all outside countries in conflict situations such as those in Africa is *not to choose sides at all, but rather to utilize the full potentialities of the UN stage to safeguard the process of transition and discourage outside interference.* (No less important is to reduce, through international publicity, the bloodshed that sometimes accompanies political change.)

In a period in which the United States supports peaceful change and opposes unilateral intervention, *the most effective US posture will be that of international champion of the principle of non-intervention, except as intervention is used by the United Nations for legitimate peacekeeping or humanitarian reasons, and helping with the orderly transition of political power in southern African countries, such as Namibia and Rhodesia.*

The Middle East wars have demonstrated that regional and even world peace at times depends on the ability of the UN Security Council to mount observation and peacekeeping missions. *The United States should sustain to the full the United Nations' authority and capacity to interpose neutral forces between fighting parties whose actions menace international peace and security.*

There should be more active recourse to the methods of pacific settlement of disputes enumerated in Article 33: negotiation, inquiry, mediation, conciliation, arbitration, judicial settlement, resort to regional agencies or arrangements, or other peaceful means of the parties' own choice.

Just listing these processes reminds one how meager their usage has been in recent years. *We strongly recommend a major effort by the US government, in concert with a coalition of similarly concerned states of all persuasions and levels of development, to re-examine the reasons for this failure and find ways to affirm a new commitment among themselves to reactivate the machinery for peaceful settlement of disputes that today languishes essentially unused.*

Some have suggested enlarging the Security Council by adding some middle powers in effect as "associate permanent members" without a veto, e.g., West Germany, Japan, India, and possibly Nigeria and Brazil. We recommend that *such "middle" powers be frequently reelected to the Council.*

The Specialized Agencies

The turbulence in the United Nations system has spilled over into some of the specialized agencies. A lively political process in these bodies is entirely legitimate and normal. But recent activities by militant blocs within technical agencies such as the International Labor Organization, the UN Educational, Scientific, and Cultural Organization, and the World Health Organization have forced the intrusion into the technical debates of extraneous issues such as Palestine and southern Africa. In some cases this has jeopardized US participation. In all cases it has hampered important work and, if continued, may threaten the future of the agencies.

Most of the specialized agencies are performing reasonably well their essential tasks of standard setting, technical assistance, and public services, ranging from epidemic control and safety at sea to international environmental standards and inspections of nuclear power reactors in scores of countries. *US interest in the continuation of these and many additional programs is strong.* In practical terms, they are major bargains for the United States, most of which would have to be invented if they did not exist today. *The US should remain in, and work to reform, them.*

Our goal now must be to insulate the agencies so that they can carry out the important technical and other tasks assigned to them in their respective charters, and proper steps can be taken to prevent them from being crippled by extraneous political issues. The United Sates should vigorously *promote these objectives through intensified collaboration with other states who share this concern.* In the worst contingency, *if an agency is genuinely stymied, states committed to its program might constitute a temporary "action coalition" within the organization to carry out some of the agency's frustrated purposes by agreeing to move ahead with common action which the majority may temporarily not be willing to pursue or adopt.*

We recommend major diplomatic efforts to try to make all the specialized agencies work better, as well as strengthen US participation, including a substantial improvement in the contributory record of the world's richest nation.

Coalitions of the Willing

Situations increasingly arise in which it is important to take collective action, but where such action is not supported by a majority, or where the majority consists of states not directly affected or responsible for implementation. This can be a blueprint for paralysis.

Ways need to be found to give more vitality to the views of states which are affected or are willing to take responsibility for constructive provisional action in the common interest, on matters that must be negotiated multilaterally, but not universally.

In the spirit of pragmatism, we recommend exploring the possibility of forming "coalitions of the willing." We see them as temporary and shifting groupings of states within the United Nations and other organizations, *who would agree among themselves to initiate commonly-needed action programs, or to act with respect to one another, at a higher standard of international behavior than the existing common level.*

Clearly such *ad hoc* group initiatives do not substitute for universal agreement. But they represent a potential device for universal agreement to get things done, among initially limited groups of states, always in the hope that others will soon join or follow suit. At times of stalemate, such coalitions might help to get a necessary global program off the ground, improve the chances for more serious bargaining among individual states, or move toward more effective dispute-settling.

Such problem-solving groupings might naturally start with democratic industrialized countries sharing common values, but they need not reflect any single bloc or region. They can and should *include states from all regions and blocs who, on a particular issue, want to see the international community make headway on a common problem—in short, an alternative to failure.*

Examples of subjects for coalition action might be: acceptance of compulsory arbitration of disputes among those agreeing; greater use of the world court and other instruments of settlement of disputes long left in disuse; formation of peace observation missions in situations where the majority refuses but the parties consent; and the establishment of a computerized conflict-prevention analysis center. The scheme might also be applied to the administration of certain international straits or waterways which are used by a limited number of countries, but which would benefit from multinational agreements over access. Other candidates for coalition action, in the event of deadlock, would be: allocation of donated global food stocks; plutonium-free zones; seabed mining rights and revenues; and establishment of multinational regional nuclear fuel reprocessing centers.

Improved Consultations

US interests require that this country be supported by others and not isolated. This implies a new degree of collaboration and compromise with other states of all persuasions.

One priority step is to *secure maximum harmony with our allies and trading partners in order to develop constructive positions in the global bargaining process now beginning to take place in multilateral forums.* The purpose of such collaboration is not to engage the rest of the world in a pitched battle over basic differences: it is to make progress, by mutually reinforcing one another's position, toward urgently needed reforms in the international economic, trading, investment, and monetary systems. In our view, the poorer and more disadvantaged countries can only benefit from a more coherent attack on these problems by the maximum number of industrialized nations.

A basic precondition is a *new willingness on the part of the United States—and of its friends—to consult early, and to compromise.* Too often the United States has not developed its policies on crucial North-South negotiations until just before or even during a conference. This prevents full support from others, or timely adjustment of the US position to secure such support. In preparing its positions for forthcoming negotiations, the United States should *consult far earlier with those who share its basic interests. Prior to negotiations such consultations should widen to secure maximum support and co-sponsorship.*

Secretary-General

US interests are well served by a strong, independent-minded Secretary General. *We recommend that the Secretary General be encouraged to use to the full his agreed authority in international diplomacy—* a capability which time has proven to be highly valuable to the maintenance of peace and security. To enhance his independence, he should be limited, in the future, to a single five-year term of office.

Regional Organizations

We recommend a major reconsideration of the division of labor between global and regional organizations. It is timely to decide afresh whether certain functions that have been automatically taken up at the global level should not rather be "regionalized," and thus dealt with only by those directly affected. The United Nations can and should set global standards; but action on many matters might be more effective at regional or subregional levels. Some regional action groupings might themselves have UN sponsorship, as is already the case in the environmental field.

[*What Future for the UN?*, 1977, pp. 11–19]

C.

THE US ROLE

IN SEARCH OF
AMERICAN POLICY

Lincoln P. Bloomfield

NATION-STATES WILL CONTINUE to act as though sovereignty were total; but the air, the water, the food sources, the quality of people's lives, the communications that enrich them, the wars and diseases that kill them, the consequences of affluence and of scientific discovery—every single one of these will turn out upon analysis to be largely indifferent to a single nation's boundaries and effectively approachable only on the basis of regional or international co-operation and ultimately of international regulation.

Even if we and other peoples are not ready for this insight, it is nevertheless a towering fact—as is the fact that only states can undertake the diplomacy essential for solving these problems. It follows that the development of genuinely effective multilateral instruments and agencies has become for the first time in history a sheer necessity instead of a luxury. . . .

The chief danger is not that the United Nations will die, but that it will settle into a condition of permanent invalidism. The heart of the problem is not that the United States and other major powers ignore the United Nations; it is that their short-run view of what will advance their individual national interests positively excludes the United Nations from a serious place in matters of moment. Their estimates of the likely headaches involved in U.N. action are all too accurate. The trouble is that their longer-range interests in a more predictable and just world order require that they run more short-term risks and pay more short-term costs—and that is precisely what they are unwilling to do. . . .

The truly hard-nosed advice may well be that which recommends interpreting the national interest far more broadly—that is, by taking bold moves to pool authority and giving a new lead to co-operative rather than unilateral directions. . . .

Today the United Nations and the regional organizations do not come close to doing the job that needs doing, and their nibbling at the fringes simply will not be sufficient. It is now time to take a new look at the bone structure of international organization on the basis of almost a third of a century of experience, in order to determine what changes are needed. We should no longer hesitate to reopen the most fundamental premises and components of the U.N. Charter. It could hardly worsen the behavior of the member states, and it might help. . . .

It is now open once again to the United States to show that a contrast exists between the cynical, power-oriented, imperialistic behavior of others, and the willingness of a democratic power like the United States to give primacy to other values such as peaceful change, political democracy, human rights, and social justice. That vision of a better world, backed by a humane and self-restrained outlook that avoids crusades but says what it thinks is right, is the first giant step back to being Number One not in arrogance but in decency. . . .

Engineers have to "design around" obstacles. A reformed foreign policy has to "design around" both the intransigeance of others and the encrustations in our own arteries.

A story is told of a French general in World War II who visited a detachment in a particularly inhospitable piece of North African desert. He ordered the captain to have a shelter of trees planted. "But, mon Général," protested the captain, "it will take twenty-five years for them to grow." "Indeed?" replied the General. "Then you have no time to lose!"

[*In Search of American Foreign Policy: The Humane Use of Power,*
1974, pp. 159–173]

BIBLIOGRAPHY

Adams, Henry, *The Education of Henry Adams,* NY: Modern Library, 1931.

Atlantic Council of the United States, "What Future for the UN? An Atlantic Dialogue." In *Atlantic Council Policy Paper,* Atlantic Council, Washington, DC, Oct. 1977.

Beaton, Leonard, *The Reform of Power.* NY: Viking, 1972.

Beer, Francis A., *Peace Against War.* San Francisco: W. H. Freeman, 1981.

Bennett, A. Leroy, *International Organizations,* 2nd ed. Englewood Cliffs: Prentice-Hall, 1980.

Black, Cyril E. "World Orders: Old and New" in C. Black et al *A New World Order,* World Order Project Occ. Paper No. 1, Center of Int. Studies, Princeton, NJ, 1977.

Bloomfield, Lincoln P., "From Ideology to Program to Policy: Carter Human Rights Policy." In *Journal of Policy Analysis and Management,* Vol. 2, No. 1, 1982.

Bloomfield, Lincoln P., *In Search of American Foreign Policy: The Humane Use of Power,* NY: Oxford Univ. Press, 1974.

Bloomfield, Lincoln P., *The United Nations and US Foreign Policy,* Boston: Little, Brown, revised ed., 1967.

Brown, Seyom, *Issues in U.S. Foreign Policy—On The Front Burner,* Boston: Little, Brown, 1984.

Brown, Seyom, *New Forces in World Politics,* Washington: The Brookings Institution, 1974.

Brzezinski, Zbigniew, "U.S. Foreign Policy: The Search for Focus." In *Foreign Affairs,* July 1973.

Camps, Miriam, *Collective Management: The Reform of Global Economic Orgs.,* NY: McGraw-Hill, 1981.

Catholic Bishops of the United States, "The Challenge of Peace: God's Promise and Our Response," in *Conference of Catholic Bishops on War and Peace,* 1983.

Chernenko, Konstantin U., "Speech to Central Committee of the CPSU," Feb. 13, 1984 in *New York Times,* Feb. 14, 1984.

Clark, Grenville and Louis B. Sohn, *World Peace Through World Law,* Cambridge: Harvard Univ. 2nd ed., 1960.

Cleveland, Harlan, "Governing a Pluralistic World," in *Wye paper.* New York: Aspen Institute, 1981.

Cleveland, Harlan, "Foreign Policy and Presidential Selection," in *Sloan Foundation project,* Vanderbilt Univ., Feb. 17, 1984.

Cleveland, Harlan and Alexander King, "The Renewable Way of Life," in *The Futurist,* April, 1980.

Council on Environmental Quality and Dept. of State, *The Global 2000 Report to the President,* Washington: U.S. Government Printing Office, 1980.

Crabb, Cecil V., Jr., *Policy-Makers and Critics,* NY: Praeger, 1976.

Diebold, William Jr., "The US in the World Economy," in *Foreign Affairs,* Fall, 1983.

Drucker, Peter F., "The Changed World Economy," in *Foreign Affairs,* Spring, 1986.

Dyson, Freeman, "Weapons and Hope", Part IV, in *New Yorker,* Feb. 27, 1984.

Falk Richard A. and Samuel S. Kim, "World Order Studies: New Directions and Orientations," in *Macroscope,* No. 10, Fall 1981.

Feinberg, Richard E., *The Intemperate Zone: The Third World Challenge to US For. Pol,* NY: W. W. Norton, 1983.

Frieman, Edward A., "The Energy Sector", in *Technological Frontiers in Foreign Relations,* Natl. Academies of Science and Engineering and Council on Foreign Relations, Washington, DC, 1984.

Grenier, Richard, "Yanqui, Si! U.N., No!," in *Harper's,* Jan. 1984.

Hamilton, Alexander, *The Federalist.* No. XVII. (1787–88) The Federalist or, the New Constitution, London: J. M. Dent, 1934.

Head, Ivan L., "North-South Interdependence" in Spiegel, Steven L., Ed. *At Issue: Politics in the World Arena,* 4th Ed. NY: St. Martin's Press, 1984.

Hobbes, Thomas, *Leviathan,* (1651) NY: E. P. Dutton, 1950.

Ispahani, Mahnaz Z., "Alone Together: Regional Security Arrangements . . in the Gulf," in *International Security,* Spring 1984.

James, Alan, "The Politics of Peace-keeping in the 1980's" in H.

Hanning, ed. Peacekeeping and Technology, NY: International Peace Academy, 1983.

Johansen, Robert C., *Toward a Dependable Peace*, NY: Institute for World Order, 1978.

Kennan, George F., "A Proposal for International Disarmament," address, May 19, 1981.

Keohane, Robert O. and Joseph S. Nye, Jr., "Two Cheers for Multilateralism," in *Foreign Policy*, Fall, 1985.

Khrushchev, N. S., "On Peaceful Coexistence," in *Foreign Affairs*, Oct. 1959.

Kirkpatrick, Jeane J., "Global Paternalism: The UN and the . . International Regulatory Order" in *Regulation*, Jan./Feb., 1983.

Kluckhohn, Clyde, *Mirror for Man*, NY: Fawcett, 1957.

Law of The Sea Treaty, "Summary of Provisions," in *New York Times*, Dec. 11, 1982.

Lebow, Richard Ned, "The Paranoia of the Powerful," in *P.S.* (American Political Science Association), Winter 1984.

Lenin, V. I., Report of the Central Committee at the Eighth Party Congress in Stalin, J. *Problems of Leninism, Moscow:* Foreign Language Publishing House, 1940.

Luck, Edward C., "The U.N. at 40: A Supporter's Lament," in *Foreign Policy*, Winter 1984–85.

Lusaka, Paul J. F., "Address to United Nations General Assembly," New York, Sept. 18, 1985.

McNamara, Robert S., "Time Bomb or Myth: The Population Problem," in *Foreign Affairs*, Summer 1984.

Mitrany, David, *A Working Peace System*, Chicago: Quadrangle Press, 1966.

Morgenthau, Hans J., *Politics Among Nations*, NY: Alfred A. Knopf, 1967, 4th ed.

Motley, James Berry, "International Terrorism: A New Mode of Warfare," in *International Security Review*, Spring 1981.

Perez de Cuellar, Javier, "Report of the Secretary-General on the work of the Organization 1983," NY: United Nations, 1983.

Puchala, Donald J., "American Interests and the UN" in Spiegel, Steven L., ed. *At Issue: Politics in the World Arena*, 4th ed., NY: St. Martin's, 1984.

Richardson, Elliot, L. Statement before Subcommittees on Human Rights and International Organizations, Committee on Foreign Affairs, House of Representatives, Sept. 27, 1983.

Rodley, Nigel S., "The UN System and Human Rights" in Gati, Toby T., ed., *The US, the UN, and the Management of Global Change*, NY: UNA-USA, 1983.

Sagan, Carl, "Nuclear War and Climatic Catastrophe," in *Foreign Affairs*, Winter 1983/84.

Schell, Jonathan, "The Abolition, II-A Deliberate Policy," in *New Yorker*, Jan. 9, 1984.

Simon, Julian, *The Ultimate Resource*, Princeton: Princeton University Press, 1981.

Speth, James Gustavus, "Environment, Economy, Security: The Emerging Agenda," in *Protecting Our Environment*. Washington: Center for National Policy June, 1985.

Toynbee, Arnold J., *A Study of History*, (Somervell abridgment). NY: Oxford Univ. Press, 1947.

Trilateral Commission, *Towards a Renovated International System*, NY: The Trilateral Commission, 1977.

U.S. State Department, "New World Information Order" in *GIST*, Bureau of Public Affairs, US Department of State, Washington, Oct., 1981.

United Nations, "Hunger," in UN Chronicle, Jan., 1983.

United Nations, "The New International Economic Order," in *UN Chronicle*, Oct., 1982.

United Nations, "The UN Role in Space" in *UN Chronicle*, July, 1982.

United Nations Association of the USA, "Issues Before the 38th UN General Assembly," NY: UNA-USA, 1983.

United Nations Association of the USA, "Report on Non-Proliferation," Multilateral Project Advisory Group, NY: UNA-USA, March 13, 1984.

United Nations Association of the USA, "UN Specialized Agencies at a Glance," in *UNA-USA*, New York.

United Nations Food and Agriculture Organization, "Mixed Picture on Food," in *UN Chronicle*, June, 1982.

Urquhart, Brian, "International Peace and Security," in *Foreign Affairs*, Fall, 1981.

Waltz, Kenneth N., "The Myth of National Interdependence" in Kindleberger, C. P. ed., *The International Corporation, A Symposium*. Cambridge: MIT Press, 1970.

Wijkman, Per Magnus, "Managing the Global Commons," in *International Organization,* Summer, 1982.

Wilson, Thomas W. Jr., "World Security and the Global Agenda," in Harlan Cleveland, ed. *The Management of Sustainable Growth.* NY: Pergamon, 1981.

Wohlstetter, Albert, "Bishops, Statesmen and Other Strategists," in *Commentary,* June, 1983.

Yost, Charles W., *History and Memory,* NY: W. W. Norton, 1980.

INDEX